UNDERSTANDING
FAMILY LAW

Cavendish
Publishing
Limited

London • Sydney • Portland, Oregon

UNDERSTANDING FAMILY LAW

ME Rodgers, LLB, BA, Solicitor

Senior Lecturer, Nottingham Law School,
The Nottingham Trent University

Cavendish
Publishing
Limited

London • Sydney • Portland, Oregon

First published in Great Britain 2004 by
Cavendish Publishing Limited, The Glass House,
Wharton Street, London WC1X 9PX, United Kingdom
Telephone: + 44 (0)20 7278 8000   Facsimile: + 44 (0)20 7278 8080
Email: info@cavendishpublishing.com
Website: www.cavendishpublishing.com

Published in the United States by Cavendish Publishing
c/o International Specialized Book Services,
5824 NE Hassalo Street, Portland,
Oregon 97213-3644, USA

Published in Australia by Cavendish Publishing (Australia) Pty Ltd
45 Beach Street, Coogee, NSW 2034, Australia
Telephone: + 61 (2)9664 0909   Facsimile: + 61 (2)9664 5420
Email: info@cavendishpublishing.com.au
Website: www.cavendishpublishing.com.au

British Library Cataloguing in Publication Data
Rodgers, ME
Understanding family law
1 Domestic relations – England 2 Domestic relations – Wales
I Title
346.4'2015

Library of Congress Cataloguing in Publication Data
Data available

ISBN 1-85941-920-8
ISBN 978-1-859-41920-5

1 3 5 7 9 10 8 6 4 2

Printed and bound in Great Britain by Biddles Ltd, Kings Lynn, Norfolk

ACKNOWLEDGMENTS

The author would like to thank the staff at Cavendish for their support and gentle persuasion to actually write this text. Ruth Massey deserves special mention for her motivation skills!

LB Curzon is also thanked for permitting the author to rifle through his *Briefcase on Family Law* for case extracts – not only saving time, but also resulting in the wheel only being invented once.

Every effort has been made to gain permission to reproduce copyrighted material. If any material has been overlooked, please contact the publisher.

INTRODUCTION

We all belong to a 'family', whether we like it or not; but you may have one idea of what your family is, and who comprises your family, and others may have a completely different idea. Distinctions in these definitions may arise due to cultural differences, historical patterns, economic factors and social values, and yet the definitions will all have some form of validity. So, for example, a family may comprise a married couple, with or without children; or a cohabiting couple, heterosexual or same-sex; or a single parent with resident children; or all relationships created by a blood link. While you may or may not class all these as being family, they can all be seen as such; but this does not mean that they are all socially or legally accepted. Although the law generally reflects social values, this is not always the case where family law is concerned. To give you an example, society is generally accepting of heterosexual cohabiting couples, and yet the law provides this type of relationship with very little in the way of family law rights. The law faces difficulties in providing legal codes to cover the family relationship precisely because the family is a potentially nebulous concept; and it is interesting to note that the law does not really define what it means by a family, but simply provides enforceable rights to specified groups or defined relationships. The interface between social values and the legal code is such that the law usually reacts to changes in social norms rather than being proactive in establishing the family unit. The acceptance, in *Fitzpatrick v Sterling Housing Association* [1999] 3 WLR 1113, of same-sex relationships creating 'family rights' demonstrates this. Throughout this text you will come across areas where developing social values raise issues for legal intervention – is it right to give same-sex couples the same rights as married couples? Should parents who do not marry have the same rights in relation to their children as those who are married? Should the fact of marriage grant special status at all? All these issues raise the question of how the law can, and should, intervene in the lives of individuals, and the extent to which state regulation in family life is desirable. While the issues can be raised, whether they can be answered is debatable, and this book does not seek to provide an absolute answer – you should try to form your own opinions on the issues based, of course, on sound legal reasoning!

Before these types of questions and issues can be posed, the existing law needs to be fully understood – and so this book will introduce you to the main areas of state intervention in family life. You should treat this almost as a story – a couple meet, marry, have children, fall out of love, decide to separate and divorce and then have to sort out the consequences of ending the relationship. They also have to consider their parenting role and how this relates to their children's rights, if any such rights exist. Finally, for good measure, the couple have to be aware of the consequences of them being classed as 'bad parents', and the powers the state has over their children in those circumstances. These are the main life events for a large sector of society and are all life events subject to legal rules and oversight by the courts and the state.

Before embarking on this story of life, a couple of general points need to be highlighted in relation to the manner in which family law operates. First, there is no single family court, despite calls for one to be created. Hence, family law rights can be enforced in a variety of forums, from the magistrates' court (which is known as the Family Proceedings Court (FPC) when dealing with family matters) through to the High Court Family Division, although the county court deals with the highest percentage of cases. Secondly, the passing of the Human Rights Act (HRA) 1998 brings the European Convention on Human Rights (the Convention) into play where family rights are concerned. Section 2(1) of the HRA 1998 provides that the various family courts must:

> take into account any judgement, decision, declaration or advisory opinion of the European Court of Human Rights ... whenever made or given, so far as, in the opinion of the court or tribunal, it is relevant to the proceedings in which that question has arisen.

Section 3(1) of the HRA 1998 dictates that the family courts must ensure that:

> [In] so far as it is possible to do so, primary legislation and subordinate legislation must be read and given effect in a way which is compatible with the Convention rights.

Hence, some of the issues for debate will require knowledge and understanding of the various Convention rights – principally, in family law, the right to a fair trial (Art 6), the right to privacy and family life (Art 8), the right to marry and found a family (Art 12) and the right not to be discriminated against (Art 14). Finally, the familiar system of precedent takes, to a certain extent, a back seat in the operation of the law. While general principles can be established through case law, the diversity of family life is so great that it is rare to find another case with exactly the same facts and issues. This does not mean that you can forget about reading cases! Throughout the text you will find extracts from a range of cases and also some references to other cases that illustrate key legal points. You will aid your studies and gain a deeper understanding by seeking out all these decisions and reading them. These cases are not always going to be groundbreaking decisions, nor will they always be the most recent, but they have been selected since they provide a good illustration of how the law is applied in practice and show how difficult it is, in some situations, to deal with relationship breakdowns or disputes. You will also see 'Questions' posed throughout the text – these are issues for *you* to think about. Try to formulate *your* opinion on the matter, since this will help you to understand the law and perform better in any assessments you have on the topic. Finally, the majority of chapters will have an 'End of Chapter Assessment' section comprising of one or more questions relating to the topic in that chapter. Do attempt them since this too will aid your understanding and assessment performance. Hence, by the time you have digested this text and done the additional directed reading you really will 'Understand Family Law'.

ME Rodgers
The Nottingham Trent University

CONTENTS

Acknowledgments   *v*

Introduction   *vii*

Table of Cases   *xi*

Table of Statutes   *xv*

Table of Statutory Instruments   *xx*

Table of International Legislation   *xxi*

1   MARRIAGE – THE STARTING POINT   1

2   NULLITY AND LEGAL SEPARATION   15

3   THE LAW ON DIVORCE   35

4   PROPERTY AND FINANCE ON DIVORCE   59

5   PROPERTY AND FINANCE WITHOUT DIVORCE   87

6   CHILD SUPPORT   107

7   DOMESTIC VIOLENCE   129

8   THE LAW RELATING TO CHILDREN   147

9   THE PRIVATE LAW RELATING TO CHILDREN   161

10 THE PUBLIC LAW RELATING TO CHILDREN   195

11 ADOPTION   245

12 THE INHERENT JURISDICTION – WARDSHIP   259

13 END OF CHAPTER ASSESSMENT – OUTLINE ANSWERS   267

Index   293

TABLE OF CASES

A v A (A Minor: Financial Provision) [1994] 1 FLR 657 126
A v A (Maintenance Pending Suit: Provision of Legal Fees)
    [2001] 1 WLR 605 62
A v N (Committal: Refusal of Contact) [1997] 1 FLR 533 189
A v UK (Human Rights: Punishment of Child) [1998] 2 FLR 959 170
AMT (Known as AC) (Petitioners for Authority to Adopt SR)
    [1994] Fam Law 225 249
Ash v Ash [1972] 2 WLR 347 . . . . 43, 274

B (A Minor) (Adoption by Natural Parent), Re [2002] 1 WLR 258 249
B (A Minor) (Wardship: Medical Treatment), Re [1981] 1 WLR 1421 262
B (Adoption Order: Jurisdiction to Set Aside), Re [1995] 2 FLR 1 257
B (Care or Supervision Order), Re [1996] 2 FLR 693 238
B v B (Mesher Order) [2002] EWHC 3106 (Fam) 82
B v B (Occupation Order) [1999] 1 FLR 715 138
Banks v Banks [1999] 1 FLR 726 138
Bannister v Bannister [1980] 10 Fam Law 240 43
Barder v Barder [1987] 2 WLR 293 81
Baxter v Baxter [1948] AC 274 . . . . 24, 26
Beach v Beach [1995] 2 FLR 160; [1995] 2 FCR 526 76
Bellinger v Bellinger [2001] EWCA Civ 1140; [2003] UKHL 21 . . . . 20, 21
Bennett v Bennett [1969] 1 WLR 430 28
Berkshire CC v B [1997] 1 FLR 171 241
Brooks v Brooks [1995] 2 FLR 13 77
Buffery v Buffery [1988] 2 FLR 365 46
Burgess v Burgess [1996] 2 FLR 34 73
Burns v Burns [1984] Ch 317 105

C (Interim Care Order: Residential Assessment), Re [1997] 1 FLR 1 . . . . 235, 236
C v C (Non-Molestation Order: Jurisdiction) [1998] Fam 70 134
CDM v CM, LM, DM (Children) [2003] 2 FLR 636 189
Chalmers v Johns [1999] 1 FLR 392 . . . . 137, 138
Cleary v Cleary [1974] 1 WLR 73 41
Coombes v Smith [1986] 1 WLR 808 102
Corbett v Corbett [1970] 2 All ER 33; [1971] P 83 . . . . 19, 22
Cossey v UK [1991] 2 FLR 492; (1991) 13 EHRR 5 20
Cowan v Cowan [2001] EWCA Civ 679; [2001] 3 WLR 684 75
Cowen v Cowen (1945) unreported 24
Crozier v Crozier [1994] 2 WLR 444 120

D, Re [1993] 2 FLR 423 238
D (A Minor) (Care or Supervision Order), Re [1993] 2 FLR 423 228
D (A Minor) (Wardship: Sterilisation), Re [1976] Fam 185 262
D (Children) (Shared Residence Orders), Re [2001] 1 FLR 495 182
D v S (Parental Responsibility) (1995) 3 FCR 783 173
Dart v Dart (1996) 2 FLR 286 . . . . 68, 72, 73
Davis v Johnson [1979] AC 264 130
Dawson v Wearmouth [1999] 1 FLR 1169 168
Drake v Whipp [1996] 1 FLR 826 . . . . 95, 102

F (In Utero), Re [1988] Fam 122 261
F v Wirral MBC [1991] 2 WLR 1132 218
Ford v Ford [1987] 17 Fam Law 232 25
Fuller v Fuller [1973] 1 WLR 730 45

G v G (Financial Provision: Separation Agreement)
    [2000] FLR 472 83
Gillick v West Norfolk & Wisbech AHA
    [1985] 3 All ER 402 . . . . 162, 163, 166, 167
Gissing v Gissing [1970] 3 WLR 255; [1970] 2 All ER 780 . . . . 99, 278
Goodwin v UK (2002) 35 EHRR 18 . . . . 20, 21
Grant v Edwards [1986] 2 All ER 426 98
GW v RW (Financial Provision: Departure from Equality)
    [2003] EWHC 611 75

H (A Minor) (Parental Responsibility), Re [1993] 1 FLR 484 188
H (A Minor) (Section 37 Direction), Re [1993] 2 FLR 541 207
H (Minors) (Local Authority: Parental Rights)
    (No 3), Re [1991] Fam 151 . . . . 172, 173, 176
H and Others, Re [1996] 1 All ER 1 227
H v H (A Child) (Occupation Order: Power of Arrest)
    (2001) The Times, 10 January 143
Hanlon v Hanlon [1978] 1 WLR 592 . . . . 64, 65
Hanlon v The Law Society [1981] AC 124 65
Hardy v Hardy [1981] 2 FLR 321 70
Hendricks v Netherlands (1983) 5 EHRR 231 186
Hirani v Hirani [1982] 4 FLR 232 . . . . 27, 272
Horner v Horner [1982] 2 WLR 914 134
Horton v Horton [1947] 2 All ER 871 25
H(T) v T (Divorce: Irretrievable Breakdown) (2002) unreported, 6 June 46, 47
Humberside CC v B [1993] 1 FLR 257 224

J (A Minor) (Child in Care: Medical Treatment), Re [1992] 4 All ER 614 260
J (Minors) (Care: Care Plans), Re [1994] 1 FLR 253 232
J (Specific Issue Orders: Child's Religious Upbringing and
    Circumcision), Re [2000] 1 FLR 571 191
J v C [1970] AC 668 156
J v C (Child: Financial Provision) [1999] 1 FLR 952 126
J v S-T (Formerly J) (Transsexual: Ancillary Relief)
    [1997] 3 WLR 1287; [1997] 1 FLR 402 . . . . 31, 76, 96

K (Adoption and Wardship), Re [1997] 2 FLR 221 . . . . 257, 263
K v K (Pre-Nuptial Agreement) [2003] 1 FLR 120 83
Keegan v Ireland (1994) 18 EHRR 342 175
Khorasandjian v Bush [1993] QB 727 132
Kiely v Kiely [1988] 1 FLR 248 124
Knibb v Knibb [1987] 2 FLR 396 64

L, Re V, Re M, Re H, Re [2000] 2 FLR 334 185
Lambert v Lambert [2002] EWCA 1685 . . . . 75, 276
Le Marchant v Le Marchant [1977] 1 WLR 559 . . . . 48, 79
Leadbeater v Leadbeater [1985] FLR 789 . . . . 70, 72
Livesey (Formerly Jenkins) v Jenkins [1985] 2 WLR 47 69
Livingstone-Stallard v Livingstone-Stallard [1974] Fam 47 42
Lloyds Bank v Rosset [1990] 1 AC 107 . . . . 97, 278
Lomas v Parle [2003] EWCA Civ 1804 145

M (A Child) (Medical Treatment: Consent), Re [1999] 2 FLR 1097 167
M (A Minor) (Care Order: Threshold Conditions), Re
      [1994] 2 AC 424 226
M (Care Order: Parental Responsibility), Re [1996] 2 FLR 84 225
M v Birmingham CC [1994] 2 FLR 141 229
M v M (Child Access) [1973] 2 All ER 81 184
M v M (Financial Provision) [1987] 2 FLR 1 70
M v W (Non-Molestation Order: Duration) [2000] 1 FLR 107 136
McFarlane v McFarlane [2004] EWCA Civ 872 79
McMichael v UK (1995) 20 EHRR 205 175
Martin v Martin [1977] 3 All ER 762 71
Matharu v Matharu [1994] 2 FLR 597 102
Mehta v Mehta [1945] 2 All ER 690 27
Midland Bank v Cooke [1995] 2 FLR 215 . . . . 100, 278, 279
Mortimer v Mortimer-Griffin [1986] 2 FLR 315 64
Mouncer v Mouncer [1972] 1 WLR 321 . . . . 44, 45, 46

Nottinghamshire CC v P [1993] 3 WLR 637 . . . . 192, 208, 217, 231

O (A Minor) (Care Order: Education: Procedure), Re
      [1992] 1 WLR 912; [1992] 2 FLR 7 . . . . 165, 224
O (Care or Supervision Order), Re [1996] 2 FLR 755 238
O (Contact: Imposition of Conditions), Re [1995] 2 FLR 124 187
O'Neill v O'Neill [1975] 3 All ER 289 43

P (Child), Re [2003] EWCA Civ 837 126
P (Emergency Protection Order), Re [1996] 1 FLR 482 219
Pao On v Lau Liu Long (1980) unreported 27
Park, Re [1954] P 112 . . . . 26, 270
Parlour v Parlour [2004] EWCA Civ 872 79
Parra v Parra [2002] EWCA Civ 1886 75
Pascoe v Turner [1979] 1 WLR 431 101
Peter Whitear v UK [1997] EHRLR Issue 3 186
Pettitt v Pettitt [1969] 2 All ER 385 96
Pheasant v Pheasant [1972] 2 WLR 353 43
Philips v Peace [1996] 2 FLR 230 119

R (A Child), Re [2001] EWCA Civ 1344 168
R (A Minor) (Wardship: Medical Treatment), Re [1992] 1 FLR 190 167

R v Lancashire CC ex p M [1992] 1 FLR 109 251
R v R [1991] 3 WLR 767. 130
R v Secretary of State for Social Security ex p West
   [1998] EWHC (Admin) 687 111
R v W and B (Children) W (Children) [2001] HRLR 50 233
Rampal v Rampal [2001] EWCA Civ 989 32
Rees v UK [1987] 2 FLR 111; (1987) 9 EHRR 56 20
Richards v Richards [1983] 3 WLR 173 131
Rose v Rose [2003] EWHC 505 (Fam). 69
Rukat v Rukat [1975] 2 WLR 201. . . . . 49, 79

S v F (Occupation Order) [2000] 1 FLR 255. 139
Schuller v Schuller [1990] 2 FLR 193. 71
Sheffield and Horsham v UK (1997) 27 EHRR 163 20
Singh v Singh [1971] 2 WLR 963 25
State v Ward (1994) 28 SE 2d 785. 2
Szechter v Szechter [1971] 2 WLR 170 . . . . 26, 27, 272

T v S (Financial Provision for Children) [1994] 2 FLR 883 . . . . 124, 126
Thurlow v Thurlow [1975] 3 WLR 161. 42
Tinsley v Milligan [1993] 3 WLR 126 96

Vicary v Vicary [1992] 2 FLR 271. 82

W (A Minor) (Contact), Re [1994] 2 FLR 441. 185
W (Minors), Re (1996) CLY 568 185
W v W [1967] 1 WLR 1554 24
W v W (Nullity: Gender) [2001] 1 FLR 324 22
Wachtel v Wachtel [1973] Fam 72. . . . . 68, 73, 76
WB (Minors: Residence), Re [1995] 2 FLR 1023 181
Westdeutsche Landesbank Girozentrale v Islington LBC
   [1996] 2 WLR 802 95
Whiston v Whiston [1995] 2 FLR 268 . . . . 32, 96
White v White [2000] 3 WLR 1571 . . . . 66, 68, 71, 73, 75, 82, 276

TABLE OF STATUTES

Access to Justice Act 1999 53

Adoption Act 1976 .... 246, 249,
253, 255, 256

Adoption of Children
Act 1926 245

Adoption and Children
Act 2002 .... 171, 174, 177, 179, 232,
245, 246, 247, 248,
249, 250, 252, 254,
255, 257, 289, 290, 291

s 1 .... 255, 290
s 1(6) 256
s 3 250
s 18 252
s 18(2) 252
s 19 252
s 19(1) 252
s 20 255
s 21 253
s 21(2)–(3) 253
s 22(3) 253
ss 26–27 257
s 42 248
s 44 254
s 44(5) 254
s 45 250
s 45(2) 250
s 46(1) 247
s 47 .... 248, 254
s 47(2) 254–55
s 47(4) 255
s 47(6) 255
s 49 248
s 50 .... 248, 250
s 51 248
s 52 253
s 52(1) 253–54
s 52(2) 249
s 52(5) 253
s 67 247
ss 69–70 247
ss 71–73 247
s 74 247
s 74(1) 248
ss 75–76 247
s 111 176
s 112 177
s 114 183
s 115 192

Child Support Act 1991 .... 64, 65, 67,
72, 107, 108–16, 118,
119, 120, 121, 122, 125,
126, 127, 163, 280, 281

s 1(1)–(2) 109
s 2 113
s 3 109
s 4 .... 112, 113, 114, 116, 279, 280
s 4(1) 112
s 4(9) 114
s 4(10) 115
s 6 .... 112, 113, 114, 115, 279
s 6(1) 112
s 6(3) 112, 113
s 6(5) 113
s 6(7) 112
s 8 280
s 8(3) 116
s 8(5) 116
s 8(5)(b) 116
s 8(6)–(8) 122
s 26(2) 111
s 44(1) 110
s 46 .... 113, 114
ss 54–55 109
Sched 1 118
    para 2(1)–(2) 117
    para 6(1) 118
Sched 4B 119
    para 4 121

Child Support Act 1995 .... 64, 65, 67,
72, 107, 108, 163

Child Support Act 1999 117

Child Support, Pensions and
Social Security Act 2000 .... 107, 111,
117, 119

Children Act 1908 .... 152, 153

Children Act 1948 153

Children Act 1989 .. 119, 123, 125–26, 147, 150
151, 153, 154, 155–60, 161, 162,
164, 165, 168, 169, 171, 174, 176,
177, 179, 180, 181, 182, 183, 184,
185, 190, 191, 192, 193, 198, 199,
200, 202, 204, 205, 206, 207, 208,
210, 217, 218, 219, 220, 223, 224,
226, 227, 229, 230, 232, 233, 234,
235, 236, 241, 243, 245, 246, 255,
256, 257, 259, 260, 261, 263, 265,
266, 280, 283, 284, 285, 286, 287, 290

Children Act 1989 (contd)—
Pt IV 192, 221, 229
Pt V 212, 216
s 1 .... 155, 161, 182, 195,
                        216, 285, 286, 289
s 1(1) 126, 155, 212
s 1(2) 155, 157
s 1(3) 155, 156, 160, 212,
                        255, 283, 284,
                        285, 286
s 1(4) 155–56, 172, 212
s 1(5) 156, 158, 159, 168,
                        181, 182, 186,
                        212, 242
s 2 .... 171, 286
s 2(7) 173, 192
s 2(8) 181
s 2(9) 176, 177
s 3 161
s 3(1) 161, 162
s 3(5) 176, 177, 242
s 4 .... 171, 172, 174, 176,
                        177, 178
s 4(1) 172
s 4(1)(a) 111
s 4(2) 172
s 4A 177
s 7 206
s 8 .... 161, 168, 178, 179, 182,
                183, 184, 192, 193, 194,
                201, 208, 217, 233, 237,
                246, 249, 250, 256, 261,
                263, 286, 287, 290, 291
s 8(1) 187
s 9 .... 179, 183, 241
s 9(2) 192
s 9(5) 192
s 10 179
s 10(1) 159
s 10(1)(b) 192
s 11(4) 181
s 11(5) 183
s 11(7) 180, 187
s 12(1) 187
s 12(2) 176–77
s 13 .... 181, 287
s 13(1) 167
s 13(1)(b) 287
s 13(2) 287

s 14A 192, 193
ss 14B–14E 192
s 14F 192, 193
s 14G 192
s 17 .... 155, 159, 198, 199,
                        200, 201, 206,
                        225, 231, 284
s 17(1) 156, 200
s 17(3) 199
s 17(7)–(8) 199
s 17(10) 199, 200
s 18(1) 200
s 18(5) 200
s 20 .... 202, 203
s 20(1) 200, 201
s 20(1)(a)–(c) 201
s 20(3) 202
s 20(4) 201
s 20(6) 202
s 20(7) 201
s 22 200
s 23 .... 200, 203
ss 23B–23C 200
s 24 .... 200, 203
s 24(1) 200
s 31 .... 165, 221, 223, 225,
                        227, 234, 263
s 31(1) 221, 222, 231
s 31(2) 221–22, 226, 230, 253
s 31(2)(a) 226, 229
s 31(3) 222, 229
s 31(5) 237
s 31(9) 223
s 31(10) 223, 224
s 31A 232
s 33 239
s 33(3) 239
s 33(6)–(7) 240
s 34 240
s 34(6) 240
s 34(11) 240
s 35 .... 241, 242
s 35(1)(c)(i) 242
s 36 .... 164, 165
s 36(1) 165
s 36(3) 165
s 37 .... 189, 206, 207, 220, 234
s 37(1) 206, 208

Children Act 1989 (contd)—
s 37(4) 207
s 38 .... 225, 234, 235, 236
s 38(2) 235
s 38(6) 235
ss 38A–38B 235
s 39 241
s 39(4)–(5) 241
s 40 243
s 41 220
s 42 221
s 43 .... 211, 212
s 43(1) 211
s 43(3) 212
s 44 .... 213, 216, 223, 263,
                                266, 289
s 44(1) 213–14
s 44(1)(a) 214, 215, 216, 225, 289
s 44(1)(a)(i) 214
s 44(1)(a)(ii) 214, 215
s 44(1)(b) 215, 216, 289
s 44(1)(c) 216
s 44(4) 216
s 44(4)(c) 218
s 44(6) 217
s 44(10) 216
s 44(13) 217
s 44A 217, 235
s 44B 217
s 45(1) 218
s 45(5) 218
s 45(8)–(10) 219
s 46 204
s 46(7) 205
s 47 .... 203, 204, 206, 207,
                          215, 216, 223, 225,
                            230, 288, 289
s 47(1) 204
s 47(3) 205
s 47(4) 205, 215
s 47(6) 205
s 47(7) 206
s 47(9) 204
s 100 .... 260, 265
s 100(2)–(3) 264
s 100(4) 264, 265
s 100(5) 265
Sched 1 284
   paras 1–2 125

para 4 126
Sched 2 198
   para 5 217
Sched 3 241
Pt II 243
   para 4(4) 241
   para 6(1) 243
   para 6(3) 243
Children (Leaving Care)
   Act 2000 203
Children and Young Persons
   Act 1933 .... 164, 166
Children and Young Persons
   Act 1969 .... 153, 154, 228, 265
Clandestine Marriages
   Act 1753 2
Crime and Disorder
   Act 1998 .... 204, 205, 207, 229, 230
s 11(3) 230
s 12 230
s 12(6)–(7) 230
Criminal Justice and Public
   Order Act 1994 130

Divorce Reform Act 1969 .... 36, 37
Domestic Proceedings and
   Magistrates' Courts
   Act 1978 .... 88, 89–90, 91, 123,
                          125, 126, 280, 281
ss 1–2 .... 89, 90
s 3(2) 89
s 3(3)–(4) 125
s 4 89
s 6 90
s 7 90
s 7(4) 90
Domestic Violence (Matrimonial
   Proceedings) Act 1976 282

Ecclesiastical Licences
   Act 1533 6
Education Act 1996 .... 164, 165
s 7 164
Equal Pay Act 1970 60

Family Law Act 1996 .... 35, 39, 50, 51, 52,
                           55, 57, 78, 82, 92, 93,
                           102, 129, 131, 133–43,
                           145, 146, 282, 283

Family Law Act 1996 (contd)—
Pt II 35, 52
Pt III 52, 53
Pt IV 129, 133, 134
s 1 .... 50, 51
s 3(6) 137
s 3(6)(a)–(d) 137
ss 30–32 92
s 33 .... 92, 136, 137, 139, 145, 283
s 33(1) 136
s 33(6)–(7) 93, 137, 138
s 33(10) 139
s 34 136
s 35 .... 136, 139, 140, 283
s 35(6) 139
s 36 .... 136, 141, 283
s 36(6) 140, 283
s 36(6)(e) 140
s 36(8) 283
ss 37–38 136
s 41 283
s 41(2) 140
s 42 .... 133, 134, 144, 282
s 42(1) 133
s 42(1)(a)–(b) 134
s 42(2)(b) 135
s 42(5) 136, 282
s 42(7) 136
s 42A 144
s 42A(1) 144
s 45 .... 141, 142, 282
s 46 142
s 46(3)–(4) 142
s 47 .... 142, 144, 282
s 47(2) 282
s 62 .... 134, 135, 144, 282
Sched 4, para 2 93
Family Reform Act 1969 111

Gender Recognition Act 2004 .... 21, 23,
                                    29, 30
s 1 21
s 1(1)(a)–(b) 21
s 2 21
s 3 21
s 3(6) 21
s 4(3) 21
s 5 22

Human Fertilisation and
 Embryology Act 1990 .... 110, 249
Human Rights Act 1998 .... 199, 234
s 2(1) vi
s 3(1) vi
Sched 1, Pt 1 233

Immigration and Asylum
 Act 1999 7
Inheritance (Provision for
 Family and Dependants)
 Act 1975 103

Law of Property (Miscellaneous
 Provisions) Act 1989
s 2 94
Legal Aid Act 1988 53
Legitimacy Act 1976
s 1 .... 31, 171
s 2 171
Local Government Act 1970 195
Lord Hardwicke's Act
 See Clandestine Marriages Act 1753

Marriage Act 1753 10
Marriage Act 1836 2
Marriage Act 1949 .... 2, 7, 8, 17
s 3 11
s 5 .... 5, 6
s 6(1) 5
s 7(1) 5
s 27(1)–(2) 3
s 27(4) 3
s 27(5) 4
s 28(1) 4
s 31(1)–(2) 4
s 41 10
s 44(3) 7, 10
s 48(1) 11
s 49 11–12
Sched 1 .... 17, 248
Marriage Acts 1949–1986 16
Marriage Act 1994 .... 8, 272
Marriage Ceremony (Prescribed
 Words) Act 1996 .... 7, 8
Marriage (Prohibited Degrees
 of Relationship) Act 1986 271
s 1 18

Marriage (Registrar-General's
Licence) Act 1970 6
Matrimonial Causes Act 1937 24
Matrimonial Causes Act 1973 .... 22, 30,
32, 35, 36, 37, 38,
39, 40, 41, 49, 50,
52, 53, 55, 56, 60,
65, 66, 72, 73, 76,
77, 78, 79, 82, 88,
89, 90, 91, 94, 102,
123, 124, 125, 126,
156, 273, 275, 276,
280, 281
s 1(1) 37, 274
s 1(2) 37, 38, 47, 274, 275
s 1(2)(a) 274
s 1(2)(b) 42, 46, 47, 274
s 1(2)(c) 274, 275
s 1(2)(d) 44, 274, 275
s 1(2)(e) 274
s 1(3) 39
s 2 .... 47, 50
s 2(1) 274
s 2(5) 275
s 3 275
s 3(1)–(2) 38
s 5 .... 48, 79, 274
s 5(1) 48
s 10 .... 48, 49, 79, 274
s 11 .... 15, 16, 269, 270, 271, 272
s 11(a)
s 11(a)(i) 16, 271
s 11(a)(ii) 19, 271
s 11(b)–(c) 271
s 11(d) 16, 22
s 12 .... 15, 23, 30, 270, 272
s 12(a)–(b) 26, 270, 272, 273
s 12(c) 28, 270, 272
s 12(d) 28, 270
s 12(e) 272
s 12(f) 29
s 12(g) 23, 29
s 13 .... 30, 271, 272
s 13(1) 272
s 13(2) 271, 272
s 13(2A) 30
s 17(2) 32
s 22 62
s 23 .... 31, 60, 62, 78, 88
s 24 .... 31, 63

s 24A 63
s 25 .... 67, 68, 71, 73,
74, 80, 83, 84,
85, 89, 276
s 25(1) 31, 66, 67–69, 76, 83
s 25(2) 66–67, 88
s 25(2)(a) 69, 74
s 25(2)(b) 74
s 25(2)(c)–(e) 73–74
s 25(2)(g) 76, 83
s 25(2)(h) 77
s 25(3)–(4) 125
s 25A 78
s 25A(2) 79
s 25B(4) 78
s 27 .... 88, 89
s 27(6)–(7) 88
s 28 .... 61, 79
s 28(1A) 80
s 28(2) 88
s 31 80
s 52(1) 123
Matrimonial and Family
Proceedings Act 1984
s 38 262
Matrimonial Homes
Act 1983 92
Mental Health
Act 1983 .... 23, 28, 241, 270

Offences Against the Person
Act 1861 .... 164, 166

Pensions Act 1995 77
Police and Criminal Evidence
Act 1984 132
Prevention of Cruelty
Act 1889 152
Protection from Harassment
Act 1997 .... 143, 145, 146
s 2 145
s 4 145
s 5A 145

Trusts of Land and Appointment
of Trustees Act 1996 .... 94, 102, 139
ss 12–14 102

Welfare Reform and Pensions Act
1999 78

TABLE OF STATUTORY INSTRUMENTS

Child Support (Maintenance
  Assessment Procedure)
  Regulations 1992
  (SI 1992/1813) 114
Child Support (Maintenance
  Calculations and Special Cases)
  Regulations 2000
  (SI 2000/155) 118
Child Support (Miscellaneous
  Amendments) Regulations 1996
  (SI 1996/1945) 114
Child Support (Variation)
  Regulations 2000
  (SI 2000/156) 121
  paras 18–20 121

Family Proceedings Rules 1991
  (SI 1991/1247) 220, 263
  Sched 2 219

Marriages (Approved Premises)
  Regulations 1995
  (SI 1995/510) 8
  reg 5(1) 8
  reg 6(1)(a) 8
  Scheds 1–2 8

Placement of Children with
  Parents etc Regulations 1991
  (SI 1991/893) 239

TABLE OF INTERNATIONAL LEGISLATION

European Convention on
  Human Rights 150, 175, 185,
                    190, 199, 210, 239
  Art 6 .... 210, 234
  Art 8 .... 20, 154, 158, 175, 185,
                    186, 199, 217, 233

Art 8(2) 186
Art 12 .... 20, 21
Art 14 175
Hague Convention on Child
  Abduction 182

CHAPTER 1

MARRIAGE – THE STARTING POINT

1.1   OBJECTIVES

By the end of this chapter you should:

- understand and be able to describe the legal rules on the process of marriage;
- be able to apply the law to client scenarios and advise on the marriage formalities; and
- be able to advise clients on the consequences of failure to comply with the formalities.

Historically, the law did not involve itself too much in the regulation of marriage. An individual was free to 'marry' merely by the exchange of vows, or by the act of sexual intercourse with their partner. This lack of legal regulation led to the term 'common law wife', which is still in use today, although having little, if any, legality or rights attached to it. The law did, however, start to become involved in marriage in the 18th century, and now legislation provides the rules surrounding the process of marriage. In this chapter you will be looking at the formalities of the marriage process and the potential consequences of failure to comply with the law, to establish how you marry, before moving on in the next chapter to look at the issue of who can marry whom.

1.2   DEVELOPMENT OF THE LAW

As you have just seen, the law has only begun to become involved with the process of marriage in the last 250 or so years, by laying down requirements on parties wishing to marry. Common law marriages, which took the form of an exchange of vows (not required to be in a church or religious place of worship), or the act of living together and having sexual relations, were the norm.

Question

Can you think of any problems that may arise from such a form of marriage?

While there may have been advantages to this system, for example, the lack of expense and the lack of state regulation over what was seen both as a religious issue and also as a personal matter, there have been some problems identified with this common law system. Cretney, Masson and Bailey-Harris in *Principles of Family Law*, 7th edn, 2002, Sweet & Maxwell, p 10, identify them thus:

The informality permitted by the common law had a number of disadvantages. First, there would often be uncertainty about the validity of a marriage. It was not so much that there might be doubts about the validity of the informal union itself; but rather that indiscreet and quickly forgotten words breathed under the influence of passion would be relied on many years later by one of the parties to a, possibly transient, relationship. The intention underlying such an assertion of an informal marriage might well be to invalidate the other party's subsequent solemn marriage with a third party.

Secondly, hasty and ill-considered marriages were facilitated. The agreement which is all that is necessary to form a valid common law marriage might – as an American writer has put it – have been entered into 'in the privacy of one's own bedroom, in an automobile after a picnic in the country, or after a night's debauch'. In such cases, it seems unlikely that there would be much point in inquiring whether the promises were in the present or future tense.

Thirdly, the creation of such a marriage might have important and undesirable legal consequences. The American case of *State v Ward* 28 SE 2d 785 (1994), provides a striking illustration of the potential evil of such 'quickie' marriages: the defendant to a charge of unlawful intercourse with a minor successfully asserted that the complainant was his wife at common law.

Consequently, legislation was passed in 1753 to regulate marriage, and the manner in which a marriage could be contracted. While the Act is commonly called Lord Hardwicke's Act, its correct title was the Clandestine Marriages Act 1753, and it succeeded in replacing the common law marriage with a marriage celebrated in church. Certain pre-marriage formalities were stipulated (such as the calling of banns), and failure to comply with them would result in the marriage being invalid.

In 1836, the Marriage Act was passed, which amended Lord Hardwicke's Act, and introduced the secular procedure for marriage. This, therefore, meant that couples could legally marry without having to go through a Church of England ceremony. This secular ceremony was not to be as simple as the common law exchange of vows, since the Act again specified the formalities to be met before the marriage would be acceptable in law. This dual system of marriage and, in particular, the dual system of pre-marriage formalities, is still with us today. The legislation has occasionally been amended, and the relevant law is contained in the Marriage Act 1949 (as amended).

1.3 THE FORMALITIES OF MARRIAGE

Within this heading, there are different areas to be considered, namely the pre-marriage requirements, the solemnisation of the marriage, and consent. However, when most people contemplate marriage they probably think more about the practicalities of getting married, and what they perceive to be the formalities – such as getting the wedding outfits, choosing the rings, arranging the reception and making sure that hostile relatives do not end up sitting next to one another. However, these sort of practicalities have nothing to do with the legality of the process; they are little more than the social etiquette that is attached to the wedding ceremony. The legal formalities refer to the giving of notice of the forthcoming ceremony and other prerequisites, and these will differ according to the type of ceremony you have, that is, a Church of England ceremony, a purely secular or civil ceremony, or a religious ceremony (other than C of E).

1.3.1 Pre-marriage requirements

1.3.1.1 Civil marriages and marriages other than in accordance with the Church of England

A secular marriage, as well as a marriage which is conducted under the auspices of a religion other than the Church of England, must only be performed after the necessary forms of notice have been given and the relevant superintendent registrar's certificate issued. Read the following extracts from the Marriage Act 1949 to establish the type and form of notice required to marry:

27 Notice of marriage

(1) Where a marriage is intended to be solemnized on the authority of certificates of a superintendent registrar ... notice of marriage in the prescribed form shall be given –

(a) if the persons to be married have resided in the same registration district for the period of seven days immediately before the giving of the notice, by each of those persons to the superintendent registrar of that district;

(b) if the persons ... have not resided in the same registration district for the said seven days ... by each of those persons to the superintendent registrar of the ... district in which he or she has resided ...

(2) A notice of marriage shall state the name and surname, marital status, occupation, place of residence and nationality of each of the persons to be married ... and –

(a) ... shall state the period, not being less that seven days, during which each of the persons to be married has resided in his or her place of residence;

...

(4) The superintendent registrar shall file all notices of marriage and ... enter the particulars given in every such notice, together with the date of the notice ... in a book furnished to him for that purpose ... and the marriage notice book shall be open for inspection free of charge at all reasonable hours.

(5) The superintendent registrar shall be entitled to a fee ... for every entry made in the marriage notice book under this section.

28 Declaration to accompany notice of marriage

(1) No certificate for marriage shall be issued by a superintendent registrar unless the notice of marriage is accompanied by a solemn declaration in writing ... made and signed at the time of the giving of the notice by the person by whom the notice is given ...

(a) that he or she believes that there is no lawful impediment of kindred or alliance or other lawful hindrance to the marriage; ...

(c) where one of the persons to be married is a child ... that the consent of the person or persons whose consent to the marriage is required ... has been obtained, that the necessity of obtaining such consent ahas been dispensed with ..., that the court has consented to the marriage ... or that there is no person whose consent is so required.

...

31 Marriage under certificate without licence

(1) Where a marriage is intended to be solemnized on the authority of certificates of a superintendent registrar ... the superintendent registrar to whom notice of marriage has been given shall suspend or affix in some conspicuous place in his office, for 15 successive days next after the day on which the notice was entered in the marriage book, the notice of marriage ...

(2) At the expiration of the said period of 15 days the superintendent registrar ... shall issue a certificate in the prescribed form unless –

(a) the superintendent registrar is not satisfied that there is no lawful impediment to the issue of the certificate ...

As you can see, any marriage that is not under the auspices of the Church of England will have to give the same notices before the couple will be granted a certificate to marry. For these non-Church of England ceremonies, the requirements for notice are as follows: the parties have resided in the district where notice is given for a period of at least seven days; they have declared that there are no lawful impediments to the marriage; they meet the residence requirements and the relevant fee is paid. Once the notice and the declarations have been given to the superintendent registrar, notice will be posted in a marriage notice book available for public inspection. A total period of 15 days will have to pass from the posting of the notice before the certificate authorising the marriage ceremony can be issued. It is important to remember that notice has to be given by both of the couples and must be in person.

1.3.1.2 Church of England (or Anglican) marriages

The formalities relating to these weddings are linked with religious tenets. It is possible that some of these requirements will be changed in the near future, perhaps due to their 'old-fashioned' nature. As before, read the following extracts from the Marriage Act 1949 to see how the notice must be given:

5   Methods of authorising marriage

A marriage according to the rites of the Church of England may be solemnized –

(a) after the publication of banns of matrimony;

(b) on the authority of a special licence of marriage granted by the Archbishop of Canterbury ...;

(c) on the authority of a licence of marriage (other than a special licence) granted by an ecclesiastical authority having power to grant such a licence (... referred to as a common licence); or

(d) on the authority of a certificate issued by a superintendent registrar ...

6   Place of publication of banns

(1) Subject to the provisions of this Act, where a marriage is intended to be solemnized after the publication of banns of matrimony, the banns shall be published –

(a) if the persons to be married reside in the same parish, in the parish church of that parish;

(b) if the persons to be married do not reside in the same parish, in the parish church of each parish in which one of them resides ...

7   Time and manner of publication of banns

(1) ... banns of matrimony shall be published on three Sundays preceding the solemnization of the marriage during morning service, or if there is no morning service on a Sunday on which the banns are to be published, during evening service ...

You will have seen that three types of marriage are permitted:

• marriage after publication of banns;

• marriage under common licence; and

• marriage under special licence.

The former is more common and is also cheaper! The requirements are for the banns to be published for three consecutive Sundays in the parish churches where the parties reside (having at least 15 days' residence) and in the church where the marriage will be conducted, if different. Publication means that the banns are both entered into a written register and also read out in the church itself during a service. Once the banns have been published the marriage ceremony can be conducted immediately. It should be noted that the Church of England has mooted the possibility of changing this type of preliminary requirement and proposed that the requirement for the reading of banns be removed. No steps have been taken towards the abolishment of the requirement.

Marriage under common licence is rarer and has different requirements. There is still the residence requirement, but in relation to only one of the parties, and it is still 15 days. Rather than the requirement for the registering and reading out of the banns, one of the parties is required to swear an affidavit stating that there is no impediment or legal reason why the couple should not marry. There is no waiting time and once the licence is granted the marriage can be conducted.

Marriage under special licence is covered below under 'other forms of notice'.

Question

Why do couples have to give notice?

According to the Efficiency Scrutiny of the Registration Service (1985), the Register Office notice board is generally used by those tradespeople who have an interest in weddings, for example, the photographer, the chauffeur, the florist, etc. The real purpose of giving notice and having the forthcoming marriage publicly displayed is to enable anyone who knows of any objections to the marriage to bring those objections to the notice of the registrar. The same is true of the calling of banns. In reality, the notification of objections is not likely to occur, since many individuals would never think to view the notice board (when did you last do so?) or go to church. Also, with a more 'mobile' population it is not as common for individuals to be well known in an area.

1.3.1.3   Other forms of notice

The above notice requirements may not be suitable for all situations, and forms of 'emergency notice' exist to deal with 'deathbed' weddings or 'prison' weddings. Under the Marriage (Registrar-General's Licence) Act 1970 it is possible to obtain a licence to marry away from a register office if one of the parties is seriously ill and not likely to recover, or if one of the parties cannot be moved to a place where marriages can be conducted. If the same situation is relevant to an Anglican ceremony then, under the Ecclesiastical Licences Act 1533, the Archbishop of Canterbury is able to grant a special licence to permit a marriage at any time of day, whether or not in a church (this is the special licence referred to in s 5 of the Marriage Act 1949 above). This is often used to permit marriages in college chapels or churches where the parties have no connection with the church in which they are to be married, and hence cannot use the traditional notification procedures.

1.3.1.4   Reform

As you have just seen, the purpose of giving notice is not, in today's society, truly met. You may ask, why bother? The ineffectiveness of notice periods has been noticed and proposals for change have recently been mooted. In the Government Green Paper, *Supporting Families: A Consultation Document*

(November 1998, TSO), it was suggested that rather than remove the notice periods, they should be increased to a minimum of 15 days. In addition, it was proposed that both parties to the forthcoming marriage should have to attend to give notice jointly. This has now been introduced via the Immigration and Asylum Act 1999.

The reasoning behind the proposed alterations gives an indication of the changing view of why notice is necessary. The Green Paper states in para 4.27 that a minimum of 15 days' notice would '... allow couples more time to reflect on the nature of the commitment they are entering into and to take up marriage preparation'. The reasons for joint notice are that it '... would test the willingness of each partner to enter into the marriage contract and would enable the registrar to provide information on available guidance and to refer both partners to pre-marriage support'. Can you see how this is focusing more on the couple themselves than on letting the public know about the marriage? The concept of pre-marriage counselling is not new, but perhaps is more important given the current high divorce rate. You may agree that it is better to know what marriage entails before you enter in to it than find out to your cost later!

1.4   THE MARRIAGE CEREMONY

While only two forms of notification procedure exist, there are four main types of ceremony that are permitted in English law. You should know of two of these: namely, the civil ceremony and the Church of England ceremony. The others are religious ceremonies not according to the rights of the Church of England, and marriages according to Jewish or Quaker traditions.

1.4.1   The civil ceremony

After the civil preliminaries have been complied with, a marriage can take place in any register office, subject to certification, although the office in the area where one of the parties resides is often preferred unless the couple are marrying in a stately home, etc. The marriage ceremony will need to be conducted by an authorised person and will need to take place between the hours of 8 am and 6 pm. In addition, the marriage should take place with 'open doors', meaning that any member of the public may enter (as required by the Marriage Act 1949). The parties to the marriage must, at some point during the ceremony, declare that they know of no impediment to the marriage and also make the 'required declaration'. This means that the parties are required to call upon the persons present at the ceremony to witness their contract with one another. The precise wording of the declaration is set out in s 44(3) of the Marriage Act 1949 although the Marriage Ceremony (Prescribed Words) Act 1996 permits another form of wording to be adopted. The reason for the very minor alterations in language under the latter Act seems to be nothing more than modernisation of the language used. Consequently, the wording is more readily understood and perhaps may be thought to be more appropriate to the individuals concerned; but other than for these reasons, there seems to be no clear reason for introducing this option.

1.4.1.1   Alternative venues for the ceremony

In addition to the changes to the wording used in the ceremony, recent changes have occurred with regard to the place where a civil marriage can be carried out. The Marriage Act 1994 amended the Marriage Act 1949 to enable marriages in 'approved premises'. These are premises approved by the relevant local authority for the purposes of a marriage ceremony.

The Marriages (Approved Premises) Regulations 1995 (SI 1995/510) set out the process for the application and registration of other 'premises'. The extracts from the 1995 Regulations that follow should enable you to see what the basic requirements are:

Schedule 1 (Regulation 5(1))

1   Having regard to their primary use ... the premises must, in the opinion of the authority, be a seemly and dignified venue for the solemnisation of marriages.

    ...

4   The premises must have no recent or continuing connection with any religion, religious practice or religious persuasion which would be incompatible with the use of the premises for the solemnisation of marriages ...

Schedule 2 Conditions to be attached to grants of approval (Regulation 6(1)(a))

    ...

7   No food or drink may be sold or consumed in the room in which a marriage ceremony takes place for one hour prior to that ceremony or during that ceremony.

    ...

9   The room in which a marriage is solemnised must be separate from any other activity on the premises at the time of the ceremony.

    ...

11   Any reading, music, words or performance which forms part of a ceremony of marriage ... must be secular in nature ...

12   Public access to any ceremony or marriage solemnised in approved premises must be permitted without charge.

A marriage will not be permitted anywhere: for example, there must be a roof, it must be a permanent structure or be permanently moored if a boat. The criteria that the premises are a 'seemly and dignified venue' are perhaps a little subjective since each individual is likely to have their own view as to what is seemly. The changes do however mean that individuals have a greater scope for marrying in surroundings that they feel to be appropriate and, perhaps, far more attractive. The popularity of these alternative venues is clear, and the number of church weddings has declined considerably since the introduction of the regulations. Most stately homes, many hotels and even football stadia can be used as a venue; but attractive as some of these are there can be potential problems with some venues, for example, the Eurostar Waiting Room at Ashford Station, which applied for permission to hold weddings in 1996.

Question

What do you think the problem may be?

If you recall the requirements for a marriage ceremony, it needs to be conducted with open doors. If guests have to go through customs (as they would at such a station) before they can witness the marriage, then is it truly open to the public?

1.4.1.2   Reform of civil marriages

As you are aware, reform of the various marriage formalities has been mooted in several government publications (for example, *Supporting Families*). In January 2002 a White Paper was published with a view, amongst other things, to changing certain aspects of civil marriage (*Civil Registration: Vital Change*). These changes are primarily directed at the nature of the marriage ceremony and the place of the ceremony. Once the changes come into force, couples will not be constrained in terms of where they marry – unless the place is deemed unsafe, such as in a shark cage or at the bottom of a bungee rope. The place of the marriage will no longer have to be registered; the fact that the marriage celebrant has the requisite licence will be the important factor.

In terms of likely implementation, the White Paper suggests that the updating of existing legislation should be completed by 2004 and that the changes should be implemented by the end of 2005. However, this will be dependent on sufficient parliamentary time being available; but some of the changes may be implemented via delegated legislation reducing the time frame for implementation, although, at the time of writing, no such changes have yet been implemented.

1.4.2   The Church of England ceremony

The nature of the ceremony is very similar to that in a register office, with the obvious emphasis on the religious nature of the ceremony. There must be a qualified clergyman to conduct the ceremony, before witnesses, with open doors, and between the specified times. Again, the prescribed words and declarations must be made, although there is little scope to amend them as with civil ceremonies.

1.4.3   Other religious ceremonies

This category will incorporate those individuals of the Roman Catholic faith, Sikhs, Hindus and Muslims. Before the ceremony the civil preliminaries must be carried out. Thereafter, the ceremony may be carried out in accordance with the relevant religion. The law requires that the building, in which the ceremony takes place, is one which is a place of meeting for religious worship (s 41 of the Marriage Act 1949). In addition, there must be an authorised person in attendance – this may in fact be the registrar but is more commonly a priest or minister of the necessary faith. Regardless of which religion is involved, the wording in s 44(3) of the Marriage Act 1949 (the required wording referred to in civil ceremonies above) must be said at some stage in the ceremony.

1.4.4   Jewish and Quaker marriages

For some reason these two faiths were exempted from the provisions of the Marriage Act 1753. Hence, today the only requirements are for couples to comply with the civil notification procedure. The ceremony takes place in accordance with the religious requirements of the relevant faith.

1.5   REGISTRATION

Formal registration of the marriage is necessary to enable the parties to have proof of their status. As you will realise, many rights and obligations, both of the parties to one another and of the state, are dependent upon the status of a married person. The marriage register must be completed and signed by witnesses. A copy of this entry in the marriage register is provided to the couple.

1.6   CONSENT

This is an issue to which you will return in the next chapter when considering the legal status of a marriage. At this point it is necessary merely to note that marriage is, in effect, a contract between the two individuals concerned, although, it is true to say, it is a contract with little by way of clear obligations on either party. As such, it is a very simple contract and most individuals are deemed capable of entering into it. The idea that individuals need to be of a certain age to enter a contract holds true for marriage: it is not permissible to marry under the age of 16. If a young person between the ages of 16 and 18 wishes to marry, they can do so only with the consent of their parents (or those who hold parental responsibility) or their guardian. If the person or persons who are required to give consent refuse to do so, the court can be asked to give consent instead. If no one is able to give consent, perhaps due to a disability, the need for consent can be dispensed with by the superintendent registrar (this is covered in s 3 of the Marriage Act 1949). However, if this consent is not given, or the consent is fabricated, and the marriage ceremony goes ahead, it will still be a valid marriage.

1.7 CONSEQUENCES OF NON-COMPLIANCE WITH THE FORMALITIES

Question

What do you think the consequences should be if the required preliminaries have not been complied with?

You may have decided that if the preliminaries were ignored then the marriage should be invalid and, hence, have no legal consequences. Alternatively, you may have looked at the nature of the requirements and decided that they were not really significant and, hence, failure to comply should not result in the marriage being deemed invalid. Unfortunately, the legislation is not so clear cut, as the extracts from the Marriage Act 1949 below illustrate:

48   Proof of certain matters not necessary to validity of marriage

   (1)   Where any marriage has been solemnized under the provisions of this Act, it shall not be necessary in support of the marriage to give any proof –

      (a)   that before the marriage either of the parties thereto resided, or resided for any period, in the registration district stated in the notice of marriage to be that of his or her place of residence;

      (b)   that any person whose consent to the marriage was required ... had given his consent;

      (c)   that the registered building in which the marriage was solemnized had been certified as required by law as a place of religious worship;

      (d)   that the building was the usual place of worship of either of the parties to the marriage; ...

      nor shall any evidence be given in to prove the contrary in any proceedings touching the validity of the marriage.

49   Void marriages

If any persons knowingly and wilfully intermarry ...

(a) without having given due notice of marriage to the superintendent registrar;

(b) without a certificate for marriage having been duly issued by the superintendent registrar to whom notice of marriage was given;

(c) without a licence having been so issued, in a case in which a licence is necessary;

(d) on the authority of a certificate which is void ...

(e) in any place other that the church chapel, registered building, office or other place specified in the notice of marriage and certificate of the superintendent registrar;

(ee) ... on any premises that at the time the marriage is solemnized are not approved premises;

(f) in the case of a marriage in a registered building (not being a marriage in the presence of an authorised person) in the absence of [the] registrar ...;

(g) in the case of a marriage in the office of a superintendent registrar, in the absence of the superintendent registrar ...;

(gg) in the case of a marriage on approved premises, in the absence of the superintendent registrar ...;

the marriage will be void.

As you will have seen, these sections set out the breaches of formalities which will have no effect on the validity of the marriage, and those which will mean the marriage is void (this is a topic covered in depth in the next chapter).

If you were to summarise these sections in a table or list form it would look something like this:

VALID	VOID
Breach of residence requirements.	No notice given to the registrar.
Lack of consent of parents/ guardians if either party below 18 years.	No certificate issued or void certificate issued.
Building not registered as a place of religious worship.	No licence issued (where one is necessary).
Building not the parties' usual place of worship.	Married in a place not specified on the certificate.
	Building not an approved place.
	Married in the absence of an authorised person or registrar.

When reading the sections did you notice the caveat to the invalid or void marriages? If not, go back and try to spot it.

You should have noticed the phrase, 'If any persons knowingly and wilfully intermarry ... the marriage shall be void'. This means that it is only where a marriage is carried out with the parties knowing that they have not fulfilled the relevant preliminaries that the marriage is not valid. It is not clear from the legislation whether or not both parties should know of the defect, although most writers (for example, Cretney, Masson and Bailey-Harris, and Hayes & Williams, *Family Law; Principles, Policy and Practice*, 1999, Sweet & Maxwell) do speak in plural terms, suggesting that both parties should know.

Earlier on in this chapter you were told that a marriage (whether secular or Anglican) had to be conducted between the hours of 8 am and 6 pm. What would be the situation if the marriage took place at 6.05 pm?

The sections extracted above are of no assistance on this particular point since the law is not clear as to the effect of failure to comply with certain of the formalities. The hours for marriage is one such formality. Others that fall into this 'vague' category include the requirement for open doors and the need to make the required declarations.

1.8   SUMMARY

In this chapter you have looked at the means by which a marriage can be conducted and legally formed. You should now be familiar with the requirements for notification of an impending marriage ceremony and the purposes for which this notice is given. The ability in today's society for this notice to achieve its aims is an issue you should be able to discuss. The actual process of the marriage ceremony itself, who may conduct it and where, is another area which you should feel comfortable discussing. Linked to this, the consequences for ignoring the legal requirements should be clear. You should also be in a position to suggest why there have been calls for reform in this area, since this is relevant to the End of Chapter Assessment.

1.9   END OF CHAPTER ASSESSMENT

'[M]any of the procedures [relating to marriage] are unnecessarily complex and restrictive': *Registration: A Modern Service*, Government Green Paper, Cm 531.

Discuss the validity of this statement.

CHAPTER 2

NULLITY AND LEGAL SEPARATION

2.1   OBJECTIVES

By the end of this chapter you should be able to:

- explain the importance of ss 11 and 12 of the Matrimonial Causes Act (MCA) 1973;
- analyse and discuss the meanings within the legislation;
- apply the law to problem scenarios and advise hypothetical clients in problem-style assessment questions;
- identify areas where the law may be capable of change and the nature of those changes; and
- explain the relevance of legally authorised separation to end a marriage.

In 2002, only 167 marriages were brought to an end by the use of the nullity procedure compared with 148,164 divorce petitions (*Judicial Statistics*, 2003, HMSO). Consequently you may be wondering why you need to study this area of law. While nullity, in particular, is little used to bring a marriage to an end, it is important to the understanding of the legal rules surrounding marriage itself and of the question, 'who can marry whom?' In addition, nullity illustrates the historical difficulties of obtaining a divorce which, in reality, is only a recent option. Legally authorised separation is also a little used provision but does retain relevance for certain individuals in society.

2.2   VOID VERSUS VOIDABLE

In the previous chapter you came across the term 'void' in respect of a marriage, but do you know what voidable means and are these terms you would expect to find in family law?

In reality, marriages fall into three categories:

- those that are *valid* and can only be brought to an end through divorce or legally authorised separation;
- those that are *void* and have, therefore, never existed as a valid marriage; indeed in law, no marriage has been created; and
- those that are *voidable* and which will be seen in law to be valid, although due to an irregularity, the marriage may be set aside and declared to be no longer in existence.

The terminology stems from the fact that marriage is seen as a contract and so terms are used that reflect contractual situations. However, we will see in this chapter that the distinctions between void and voidable marriages, in so far as the consequences are concerned, are not that great.

2.3   VOID MARRIAGES

Those marriages that are deemed void are covered in s 11 of the MCA 1973, which you will find below. Have a look at the section and list those types of marriages that are void:

11   Grounds on which a marriage is void

A marriage celebrated after 31st July 1971 shall be void on the following grounds only, that is to say –

(a)   that it is not a valid marriage under the provisions of the Marriages Acts 1949 to 1986 (that is to say where –

(i)   the parties are within the prohibited degrees of relationship;

(ii)   either party is under the age of sixteen; or

(iii) the parties have intermarried in disregard of certain requirements as to the formation of marriage);

(b)   that at the time of the marriage either party was already lawfully married;

(c)   that the parties are not respectively male and female;

(d)   in the case of a polygamous marriage entered into outside England and Wales, that either party was at the time of the marriage domiciled in England and Wales.

For the purposes of para (d) of this sub-section a marriage is not polygamous if at its inception neither party has any spouse additional to the other.

Question

Do you agree with the inclusion of all these categories?

It is one thing to know what the law says, another to know what it means, so now let's consider what each of the categories cover and look at some of the difficulties that they throw up.

2.3.1   The prohibited degrees

The first to consider is that the 'parties are within the prohibited degrees of relationship' (s 11(a)(i)). There are two types of prohibited degrees within the law and they clearly reflect the question 'who can marry whom?' The first category is the prohibited degrees of consanguinity, that is, relationships by blood. The second category is the prohibited degrees of affinity and these are relationships created by marriage.

Question

Who do you think should be covered by this sort of prohibition and why?

Schedule 1 to the Marriage Act 1949 lists those individuals who are prevented from marrying due to their being in these categories. Below you will find a summary of the prohibitions in this Act.

Prohibited degrees of consanguinity:

- A man may not marry his:

  mother, adopted mother or former adopted mother, daughter, adoptive daughter or former adoptive daughter, father's mother, mother's mother, son's daughter, daughter's daughter, sister, father's sister, mother's sister, brother's daughter, sister's daughter.

- A woman may not marry her:

  father, adoptive father or former adoptive father, son, adoptive son or former adoptive son, father's father, mother's father, son's son, daughter's son, brother, father's brother, mother's brother, brother's son, sister's son.

Prohibited degrees of affinity:

- A man may not marry his:

  daughter of a former wife, former wife of his father, former wife of his father's father, former wife of his mother's father, daughter of the son of his former wife, daughter of the daughter of his former wife, mother of his former wife, former wife of his son.

- A woman may not marry:

  son of her former husband, former husband of her mother, former husband of her father's mother, former husband of her mother's mother, son of the son of her former husband, son of the daughter of her former husband, father of her former husband, former husband of her daughter.

The justifications for these restrictions span a variety of considerations. As you may know, the potential for genetic defects in offspring is greater the closer the blood link between parents. Genetically, therefore, marriage within the prohibited degrees of consanguinity may increase the risks of inherited disease. The morality and social policy considerations of marrying a member of one's close family are also relevant, especially in the degrees of affinity where step-parents or step-children and other affines are concerned. It would not be acceptable in the majority of circles for a child to be raised by someone acting as a parent and then for those two parties to marry subsequently and create a totally different relationship.

Question

Do you think that the same prohibitions should apply if the step-parent and step-child (in the list of prohibitions above, being daughter or son of former spouse) had not actually lived in the same household in a parent/child relationship?

Clearly, here there is less of a 'family' relationship and so you might agree that the law should treat such a case differently; yet the degrees of affinity have been relaxed only in the recent past. There are now limited situations where marriage across the degrees is permissible. These are set out in s 1 of the Marriage (Prohibited Degrees of Relationship) Act 1986, which relaxes the prohibition where:

- both parties are over 21 (in all cases);
- the marriage is between step-parent and step-child and the child had not been treated as a child of the family before reaching the age of 18;
- the marriage is between an individual and their parent-in-law, or child-in-law, and the respective spouses are dead.

2.3.2 The age of the parties

The terms of this restriction are not difficult to understand, but the rationale is less clear. It would appear that social mores affect this principle. You may not be aware that in the early part of the 20th century it was permissible for a girl to marry at the age of 12 (this age was raised in 1929), something that would seem quite unacceptable today. The fact that there is a minimum age for marriage does not seem too important, with only a minority of individuals marrying in their teens.

If a child of 16 or 17 wishes to marry, this is permissible subject to the consent of their parents (or persons with parental responsibility). However, in the event that this consent is not forthcoming the court can be asked to give consent instead. If consent is not given, the child lies about their age, or a parental consent is invalid, but the marriage goes ahead, then the marriage is still valid in law. No challenge may be made regardless of the breach of the requirements. You must remember that this only applies to marriages where the minimum age of 16 is met.

2.3.3 The disregard of certain formalities

You should recall the situations and the types of breach that will invalidate the marriage from the previous chapter – if you can't, go back and re-read that section of the book.

2.3.4   Already lawfully married

As with the s 11(a)(ii) of the MCA 1973 prohibition, this prohibition should not cause too many problems. The restriction on marriage, when already lawfully married, is in connection with the second marriage. The first marriage will remain valid (always assuming it was valid to start with); the second marriage will automatically be void. As you may be aware, if one of the parties to a marriage is already married, a criminal charge of bigamy may result.

2.3.5   The parties are not respectively male and female

This again would appear to be an uncontroversial aspect of the legislation since it reflects the notion of marriage as being the union of one man and one woman. In reality, there has been continued debate on this provision and the issue of what is meant by 'male' and 'female'.

The starting point in case law on this issue is *Corbett v Corbett* [1970] 2 All ER 33 and the opinion of Ormrod J. The facts of the case, briefly, were that the respondent, April Corbett, nee Ashley, was born and their birth registered under the name of George Jamieson. In 1960, the respondent underwent a 'sex change' operation to reassign his sex to female. The parties married in 1963. In the proceedings to establish if the marriage was void due to the parties being of the same gender Ormrod J stated:

> Since marriage is essentially a relationship between man and woman, the validity of the marriage in this case depends, in my judgment, on whether the respondent is or is not a woman ... The question then becomes what is meant by the word 'woman' in the context of a marriage, for I am not concerned to determine the 'legal sex' of the respondent at large. Having regard to the essentially heterosexual character of the relationship which is called marriage, the criteria must, in my judgment, be biological ... the law should adopt, in the first place, the first three of the doctors' criteria, ie, the chromosomal, gonadal and genital tests, and, if all three are congruent, determine the sex for the purpose of marriage accordingly, and ignore any operative intervention.

Hence, applying this to the respondent they had at the time before the marriage:

> ... been shown to have XY chromosomes and, therefore, to be of male chromosomal sex; to have had testicles prior to the operation and, therefore, to be of male gonadal sex; to have had male external genitalia without any evidence of internal or external female sex organs and, therefore, to be of male genital sex.

As a result, the marriage was held to be void since, despite the respondent undergoing reassignment surgery, the test for maleness or femaleness was taken to be the sex determining factors at birth.

Although the issue of 'gender' has been raised in the European Court of Human Rights, when arguing a breach of Art 12, the right to marry and found a family, the traditional approach of Ormrod J was upheld as being within the scope of national law for many years. This approach was demonstrated in *Cossey v UK* [1991] 2 FLR 492; (1991) 13 EHRR 5. Here, Cossey had been born male and her birth certificate stated this fact. She developed psychologically as a female and received gender reassignment surgery. Cossey's request for a change to her birth certificate was refused. She later married Mr X but the marriage was declared to be void because the parties were not male and female. On an application to the European Court of Human Rights, when it was argued that there had been a violation of Art 8 (right to family life) and Art 12 (right to marry) it was held, by a majority, that the refusal to alter Cossey's birth certificate was *not* a violation of Art 8. The UK's birth registration certificate was a public record and respect for Cossey's private life did not impose an obligation on the UK to alter existing records. There was no violation of Art 12 which, as you recall, lays down that a person's right to marry is subject to domestic law. The UK's restriction of the right to marry to persons of the opposite biological sex did not affect Art 12, which concerned traditional marriage between male and female. Judge Palm and two colleagues, dissenting, argued that there had been significant changes in public opinion as regards the full legal recognition of transsexualism which should be taken into account in the interpretation of Art 12.

Again, in *Bellinger v Bellinger* [2001] EWCA Civ 1140, the Court of Appeal accepted that the assignment of gender at birth, in accordance with the Ormrod J criteria, must stand, and while they acknowledged the psychological aspects of transsexualism, together with the fact that it is medically recognised as a psychological condition, they did not feel able to give these 'secondary factors' priority over the biological ones. There was however a clear statement that the present state of affairs was unsatisfactory and that it may not match the changing views of the European Court of Human Rights as evidenced in the case of *Sheffield and Horsham v UK* (1997) 27 EHRR 163.

Mrs Bellinger appealed to the House of Lords but, before this hearing took place, the European Court of Human Rights heard the case of *Goodwin v UK* (2002) 35 EHRR 18. In the *Goodwin* case several issues were raised with regard to the treatment of post-operative transsexuals under the law of England and Wales. With reference to the right to marry, enshrined in Art 12 ECHR, the Court found:

> The Court recalls that in the cases of *Rees, Cossey* and *Sheffield and Horsham* the inability of the transsexuals in those cases to marry a person of the sex opposite to their re-assigned gender was not found in breach of Article 12 of the Convention. These findings were based variously on the reasoning that the right to marry referred to traditional marriage between persons of opposite biological sex, the view that continued adoption of biological criteria in

domestic law ... was encompassed within the power of Contracting States to regulate by national laws ... Reviewing the situation in 2002, the Court observes that Article 12 secures the fundamental right of a man and woman to marry and to found a family. The exercise of the right to marry gives rise to social, personal and legal consequences. It is subject to the national laws of the Contracting States but the limitations thereby introduced must not restrict or reduce the right in such a way or to such an extent that the very essence of the right is impaired.

The Court has found ... that a test of congruent biological factors can no longer be decisive in denying legal recognition to the gender of gender of a post-operative transsexual.

One of the consequences of this declaration, and the fact that *Goodwin* had declared refusal to accept a transsexual in their new gender for the purposes of marriage to be unlawful, was the publication of a draft Gender Recognition Bill in July 2003. It should be noted, however, that this was not sufficient for Mrs Bellinger's case to be successful in the House of Lords ([2003] UKHL 21).

The Gender Recognition Bill was introduced in the House of Lords on 27 November 2003, and gained Royal Assent on 1 July 2004. Its aim is to enable individuals to gain formal recognition of their change of gender via application for a 'gender recognition certificate' (s 1). The applicant will have to be over 18, and be accepted as 'living in the other gender' (s 1(1)(a)), or having 'changed gender under the law of another country or territory outside the UK' (s 1(1)(b)). Any such application will be determined by a new body, the Gender Recognition Panel, which will be required under s 2 to grant the certificate if satisfied the applicant:

(a) has or has had gender dysphoria;

(b) has lived in the acquired gender throughout the period of two years ending with the date on which the application is made;

(c) intends to continue to live in the acquired gender until death; and

(d) complied with the requirements imposed by s 3.

Section 3 sets out the nature of the evidence needed to substantiate the application. It is not a requirement of s 3 that the applicant actually undergoes surgery, or such treatment, for the gender dysphoria – a diagnosis alone can be sufficient. Section 3(6) also requires the applicant to indicate if they are married (this can only be in the original gender unless, of course, the applicant is seeking a certificate under s 1(1)(b) where the marriage may be in the acquired gender). In addition, birth certificates must be submitted with the application.

If the evidential aspects are met the Panel must grant the certificate, but if the applicant is married, only an interim gender recognition certificate can be granted (s 4(3)). The interim certificate can be made into a full one if the marriage is ended by virtue of nullity proceedings or the spouse dies. There is a time limit of six months after the ending of the marriage or death of the spouse for the certificate to be made into a full gender recognition certificate (s 5).

Amendments will also be made to the MCA 1973 to increase the situations when a marriage may be deemed voidable. These will be covered later in the chapter.

There are, however, some situations where the 'sex at birth' and the application of the biological tests are not conclusive. These are cases where the individual is deemed 'intersex' and, hence, are not covered by the test in *Corbett*. In these situations, the secondary factors can legitimately be used to assign the individual to the 'correct' gender as in *W v W (Nullity: Gender)* [2001] 1 FLR 324. Here, H and W had married in 1993. In 1997 a decree absolute had been granted following W's petition. H did not contest the divorce but later sought a decree of nullity on the ground that at the time of the marriage the parties had not been male and female respectively. He contended that the marriage was void in that W was not a woman but a physical intersex. Although W was registered at birth as a boy, and in spite of treatment with testosterone injections from an early age, her general appearance had been more female than male. From the time she was able to choose, she had lived as a female. In 1987, following oral oestrogen treatment, W had undergone gender reassignment surgery. The court held that H's application should be dismissed. Charles J stated that the factors determining a person's sex for the purpose of marriage, as set out in *Corbett v Corbett* (1971), were biological and, if the gonadal, chromosomal and genital tests were congruent, that was determinative of an individual's sex. W's genetic and gonadal sex was male but her genitalia were ambiguous, hence she did not fulfill the *Corbett* criteria. Partial androgen insensitivity caused her to be in a physical intersex state. Given such insensitivity, its cause and effect, evidence of W's final choice to live as a woman before the oestrogen treatment, her gender reassignment surgery, and her capacity to consummate the marriage, Charles J was satisfied that this was sufficient to demonstrate that, for the purposes of the marriage, W was a woman.

2.3.6 Polygamous marriages

The restriction on polygamous marriages would appear to overlap with that of bigamy and this is true to the extent that both concern marriages to more than one person. However, polygamy is not automatically a criminal offence; in other words, a polygamous marriage may be valid in England and Wales.

Section 11(d) of the MCA 1973 often causes confusion and yet it is not a complicated provision. The key issue in deciding whether or not a marriage will be void for polygamy is the question of where the parties are domiciled. If the country of domicile permits polygamy (for example, Pakistan), then as long as all the parties to the polygamous marriage, ie, husband plus two wives, are domiciled within that jurisdiction at the time of the ceremonies, there will be no question of the marriage being invalid. If one of the parties is domiciled in England and Wales and the other is not, for the marriage to be valid it must be between single people.

2.4   VOIDABLE MARRIAGES

Those marriages that are deemed voidable are covered in s 12 of the MCA 1973, which you will find below. Have a look at the section and list those types of marriages that are voidable.

12   Grounds on which a marriage is voidable

A marriage celebrated after 31 July 1971 shall be voidable on the following grounds only, that is to say –

(a) that the marriage has not been consummated owing to the incapacity of either party to consummate it;

(b) that the marriage has not been consummated owing to the wilful refusal of the respondent to consummate it;

(c) that either party to the marriage did not validly consent to it, whether in consequence of duress, mistake, unsoundness of mind or otherwise;

(d) that at the time of the marriage either party, although capable of giving a valid consent, was suffering (whether continuously or intermittently) from mental disorder within the meaning of the Mental Health Act 1983 if such a kind or to such an extent as to be unfitted for marriage;

(e) that at the time of the marriage the respondent was suffering from venereal disease in a communicable form;

(f) that at the time of the marriage the respondent was pregnant by some other person other than the petitioner.

In addition, under the Gender Recognition Act 2004 it has been inserted into the MCA as sub-para (g):

that an interim gender recognition certificate under the Gender Recognition Act 2004 has, after the time of the marriage, been issued to either party to the marriage.

2.4.1   Incapacity to consummate or wilful refusal to consummate

Although these two categories are separate, their similarities mean that it is easier to consider them together.

Question

How would you define consummation?

The condition of consummation is one that requires sexual intercourse to take place between the parties. Intercourse does not have the same definition as it would in criminal law for the purposes of rape. Sexual intercourse must be 'ordinary and complete'. A marriage will be consummated regardless of whether or not ejaculation occurs, and does not depend upon the use of contraception: what is at issue is not the ability to conceive, but the ability to have sexual relations. For example, in *Baxter v Baxter* [1948] AC 274, H and W married in 1934. Some 10 years later H left W. H petitioned for a decree of nullity on the ground of non-consummation due to W's wilful refusal. H stated that W refused sexual intercourse unless he used a contraceptive. The court held that consummation of the marriage was *not prevented* by the use of contraceptives. *Per* Lord Jowitt:

> I am unable to believe that Parliament, by using the word 'consummate' in connection with this new ground of nullity, intended that the courts should be involved in enquiries of this kind. Long before the passing of the Matrimonial Causes Act 1937, it was common knowledge that reputable clinics had come into existence for the purpose of advising spouses on what is popularly called birth control and ... it is also a matter of common knowledge that many young married couples agree to take contraceptive precautions in the early days of married life. I take the view that in this legislation Parliament used the word 'consummate' as that word is understood in common parlance and in the light of social conditions known to exist, and that the proper occasion for considering the subjects raised by this particular appeal is when the sexual life of the spouses, and the responsibility of either or both for a childless home, form the background to some other claim for relief. On this basis I am constrained to say that, in my opinion, there is no warrant for the decision in *Cowen v Cowen* (1945) [(unreported) in which the Court of Appeal had held that there had been no consummation where a husband had persisted in the use of a contraceptive]. The result is I would dismiss this appeal.

In the case of *W v W* [1967] 1 WLR 1554 the court considered a petition in which evidence was given suggesting that penetration had not led to ordinary, complete intercourse. The court held a decree of nullity would be granted. As Brandon J stated:

> There are binding decisions that the emission of seed, or possibility of procreation, are not necessary ingredients as a matter of law to ordinary and complete intercourse, and there are authorities which seem to me to be right, if not binding, that full and complete penetration is an essential ingredient to complete intercourse.
>
> I do not think that there is any authority which binds me to hold that any penetration amounts to consummation of a marriage, and in the absence of

such authority I do not see why I should not make a finding of fact in accordance with what seem to me to be the realities of the case. On those grounds, in my judgment, this marriage has not been consummated and I am satisfied that the cause of that non-consummation is the impotence of the husband which existed at the date of the marriage and continued at all material times. There will, accordingly, be a decree of nullity of marriage on the ground of incapacity.

Incapacity to consummate can be due to the 'defects' of either party, and an individual can rely on their own incapacity, but it is always for the petitioner to prove that incapacity exists. The common perception of incapacity would relate to physical difficulties in consummating the marriage. This does not have to be the case, and psychological aversion can suffice. In the case of *Singh v Singh* [1971] 2 WLR 963, H and W, aged 21 and 17, were Sikhs who were married in a register office. W's parents had arranged the marriage and she had never seen H before the ceremony. It was intended that the civil ceremony would be followed by a religious ceremony. W took a dislike to H when she first saw him at the register office and she refused to participate in the religious ceremony or to live with him. W's subsequent petition for a decree of nullity was based upon duress and incapacity to consummate because of her 'invincible repugnance'. The petition was dismissed. Karminski LJ stated:

> There is the matter of repugnance. It is true that W never submitted herself to the physical embraces of H, because after the ceremony of marriage before the registrar it does not appear that she saw him again or went near him. Having taken the view which she did, that she did not want to be married to him, it is understandable that she did not want to have sexual intercourse with him: but that seems to be a very long way from an invincible repugnance ... Here W abandoned the idea of her marriage altogether, and there is nothing of a psychiatric or sexual aversion on her part which is in any way established. In my view that ground of nullity fails completely.

By contrast, for wilful refusal to be proven the petitioner must prove that the respondent has reached a 'settled and definite decision without just excuse' (*per* Jowitt LC in *Horton v Horton* [1947] 2 All ER 871, at p 874) not to have intercourse. The assessment of the settled decision is a question of fact for the court.

Question

When do you think a respondent would have a just excuse not to consummate the marriage?

An example of when it may be deemed 'just excuse' can be found in the case of *Ford v Ford* [1987] 17 Fam Law 232. Here H was in prison and despite being able to engage in intercourse with W (albeit against prison rules) the court held that his failure to consummate the marriage whilst still in prison would have equated to a just excuse: it was a valid reason for not having intercourse. The existence of other evidence for non-consummation meant that the marriage was, nevertheless, held to be void. The case of *Baxter v Baxter* [1948] AC 274 (above) demonstrates a situation where there was no just excuse.

Question

Would it make a difference to this ground if the parties had had sex before the marriage?

Given that the focus of both s 12(a) and (b) of the MCA 1973 is on the ability of the couple to have sexual intercourse it would be logical to answer this question in the affirmative. However, what is at issue is whether or not the marriage has been consummated and therefore the ability or desire of the parties prior to the ceremony is irrelevant.

2.4.2   Consent

The legal requirements for consent cover three main areas.

Starting with unsoundness of mind, the first thing you should be aware of is that this is not automatically the same as mental illness, although it may include it. The real concern here is that due to the individuals' mental incapacity they are unable to enter a contract; marriage is a contract. The level of understanding and therefore capacity that is needed is quite low since marriage is a simple contract (*per* Hodson LJ in *Re Park* [1954] P 112, at p 136).

Turning to duress, this fact has had a variety of approaches taken in the courts as to what actions will constitute duress, and hence vitiate consent.

In *Szechter v Szechter* [1971] 2 WLR 170, P, a Polish national, was arrested and imprisoned in Warsaw, having been charged with anti-state activities. R, an eminent Polish scholar, to whom the authorities had given permission to emigrate, assisted in effecting P's release by divorcing his wife and marrying P while she was in prison. P, R and his former wife came to England. P petitioned for a decree of nullity on the ground of fear and duress, in order that R and his first wife might remarry. Simon P stated that:

> It is, in my view, insufficient to invalidate an otherwise good marriage that a party has entered into in order to escape from a disagreeable situation, such as penury or social degradation. In order for the impediment of duress to vitiate an otherwise valid marriage, it must, in my judgment, be proved that the will of one of the parties thereto has been overborne by genuine and reasonably-held fear caused by threat of immediate danger (for which the party is not himself responsible) to life, limb or liberty, so that the constraint destroys the reality of consent to ordinary wedlock.

In the later case of *Hirani v Hirani* [1982] 4 FLR 232 P, aged 19 and a Hindu, was living with her parents, also Hindu, in England. There she met X, an Indian Muslim. The parents opposed the friendship of P and X and arranged for P to marry a Hindu; neither P nor the parents had met him. P was threatened with expulsion from the family home unless she married in accordance with her parents' wishes. The marriage was not consummated and P left her husband after six weeks. She petitioned for nullity on the grounds of duress. The judge refused to grant a decree because there had been no threat to P's life, limb or liberty. P appealed. The appeal was allowed and a decree was granted. Ormrod J stated:

> It is clear that the judge was greatly influenced by the judgment of Simon P in *Szechter v Szechter* (1971) ... Reading that passage – and one can understand what the judge had in mind – he felt that he had to find a threat to life, limb, liberty in order to find duress. With respect, I do not for one moment think that the President intended that result. He was merely contrasting a disagreeable situation with one which constituted a real threat. The matter can be dealt with quite shortly by referring to *Pao On v Lau Liu Long* (1980) unreported in which Lord Scarman said: 'Duress, whatever form it takes, is a coercion of the will so as to vitiate consent.'

> The crucial question in these cases, particularly where a marriage is involved, is whether the threats, pressure or whatever it is, is such as to destroy the reality of consent and overbears the will of the individual. It seems to me that this case of a young girl, wholly dependent on her parents, being forced into a marriage with a man she has never seen in order to prevent her (reasonably from her parents' point of view) continuing in an association with a Muslim which they would regard with abhorrence. But it is as clear a case as one could want of the overbearance of the will of the petitioner and thus invalidating or vitiating her consent.

In the first of these cases the court's view was that to establish duress the petitioner had to show that their will had been overborne by genuine and reasonably held fear that was caused by an immediate threat to life, limb, or liberty. In the case of *Hirani*, the interpretation of duress was that it will be found where pressure, of whatever kind, had been such as to destroy the reality of the consent given to the marriage.

Of the two interpretations the latter is preferable since it looks at duress in a more common sense way and focuses on the subjective element of consent.

Mistake is the final reason for obviating consent to marriage.

Question

Can you think of any situations where a mistake would mean that a marriage could be avoided?

There are two types of situations where a mistake might occur. You may have thought of a situation where one does not realise that what they are doing is getting married. In a case in 1945 (*Mehta v Mehta* [1945] 2 All ER 690) the petitioner wrongly believed that they were going through a ceremony of religious conversion. This mistaken belief was held to vitiate consent.

Alternatively, you may have considered the situation where one wrongly believes their spouse to be a millionaire when, in reality, they are a pauper. In this case, if it is merely a mistake as to the attributes of the person one marries, one cannot plead mistake. If, however, one marries Tom, believing him to be Fred, his twin brother, mistake would be a valid claim.

2.4.3   Mental illness

Again, the mental capacity of one of the parties to the marriage is the main issue, but here the requirement is that the party is suffering from a mental illness within the meaning of the Mental Health Act 1983. The important point to note is that in s 12(d) of the MCA the mental illness is more specifically defined than in s 12(c), which refers to unsoundness of mind, a much wider and potentially vague concept. It is also important to note that the consequence of the mental illness is relevant. The party must be 'unfitted for marriage' for s 12(d) to apply; by contrast s 12(c) is simply looking at consent. You should remember that an individual may have a mental illness but still be capable of giving consent. After the marriage it may be found that such an individual is 'unfitted', and the marriage can be avoided by use of s 12(d).

In *Bennett v Bennett* [1969] 1 WLR 430, H had married W in 1965 but they spent only very short periods of time with each other because H was abroad on active service. W had been admitted twice to a mental hospital before the marriage, once for a month and, later, for a fortnight during which she was given shock treatment. H was not aware of these facts when he married W. When he returned home in December 1965 he learned from a doctor that W had been receiving treatment in a mental hospital. Following another tour of duty abroad, he filed a petition of nullity. The court held that whilst accepting W's behaviour was likely to be difficult over a relatively short period of time, it was clear that W was suffering from no more than a temporary neurosis. The marriage of H and W was valid. *Per* Ormrod J:

> Concerning the definition of mental disorder [in the Mental Health Act] the question is, what did Parliament mean by the phrase 'unfitted for marriage and the procreation of children', because they are conjunctive and not disjunctive. 'Unfitted' is a word which is not easily construed. It might be given a very wide interpretation or a very narrow one. It is quite plain to me, having regard to the context, with the background of mental deficiency in mind, that Parliament cannot possibly have intended to use the word 'unfitted' in an extensive sense. This must really mean something very much like the test of unsoundness of mind although perhaps not quite the same, it really must mean something in the nature of: 'Is this particular person capable of living in a married state and of carrying out the ordinary duties and obligations of marriage?' I do not think it could possibly be given any wider meaning than that.

2.4.4   Venereal disease

This reason for avoiding a marriage is little used and is perhaps anachronistic given the ability of medicine to cure venereal disease (VD). Today the sub-section has generated debate in relation to HIV and AIDS and whether this would be within the terms of the provision.

Question

Do you think HIV or AIDS fall within this provision? Should it?

No cases on nullity, to date, seem to have focused on HIV or AIDS. The problem would be that HIV itself is not really a disease, it is a virus, and also both HIV and AIDS are deemed to be blood disorders, and not VD. To a degree this would make sense since HIV can be transmitted in manners other than sexual contact. Given this doubt it may be preferable for an individual to seek a divorce rather than use the nullity provisions.

2.4.5   Existing pregnancy

The presence of this ground for annulling a marriage is rooted in history when fraudulent or wilful concealment of a relevant fact was ground for annulment. If a wife was pregnant by another man and had not revealed this to her husband before the marriage it did not amount to fraud or concealment and hence would not enable the husband to end the marriage. An existing pregnancy would also not be sufficient to enable the husband to divorce the wife. Consequently, the law had to be changed to ensure that men who had been deceived into marriage could break those legal ties; hence, the provision now found in s 12(f) of the MCA 1973. Today it seems more to highlight the potential discrimination in the law: do you think a wife could petition for nullity because her husband had caused another woman to become pregnant before the marriage?

2.4.6   The new gender grounds

As you will remember, from earlier in the chapter, the Draft Recognition Act 2004 increases the grounds upon which a marriage will be voidable. Under s 12(g) the court will be able to end a pre-existing marriage by means other than divorce, where one of the parties is seeking a full gender recognition certificate but, due to the marriage, has only been able to obtain an interim certificate.

2.5 BARS TO THE ANNULMENT

Section 13 of the MCA 1973 does, to a degree, temper the effects of s 12. The basic premise is that if an individual is seeking to set their marriage aside as voidable, but that individual had, despite knowing it would be possible to set the marriage aside, conducted themselves in a manner which suggested they did not intend to set the marriage aside, it would be unjust for the court to set the marriage aside, in which case the court can refuse to make the order. Section 13 also limits the scope for annulment in relation to the consent, mental illness, VD or pregnancy grounds. The proceedings must be commenced within three years of the marriage. Also, if the petition is brought under the VD and pregnancy grounds, the petitioner must satisfy the court that they did not know of the illness/pregnancy at the time of the marriage. The Gender Recognition Act 2004 inserts s 13(2A) into the MCA 1973, providing a limit of six months in which proceedings can be brought by virtue of one of the parties obtaining an interim gender recognition certificate. Presumably, if this timescale is not met, the parties would have to bring the marriage to an end via divorce. You should note that this would not entitle the party changing gender to obtain a full recognition certificate unless the divorce was instituted within six months of the gaining of the certificate – in which case why not just go for nullity?

2.6 WHO CAN APPLY FOR THE MARRIAGE TO BE ANNULLED?

Question

Who do you think can apply to end the marriage under the nullity provisions?

If you looked back at the relevant sections of the MCA 1973, you will probably have noticed that s 12 indicates who can petition on which ground, but that s 11 is silent on the matter.

Where a marriage is void the number of potential applicants is much wider. It includes not just the parties to the marriage, but also any other interested individual (for example, a child) who may wish to have the marriage set aside. This can happen, not just in the parties' lifetime, but also posthumously. A reason why this might occur is in relation to rights of inheritance.

If the marriage is voidable only the parties to the marriage can annul it and only in accordance with s 12. You should, therefore, make sure you are fully aware of who can petition on which ground. For example, under incapacity to consummate either party can petition and an individual's own incapacity can be relied on.

2.7 CONSEQUENCES OF NULLITY

Apart from the obvious consequence that once a marriage is annulled it will be brought to an end, other consequences flow.

2.7.1 Parties' rights: void marriages

Where the marriage is void, that is, has never been valid, it may still give the parties rights. If any children are born to the parties, then if one of the parties reasonably believed the marriage to be valid, the child will be treated as being legitimate (s 1 of the Legitimacy Act 1976). When a marriage is ended there are inevitably financial considerations. The ability to seek financial remedies is not restricted to divorce, but can also be extended to nullity (ss 23 and 24 of the MCA 1973). The willingness of the court to do so will depend on the reason for declaring the marriage to be void. The courts have, in the past, considered the public policy aspects of benefiting from ones own crime crime, when deciding these cases, and have refused, for example, to grant financial relief to someone who deliberately committed bigamy. This has also been taken to cover the fact of perjury where a party claimed to be male when they were in fact female! This trend is however not really a trend, with the courts returning to their traditional discretionary approach and looking at the individual facts of the case rather than simply stating the committing of a 'marital crime' should automatically deprive the party committing that crime of financial relief at the ending of a marriage. You will be looking at financial remedies on the ending of a marriage in a later chapter. For now, look at the following cases that cover both nullity and the ability to seek financial awards when the marriage is annulled.

In *J v S-T (Formerly J) (Transsexual: Ancillary Relief)* [1997] 1 FLR 402, the defendant (D) was a transsexual male who had been born a female and had concealed his true gender from the registrar and his 'wife' (the plaintiff (P)) for some 17 years. The true facts became known to P only when she examined D's birth certificate. A decree of nullity was granted in 1994 and D applied for ancillary relief (periodical payments and a property adjustment order). P then challenged D's right to apply. In January 1996, the judge held that D was debarred from continuing the claim for ancillary relief on the ground that it was contrary to public policy. D appealed and the Court of Appeal held that D's claim would be dismissed. Sir Brian Neill stated that, in the exercise of the court's discretion under s 25(1) of the MCA 1973, it was legitimate to take into account principles of public policy. The applicant (D) had been guilty of a serious crime (perjury) and had practised deception of a grave nature on P; these matters constituted relevant circumstances which were to be taken into account. It was possible to make the necessary assumptions of hardship in D's favour – P was very rich, whereas D had nothing except assets given by P and, perhaps, an equitable interest in the sale of the matrimonial home. However, no court could, in the proper exercise of its discretion, grant ancillary relief of the kind claimed by D. D's conduct at the time of the marriage ceremony (when he described himself as 'a bachelor'), when judged by principles of public policy, tipped the scales in decisive fashion against the grant of any relief.

In the earlier case of *Whiston v Whiston* [1995] 2 FLR 268, the court had also used public policy as a means to prevent a female bigamist from seeking a financial award when the marriage was annulled. However, in *Rampal v Rampal* [2001] EWCA Civ 989, the Court of Appeal confirmed that the conduct of the party in relation to a void marriage must be seen in the round – hence being a bigamist will not always prevent a financial award being granted as *Whiston* suggests.

2.7.2 Parties' rights: voidable marriages

Where the marriage is voidable, the same consequences will apply as for a void marriage. However, this is due to the fact that the marriage is valid unless and until it is annulled.

2.8 LEGAL SEPARATION

Legally authorised separation operates as a sort of halfway house between marriage and divorce. It does not totally rescind the marriage contract, but merely absolves the parties from certain requirements, for example, living together. The grounds for seeking a legal separation are currently found in the MCA 1973 and are the same as for divorce, with the exception that the court is not required to establish an irretrievable breakdown in the marriage (s 17(2)). As you will see in the next chapter, the applicant for a legal separation need, therefore, only show that a 'matrimonial offence' has occurred or that separation has already taken place. As legally authorised separation is not designed to terminate the marriage there is no need to go that one stage further and prove the marriage has ended completely.

If a couple uses legally authorised separation, there are certain advantages or consequences:

- a divorce petition can be brought at any future point during the marriage;
- financial relief can be sought;
- the parties do not have to cohabit;
- the parties are not free to remarry another person;
- for intestacy purposes the separated spouses are treated as being dead;
- the order can be converted to a divorce provided the remainder of the legal rules pertaining to divorce are met.

2.9   SUMMARY

The annulment of marriage is, at best, the confirmation of necessary rules relating to marriage and, at worst, the continuation of a set of anachronistic provisions with little, if any, real role to play in marital law. As you have seen, there exist a number of reasons or grounds for annulment, some of which may continue to be highly relevant, others less so. You should be familiar with their definitions and the consequences of a petition.

2.10   END OF CHAPTER ASSESSMENT

Here are a selection of smaller advice and essay type questions rather than one long question.

1   Alfred has been undergoing medical treatment for clinical depression. The drug regime has made him intermittently 'hazy' and he has difficulty in understanding or making sense of things. Last week Alfred went through a register office wedding with Bernadette. After the ceremony they booked in to a hotel nearby and the marriage was consummated. They have not lived together beyond that first night. Alfred has now sought your advice on bringing the marriage to an end.

2   To what extent can an individual marry whomsoever they wish, wherever they wish?

3   Andre is married to Steffi and the marriage took place eight months ago. Shortly after the marriage Andre confessed he was bisexual. Due to this, Steffi insisted that Andre must have an HIV test. This has been returned with a positive result. No sexual intercourse has taken place. Advise Andre, who wishes to set up home with Phillip and to relinquish all his marriage ties.

4   Four years ago Paramjit and Ravi married in their local temple, the marriage having been arranged by their respective families. The couple had not met prior to the ceremony. Ravi was not keen on the prospect of marrying but, due to her age at the time (28), her parents were constantly telling her of the shame that she was bringing on the family. The marriage has never been a happy one; Ravi has never felt able to have physical contact with Paramjit, and sexual intercourse has never taken place. Again, due to the family concerns, Ravi agreed to be artificially inseminated and has borne one child, Amandeep, now eight months old. Advise Ravi on her chances of bringing the marriage to an end.

CHAPTER 3

THE LAW ON DIVORCE

3.1   OBJECTIVES

By the end of this chapter you should be able to:

- explain the legal provisions that enable a divorce to be granted;
- evaluate the proposed changes to the legal regime;
- evaluate the effectiveness of, and any problems with, the provisions; and
- advise hypothetical clients as to their rights.

As you may be aware, the law on divorce has been subject to review over the last few years. The Family Law Act (FLA) 1996 was enacted with one of its aims being to change the divorce regime and to support the institution of marriage. While a large part of the FLA has been brought into force, Pt II, the part that dealt with divorce, was left unimplemented. Primarily this was to enable pilot studies to be carried out as to the best method for implementation. These pilot studies, and the accompanying research, were not favourable and hence Pt II of the FLA 1996 will, at some point, be repealed. This means that the Matrimonial Causes Act (MCA) 1973, despite criticism, remains in force and it is this Act's provisions that establish how a divorce can be obtained. In addition to studying the MCA 1973 you will look briefly at the FLA 1996, but this will be to enable you to understand why the reform failed and it will assist you in learning how to evaluate the law in a critical way. You should try to approach this part of the text on the basis of why the FLA's principles were so unworkable, and whether anything beneficial could come from it, etc. You will also be looking at mediation, a FLA concept for resolving issues in divorce, this being one of the parts of the FLA 1996 that are fully in force and operational.

3.2   A HISTORICAL PERSPECTIVE

England and Wales are perceived to have a high divorce rate – the number of divorces granted in 2003 being in excess of 148,000, although this is a fluctuating figure. This number of divorces is seen as being detrimental to the stability of family life and, indeed, detrimental to the family *per se*. The ability to seek a divorce, for the majority of couples who wish to do so, is a relatively recent development. Historically, divorce was available only to a few, those rich enough to obtain a Private Act of Parliament, and was often only an option for the male partner. In 1857 the concept of judicial divorces was introduced, being available where one party to the marriage was guilty of adultery and the petitioning spouse was free from any guilt. A move away from adultery as a basis for divorce came in 1937 with a widening of the categories, although the categories were all a 'matrimonial offence', such as cruelty, desertion, insanity or adultery. The modern law stems from the Divorce Reform Act (DRA) 1969 and was re-enacted without change in the MCA 1973. This change was intended to move away from the idea of a matrimonial offence as a basis for bringing the marriage to an end.

Following the full introduction of the DRA 1969, the number of divorces increased although not immediately. However, there was over a threefold increase in decrees granted between 1968 and 1978. The Law Commission has pointed out that whilst it may be easy to blame changes to the divorce laws for increasing marital breakdown, a change to divorce law and the number of divorces are not necessarily linked and you may find it useful to look at the paper (Law Commission Discussion Paper, *Facing the Future – A Discussion Paper on the Ground for Divorce* No 170, 1988, HMSO).

The increasing number of divorces does not predicate that marriage is unpopular, although it is true that marriage for the never-married category of individuals is decreasing. This, in part, could be due to the increasing acceptability of cohabitation instead of marriage: but it is also true that many individuals who divorce will go on to remarry, hence the term 'serial monogamy'.

3.3   THE BASIC PRESUMPTIONS OF THE MODERN DIVORCE

The forerunners of the DRA 1969 Act were the reports entitled *Reform of the Grounds for Divorce: The Field of Choice* (Law Commission, No 6, 1966) and *Putting Asunder*, produced by a committee set up by the Archbishop of Canterbury and also published in 1966. These reports set out to establish what purpose a 'good' divorce law should serve.

Question

What do you think the purpose of the divorce law should be?

The main planks upon which the new divorce law was to be built were that the law should 'buttress, rather than undermine, the stability of marriage' and 'enable the empty shell of a marriage to be destroyed with the maximum fairness and the minimum bitterness, distress and humiliation'.

Question

Can the divorce law achieve these aims? If so, how?

To achieve these ends the legal basis upon which a divorce should be granted was to be changed. The methods for change suggested by the Law Commission were:

- removing the references to matrimonial offences and replacing that ground with 'irretrievable breakdown' either with or without the need to carry out a thorough inquest into the breakdown;

- allowing divorce by consent, noting problems where children are involved; and

- allowing divorce where there has been a minimum of six months' separation, although possibly longer (but this was perceived to be an *additional* ground to the existing matrimonial offences).

Several safeguards were suggested, including the need for a minimum duration of marriage of three years, adjournment of the proceedings for reconciliation to be attempted and improving the rules in relation to arrangements for children born to the marriage. The resulting legislation, did not, however, reflect the Law Commission's proposals in all respects and was in reality a mixture of the approaches in the Law Commission and the Archbishop's report.

3.4 THE GROUNDS FOR DIVORCE – THE MATRIMONIAL CAUSES ACT 1973

The DRA 1969 implemented the changes and these were re-enacted in the MCA 1973. A divorce may be sought on the following grounds:

1   Divorce on breakdown of marriage

(1) Subject to section 3 below, a petition for divorce may be presented to the court by either party to a marriage on the ground that the marriage has broken down irretrievably.

(2) The court hearing a petition ... shall not hold the marriage to have broken down irretrievably unless the petitioner satisfies the court of one or more of the following facts, that is to say –

(a) that the respondent has committed adultery and the petitioner finds it intolerable to live with the respondent;

(b) that the respondent has behaved in such a way that the petitioner cannot reasonably be expected to live with the respondent;

(c) that the respondent has deserted the petitioner for a continuous period of at least two years immediately preceding the ... petition;

(d) that the parties to the marriage have lived apart for a continuous period of at least two years immediately preceding the presentation of the petition ... and the respondent consents to a decree being granted;

(e) that the parties to the marriage have lived apart for a continuous period of at least five years immediately preceding the presentation of the petition.

...

3   Bar on petitions for divorce within one year of marriage

(1) No petition for divorce shall be presented to the court before the expiration of the period of one year from the date of the marriage.

(2) Nothing in this section shall prohibit the presentation of a petition based on matters which occurred before the expiration of that period.

As you will see from the above extract, there is only one ground on which a divorce can be granted, namely that the marriage has broken down irretrievably.

Question

Does this ground include fault, or require the party petitioning for divorce to allege fault to end the marriage?

In the attempt to move away from the idea of matrimonial offences, the ground for divorce was intended to be 'fault free' and, notionally, irretrievable breakdown does achieve this aim. However, there are two major inroads into the idea of dissolving the 'empty shell' of a marriage: in s 3(1) of the MCA 1973 the prohibition on being able to seek a divorce until the marriage has existed for at least one year; and in s 1(2) the need to prove irretrievable breakdown by reference to one or more of five facts.

3.4.1   The five facts

Of the five facts, the first three (adultery, behaviour and desertion) are normally perceived as continuing to emphasise fault in the divorce process. The two separation facts are less clearly rooted in the fault mould and perhaps can be seen to be more consistent with the aims of the legislation. When you look at what needs to be proven and how this is done under the MCA 1973 process, the importance of fault seems to be minimal in the sense of the law and even for the parties themselves.

 ## 3.5   THE DIVORCE PROCESS

The method adopted during the 1970s to process the majority of divorce petitions is called the 'special procedure'. The procedure is, in effect, a purely documentary process. Under the special procedure the party seeking the divorce files their petition with the court and serves it on the respondent (although the court automatically serves the petition unless specifically asked not to do so). The respondent files an answer, normally agreeing to the divorce and confirming the facts alleged to be true. The documentation is then placed before a district judge to 'check' that everything is in order and to confirm that the ground and fact for divorce have been proven. In the checking of the paperwork it is unlikely that anything other than procedural errors will be spotted and no real investigation into the facts will take place. This is despite a requirement in s 1(3) of the MCA 1973 for the court 'to enquire, so far as it reasonably can, into the facts alleged by the petitioner and into any facts alleged by the respondent'. The reliance on the special procedure, and the failure of the court to meet its theoretical obligation in investigating the truth of the statement of irretrievable breakdown, has caused concern and helped drive the reforms contained in the FLA 1996. Indeed the Law Commission has stated that '[district judges] act as little more than rubber stamps' (*Facing The Future – A Discussion Paper on the Ground for Divorce*).

Given that the Law Commission was clearly of the view that the special procedure has resulted in a 'rubber stamp' exercise they concluded that individuals who want a divorce can gain one relatively easily – especially where adultery or behaviour is cited as the fact to support the breakdown. The fact that the special procedure cannot 'pick out' those cases of collusion means that divorce can be obtained, in effect, by consent.

Question

If divorce can thus be gained by consent if the parties are willing to collude, what does this say about fault?

As you know, the MCA 1973 was deemed to introduce 'no fault' divorce, and yet has been criticised for retaining 'fault based' facts to prove irretrievable breakdown. However, if couples who no longer wish to live together and wish to end their relationship can collude and pretend that adultery has taken place or that one party's behaviour is such that the other party cannot reasonably live with them, then is there any 'fault'? There may be fault in the sense of perjury but this is not the criticism that has been levelled at the legislation.

There is potential evidence to support the claim about collusion in the statistics on the facts used to support a divorce petition. There is a clear distinction between the genders when considering the number of applications for divorce, with women accounting for two-thirds of the applications. Women are more likely to apply on the basis of their husband's behaviour (51,982 compared to 12,786 in 2001) or his adultery (20,766 compared to 12,073 in 2001). In relation to the separation facts, 25,822 petitions, petitions based on these facts, were granted to women in 2001 and 19,236 granted to men in the same year. While the statistics do not show that the couple is consenting to the use of the 'fault' facts, they are clearly more popular than the 'non-fault' separation facts. The Law Commission has commented thus: '... the evidence suggests that behaviour and adultery are frequently used because of the need to obtain a quick divorce.'

In relation to the facts for separation, the time limits may be important (it will take a minimum of two years) but so will the economic realities of trying to establish two separate homes before divorce proceedings commence, although this is in fact a problem for many divorces anyway and many couples will not be in a position to enter into a separation deed. You may also like to think about whether the separation facts are truly fault free. While some couples may simply 'grow apart' and hence separate, is it not also the case that many separations will arise due to some act, or fault, on the part of one or both of the parties?

3.6   OTHER DIFFICULTIES

The inability of the special procedure to prevent cases of collusion and the inconsistency of a fault free divorce law primarily founded on fault based facts are merely two of the problems with the MCA 1973. Closer examination of the facts themselves should reveal additional conceptual and legal difficulties, in particular that the MCA 1973 is confusing and misleading.

3.6.1   The respondent has committed adultery and the petitioner finds it intolerable to live with the respondent

This fact, as you will see, involves the proving of two distinct elements:

- the fact of adultery; and
- the fact that there is a level of intolerability.

The first is easily defined: there must be an act of sexual intercourse between the respondent and another person, not being the respondent's spouse. Intercourse does not have the same definition as in nullity proceedings, and all that is required is some degree of penetration.

Question

Do you think this is an adequate definition? What are the shortcomings?

The idea of adultery comprising sexual intercourse is a very common sense approach, but the definition ignores the fact that sexual conduct less than intercourse may be just as distressing to the petitioner and yet they would not be able to petition. Also, the definition applies only to heterosexual intercourse and, therefore, there would be no means of redress through this fact for the petitioner if their partner had had a homosexual or lesbian relationship.

Turning to the second element, intolerability, this is a subjective issue in that the MCA 1973 states that 'the petitioner finds it intolerable'. As the Law Commission have explained:

> ... this requires some finding of incompatibility ... it has been held that there need be no causal link between the two requirements. Thus, the petitioner may find it intolerable to live with the respondent for any reason, not necessarily because he has committed adultery. The court or registrar is in no position to gainsay the petitioner ... (*Facing the Future – A Discussion Paper on the Ground for Divorce*).

The fact that no link is needed between the two elements of the adultery fact is certainly problematic. In *Cleary v Cleary* [1974] 1 WLR 73, H and W married in 1964. In 1971, W left H and went to live with another man. A month later W returned to H and stayed for six weeks, then leaving to live with her mother. H petitioned in 1972 on the ground of irretrievable breakdown of the marriage, arguing that H had behaved in a manner making it intolerable for her to live with him. H admitted the breakdown of the marriage and asked for a dissolution on the ground of W's adultery. The court heard evidence showing that W's adultery was proved and H submitted that, because there was no longer any real basis for the marriage, he could no longer live with W. His petition was dismissed and he appealed. On appeal it was held that H's appeal should be allowed. *Per* Lord Denning:

> As a matter of interpretation I think that the two facts in the section [adultery and intolerability] are independent and should be so treated. Take this very case. H proved that W committed adultery and that he forgave her and took her back. That is one fact. He then proves that, after she comes back, she behaves in a way that makes it quite intolerable to live with her. She corresponds with the other man and goes out at night and finally leaves H, taking the children with her. That is another fact. It is in consequence of the second fact that he finds it intolerable – not in consequence of the previous adultery. On that evidence it is quite plain that the marriage has broken down irretrievably. He complies with the section by proving (a) her adultery which was forgiven; and (b) her subsequent conduct (not adultery) which makes it intolerable to live with her ...

> A judge in such cases as these should not accept the man's bare assertion that he finds it intolerable. He should inquire what conduct on W's part has made it intolerable. It may be her previous adultery. It may be something else. But whatever it is, the judge must be satisfied that H finds it intolerable to live with her. On the facts of this case I think that the judge could and should have found on the evidence the two elements required: (1) W's adultery, and (2) H found it intolerable to live with her.

3.6.2 The respondent has behaved in such a way that the petitioner cannot reasonably be expected to live with the respondent

This is commonly called the unreasonable behaviour fact, but you should not fall into this shorthand description. When looking at the words used it is, or should be, clear that it is not the behaviour that is unreasonable, but the expectation of cohabitation. There are, again, two conditions to be satisfied:

- that there has been some form of 'behaviour'; and
- that it is unreasonable for the petitioner to continue living with the respondent.

With regard to the first condition, almost all types of behaviour will have been cited by a petitioner somewhere, at some time. In general, behaviour such as violence and excessive drinking are the ones that spring to mind, but the continued occurrence of minor or trivial incidents will often be sufficient. In one case the court had to consider, under the behaviour element, the parties' methods of washing their underwear. This is hardly what one would consider to be adequate to gain a divorce!

Turning to the unreasonableness of cohabitation, you are again looking at a type of subjective test – it is what is *reasonable for this petitioner* – but with aspects of objectivity. The test was formulated, in *Livingstone-Stallard v Livingstone-Stallard* [1974] Fam 47, at p 54, thus:

> Would any right-thinking person come to the conclusion that this husband has behaved in such a way that this wife cannot reasonably be expected to live with him, taking into account the whole of the circumstances and the characters and personalities of the parties?

Can you see the two aspects of the test?

Other cases where the nature of the test have been considered include:

> *Thurlow v Thurlow* (1975) 3 WLR 161, the W's epileptic fits, from which she suffered at the time of the marriage, meant that she was increasingly confined to her bed. She became very aggressive and damaged the home. It was obvious that she was in need of permanent institutional care. H petitioned for a decree of divorce on the ground that W's behaviour was such that he could not reasonably be expected to live with her. W contended that this did not amount to behaviour under s 1(2)(b) of the MCA 1973.

The court held that passive behaviour, for example, that caused by medical illness, *can* amount to 'behaviour' within s 1(2)(b). Taking into account the strain undergone by H a decree was granted. *Per* Rees J:

> I am satisfied that by July 1972 the marriage had irretrievably broken down and since the wife, tragically, is to spend the rest of her life as a patient in a hospital, the husband cannot be expected to live with her. But the question remains as to whether the wife's behaviour has been such as to justify a finding by the court that it is unreasonable to expect him to do so.

> As to the distinction which has been made between 'positive' and 'negative' behaviour, I can find nothing in the statute to suggest that either form is excluded. The sole test prescribed as to the nature of the behaviour is that it must be such as to justify a finding that the petitioner cannot reasonably be expected to live with the respondent. It may well be that in practice such a

finding will more readily be made in cases where the behaviour relied upon is positive than those where it is negative.

In reaching a decision, the judge will have regard to all the circumstances including the disabilities and temperaments of both parties, the causes of the behaviour and whether the causes were or were not known to the petitioner, the presence or absence of intention, the impact of it upon the petitioner and the family unit, its duration and the prospect of cure or improvement in the future. If the judge decided that it would be unreasonable to expect the petitioner to live with the respondent then he must grant a decree of divorce unless he is satisfied that the marriage has not irretrievably broken down.

Approaching the facts in the instant case upon the basis of these conclusions I feel bound to decide that a decree nisi should be granted. This husband has conscientiously and courageously suffered the behaviour of the wife for substantial periods of time between 1969 and 1972 until his powers of endurance were exhausted and his health was endangered. This behaviour stemmed from mental illness and disease and no blame of any kind can be attributed to the wife.

In *Ash v Ash* [1972] 2 WLR 347, W filed a petition for divorce on the ground of irretrievable breakdown of the marriage, citing H's various acts of violence and drunkenness. H admitted the acts but denied irretrievable breakdown. The court held that W did not appear, clearly, to be of such a character that she could be expected to live with H. The marriage had broken down irretrievably and a decree should be granted. *Per* Bagnall J:

In order to answer the question whether the petitioner can or cannot be reasonably expected to live with the respondent, in my judgment, I have to consider not only the behaviour of the respondent as alleged and established in the evidence, but the character, personality, disposition and behaviour of the petitioner. The general question may be expanded thus: can this petitioner, with his/her character and personality, with his/her faults and other attributes, good and bad, and having regard to his/her behaviour during the marriage, be reasonably expected to live with this respondent? It follows that if a respondent is seeking to resist a petition on the first ground on which the husband in this case relies, he must in his answer plead and in his evidence show the characteristics, faults, attributes, personality and behaviour on the part of the petitioner on which he relies. Then, if I may give a few examples, it seems to me that a violent petitioner can reasonably be expected to live with a violent respondent; a petitioner who is addicted to drink can reasonably be expected to live with a respondent similarly addicted ... and if each is equally bad, at any rate in similar respects, each can reasonably be expected to live with the other.

Other cases you may like to look at include: *O'Neill v O'Neill* [1975] 3 All ER 289; *Bannister v Bannister* [1980] 10 Fam Law 240; *Pheasant v Pheasant* [1972] 2 WLR 353.

> **Question**
>
> Would Mr and Mrs Average understand the true legal concept of this fact?

3.6.3 The respondent has deserted the petitioner for a continuous period of two years

Desertion is an infrequently used fact and accounts for less than 0.5% of divorce petitions. For desertion to be proved it requires the respondent's withdrawal from the state of marriage, without just cause. Hence, there needs to be a mental withdrawal from the marriage which, in most cases (although not necessarily in all), is accompanied by a physical withdrawal. If the respondent has a reason for not being with the petitioner, for example, if he or she is imprisoned, or has to work abroad for a lengthy period, then desertion will not be proven. Again, as with the 'behaviour fact', the legal elements are unlikely to be understood by Mr and Mrs Average.

In addition, the desertion fact overlaps greatly with s 1(2)(d) of the MCA 1973 and it is generally the case that the separation fact will be used in preference.

3.6.4 The parties have lived apart for a continuous period of two years preceding the presentation of the petition and the respondent consents

This fact is similar to the desertion fact, except that consent is required. There is still a requirement of withdrawal from the marriage – the separation – which must last for two years. It is possible for parties to be living in the same house, but to be separated from each other. This reflects the common economic reality that it is often hard for couples to physically move out from the matrimonial home, but it can cause problems in relation to separation. If the parties share any community of living then they will not be deemed to have separated. What is important to proving separation in this situation is that no shared activities take place, for example, cooking and eating meals together, or, if they are, that it is under a clearly differently constituted relationship, for example, as a lodger with the spouse and their new partner. To prove this fact, there must be unconditional consent from the respondent, they must know what they are consenting to, and if induced to consent, the divorce may be set aside.

In *Mouncer v Mouncer* [1972] 1 WLR 321, H and W were married in 1966. The relationship became unsatisfactory and from 1969 to mid-1971 they moved into separate bedrooms although they shared other rooms in the house and ate meals together with the children and participated in keeping the house clean. H argued that he stayed in the house only in order to be involved in the upbringing of the children. H left in mid-1971 and petitioned for divorce. The court held that H and W had *not* been 'living apart'. Indeed, they had shared the same household. The fact that they did this with the 'wholly admirable motive' of caring properly for their children could not alter the result of what they did.

By contrast, in *Fuller v Fuller* [1973] 1 WLR 730, H and W, who had been married in 1942, separated in 1964, W going to live with another man. In 1968 H became unwell and was told he could no longer live alone for health reasons. H then moved in with W and her partner. He took one meal with the 'family' and his other cooking was done by W, but he paid a regular amount for board and lodgings. On a petition for divorce based on five years separation the court held that H and W were in fact separated even though living in the same house. *Per* Lord Denning:

> From 1964 to 1968 the parties were undoubtedly living apart. From 1968 to 1972 the husband came back to live in the same house but not as a husband. He was to all intents and purposes a lodger in the house. I think the words 'with each other' mean 'living with each other as husband and wife'. In this case the parties were not living with each other in that sense. It is impossible to say that husband and wife were or are living with each other in the same household. It is very different from *Mouncer v Mouncer* where the husband and wife were living with the children in the same household – as husband and wife normally do – but were not having sexual intercourse together. That is not sufficient to constitute 'living apart'. I do not doubt the correctness of that decision. But the present case is very different.

Question

Having read the facts of *Mouncer*, do you think that they should have been successful in their petition since they had lived in the way they did purely in the interests of the children? Do you think that this is a state of affairs other couples could find themselves in?

3.6.5 Separation for five years without consent

This fact is basically the same as the separation fact discussed above, with the exception of the time period and the absence of consent. The purpose of the longer period is to prevent unilateral divorce being too easy, although as you have seen, and will see later, perhaps this does not work appropriately.

3.7 RELATIONSHIP BETWEEN THE GROUND FOR DIVORCE AND THE FACTS

Question

How do you think the ground for divorce and the facts interrelate?

You should remember that the ground for divorce is 'irretrievable breakdown of the marriage' and that proving one of the five facts evidences that breakdown.

Question

What would be the position if you could not prove a fact to the court's satisfaction, but still felt your marriage had broken down irretrievably?

The simple answer is that even if you can prove a breakdown of your marriage, but cannot prove the fact, you cannot get your divorce. Equally, if you can prove a fact, but the court is not convinced that the marriage has broken down irretrievably, you cannot get your divorce. However, it is one thing for a respondent to claim their marriage has not broken down, another to get the court to believe it, as the following illustrates:

In *H(T) v T (Divorce: Irretrievable Breakdown)* (2002) unreported, 6 June, H, whose defence to W's divorce petition itself alleged that W had committed adultery, that W had entered into the marriage purely for financial gain, and that she was a bad mother, an unsupportive wife and a drug taker, could not convincingly argue that the marriage had not broken down irretrievably. H had, in his defence, pulled away every foundation and cornerstone of the matrimonial relationship, and it said much about his attitude to W that he could begin to think that a reconciliation might be possible.

Here also, *Mouncer v Mouncer* is relevant since there the marriage had broken down irretrievably, but the pleaded fact could not be proven.

In *Buffery v Buffery* [1988] 2 FLR 365, H and W had been married for 20 years and had three children who, having grown up, had left the family home. W complained that, while the children were at home, she and H rarely went out together. Furthermore, she complained of H's control of the family finances. H and W appeared to have moved apart and had lost the capacity to communicate with each other. W sought to divorce H on the ground of his behaviour under s 1(2)(b) of the MCA 1973. The recorder held that H and W had 'merely drifted apart'. W's petition was dismissed as she had failed to prove her case under s 1(2)(b). She appealed and the court held W's appeal would be dismissed. *Per* May LJ:

> Reading the judgment of the recorder in full, I conclude that in so far as any dissension over money matters was concerned, although H had been somewhat insensitive, nevertheless this did not constitute sufficient behaviour within the relevant statutory provision. In truth, what has happened in this marriage is the fault of neither party; they have just grown apart. They cannot communicate. They have nothing in common, and there lies, as the recorder said, the crux of the matter.

> It was submitted that if the matter went back to the recorder he could make various findings on the evidence about the sensitivity of W in relation to these matters and various further findings of fact about the nature and extent of H's behaviour complained of. I, for my part, do not think that he could. He heard all the evidence, and the conclusion to which he came was that nobody was really at fault here, except they both had grown apart. In these circumstances, in my judgment, W failed to make out her case under s 1(2)(b), although she satisfied the recorder that the marriage had broken down irretrievably. I do not think that any advantage would be gained by sending this matter back for a retrial. The matter was fully investigated and the recorder made the findings to which I have referred. In those circumstances I would reach the same conclusion as did the recorder, namely that the petition should be dismissed.

It does seem somewhat unfair that a marriage may be accepted as having broken down and yet cannot be ended due to the failure to prove the fact or that one can prove the fact but not the breakdown. Also, can you see that this aspect of divorce law could result in confusion to the parties?

Question

How do you think this approach fits with the idea of divorce law ending the empty shell of the marriage?

3.8   DEFENDING THE DIVORCE

As the case of *H(T) v T*, above, shows, it is possible to defend the divorce petition, although this is very rarely done and is even more rarely successful! One of the main reasons for defending the petition is to dispute the evidence relied on to support the fact in s 1(2) of the MCA 1973; for example, to dispute that the respondent has behaved in a certain way. Most cases like this will also include a cross-petition, alleging the breakdown to be the 'fault' of the original petitioner. In such a situation both parties have clearly accepted that the marriage has broken down and it is then a case of negotiation to find an acceptable fact or evidence upon which to proceed to obtain the divorce.

3.9   BARS TO DIVORCE AND STOPPING THE CLOCK

Can you remember the first principle of a good divorce law? If not, go back to the beginning of the chapter and refresh your memory. The manner in which the law tries to promote the stability of marriage is found in s 2 of the MCA 1973, which establishes a range of time bars to the different facts and also permits the parties to stop the fact clock from running in separation cases, hence promoting attempts at reconciliation. The way the section works differs for each fact so, for example, with adultery a petition must be lodged within six months of the petitioner's knowledge that the respondent has committed adultery. This clearly goes to the root of the intolerability criterion, for if cohabitation continues, it cannot be intolerable. For behaviour, the length of continued cohabitation after the behaviour complained of would affect the assessment of the reasonableness of continued cohabitation. For the other three facts the reconciliation provisions will stop the clock for a maximum of six months, although the time spent attempting reconciliation will not be taken into account in computing the length of desertion or separation. The parties must however ensure that if their reconciliation fails they separate within the six months, since if they exceed this time they will lose the benefit of any previous period of separation in calculating the total time to prove the fact.

Sections 5 and 10 also provide a means to prevent a divorce, or delay it being granted.

These sections relate only to petitions under the separation facts and, only s 5 can prevent the divorce from going ahead; s 10 being a delaying tactic. For s 5 to operate, it must be shown that there will be a 'grave financial or other hardship' to the respondent if the divorce is granted. The hardship must relate to the divorce. Where financial matters are concerned, it is generally the case that the court's power to make financial awards will negate any hardship claimed to exist.

In *Le Marchant v Le Marchant* [1977] 1 WLR 559, H, a post office employee, petitioned for divorce on the basis of five years separation without consent. W claimed, under s 5(1), that the divorce would cause grave financial hardship due to the loss of the index-linked widow's pension from the post office pension scheme. The court found in H's favour and W appealed. The appeal was dismissed. *Per* Ormrod LJ:

> It would be quite wrong to approach this kind of case on the footing that the wife is entitled to be compensated pound for pound for what she will lose in consequence of the divorce. She has to show, not that she will lose something by being divorced, but that she will suffer grave financial hardship, which is quite another matter altogether. It is quite plain that, prima facie, the loss of the pension, which is index-linked ... is quite obviously grave financial hardship. [if the respondent] should set up a *prima facie* case of financial hardship ... the petition should be dismissed unless the petitioner ... [puts] forward a proposal which is acceptable to the court as reasonable in all the circumstances, which is sufficient to remove the element of grave financial hardship which would otherwise lead to the dismissal of the petition.

> The view which I have formed is that the present offer is a reasonable one in the sense that it will, if implemented, remove the element of grave financial hardship so far as the wife is concerned, and remove therefore the defence which she has to the present petition.

Where 'other hardship' is concerned, cases often reflect religious factors, but the court's attitude is such that this will generally be insufficient to meet the requirements and prevent divorce.

In *Rukat v Rukat* [1975] 2 WLR 201, H, a Pole, and W, a Sicilian, both Catholics, were married in Italy in 1946. They came to England where their daughter was born. W returned to Sicily and H told her not to return to England because he had fallen in love with another woman. W came back to England when the other woman died and sought to revive the marriage. In 1972, H petitioned for divorce but W opposed the petition, contending that in Sicily she would suffer hardship on social grounds if she, a Catholic, were known to be a divorced woman. A decree was granted and W appealed. The court held that W's appeal would be dismissed. There was no evidence as to the reality of W's fears. *Per* Lawton LJ:

> The learned judge ... found that W was feeling at the time of the judgment that she could not go back to Sicily. That, if it was genuinely and deeply felt, would undoubtedly be a 'hardship' in one sense of that word. But one has to ask oneself whether sensible persons, knowing all the facts, would think it was a hardship. On the evidence, I have come to the conclusion that it would not ...

Per Ormrod LJ:

> The court has first to decide whether there was evidence on which it could properly come to the conclusion that W was suffering from grave financial or other hardship; and 'other hardship' in this context, in my judgment ... must mean other grave hardship. If hardship is found, the court then has to look at the second limb and decide whether, in all the circumstances, looking at everybody's interests, balancing respondent's hardship against the petitioner's interest in getting his or her freedom, it would be wrong to dissolve the marriage.

Section 10 of the MCA 1973, by contrast, permits the respondent to a divorce petition founded on five years separation to request that the divorce is not made final until all the financial and property aspects of the case have been concluded. As these may take some time to complete, this can delay the divorce for the petitioner quite considerably unless they co-operate.

3.10   THE REFORMS OF THE 1990s

Question

What do you think are the defects of the MCA 1973?

When the Law Commission continued its work on the reform of family law, it set out its criticisms of the MCA 1973 thus:

- The law is confusing and misleading – for example, irretrievable breakdown does not appear to involve fault yet the facts do. The fact relied on does not have to have any relationship to the breakdown. The law suggests an inquiry is being made into the breakdown and yet this does not occur.

- The law is discriminatory and unjust – for example, the only non-fault based facts require separation, which may not be economically possible. The inability to cross-petition or defend a divorce means that agreeing to the divorce requires acceptance of blame that may not be truly felt.

- The distorts the parties' bargaining powers – for example, the party who alleges fault will perceive themselves to be in a better position to bargain on financial matters.

- The law provokes unnecessary hostility and bitterness – for example, the system of making allegations in the petition must increase hostility; the allegations may be exaggerated and may not be contradicted by the other party.

- The does nothing to save the marriage – for example, the making of allegations may destroy any chance of reconciliation.

- The existence of s 2 of the MCA 1973, which permits time for reconciliation, is contrary to the facts.

- The law can make things worse for the children – for example, the system encourages antagonism between the parents which continues into issues surrounding the children. The system does not emphasise the needs of the children (Law Commission, No 192, *Family Law: The Ground for Divorce*, 1990, HMSO).

The Commission concluded that this long list of criticisms 'would amount to a formidable case for reform'. This is at odds with an earlier comment in the report where it was stated that 67% of the people questioned in a public survey found divorce under the present law 'acceptable'. Surely this must raise the question, 'Why the change?' Perhaps the prevalence and general acceptance of divorce is of concern. Also, there were concerns expressed by the Law Commission as to the cost to the state of legal aid payments for divorcing couples and the cost of the welfare benefits system. Finally, the adversarial nature of divorce proceedings has been seen as contrary to the interests of the couple and any children.

3.10.1   Options for reform and basic principles

The Law Commission perceived there to be three possible options for reform:

- retention of a 'mixed' system along the present lines, perhaps with some modification;

- divorce after a fixed minimum period of separation; and

- divorce after a fixed minimum period for reflection and consideration of the arrangements, referred to as 'divorce by a process over time'.

Of these three, the last was the preferred option and was taken through to the legislature in the FLA 1996.

The aims of the FLA 1996 were similar to those in the MCA 1973 but, unlike the MCA 1973, the FLA 1996 has incorporated some of the aims in the Act itself. Hence, s 1 of the FLA 1996 required the court, and anyone exercising functions under the Act, to have regard to the following:

- supporting the institution of marriage;
- encouraging the parties to save the marriage;
- where a marriage is to be ended, doing so with the minimum distress to the parties and any children, and reducing the impact on the children of the end of the marriage;
- reducing costs; and
- reducing the risk to the parties, or children, from domestic violence.

Although the reform proposed in the FLA 1996 to the divorce process itself will not be coming into force, the remainder of the Act is in force, so these basic principles must be applied by the court, lawyers and 'other professionals' involved in matrimonial disputes. These 'other professionals' are mediators, who have, thanks to the FLA 1996, an increased role in the divorce process. The matters to be borne in mind under s 1 of the FLA 1996 will also potentially introduce difficulties and conflicts. To what extent will a solicitor be required to encourage the supporting of a client's marriage and give referrals to counselling when consulted on divorce? Will it require all professionals to fulfil a role of marriage counsellor?

Question

Will the inclusion of s 1 of the FLA actually assist in the saving of marriages?

3.10.2   The framework for divorce

The FLA 1996 framework for the divorce process was intended to reduce the scope for allegations of fault being made to the court and to change the procedure to a series of steps to be completed at specified times by the parties. Irretrievable breakdown of marriage remained the sole ground for divorce or a separation order, but the link between irretrievable breakdown and a 'fact' was disposed of. The primary means to prove irretrievable breakdown was to be that a substantial period of time had elapsed and, together with successful completion of the required steps, would result in a divorce being granted. It was to be a paper based exercise, amounting almost to divorce on demand. Parties were to be encouraged to save their marriages by, first, being given information on the divorce process – presumably the thinking being that if they know how difficult the process is, they are less likely to want to go down that route. This information stage – the information meeting – was piloted to establish the best way of getting information across to the parties but the results were not as expected. The research, from the pilot projects, found that those attending an information meeting were more likely to seek a divorce, having received the information, and were unlikely to want to utilise mediation to assist in the divorce process. The fact that only one party to the marriage was required to go to a meeting was also criticised as it was seen as reducing the scope for reconciliation.

Following an information meeting, the parties would commence a divorce by filing a statement of marital breakdown, which would not declare the marriage had ended as it was believed that this would to leave the door open for reconciliation. Having filed the statement the parties would then have to spend time 'reflecting and considering' the breakdown, trying to reconcile and, if unsuccessful, making arrangements for the future – these being financial and property arrangements and also those relating to children. It is difficult to predict how effective the period for reflection and consideration would have been in addressing reconciliation versus arrangements. How long would couples be expected to take to reconcile before realising that it was not possible? Would couples try to reconcile on Monday to Wednesday, make arrangements Thursday to Saturday and have a day of rest from negotiations on Sunday? Also, would it be fair to make couples wait the full period of time (as the FLA 1996 required) if they have made their arrangements in less than a month? At the end of the required period, provided the criteria were met, the divorce order would be granted.

While the reforms in the FLA 1996 do aim to meet the criticisms of the MCA 1973, they do not do so absolutely. Fault may be removed from the requirements needed by the court, but that does not remove it from the parties' own explanation of what went wrong. The court based process may not require allegations to be made relating to the breakdown, but this would not stop the parties making these allegations to one another. The additional time taken to end the marriage, due to the need to go through a period of reflection and consideration, may add to the distress felt by the parties because they are being kept in an unhappy marriage. While the system aims to put children and their needs to the fore, there is nothing to actually ensure that this is being done. The changes and procedures highlighted above are not, due to the perceived problems with them, to be brought into force.

3.11 MEDIATION

The introduction of mediation was seen as being central to the conceptual changes to be brought about by the FLA 1996 and to the promotion of party-led resolution of issues. Mediation for family disputes is covered in Pt III of the FLA 1996 and it is important to remember that this Part of the Act was brought into force on 21 March 1997, originally to enable pilot studies to be carried out. Mediation, and its effectiveness, has been evaluated and although, as you will see later, it has not been 'revolutionary' and despite the fact that Pt II of the FLA 1996 is NOT being brought into force, *mediation is here to stay* and is currently being used in relation to divorce under the MCA 1973 framework.

Question

What do you understand mediation to be about?

The process of mediation is to enable the parties to resolve disputes and make arrangements themselves, with a third party acting to facilitate communication. The mediator (who may or may not have legal qualifications) should not pressure couples into agreements, should not suggest ways to resolve problems and should not give advice. Mediation is deemed to be a voluntary process, and yet this may not be entirely accurate when you consider who has to use mediation. In addition, it is useful to note that most mediators, whether legally qualified or not, expect their mediation clients to have access to independent legal advice to evaluate the appropriateness of any solutions proposed as a consequence of mediation.

3.11.1   Who will have to use mediation?

To establish who has to use mediation, it is important to understand how mediation has been brought into effect in the family law system. The FLA 1996 deals with mediation in Pt III, but this Part simply amended the legislation in relation to state funding for legal services – initially by amending the Legal Aid Act 1988. The Legal Aid Act was subsequently repealed and replaced with the Access to Justice Act (AJA) 1999; however the substantive detail on who must use mediation is found in the Funding Code, which is imposed by the AJA 1999. A detailed explanation of the working of the Funding Code is beyond the scope of this text, hence, at its most simple, where divorce is concerned, the only people who are required to use mediation will be those who are seeking state funding for the ancillary procedures to divorce – meaning the financial and property orders or orders in relation to children. (You should note that the divorce itself under the MCA 1973 is generally paid for as a private client. The Legal Help Scheme under the AJA 1999 only permits help to be provided to the client in completing the divorce petition. The solicitor should not draft the petition or institute proceedings.)

Question

If mediation is supposed to be the 'best' method for resolving family disputes, and hence financial issues arising from divorce, why is it only aimed at those individuals seeking state funding?

Despite calls for mediation to be used more widely throughout the justice system and family justice in particular (see, for example, *Parental Separation: Children's Needs and Parent's Responsibilities*, Cm 6273, 2004, TSO) it is going to be hard to encourage the clients or users of the system to try something new, or something they are not familiar with. While most people will not divorce or be involved with legal proceedings, most have some idea of how law is implemented and mediation does not necessarily fit within that idea. Hence, one way to encourage use of mediation is to link it to something that is controlled, or underpinned, by government – the Community Legal Services Fund – which receives it's funding from the Treasury. Arguably, then, the reason for implementing mediation is as a means to reduce costs since lawyers are perceived as being too adversarial and hence likely to drive up costs.

So, if a client is seeking state funding for their family law problem, they must be assessed for suitability according to the Funding Code, which sets out a variety of services available to them. Although limited help may be available from a lawyer, the emphasis is on mediation and this will require the applicant to be referred to a mediator to assess if mediation is suitable to deal with the dispute. If the mediator decides the dispute is one that can be dealt with by mediation, the applicant will be assisted in applying for state funding to pay for the costs of mediation. If this application is successful, the funding granted will pay for mediation services – it will not pay for legal advice alongside the mediation. If such legal advice is required, the client will have to apply for funding to cover this and it should be noted that such funding has only limited scope – for example, to provide help in drafting an agreement reached by mediation.

Where mediation is deemed suitable, and the client reuses to go down this route, although they may then apply for funding to cover legal advice and help, the reasonableness of the refusal to mediate will be considered as part of the decision as to whether legal help will be funded. This may therefore reduce the level of voluntariness to mediate, since there is no certainty that funding for a lawyer will be forthcoming if mediation has been refused.

If mediation has been attempted and has failed, again the client can apply for funding for legal help. Once more, before funding will be granted, the reasons for the failure of mediation will be considered, so here too there is no certainty that more funding will be available.

Question

Can you think of any situations where mediation will automatically be seen as unsuitable?

The Funding Code does recognise that there are some situations where mediation can be seen as unsuitable without necessarily going through the mediation intake assessment. These 'exceptions' are as follows:

- where the case is a matter of urgency;
- where there is no recognised mediator available to hold the assessment meeting;

- where the mediator is satisfied that mediation is not suitable because another party to the dispute is unwilling to attempt mediation;
- where family proceedings (this is wider than divorce and ancillary matters and will cover a range of issues within family law) are already in existence and a court hearing date is set to take place within eight weeks of the application for state funding; and
- where the client has a fear of domestic abuse from a party to the mediation and is therefore unwilling to participate in mediation.

These exceptions do attempt to ensure only suitable cases are put forward for a mediation assessment meeting. The inclusion of the exception where one party is unwilling to mediate is welcome, since this would cover cases where one party to the divorce proceedings is privately funded and the other not, and the privately funded party does not want to mediate. As a privately funded party there is no requirement to mediate and it would be ridiculous to expect a party to mediate by themselves.

As has been made clear, the Funding Code is operational now and is being applied to applications under the MCA 1973 divorce regime. On a conceptual level it must be questioned whether a process founded within a fault free approach to divorce (the FLA 1996) can work effectively within a so called fault based approach to divorce (the MCA 1973).

3.11.2 Mediation, the MCA 1973 and the role for lawyers

The effectiveness of mediation should be assessed against the ability of participants to reach, and comply with, agreements on their future. However, the reality is that mediation is being assessed by way of its cost effectiveness and its ability to speed up the settlement process. When first introduced, mediation was also seen as being a useful way of reducing the reliance on lawyers in the divorce process – another way to save costs but dressed up as 'party participation'. As you will recall, from earlier in the chapter, the use of mediation will not automatically reduce the lawyers' role – mediators usually expect their clients to have legal advisers too.

Question

Why else will lawyers be needed even if mediation is used?

The function of mediation, to try to achieve a voluntary arrangement, depends on the willingness of the parties to co-operate. Even if this willingness is present, total agreement is not always going to arise, or the talks may break down. In such situations, recourse to legal advice will be needed. Remember, though, that if state funding has been granted for the mediation, which does not succeed, the Community Legal Service Fund will not automatically give assistance for legal advice. Even if agreement is reached, lawyers will still be needed. While many legal practitioners are seeking to become qualified mediators, it is still the case that most mediators have no legal qualifications at all. As you will learn, when you look at financial arrangements later, the courts are required to take into account certain factors when dealing with ancillary arrangements. The question is: to what extent will mediators make these factors known to the parties? Will parties find an agreement being thrown out when the application to ratify the mediated agreement is presented at court. Will parties be able to re-open a negotiated agreement if they later find that they could have got more? To prevent these potentially drastic situations arising, it must be the case that it is appropriate for legal advice to be sought alongside the mediation. Finally, if agreement is reached there will be no means of enforcement unless and until the agreement is formalised by way of a court order. Lawyers will be needed, in most cases, to assist the parties to achieve this outcome, and the limited scope of legal advice funded via the Funding Code may not be truly adequate.

Question

Why might it be difficult for an individual who is mediating to access the services of a lawyer?

It might not be possible to access legal advice purely due to the inability to pay, especially if the party is making a contribution to the costs of mediation or because of refusal or a limitation of state funded legal advice. Can you see how this reference to mediation (and the lack of legal advice) may create a two-tier service for divorcing individuals?

The pressure to remove lawyers from the process of divorce may simply be cost driven since mediation is perceived to be cheaper than legal advice from lawyers. If mediation is cheaper, what better way to reduce the amount of state funding on divorce? The backlash may be an increase in litigation after divorce, relating to failure to meet the legal considerations in the MCA 1973 on financial issues.

The question of whether mediation is effective has been considered in research by Gwynn Davis *et al* in *Monitoring Publicly Funded Family Mediation* (2000, Legal Services Commission). The findings from this research suggest that use of mediation has increased but not dramatically so. The agreement rate amongst couples who mediate was low – less than half agreed where the dispute related to children and only a third agreed where the dispute was about financial matters. The costs involved in mediation were generally less than in a non-mediated dispute with the not-for-profit sector being significantly cheaper, but this did not take into account additional costs for implementing the agreement. The authors concluded that while mediation may have something to offer to some parties at a particular time, mediation could not be seen as a panacea for all the problems associated with divorce and state funding. This conclusion, taken together with figures to show the limited numbers of mediators available, indicates that the immediate future for mediation is not that rosy.

3.12   SUMMARY

You have now finished a difficult chapter: you are dealing, in part, with areas of law reform and failed law reform at that! However, you should now be able to advise hypothetical clients on divorce, but also understand the criticisms levelled at the divorce regime. You will also be able to comment briefly on the nature of the changes proposed by the FLA 1996 and evaluate why they were not implemented following the relevant pilot studies and evaluate why they have been unsuccessful.

3.13   END OF CHAPTER ASSESSMENT

1   Joyce and Ralph married 10 years ago and approached their relationship on an 'open marriage' basis. Consequently, both partners have had casual relationships outside the marriage. Last year Ralph began to have a change of heart and decided that he would not participate in any such casual relationships. Joyce did not concur with this decision and has continued to act in the same way, much to Ralph's disgust. Recently he learnt that for the last seven months Joyce has been having an affair with Anne-Marie.

Advise Ralph on his rights in relation to divorce. Is there any way that Joyce could prevent a divorce?

2   Peggy and Tony married 15 months ago and stayed together for two months before Tony left the matrimonial home. He has recently contacted Peggy and asked to give the marriage a second chance. Advise Peggy how this would affect her potential right to seek a divorce.

3   Anne and Ben married four years ago, having cohabited for the 14 years preceding the marriage. Carl, their son, was adopted by Anne seven years ago, and Ben has a joint residence order with Anne. Three years before they married, Anne adopted Carl.

Their relationship was deteriorating when the adoption took place – not having a child was one reason why the difficulties were occurring. The situation did improve for a while, but not for long. The marriage was a method to achieve a reconciliation. This has not happened. Anne and Ben have slept in separate rooms for the last five years. Ben has now met Diana and would like to commence a relationship with her.

Advise Ben on ending his marriage

CHAPTER 4

PROPERTY AND FINANCE ON DIVORCE

4.1   OBJECTIVES

By the end of this chapter you should be able to:

- explain the nature of the orders that can be made on divorce, both for property and finance;
- list the criteria and factors that the court will have to consider when making orders;
- provide an analysis of those criteria;
- apply the law to hypothetical problems; and
- highlight and discuss any defects in or criticisms of the legal rules.

The granting of a divorce does not end the legal relationship between a spouse and their partner. The existence of children and jointly held assets will ensure that further contact or legal action is needed. In this chapter you will be considering the nature of the orders that can be made and the principles upon which such orders are made. Remember, in this chapter you are learning the rules with regard to spouses and not children; child support will be covered later in Chapter 6. This area is not complicated but does need to be considered methodically to ensure you really do understand it.

4.2   THE CONCEPT OF MAINTENANCE

Before you start to study the nature of the orders that can be made for financial and property assets when a couple divorce, it is perhaps wise to think about why these orders are needed. The law operates on the basis that there is a mutual obligation on spouses, and ex-spouses, to maintain one another. The extension of the obligation after divorce may strike you as strange: if the obligations arise from the entering into of a marriage contract, surely they should end when that contract is ended?

Question

Why should these obligations be extended beyond the divorce?

If you consider the marriage contract purely from a contractual position then, arguably, the maintenance that is sought equals the damages that could be claimed when a contract is brought to an early end. However, the notion of maintenance also illustrates the unequal status of women in society, especially those women with childcare responsibilities. Women who marry, and have children, will often (although not always) face a loss of marketability in employment terms, a career may have been broken or entirely given up on marriage. Despite the Equal Pay Act 1970, women's salaries are still consistently lower than men's and this will inevitably place women at a disadvantage after divorce. If a couple do have children, the law places an obligation upon the parents to care, or to pay for care, for them. The societal constraints within the family see the mother as the primary carer and the man as the breadwinner and the mother will often retain this primary carer role after any separation. If unable to work as well, she will need some form of support. Politically it is not acceptable for that 'provider' to be the state.

4.2.1   Amendments to the MCA 1973

The concept of permanent maintenance, whilst being in accordance with the above hypothesis, is equally one which the law is loath to accept, unless necessary. The Matrimonial Causes Act (MCA) 1973 was amended in 1984 to introduce the 'clean break' provisions, which you will look at later. These provisions require the court to reflect upon the possibility of ex-spouses gaining financial independence from one another after divorce, in other words moving away from the idea of a long term right to be maintained. The courts do not impose clean breaks in all cases, the reality of the situation in each case is always considered.

4.2.2   The orders available

The orders that can be sought under the MCA 1973 cover financial and property matters. A mixture of financial and property orders are the norm. The term applied to these types of proceedings is 'ancillary relief proceedings', since the proceedings are ancillary to the divorce; in reality these are often the more contentious issues, along with proceedings relating to children which you will look at later.

4.3   FINANCIAL ORDERS: s 23

Section 23 of the MCA 1973 establishes the range of financial orders that may be sought and they fall into the following three categories:

* periodical payments;
* secured periodical payments; and
* lump sum orders.

If you look at all of s 23 you will note that it does cover orders for children – this will be returned to later when looking at maintenance for children.

4.3.1   Periodical payments

Periodical payments are the most common form of maintenance awarded. This form of maintenance covers the making of regular payments of specified amounts from one spouse to the other. These payments may be substantial or only a nominal figure (such as five pence per annum). An order which is nothing more than nominal will enable the recipient to return to court for an increase in the amount in the event that their, or their ex-spouse's, situation changes. When the payments are 'periodical', if the payer fails to comply with the terms of the order the payee must seek to enforce the order through court action. If the order is secured, as in the second category, in the event of non-payment the payee has a means to obtain payment. This is because a secured periodical payments order will require the payer to set aside a capital fund, which may comprise shares or other forms of interest-bearing capital, but could even be property, such as a home, to act as a 'pot' into which the payee can dip if the payments are not made as ordered.

Question

How long do you think periodical payments will last?

There are a variety of potential cut-off points for periodical payments. The most drastic is where either party dies. If the order has been secured, while the order may not extend beyond the death of the payee (the recipient) it may in fact extend beyond the death of the payer. This does in fact make sense since the 'pot' will still exist and is likely to be in the hands of trustees.

The order will also end on the remarriage of the payee, and this is a factor to be borne in mind when advising clients. The same is not true of cohabitation and it has been suggested that this fact will result in a disincentive to marriage (see Cretney, Masson & Bailey-Harris, *Principles of Family Law*, 7th edn, 2003, Sweet & Maxwell). In addition, there may be a detriment to the payee and any children from the first marriage if a second marriage results in an overall lower standard of living. In this case, the only option would be to endeavour to increase maintenance for the children. If cohabitation is favoured as a means to avoid the provision, the payer may seek to vary the order, in any event, to reflect the changed situation if the order itself does not provide for the possibility of cohabitation. Regardless of marriage or cohabitation, it could be argued that periodical payments merely continue to highlight the attitudes of society to the roles and dependencies of men and women.

Clean breaks may also be mentioned in the duration of the order. A clean break does not have to be effective immediately, and can be deferred. In this situation maintenance will end at the time specified in the order itself. The rules relating to deferred clean breaks are found in s 28 of the MCA 1973.

4.3.2   Lump sum orders

An applicant can only seek one lump sum order, although s 23 uses the term 'lump sums'.

Question

Why do you think this is?

Lump sums can be useful where a couple has substantial financial assets, and these sorts of payments promote the idea of a clean break. A court may order the payment of a lump sum and dismiss periodical payments if the lump sum could generate sufficient income on a regular basis. The ordering of a lump sum does not have to be to the exclusion of periodical payments however; it may be appropriate in a particular case to order both.

When lump sum orders are made, the court has the power to direct that payment be made by instalments, hence the reference to 'sums' in the section. This might be suitable where the payer is likely to have difficulty raising sufficient capital immediately. An instalment order may also be useful to take into account future realisation of assets, such as a pension, which may account for a large sum. If instalments are ordered then there is a power to ensure the payments are secured.

An advantage for the payee is that the lump sum, once made, is virtually irrevocable, and the remarriage of the payee will not affect the payment made.

4.3.3   Maintenance pending suit

Under s 22 of the MCA 1973 an order for maintenance can be sought prior to the divorce being made absolute. This is useful if the couple has separated and one individual is not in employment or, if so, has a lower income than is needed. The court can only make periodical payments orders under this section which highlights that the order is intended to be a temporary one, pending final resolution of the divorce process. While the order will not last beyond the granting of the divorce (the decree absolute), the amount of the maintenance may be influential in any final settlement. It is also interesting to note that s 22 of the MCA 1973 can be used to claim sums to cover legal costs being incurred in connection with a divorce. This point was considered in *A v A (Maintenance Pending Suit: Provision of Legal Fees)* [2001] 1 WLR 605. H and W were involved in divorce proceedings with substantive issues still to be decided. W had been in receipt of state funding for the proceedings but, upon being awarded maintenance pending suit under s 22, her state funding was withdrawn resulting in increasing legal costs to be paid by her. W sought to increase the maintenance pending suit to include an amount towards the ongoing legal costs. The court held that the sums should be increased to assist W to pay her legal fees. *Per* Holman J:

The periodical payments must be 'such ... as the court thinks reasonable' but must also be 'for his or her maintenance' ie the maintenance of the payee ... There is no doubt that in all sorts of ways 'maintenance' does extend to, and orders for maintenance pending suit have for many years been intended to cover, matters which are not ones of 'daily living'. Provision may be included, if there has been a history of it, to enable the payee to make charitable payments or payments to a third party ... Such payments are not part of the 'living' expenses of the payee at all, but may be a component of the order. Further, provision can clearly be made to cover legal costs as such ...

4.4   PROPERTY ORDERS: s 24

Section 24 of the MCA 1973 establishes the range of property orders that may be sought and they fall into the following four categories:

- property transfers;
- property settlement;
- sale of property; and
- variation, extinguishment or reduction of interest in an ante- or post-nuptial settlement.

4.4.1   Transfers and settlement of property

In the majority of marriages the home will be the largest asset that is possessed by the couple. On divorce the court, under s 24, has considerable powers to re-order the ownership of family property or even to order its sale. The order made will depend on the individual circumstances. It is obvious that one household is unlikely to become two in an easy way, and deciding who shall occupy the family home will inevitably result in loss to one party. The need to house children will weigh heavily on the court's mind when deciding on the appropriate order.

4.4.1.1   Types of property adjustment orders

Question

What type of adjustment orders might the court make? What are the advantages or disadvantages of the different orders?

Taking the types of arrangements, in no particular order:

(a) The court might order an immediate sale of the property concerned. This can be coupled with an order that the proceeds of sale be divided between the parties. Whilst this has the advantage of promoting a clean break for the couple, it can only be used in limited situations. To start, you should notice from s 24A, it can only arise as part of other orders –

the court must be making a secured periodical payment order, or a lump sum order, or a property adjustment order. Both parties need to be in a position to secure alternative housing; this is especially so if there are children involved, and so invariably there will need to be sufficient equity or other capital available.

(b) The court may transfer complete ownership of property to one party. To reflect the potential loss of a large asset there may be compensation in the form of reduced maintenance or a lump sum payment back or a charge being placed on the property.

In *Hanlon v Hanlon* [1978] 1 WLR 592, H and W separated after a marriage of 14 years. W continued to care for the four children from the marriage. Both H and W were in full-time employment with gross incomes that were almost equal. W remained in the matrimonial home and H lived rent free in accommodation provided by his employer. In the earlier hearings different orders had been made in relation to the matrimonial home: an outright transfer to W subject to her paying H £5,000, with reduced maintenance payable by H. On appeal the property was ordered to be held on trust for sale in equal shares with the sale delayed for five years, with maintenance being increased from the original order. W appealed and the Court of Appeal agreed that postponing the sale would result in both parties being potentially homeless as the sale would not produce sufficient equity to fund the purchase of a home. H was in a better financial position regarding the future compared to W and hence the proper order would be for the matrimonial home to be transferred outright to W with a reduced maintenance order being made.

Other cases of interest include *Mortimer v Mortimer-Griffin* [1986] 2 FLR 315 and *Knibb v Knibb* [1987] 2 FLR 396.

There are advantages to property adjustment orders; they will achieve certainty, and enable a clean break to be achieved in so far as housing is concerned. However, there are the following difficulties:

- the introduction of the Child Support Acts (CSAs) in 1991 and 1995 means that it is virtually impossible to offset maintenance for children against a capital transfer;

- the party gaining the property may not be in a position to pay back a lump sum or may be unable to get a loan or mortgage to do so; and

- the party in receipt of the charge-back will have to wait, potentially some considerable time, before being able to benefit from the property.

(c) The court may settle the property on one party until a specified event occurs and establish the division of proceeds for when this event happens. This often used to be set at the date that the youngest child of the family reaches 18 years or leaves full-time education. Orders of this type are called *Mesher* orders. Whilst it is common for a *Mesher* order to reflect the children's situation, the specified event may be the wife's subsequent cohabitation or marriage, or death if neither of the former occurs. As you can see, this is quite a flexible order.

Question

What are the disadvantages?

A major criticism of the *Mesher* order, and one of the reasons why it has lost favour with the courts, is the fact that it merely delays the time when the parties will have to consider rehousing themselves. If the order is to last until the youngest child reaches 18, and then the property is to be sold, the wife may find herself, literally, without a roof over her head, and if the equity is insufficient to rehouse her. In addition, by virtue of the time delay, she may be unable to obtain employment as her role as carer of the children may reduce her earning capacity, again impacting upon the ability to obtain a mortgage. The order also ignores the fact that many children do not leave home when they reach 18 and the home may still be needed for the wife and children. If the event specified is cohabitation or re-marriage, it may be the case that the new partner is not financially able to support the wife, and children of that relationship if there are any. Again, it would seem unfair for a wife to have to continue to support the children but with the loss of the property. Finally, you should have noted that the *Mesher* order does not accord with the principle of the clean break. Some of these disadvantages were raised in *Hanlon v Hanlon* (above).

The impact of the CSAs 1991 and 1995 has also affected the potential use of this order. It has been suggested that the *Mesher* order may come back into favour since it can run alongside the husband's continuing obligation to his children under the CSAs 1991 and 1995. Given the inability to utilise clean breaks to offset child maintenance, the *Mesher* order may be preferred.

4.5   HOW WILL THE COURT REACH ITS DECISION?

The court will need to have regard to the criteria set out in the MCA 1973, which you will look at shortly. However, the court operates in a pragmatic manner and, as you have seen from the types of orders that can be made, can act without necessarily having regard to who owns what in a legal sense.

The best explanation of the court's approach was by Lord Denning MR in *Hanlon v The Law Society* [1981] AC 124, where he stated (at p 147):

> [The law] takes the rights and obligations of the parties all together and puts the pieces into a mixed bag. Such pieces are the right to occupy the matrimonial home or to have a share in it, the obligation to maintain the wife and children, and so forth. The court then takes out the pieces and hands them to the two parties – some to one party and some to the other – so that each can provide for

the future with the pieces allotted to him or to her. The court hands them out without paying any too nice a regard to their legal or equitable rights but simply according to what is the fairest provision for the future, for mother and father and the children ...

The House of Lords decision in *White v White* [2000] 3 WLR 1571, covered in depth later, has added a gloss to this notion of 'fairest provision' by reference to the 'presumption of equality' elucidated by Lord Nicholls. This does not mean that spouses, on divorce, will automatically share the assets, but simply that there must be close consideration of the statutory criteria to establish how close to equality the award will be.

4.5.1   The statutory criteria

When the court is making decisions with regard to property and financial claims the MCA 1973 provides a checklist of factors to assist the court in making its decision. The factors are not prescriptive, nor is the list exhaustive. You should also remember that more often it is the legal advisers who will be considering the checklist because the court's role should be kept to the minimum. The Solicitors Family Law Association's Code of Practice works on the basis that the legal adviser will endeavour to deal with matters in a non-antagonistic and non-confrontational manner. Court action is perceived to heighten emotions and often to be contrary to the clients' respective needs – it does not promote good future relationships. This is not to say that court action should never arise, in some cases the only option will be to go to court. It is also important to note that the court will also question the need for its involvement if the issue in dispute is not very significant. Increasingly, the court is critical of parties who litigate and incur costs to such an extent that most of the assets are eaten up – the antithesis of the aim of family lawyers.

Section 25 of the MCA 1973 sets out the factors for the courts consideration thus:

(1) It shall be the duty of the court in deciding whether to exercise its powers under sections 23, 24 or 24A ... to have regard to all the circumstances of the case, first consideration being given to the welfare while a minor of any child of the family who has not attained the age of 18.

(2) As regards the exercise of the powers of the court ... in relation to a party to the marriage, the court shall in particular have regard to the following matters –

(a) the income, earning capacity, property and other financial resources which each of the parties to the marriage has or is likely to have in the foreseeable future, including in the case of earning capacity any increase in that capacity which it would in the opinion of the court be reasonable to expect a party to the marriage to take steps to acquire;

(b) the financial needs, obligations and responsibilities which each of the parties to the marriage has or is likely to have in the foreseeable future;

(c) the standard of living enjoyed by the family before the breakdown of the marriage;

(d) the age of each party to the marriage and the duration of the marriage;

(e) any physical or mental disability of either of the parties to the marriage;

(f) the contributions which each of the parties has made or is likely in the foreseeable future to make to the welfare of the family, including any contribution by looking after the home or caring for the family;

(g) the conduct of each of the parties, if that conduct is such that it would in the opinion of the court be inequitable to disregard it;

(h) in the case of proceedings for divorce or nullity of marriage, the value to each of the parties to the marriage of any benefit (for example, a pension) which, by reason of the dissolution or annulment of the marriage, that party will lose the chance of acquiring.

Question

From looking at the above list, are there any factors you think are unnecessary? If so, why?

4.5.2 Section 25(1): an overview

This sub-section reflects the non-exhaustive nature of the list that follows in s 25(2). It also highlights the importance of children of the family and this, again, can be linked with the priorities of the CSAs 1991 and 1995, which include the duty of a parent to maintain their child. It also emphasises the notion that a parent may be able to divorce their spouse, but not their child. However, you should note that the child's welfare is not the court's paramount consideration, but only the first consideration.

Also part of the consideration of 'all the circumstances of the case' is the desire of the court to provide 'fairness' to the parties in the event of divorce. As you will see, fairness will not mean granting equality, although many cases will refer to the principle of equality when looking at whether the award is fair. Fairness requires the court to investigate the s 25 factors thoroughly; this will reduce the scope for precedent in this area of the law. General principles may apply from one case to another, but the fact that each family situation is different means that only the general trends can be followed, detailed amounts cannot.

Fairness and equality appear to have replaced the judicial debate on the starting point for financial and property division. In the past, the court has held that it was appropriate for the starting point for division of finances and property, before considering any plus or minus factors from s 25, to be two-thirds of the assets to the husband and one-third to the wife.

Question

Can you think why these fractions were cited?

The one-third rule, now clearly inapplicable, was adopted because, according to Lord Denning MR in *Wachtel v Wachtel* [1973] Fam 72:

> [T]he husband will have to go out to work all day and get some woman to look after the house – either a wife ... or a housekeeper ... The wife will not usually have so much expense ... she will do most of the housework herself ... Or she may remarry, in which case her new husband will provide for her ...

That this attitude has not prevailed is perhaps understandable in today's society!

So now a 50:50 division may just as easily be seen as the appropriate starting point before adding and subtracting the s 25 factors. The important thing to note is that the recent case law is simply looking at the different weight to be attached to the various factors to be considered, not seeking to replace s 25, despite the fact that s 25 is seen as being a poor tool to use in today's divorce regime.

In *White v White*, H and W, who had divorced, had been considered by the court as 'equal partners' throughout their 33-year marriage, during which they had managed a very prosperous farming business. H's father had made a large contribution to the finances of the farm in its early years. In an application for ancillary relief W had received 40% of the total property. H had argued that this was an overgenerous award because it represented much more than W's financial needs within the meaning of s 25 of the MCA 1973, even if financial needs were to be interpreted as 'reasonable requirements' (see *Dart v Dart* [1996] 2 FLR 286). H appealed and W cross-appealed, contending that the resources ought to have been divided equally.

The appeal and the cross-appeal were dismissed by the House of Lords. The House of Lords took the view that although there was no presumption of equal division, the principle of equality ought to be departed from only if and to the extent that there was good reason for doing so. A judge would be well-advised to check, prior to reaching their decision, their tentative views against the yardstick of equal division. The financial needs of the parties, even when considered as 'reasonable requirements', were not to be considered determinative; they constituted only one of the factors to be taken into account. H and W had built up a sound business partnership in which W had looked after the family and the home and H had concentrated on business matters. Where, as in this case, assets exceeded financial needs of both parties there could be no justification for considering W's share as reflecting her actual needs while H was to be allowed to keep any surplus assets. Attention would be paid to the contribution made by H's father and to W's express wish that she might be able to make appropriate provision in her will for the children. *Per* Lord Nicholls:

Confusion might be avoided if the courts were to cease using the expression 'reasonable requirement' in cases of this type. There is much to be said for a return to the language of the statute. This would not deprive the courts of the necessary degree of flexibility. The end product of the court's assessment of financial needs should be seen and treated for what it was, namely, only one of the several factors to which the court was to have regard.

4.5.3 Resources and earnings

As you have seen, s 25(2)(a) relates to the resources that each party to the marriage has, whether it be income, property, earning capacity, or resources that the parties will conceivably have in the future. While the current assets and earning capacity should be easy to establish, subject naturally to the party's co-operation, the future earning capacity requires a court to gaze into its crystal ball.

Dealing first with disclosure and establishing the existing financial and property assets, parties are under a duty to make a full disclosure of assets and liabilities, and not just in contested cases but also where the court is being asked to endorse an agreement by way of a consent order. Failure to disclose leads to delay, extra cost and the possibility of later appeals, so is certainly not approved of!

In *Livesey (Formerly Jenkins) v Jenkins* [1985] 2 WLR 47, W was granted a decree nisi on 1 March 1982, made absolute on 14 April. On 12 August 1982 solicitors for H and W agreed on a consent order for property adjustment and financial provision. H's half-share in the matrimonial home would be transferred to W, subject to her accepting future responsibility for the existing mortgage. On 18 August 1982 W became engaged to X, a matter which had not been disclosed to anyone. On 2 September 1982 a consent order was made by the registrar. On 22 September 1982, H conveyed his half-share to W. On 24 September 1982 W remarried. H became aware of this and on 3 April 1983 made an application for leave to appeal out of time and for the order to be set aside. H's appeal was dismissed, as was a further appeal to the Court of Appeal. H appealed to the House of Lords. The House of Lords held that H's appeal would be allowed. The discretion of the court could not be exercised properly under s 25(1) of the MCA 1973 unless the court had been provided with information which was correct and up to date. H and W were under a clear duty to make a complete disclosure of all material facts to each other and to the court. Furthermore, that principle applied also to any exchanges of information leading to consent orders. W's remarriage ought to have been disclosed: it was one of the 'circumstances' mentioned in s 25(1). Because it was not disclosed, the consent order would have to be set aside.

Another useful case on this point is *Rose v Rose* [2003] EWHC 505 (Fam).

Looking now at the crystal ball gazing the court will undertake, this primarily affects women who may be expected to return to the work force.

However, you should not disregard the potential increases in men's salaries through promotion, etc.

Question

How easy is it for women to return to the workforce? What difficulties may they face?

The courts appear to recognise the difficulties for a woman when it comes to returning to the workplace given the nature of the economy, both in terms of availability of employment and the income that a woman can generate, but still feel able to make judgments on quantification of earnings. Statistics show that more women will work on a part-time basis than men, with the resultant reduction in earning capacity and long term benefits. This is especially so if the woman has care of any children. A factor that seems to be ignored by the judiciary (perhaps because the majority of judges are men, one could suggest) is the difficulty of working as a single parent. Many employers do not operate on a sufficiently flexible basis to accommodate employees' needs for time off work to deal with children's illnesses, or school holidays. However, the courts do take into account the problems of retraining and lack of skills that women may have.

There are a range of cases that illustrate this point; for example, in *M v M (Financial Provision)* [1987] 2 FLR 1, W had, before her marriage, worked as a secretary but had only done limited part-time work during the marriage. After 20 years of marriage, and following the divorce, the court felt that, even with training, W would be unable to achieve anything other that a low grade secretarial position since she lacked crucial skills and experience. Again, in *Leadbeater v Leadbeater* [1985] FLR 789, the court felt it was not reasonable to expect W to familiarise herself with modern technology after several years of part-time employment, but that it was reasonable to expect her to increase her part-time hours. Finally, in *Hardy v Hardy* [1981] 2 FLR 321, the court assessed H's ability to pay maintenance to W not on his actual salary but on the salary H could have obtained on the open market, as H worked for his father at 'reduced rates'.

Crystal ball gazing may also include examining aspects of potential inheritance for one of the parties. If it is expected that a party will inherit property or assets in the near future the court may take this into account. This also raises the issue of what resources can be considered. What should happen if a marriage has broken down several months or years earlier and then one spouse inherits after the breakdown, but before a divorce?

Question

Should these assets, acquired after marriage breakdown, be excluded from the 'matrimonial pot'?

It may seem a little unfair to take account of a windfall gained after breakdown; after all it is not a matrimonial asset. Unfortunately for the recipient, the court can take into account any resources, whether gained pre- or post-breakdown, if obtained before the ancillary proceedings.

In *Schuller v Schuller* [1990] 2 FLR 193, H and W were married in 1956 and separated in 1977 when W left the matrimonial home to keep house for an elderly friend, X. In 1987 a decree absolute was granted. On X's death W inherited his flat, which was worth £130,000. She became a residuary beneficiary of X's estate, which was valued at £5,000. H remained in the matrimonial home, worth £127,500 with an outstanding mortgage of some £5,000. W contended that X's flat was an after-acquired asset which was not related to the marriage in any way and which ought not to be taken into account. W appealed against a lump sum order awarded on the basis of a 'clean break'. W's appeal was dismissed. W appealed to the Court of Appeal.

The court held that W's appeal would be dismissed. The word 'resources' in s 25 of the MCA 1973 was not qualified in any way; it could not, therefore, be limited in any way. The court had to approach the matter of parties' assets realistically; *all* available assets based on real figures must be taken into account. Neither the registrar nor the judge had been in error in treating W's after-acquired assets in the way they did; the flat was a highly relevant factor in their decision.

In *White v White* [2000] 3 WLR 1571, however, the House of Lords did take into account the fact that some of the assets held by H did in fact result from a transfer from H's father. Consequently, it was deemed inappropriate to transfer these assets to W.

4.5.3.1   New partners

Question

To what extent do you think the court will take into account the earnings of a new partner when dealing with ancillary matters?

With regard to new partners, on a general level the court will take into account any assets or earnings that the new partner possesses when deciding on maintenance for the first spouse. However, this is not to say that a second partner will be made to *pay* maintenance to the former spouse. The court approaches the matter by asking, 'to what extent does the second partner's financial situation free up the income and assets of the spouse?'. To give you an example, in the case of *Martin v Martin* [1977] 3 All ER 762, H had commenced cohabitation with another woman, intending to marry. H lived in his new partner's council house, the tenancy of which could be transferred to them jointly. When the ancillary matters were decided, the court took account of the availability of accommodation for H and treated it as a resource of his own. Consequently, the wife was awarded a life interest in the former matrimonial home.

It is potentially easier for the court to assess resources where the asset in question is property rather than earnings. While the court can consider a new partner's financial status, this new partner cannot be compelled to give precise details of their economic position in writing but they may be required to give evidence in court. The danger of new partners making no disclosure is that the court will make assumptions about the wealth or otherwise of the partner.

4.5.4 The financial needs, obligations and responsibilities

These three categories are not synonymous but all have to be balanced in so far as is possible. The main need, in the majority of cases, will be to rehouse the parties and to ensure that any children are adequately provided for. There is, of course, a possible conflict if there are two families that need providing for, a fact that will need to be taken into account although the child support legislation may make important inroads here. The MCA 1973, due to the manner of its interpretation by the court, permits the husband to maintain his second family as a first priority and his prime responsibility, thereby reducing his capacity to support his first family. It is suggested, however, that while the needs of, and obligation to, a new family may result in a reduction in maintenance to the first wife, it may not significantly reduce the maintenance payable to the children under the CSAs 1991 and 1995.

4.5.4.1 What is the test of 'need'?

Question

How would you determine need? Would you apply a subjective or objective test?

For the purposes of the MCA 1973 the needs of a party will be considered subjectively, that is, what does this party need, having regard to the financial status of the parties? Need is, therefore, relative and a rich spouse will 'need' a more expensive lifestyle than a poor one, although the courts do draw the line somewhere – even if the family has been well off, claims for maintenance to include top of the range cars, holiday homes in Florida, etc will be looked at carefully. In *Leadbeater v Leadbeater*, W claimed that she needed a three-bedroomed property and around £20,000 to furnish it. H had claimed the property was too large and also in an area that was too upmarket. H had offered the sum of £6,000 to furnish the property. The court held that W's reasonable needs required a two bedroomed property and £10,000 to furnish it. In *Dart v Dart*, the Court of Appeal was faced with a dispute in what is often called a 'big money case'. H's assets were more than sufficient to meet the claim from W. The parties had enjoyed a lavish lifestyle during the marriage and following the divorce W sought an order for in the region of £122 million together with a property in the US. When assessing W's needs the court held that needs should be taken to mean the reasonable requirements of the spouse seeking the order. Once those reasonable needs, founded upon the consideration of W's need for a home, provision for the children and lifestyle, had been met there was nothing in the MCA 1973 to justify further capital distribution.

Even where the couple is of more modest means, the matter will still need to be assessed on a subjective basis, although more notice will need to be taken of the actual financial standing of the couples in question.

4.5.4.2 How are needs calculated: what is the starting point?

As indicated earlier, the court often wants to have a 'starting point' for the distribution of assets. The one-third rule was highlighted in *Wachtel v Wachtel* (above) and the move to an equality based approach was seen through cases such as *Burgess v Burgess* [1996] 2 FLR 34 (not extracted) and *White v White* (above).

However, while it is often advantageous to have some sort of starting point in the assessment of needs and division of assets, the court cannot fetter itself by applying a blanket formula. (You may want to compare this with the approach taken in cases under the child support legislation.) In the three cases mentioned, the court was able to use other factors from s 25 to justify the distribution that was made, rather than simply 'equality'.

Insofar as needs are concerned, *White v White* does highlight the view that where the assets are more than sufficient to meet needs there should be no reason why the husband is permitted to keep the excess after a wife's reasonable needs have been met. It appears that the court is clearly moving away from the view in *Dart v Dart* (above). In the *White* case, the House of Lords, *per* Lord Nicholls, felt that:

> [where the] husband and wife by their joint efforts over many years, him directly in his business and hers indirectly at home, have built up a valuable business from scratch, why should the claimant wife be confined to the court's assessment of her reasonable requirements, and the husband left with a much larger share? Or, to put the question differently, in such a case, where the assets exceed the financial needs of both parties, why should the surplus belong solely to the husband?

This argument does seem to make sense, although this is only applicable where assets are extensive – it would not apply necessarily to Mr and Mrs Average.

4.5.5 Section 25(2)(c), (d) and (e): the standard of living, the age of the parties, the duration of the marriage and physical and mental disabilities

The criteria covered in these three sub-sections can be taken together, since they are not problematic. Indeed, these criteria should have been identified by you as being potentially unnecessary when you first considered the s 25 checklist. However, by specifically raising them as considerations it ensures that relevant factors are not overlooked by the courts.

4.5.5.1 The standard of living

It has long been recognised that normally one household cannot be divided into two and result in the parties enjoying the same standard of living. The court is only required to see what standard of living was in existence during the marriage, and this will affect the consideration of each party's relative needs under s 25(2)(b) above.

4.5.5.2 Age of the parties and duration of the marriage

Again, you should see how these two considerations reflect other factors in the checklist. The age of the parties and the duration of the marriage will affect the assets that the parties have available and will also reflect their ability to seek employment, rehouse themselves and meet their needs.

4.5.5.3 Physical or mental disability

If one party has either a physical or mental impairment, the same arguments as raised above concerning ability to gain employment and rehousing will arise. The individual's ability to become more self-sufficient may be limited and their needs may be considerably greater. Therefore, this factor could easily be subsumed into the others.

4.5.6 Contributions made to the marriage

Question

What sort of contributions will be relevant here?

There are many contributions that are relevant – the sub-section itself refers to contributions to the welfare of the family and these will include looking after the home and the family. Principally, this is directed at the 'housewife' who should not be at a disadvantage from not working in the public economic sphere. As Lord Simon of Glaisdale expressed it: 'The cock bird can feather his nest precisely because he is not expected to spend most of his time sitting on it' (*With All My Worldly Goods*, 1964, Holdsworth Club).

Once more, there is an overlap between this factor and s 25(2)(a) and (b). While the sub-section highlights time spent caring for the family, other contributions, perhaps helping build up a family business, can be included under this head. In many cases, however, this latter type of action would also be referred to under the next sub-section.

What is certain following *White v White* is that contributions will become far more important in future cases. The cases that have come before the courts post-*White* have illustrated this; but it is important to note that the parties' skills in creating monetary wealth have seemed to predominate, emphasising the business skills over and above the homemaking skills of the wife. In the case of *Cowan v Cowan* [2001] EWCA Civ 679, [2001] 3 WLR 684, the husband's business skills were described as 'stellar', hence justifying an unequal distribution in the husband's favour. In *Lambert v Lambert* [2002] EWCA 1685, the court (Thorpe LJ) stated that:

> The authority of *Cowan v Cowan* cannot be elevated nearly as high ... the danger of gender discrimination resulting from a finding of special financial contribution is plain. If all that is regarded is the scale of the breadwinner's success then discrimination is almost bound to follow since there is no equal opportunity for the homemaker to demonstrate the scale of her comparable success.

And hence that:

> If the decision of this court in *Cowan* ... has indeed opened ... a forensic Pandora's Box then it is important that we should endeavour to close and lock the lid.

Whether the judgment of Thorpe LJ will be successful in reducing the forensic evaluation of business skills has not been thoroughly tested, but there does appear to be less reference to it in the reported cases. In *Parra v Parra* [2002] EWCA Civ 1886, H and W had been married for 20 years and had two children attending fee paying schools. W had been rehoused with the proceeds of the sale of the former matrimonial home and H was living in a property related to H's business. The original order left W with 54% of the overall assets and H with 46% and H was to be responsible for the children's school fees. On H's appeal, the court held that throughout the marriage the parties had arranged their financial affairs so as to be equal and the court could see no reason why this equality should not be maintained following divorce since there was nothing that would suggest fairness between the parties required reordering. Hence, W's lump sum was reduced. In *GW v RW (Financial Provision: Departure from Equality)* [2003] EWHC 611 (Fam), most of the assets had been accumulated from savings, not through business-making ventures. H had raised the argument of 'special contribution' to justify an unequal division between H and W. The court stated: 'The class of case where a special contribution can now be taken into account must be very narrow indeed.' In paragraph 46 of his judgment, Lambert Thorpe LJ stated:

> However for the present, given the infinite variety of fact and circumstance, I propose to mark time on a cautious acknowledgement that special contribution remains a legitimate possibility but only in exceptional circumstances. It would be both futile and dangerous to even attempt to speculate on the boundaries of the exceptional ... Certainly the mere fact of making a large amount of money cannot of itself demonstrate the existence of a special contribution.

4.5.7 The conduct of the parties

Under the MCA 1973, conduct will be taken into account when it is such that it would be inequitable to disregard it.

Question

When will that be likely to happen? What sort of conduct will it be?

Both positive and negative conduct has been considered by the courts under s 25(2)(g) of the MCA 1973. In *Wachtel v Wachtel* it was held that conduct would only be taken into account to reduce a financial award if the conduct were 'both obvious and gross' (*per* Lord Denning, at p 835). The difficulty for the courts would otherwise be that a full investigation into who was responsible for the breakdown, or whose conduct was worse, would be needed. This would also be contrary to the ethos of the MCA 1973 and 'fault free divorce'. It is not the case that only conduct leading to the breakdown of the marriage will be considered. A husband's reckless dissipation of assets has been classed as 'conduct that was inequitable to disregard', but generally there will be some link to the breakdown.

In *J v S-T (Formerly J) (Ancillary Relief)* 3 WLR 1287, the defendant (D), a transsexual male who had been born a female, had concealed his true gender from the registrar and his 'wife' (the plaintiff (P)) for some 17 years. The true facts became known to P only when she examined D's birth certificate. A decree of nullity was granted in 1994 and D applied for ancillary relief (periodical payments and a property adjustment order). P then challenged D's right to apply. In January 1996, the judge held that D was debarred from continuing the claim for ancillary relief on the ground that it was contrary to public policy. D appealed.

The court held that D's claim would be dismissed. Sir Brian Neill stated that, in the exercise of the court's discretion under s 25(1) of the MCA 1973, it was legitimate to take into account principles of public policy. The applicant (D) had been guilty of a serious crime (perjury) and had practised deception of a grave nature on P; these matters constituted relevant circumstances which were to be taken into account. It was possible to make the necessary assumptions of hardship in D's favour. P was very rich, whereas D had nothing except assets given by P and, perhaps, an equitable interest in the sale of the matrimonial home; but, no court could, in the proper exercise of its discretion, grant ancillary relief of the kind claimed by D. D's conduct at the time of the marriage ceremony (when he described himself as 'a bachelor'), when judged by principles of public policy, tipped the scales in a decisive fashion against the grant of any relief.

In *Beach v Beach* [1995] 2 FLR 160, [1995] 2 FCR 526, H and W were involved in farming although this did not prosper. The parties agreed that W would receive £450,000 from the sale of the farm to meet her claim under the MCA 1973 for ancillary relief. H failed to sell the farm and was declared bankrupt leading to W receiving less that the agreed sum. H claimed a lump sum from W. The court held that H's claim should fail. *Per* Thorpe J:

> The history is a financial tragedy, and one of the ingredients of that tragedy is the wife's forbearance. Time and time again, she was talked round. Had the farm been sold in 1983, there would have been money. Had the farm been sold in 1989, there would have been substantial money ... I think Miss Ralphs is fully entitled to suggest that the husband's conduct amounted to conduct which it would be inequitable to disregard. He obstinately, unrealistically and selfishly tailed on to eventual disaster, dissipating in the process not only his money but his family's money, his friends' money, the money of commercial creditors unsecured and eventually his wife's money ... The responsibility is, in my judgment, not shared, not hers, but his.

4.5.8   The loss of future benefits, especially pensions

The matrimonial home is normally perceived to be the largest matrimonial asset that a couple will possess. Today, with the growth of company pensions and private pensions, more couples will find themselves with another major asset, that is, a pension. Although sub-s 25(2)(h) of the MCA 1973 does not concentrate purely on pensions, these provide the focus of this section.

Question

How might a court deal with potential loss of a benefit such as a pension?

Under the MCA 1973, the loss of benefit could be dealt with by compensating the loser in another manner. Lump sum orders should spring to mind as possible remedies. This might not be an option if, for example, the husband does not have sufficient capital assets. The making of a property transfer order, giving all the equity in the home to the wife, may also be possible subject to the husband's ability to rehouse himself. In some situations the compensation has taken the form of an annuity

4.5.8.1   The Pensions Act 1995

Until the introduction of this Act and its amendments to the MCA 1973, the scope for the court to intervene with pension rights *per se* was limited. A pension fund had been divided between divorcing spouses in the case of *Brooks v Brooks* [1995] 2 FLR 13, but the circumstances of the fund itself had been unusual in this case. This uniqueness had enabled the court to hold the pension fund as being a post-nuptial settlement and, hence, capable of reallocation under the MCA 1973.

In addition to the powers of the court to make adjustment for pensions in the ways outlined above, the 1995 amendments introduced the concept of pension 'earmarking' or 'pension attachment' with regard to the pension itself. Under s 25B(4) of the MCA 1973, if the court makes a s 23 order it can require the pension fund trustees or managers to make payments from the fund to the non-fundholder. These payments may be periodical or lump sum, and are dependent on the type of pension fund benefits for the fundholder. In effect this power permits the court to divide future pension benefits between the parties, albeit only one has contributed. Problems do exist; what is the situation if the fundholder dies before the beneficiary where the pension has not 'kicked in'; can the court do anything if the fundholder simply stops paying in to the fund and starts another pension fund elsewhere; can the fundholder prevent the court taking the pension value as a whole if a large proportion of the fund was built up prior to the marriage?

A further order in respect of pensions was introduced in December 2000 due to the Welfare Reform and Pensions Act 1999, although the plans for the order were first mooted in the Family Law Act 1996. The order introduced is for pension sharing which differs from 'attachment' in that the pension fund will be split into shares and the shares allocated to each party. Sharing pensions in this manner would prevent some of the problems identified with attachment: a shared pension may be transferable to other pension providers and it will not disappear on the death of the fundholder and provides fairness in that contributions after divorce will benefit the individual making the payments. The extent to which this order is being used is unclear, but it has added to the range of options available to reach the fairest outcome. The difficulty with the expansion of options is that if a couple are mediating on their divorce settlement, without the aid of legal advice, they may fail to take pension assets into account. Not only is this a problem, but so too is establishing the value of the pension fund.

4.5.9   The clean break

As you have read earlier, the clean break provisions were introduced due to the need to encourage ex-spouses to be independent and also self-sufficient after divorce. When a court is exercising its powers under the MCA 1973, it is under a duty imposed by s 25A to consider if financial obligations can be ended immediately or at some time in the future. This fits with the notion that a divorce should end the empty shell of a marriage and allow the individuals to move on to another life without any ties from the relationship. Some of the orders you have studied in this chapter are naturally suited to this concept.

Question

Which of the orders that you have looked at support the concept of a clean break?

If the court does not feel that the parties can be financially independent, despite the wide range of orders available, it may believe that this independence will be possible in the future. Consequently the court can, under sub-s (2) of s 25A, make a periodical payments order for a specified period of time. At the end of this period the payments may end automatically without the possibility of the recipient seeking a continuance. The court can, and often will, impose a prohibition upon the right to obtain a continuation of the order under the provisions of s 28 of the MCA 1973. In some cases this prohibition is not placed on the order. If so, a further application for maintenance can be made.

You should note that following *McFarlane v McFarlane* and *Parlour v Parlour* [2004] EWCA Civ 872, these periodical payments can be ordered to enable the recipient to build up capital which will then mean a clean break is feasible in the future.

4.6   WHEN WILL THE ORDERS BE MADE?

Under the MCA 1973, financial and property orders are normally made after the decree of divorce has been made absolute (final). These ancillary proceedings may take quite some time to conclude in comparison with the speed with which an agreed divorce can be granted.

4.7   PREVENTING OR DELAYING THE DIVORCE

4.7.1   Preventing the divorce

Under the MCA 1973 there is a possibility of preventing the divorce from being made absolute, or of delaying it, to enable financial matters to be settled.

Under s 5 of the MCA 1973 the court can refuse to grant the divorce where:

... the respondent to a petition ... in which the petitioner alleges five years' separation may oppose the grant of a decree on the ground that the dissolution of the marriage will result in grave financial or other hardship ... and it would be wrong in all the circumstances to dissolve the marriage.

Financial hardship must relate to the ending of the marriage, not the fact of separation. As you have seen, in the previous chapter, it is unlikely that financial hardship will succeed to prevent divorce since the court has considerable powers to deal with the financial aftermath of separation. If 'other hardship' is cited, again this is unlikely to be successful. The cases of *Le Marchant v Le Marchant* [1977] 1 WLR 559 and *Rukat v Rukat* [1975] 2 WLR 201, which you read in Chapter 3, are relevant here.

4.7.2   Delaying the divorce

Again, this provision has been highlighted in the previous chapter but, to remind you, s 10 of the MCA 1973 provides that where the divorce is proceeding on either of the two separation facts, the respondent can apply to the court for their financial situation to be continued, resulting in the court being unable to:

> ... make the decree absolute unless it is satisfied (a) that the petitioner should not be required to make any financial provision for the respondent, or (b) that the financial provision made by the petitioner for the respondent is reasonable and fair or the best that can be made in the circumstances (s 10 (3)).

This is simply a delaying mechanism to ensure that the ancillary relief has been settled before the divorce is completed.

4.8   VARIATION AND APPEALING OF ORDERS

Variation and appeal of orders are often possibilities in family proceedings, reflecting the fact that family life can change post-divorce. Variation will normally only be possible if the orders are of a certain nature and in the absence (normally) of a clean break.

Question

Why might someone wish to change the financial order made by the court or agreed by the parties?

Two types of situation, which generally give rise to the wish to change the order made, are as follows:

- a change in circumstances; or
- a lack of full and frank disclosure.

Although s 31 of the MCA 1973 lists all the orders capable of being made by the court as open to variation or discharge, in reality periodical payments are most commonly varied and for this reason it is often tactically useful to get a nominal periodical payment that may be revived at a later date if circumstances change. If the order was specified for a fixed period of time, as can be done under the clean break provisions, the court may be prevented from reopening that arrangement due to the use of the restriction in s 28(1A) of the MCA 1973.

The criteria to be considered by the court when faced with a variation application are all the circumstances of the case with first regard being had to the welfare of children under 18. However, in practice the court will take into account all the factors of s 25 of the MCA 1973 anew.

In terms of how orders can be varied, the court does have discretion – it can replace orders with clean breaks, change periodical payments to lump sums or even grant a property adjustment order.

The parties to the proceedings will have the right to appeal against the decision made, although any client wishing to do so will need to be advised of the costs involved in so doing. Only if it is clear that the appeal is warranted should it be attempted. Appeals will lie from the county court to the Court of Appeal.

Appeals may be based on either a change in circumstances or fraud, with the latter more likely to be successful. Regardless of the reasons for seeking the appeal, as with other civil matters, there is only a limited time in which to do so before leave of the court is required. If an appeal is sought after the time limit has expired the Court of Appeal will need to grant leave to appeal. The criteria upon which an appeal out of time will be permitted include that:

- the basis or fundamental assumption underlying the order had been falsified by a change of circumstances;
- such change had occurred within a relatively short time of the making of the original order;
- the application for leave was made reasonably promptly; and
- the granting of leave would not prejudice unfairly third parties who had acquired interests for value in the property affected.

For an application for leave to appeal out of time to be successful, all of the criteria must be satisfied.

One difficulty with these criteria is the issue of whether they would apply fully to an appeal out of time where the applicant has discovered that the other party has been acting in a fraudulent manner by virtue of, say, failure to disclose.

In *Barder v Barder* [1987] 2 WLR 293, during divorce proceedings a consent order was made whereby H would transfer his interest in the matrimonial home to W absolutely, and periodical payments would be made to the children. Five weeks later, while the order was not yet in operation, W killed the children and then committed suicide. At this time the period for appealing had passed. The sole beneficiary of W's estate was X, W's mother. H's application for leave to appeal out of time was granted. His appeal was allowed and the consent order was set aside on the ground that it had been based on the underlying assumption that W and the children would need the home for some years ahead. An appeal by X, as intervener, was allowed by the Court of Appeal. H appealed to the House of Lords.

The House of Lords held that H's appeal would be allowed. The judge's decision had been correct: he had jurisdiction to hear an application for leave to appeal out of time and he had made the right order. There had been an implicit and basic assumption by H and W, and their solicitors, that W and the children would require a house for several years after the making of the order, but this assumption had been totally invalidated. An order giving leave to appeal out of time ought to be made only where the appeal, if it were heard, had a strong likelihood of success, if the supervening event had happened within a short period after the making of the order, and if the application had been made promptly. No application for leave to appeal should be made where it would prejudice a third party who had obtained, in good faith and for valuable consideration, an interest in the property which was the subject of the order in question. These conditions had been fulfilled in this particular case.

Other cases where appeals have been considered include *Vicary v Vicary* [1992] 2 FLR 271 and *B v B (Mesher Order)* [2002] EWHC 3106 (Fam).

4.8.1   Procedural changes

In an attempt to clarify proceedings in ancillary relief matters, the Ancillary Relief Protocol has been introduced. This protocol limits the extent of disclosure, although requests for additional information (with reasons for the request) will be permissible. The scope for more appeals, or claims against lawyers for negligence, cannot be ruled out.

4.9   REFORM

While the FLA 1996 raised the issue of change to the procedure for ancillary relief, the debate arising from the case of *White v White* has perhaps been more influential in bringing the current problems with the way in which the MCA 1973 deals with the question of ancillary relief. This is not to say that discussions on change have not been taking place elsewhere. For example, in 1998 Geoff Hoon, MP, raised the possibility of changes to incorporate the possibility of making pre-nuptial agreements legally binding. This proposal was followed by including the possibility of binding pre-nuptial agreements in the government Consultation Paper *Supporting Families* in November 1998.

Question

What do you understand pre-nuptial agreements to be? What do you think the court's attitude would be to enforcing a pre-nuptial agreement?

A pre-nuptial agreement is simply an agreement entered into by a couple prior to their marriage, setting out the ownership of property and financial assets. These assets may be taken into the marriage or 'after acquired' assets such as furniture or other goods bought during the relationship. These agreements can be entered into now, but the difficulty with them is that the court will not automatically uphold the agreement, because without legislation the court's jurisdiction under the MCA 1973 cannot be ousted. What the court is likely to do is to use a pre-nuptial agreement as evidence of intention only, although where the parties' agreement has been entered into with the benefit of full understanding and legal advice the courts will, if considered appropriate, uphold the terms of the agreement.

In *G v G (Financial Provision: Separation Agreement)* [2000] FLR 472, H and W had been married for just over four years. H had a successful business and was wealthy whilst W had only a modest income. Before the marriage they signed a pre-nuptial agreement with W undertaking not to claim against H's business in the event of separation and with H providing capital for a property and sums to provide for daily expenses and the education of W's children from a previous marriage. Upon separation H purchased a house for W and provided regular maintenance. W subsequently sought ancillary relief. The court held that the matter was one for a clean break and ordered H to pay W a lump sum. Connell J found that the pre-nuptial agreement was one of the most important factors to be considered in relation to s 25(1) and s 25(2)(g) of the MCA 1973 – the fact that the parties had not received legal advice did not affect the consideration of the agreement. The parties had thought the agreement fair and there was nothing in the parties' conduct that would render the agreement inappropriate for establishing the starting point for resolving the issue. Connell J did make it clear that the agreement was highly persuasive but not conclusive of the matter.

To illustrate how far the court has moved on pre-nuptial agreements, in *K v K (Pre-Nuptial Agreement)* [2003] 1 FLR 120, H and W had been married for 14 months. Both were wealthy, W by virtue of a trust fund, H by way of property dealing. W sought a lump sum of £1.6 million and periodical payments of £57,000 per annum. Prior to the marriage the couple had entered into a pre-nuptial agreement. The court upheld the agreement in relation to the capital element, having posed a series of questions to establish if the agreement was binding or influential:

- Did W understand the agreement?
- Was W properly advised as to its terms?
- Did H put W under any pressure to sign it?
- Was there full disclosure?
- Was W under any other pressure?
- Did W willingly sign the agreement?
- Did H exploit a dominant position, financial or otherwise?
- Was the agreement entered into in the knowledge that there would be a child?
- Has any unforeseen circumstance arisen, since the agreement was made, that would make it unjust to hold the parties to it?
- What does the agreement mean?
- Does the agreement preclude an order for periodical payments to W?
- Are there any grounds for concluding that an injustice would be done by holding the parties to the terms of the agreement?
- Is the agreement one of the circumstances of the case to be considered under s 25 of the MCA 1973?

- Does entry into the agreement constitute conduct which it would be inequitable to disregard under s 25 of the MCA 1973?

Having considered these points, the court upheld the agreement and, in addition, periodical payments were ordered (which were not, on the court's interpretation, forbidden by the agreement) suggesting, in effect, that the agreement was treated as being binding rather than being influential.

Whilst pre-nuptial agreements may be a good idea, and certainly continue the theme of pre-marriage guidance reflected in the consultation paper, there are difficulties with them.

Question

What are the problems you can think of?

Any list of difficulties should include things such as:

- the birth of children after the marriage when this was not covered in the agreement;
- a change in circumstances, whether for better or worse;
- failure to get legal advice before signing the document;
- duress or pressure exerted by one of the parties; and
- undisclosed assets.

All of the above are valid reasons for questioning the contents of a pre-nuptial agreement and hence the need to keep some form of oversight by the court. In its Green Paper, *Supporting Families: A Consultation Document*, the government set out the situations when a pre-nuptial agreement would not be legally binding as follows:

- where there is a child of the family, whether or not that child was alive or a child of the family at the time the agreement was made;
- where under the general law of contract the agreement is unenforceable;
- where one or both of the couple did not receive independent legal advice before entering the agreement;
- where the court considers that the enforcement of the agreement would cause significant injustice to one or both of the couple or a child of the marriage;
- where one of both of the couple have failed to give full disclosure of assets and property before the agreement was made;
- where the agreement is made less than 21 days prior to the marriage.

These caveats to the enforceability of the agreement are in some cases far too liberal. For example, surely if a child of the family was already in existence at the time the agreement was made, the parties would take this into account? The extent of the exceptions is such that legislation along these lines would add nothing to the existing situation that has been developed through the court and would, therefore, be almost meaningless.

4.10   SUMMARY

In this chapter you have covered a great deal of ground. The information itself is not complicated, although you may feel it is having read so much! It is important to realise that, where financial settlements are concerned, the prime objective is to reach a suitable agreement without the need to go to court. This achieves a better relationship between the parties and also a reduction of costs. When advising clients, you should always keep the s 25 factors in mind, but the approach must be holistic. You cannot focus purely on one or two of the factors to the exclusion of others – the approach must relate to the net effect on the couple. Matrimonial assets that once kept *a* family are unlikely to keep *two* families. You should also remember that, unless the parties are very well off, no situation will be ideal and invariably both parties will lose out.

4.11   END OF CHAPTER ASSESSMENT

Anna and Bob have been married for 18 years and together have built up a successful business. They have two children: Carmen, 20, and David, 16. Both children live in the matrimonial home. Carmen is currently finishing her university degree and David is soon to start college.

Anna has worked in the family business since the time of the marriage, although she has never received a proper salary. The matrimonial home is owned jointly in equal shares, although Bob has been the major contributor financially to the acquisition and upkeep of the house.

The marriage began to deteriorate several years ago and Bob has been living in a separate annex to the matrimonial home for the last six years.

Advise Anna on:

(a) her ability to seek a divorce;

(b) the principles the court would apply in assessing her claims for ancillary relief; and

(c) the types of order the court could make.

CHAPTER 5

PROPERTY AND FINANCE WITHOUT DIVORCE

5.1   OBJECTIVES

By the end of this chapter you should be able to:

- describe the legislative provisions for obtaining maintenance in the absence of a divorce or legal separation;
- evaluate the effectiveness of the provisions;
- advise hypothetical clients as to the preferred options;
- discuss the rules relating to occupation of property by virtue of spousal status;
- outline the factors used by the court to assess property ownership rights within equity; and
- consider the case for reform of cohabitees' rights.

Having spent time looking at what happens after divorce, you will now turn to the position of couples who may part and lead separate lives, but who do not wish to divorce or separate. Indeed, some couples may utilise the legal provisions to obtain maintenance or property rights without thinking about separating at all! As well as financial orders, the rules in relation to property, both occupation rights and ownership, will be discussed. Many of these property provisions will be equally relevant to cohabitees and you will also look at the proposals for legislative reform for cohabitees rights.

5.2   MAINTENANCE WITHOUT DIVORCE

As you will recall there is a common law duty of a spouse to maintain the other spouse and it is this duty which forms the basis of the existing laws on maintenance in divorce. However, what happens if a couple do not wish to divorce but merely prefer to live apart? Should the same rules apply or should the law recognise this as a different category and provide other remedies? Is it practicable for spouses to seek to enforce the common law duty whilst still living with their partner, or do you think that this would create too much antagonism?

In fact, the law treats the question of maintenance without divorce in only a slightly different manner to maintenance with divorce. The principles relating to issue of property are, by contrast, more akin to land law principles than it is to matrimonial law. If a couple have not separated, there is nothing, legally, to prevent property claims being made under land law, provided the criteria for the application can be met. You should note that a full discussion of land law principles is beyond the scope of this text – all you will cover here are the bare bones of the topic.

5.2.1   Claiming maintenance

Spouses are able to seek maintenance under two statutes, the Matrimonial Causes Act (MCA) 1973, with which you are already familiar, and the Domestic Proceedings and Magistrates' Courts Act (DPMCA) 1978. Neither of these Acts is available to cohabitees, and this is an important fact to remember. Although the general thrust of both Acts is the same, there are however some subtle differences that must be borne in mind when deciding which is the most appropriate to use.

5.2.1.1   The MCA 1973

Section 27 of the MCA 1973 allows maintenance to be sought where the other party has 'failed to provide reasonable maintenance for the applicant'. This is the sole trigger factor. When assessing what reasonable maintenance is, the criteria are in fact the same as for any other maintenance application under the MCA 1973. Consequently, what you learnt in the previous chapter is relevant here. A major difference to be aware of is that the court is only reflecting upon the maintenance situation under s 27; the holistic approach, which takes in property requirements, does not automatically apply. If couples are separating without divorce or legal separation, and they wish to deal with the matrimonial home, land law principles are applicable.

The types of orders that can be granted, again, are very comparable to those under s 23 of the MCA 1973. The court can make a periodical payments order, which may or may not be secured, or a lump sum order (s 27(6)). There is no set limit on the amount that may be awarded; the court will assess the 'reasonableness' purely on the s 25(2) factors. In addition, lump sum orders may be made, again with no limit as to amount (s 27(7)). What is important to remember is that this only covers financial orders.

Question

How long should the orders last? Would the fact that the couple have not separated make a difference?

The orders that can be made under s 27 can be for any term that the court may specify. Hence, the notion of fixed term payments is clearly anticipated. If a spouse is merely trying to force the other into paying maintenance, a short term order may be appropriate. In any event, the court may be loath to grant an unlimited duration order if the parties are still cohabiting, but a long term order is not outside the realms of possibility. If an unlimited term order is made, the only restrictions on duration are set out in s 28(2) which provides that:

> ... where a periodical payments ... order in favour of a party to a marriage is made otherwise than on or after a grant of [divorce or nullity], and the marriage is subsequently dissolved but the order continues in force, the order shall, notwithstanding anything in it, cease to have effect on the remarriage of that party.

Clearly, the remarriage of one of the parties will not be the only situation that ends a s 27 order. The couple may resume cohabitation, or maintenance may be paid more willingly and an application to terminate the order be made, one of the parties may die or, perhaps less tragically, the couple may divorce and another order be made in those proceedings. You should note that the divorce of a couple, which has obtained a s 27 order, does not automatically end that order.

5.2.1.2　The DPMCA 1978

This is the alternative source of remedies for spouses who seek maintenance where a divorce is not contemplated. Indeed, this Act is only applicable where spouses are currently cohabiting or are separated. The criteria in s 1, which trigger the jurisdiction of the court, are that the other party to the marriage has:

- failed to provide reasonable maintenance for them;
- has behaved in such a way that the applicant cannot reasonably be expected to live with the respondent; or
- has deserted the applicant.

When the magistrates are assessing whether to make the order they must consider the factors in s 3(2) of the DPMCA 1978. These will be familiar to you since they are the same as the s 25 of the MCA 1973 factors.

The scope of the orders is where the constraints of the DPMCA 1978 become apparent. A court may make both periodical payments and lump sum orders under s 2 but the court can only make *unsecured* periodical payments, whilst those under s 27 of the MCA 1973 may be *secured*. Additionally, the magistrates' powers only extend to the making of a lump sum order to a total of £1,000. There is no such restriction under the MCA 1973.

In relation to the duration of the order the restrictions included within s 4 of the DPMCA 1978 are the same as for s 27 of the MCA 1973. It is interesting that the magistrates' orders can survive divorce when the input this court has into divorce *per se* is very small. Unlike the MCA 1973, however, any order made for periodical payments will cease if the couple remains in, or recommences, cohabitation for a period in excess of six months (s 25). This is more logical than the MCA 1973; if the parties are living together, the state should not have to intervene in this way; it should be for the individuals themselves to sort out their financial affairs.

> **Question**
>
> Why would you advise a client to use the DPMCA 1978 rather than the MCA 1973?

This is the type of question you will need to reflect upon if you intend to work within the family law. Where there are jurisdictional options for legal proceedings, the legal adviser must explain the best option for that particular client. The advantages of using the magistrates' jurisdiction are that the court is generally quite quick to deal with the application, the court is often easier to access since there are more magistrates' courts than county courts, and the application will result in lower costs for the client. However, a disadvantage of the magistrates' courts is that state funding may not be granted for the application since it might be perceived to be a simple application where no legal assistance is warranted (however, it is true to say that in the future with the restrictions on state funding in all courts this may not be a factor for consideration).

5.2.1.3   Other orders in the magistrates' courts

In addition to the orders available under s 1 of the DPMCA 1978 criteria, the magistrates have a slightly extended jurisdiction by virtue of ss 6 and 7. Taking s 6 first, this provides the magistrates with the power to make consent orders (that is, orders when the court accepts an arrangement reached by the parties themselves and hence not requiring a full contested hearing). Without this section a consent order could not be made under the DPMCA 1978. The court is not required to go behind the agreement, merely to consider whether the making of the order is contrary to the interests of justice. By implication, this would involve some investigation to ensure that any provision within the consent order was reasonable.

Section 7 is a very useful section. Under the provisions of s 7 the couple must have been living apart for more than three months. The court can make an order, without consent, where one party has paid maintenance to the other party voluntarily for three months or more. The aggregate amount of maintenance will dictate the amount that can be ordered (subject to s 7(4)). So, for example, if the absent spouse has paid £500 in month one, £300 in month two and £400 in month three, then the maximum award would be £400 per month, which is the total amount divided by three, that being the period over which voluntary payments have been made.

There is a proviso in sub-s (4) which is important since the mean amount may be deemed inadequate by the magistrates. Under this sub-section the magistrates can treat the application as made under s 2 and, hence, increase the amount awarded.

5.2.2   The welfare state

In addition to the MCA 1973 and the DPMCA 1978, the influence of the social security legislation may be felt. In the event of a couple separating, and maintenance being unforthcoming, one party is potentially reliant on welfare benefits. If this is so, under social security legislation the non-claiming spouse will be classed as a 'liable relative' and thus 'liable to maintain his wife [and any children of whom he is the father]'. The same liability applies to a wife. The Benefits Agency may 'persuade' the claimant to apply for maintenance under the MCA 1973 or the DPMCA 1978. Alternatively, the Benefits Agency may contact the liable relative directly to request 'voluntary payments' to be made. If no maintenance is paid the Secretary of State has the right to apply in the magistrates' court for an order against the non-claiming spouse.

It was explained earlier that the MCA 1973 and the DPMCA 1978 are not applicable to cohabitees who separate or who do not maintain each other: the same is *not* true of the social security provisions. A partner in a heterosexual relationship who wishes to seek benefit may be prevented from doing so if the Benefits Agency believes he or she is living in the 'same household' as their partner. Only one partner in a heterosexual couple can claim benefits. The social security legislation implies a dependency between cohabitees, but if benefits are paid to one partner that partner cannot legally be 'forced' to hand over any money to the partner unable to claim. This is a clear illustration of how the law currently treats cohabitees differently and, arguably, may here be acting in a discriminatory manner.

While you need to know these distinctions, detailed knowledge of welfare benefits is beyond the scope of this book.

5.3   OCCUPATION RIGHTS AND THE MATRIMONIAL HOME

The right to occupy the matrimonial home is not the same as the right of ownership, the latter of which you will be considering later in this chapter. For many spouses (and indeed cohabitees) the matrimonial home will be owned jointly and, as such, occupation rights will be bound up with rights of ownership. While joint ownership is more common, there are cases where only one spouse owns the matrimonial home. For the non-owning spouse this may cause problems when the relationship ends but divorce is not contemplated, or perhaps a third party becomes involved, for example, when a bank forecloses on a mortgage. To ensure some form of protection for the non-owning spouse, legislation has stepped in to grant rights of occupation. You need to remember that these rights primarily apply to spouses only and that cohabitees have more limited rights. You will cover these rights further when looking at domestic violence.

5.3.1 The Family Law Act 1996

This is the latest of several Acts designed to provide a non-owning spouse with rights of occupation in the matrimonial home with the provisions in ss 30–32 of the FLA 1996 replacing the Matrimonial Homes Act 1983, although the provisions are substantially the same. This part of the FLA 1996 came into force in October 1997, so has already been in operation for several years.

Section 30 of the FLA 1996 sets out the rights available – they are only rights of 'occupation' and not of ownership. The occupation derives purely from the status of marriage, and will only arise where one spouse has no ownership rights but the other spouse does, these ownership rights being legal or beneficial (that is, those ownership rights that exist behind the legal title and arise from principles of equity).

The rights to occupy under the Act mean that the spouse with no ownership rights can remain in the property and cannot be evicted by the owning spouse unless the court orders otherwise, or gives the non-owning spouse the right to be admitted into the property (if already evicted) subject to the agreement of the court.

5.3.1.1 Seeking an order

If a spouse needs to enforce their rights to occupation under the FLA 1996, they need to look to s 33 for the relevant order: the 'occupation order'. Occupation orders are wide in scope and permit the court to do a variety of things in relation to the occupation of the matrimonial home, including:

- enforcing the applicant's entitlement to remain in occupation;
- requiring the respondent to permit the applicant to enter and remain in occupation;
- regulating the occupation by one or both of the parties;
- prohibiting, suspending or restricting the respondent's right of occupation in the home; and
- requiring the respondent to leave the home and/or excluding the respondent from the vicinity of the home.

Before the courts decide on the appropriate course of action, they must be certain that the order is warranted.

5.3.1.2 Criteria to be applied

> **Question**
> What criteria would you use?

When considering a s 33(6) application the court must have regard to all the circumstances of the case, the housing needs and resources of the parties and relevant children, the financial resources of the parties and any relevant child, and the effect of any order or decision on the health, safety or well being of the parties and of any relevant child. In addition, the FLA 1996 requires the court to balance the needs of the applicant in gaining an order against the potential effects on the defendant. This balance of harm test is set out in s 33(7) of the FLA 1996. For cases on this area of the law you should look at the chapter on domestic violence (Chapter 7).

5.3.2 Protecting rights of occupation

Question

Other than gaining an occupation order, can these occupation rights be protected?

The right to occupy premises by virtue of status is, under common law, a personal right that can be enforced only against the other spouse. This would have the consequence of making the wife's position insecure against third parties. To overcome this difficulty, the FLA 1996 provides that a spouse with occupation rights can register this right against the title of the property. If the land is registered, the spouse can place a notice on the Register. If the land is unregistered, the rights of occupation can be secured by way of a land charge. Only one property may be subjected to a charge, so if two or more houses exist, a choice will need to be made before registration occurs (Sched 4, para 2 of the FLA 1996).

Question

Will a notice or land charge protect the non-owning spouse against a mortgagee granting a mortgage on completion of the purchase?

The difficulty for a non-owning spouse in this common situation is that the mortgagee will have no notice of the wife's right to occupy. She will not be in occupation at the time the mortgage is completed, hence her rights are not capable of overriding or binding those of the mortgage company. The registration of a charge or notice will only be effective against later creditors. Despite this limitation it is true to say that, in a failing relationship, it will be normal for a non-owning spouse to protect their rights of occupation by registration. This will hopefully prevent or discourage the owner from selling the matrimonial home or from asking the non-owning spouse to leave the premises.

5.4   RIGHTS OF OWNERSHIP

Above, we concentrated purely on occupation, which may be nothing more than a temporary right. The right of ownership is clearly of greater significance.

Question

Why?

Owning property, whether by way of a joint tenancy or a tenancy in common, is a more permanent arrangement. Alongside the ownership rights will run rights of occupation. An owner has a stake in the equity (profit) that is built up within the asset. In times of falling house prices, this benefit may become the detriment of a share in negative equity. A joint owner may request an order for the sale of the property from, or be ordered to sell by, the court under the terms of the Trusts of Land and Appointment of Trustees Act (TLATA) 1996.

A legal interest in land generally has to be created by a deed. Any other interest in land, which primarily will be an equitable interest, must be created by a written contract signed by all of the parties (s 2 of the Law of Property (Miscellaneous Provisions) Act 1989). However, within the matrimonial sphere, the situation will sometimes arise where one party has no legal or equitable interest in accordance with the above principles. If this is the case, a non-owning spouse may utilise the law of trusts to seek ownership rights through the means of an informal trust. The same will be true for cohabitees who do not jointly own property. The question of who owns property is perhaps less significant for married couples who, as you have learnt, have the MCA 1973 to fall back on if they divorce. Cohabitees have to rely on property law, which is less flexible in its approach.

5.5   INFORMAL TRUSTS OF LAND

The term informal trust is being used here to cover resulting and constructive trusts, both of which may be used to gain a beneficial interest in property by a legal non-owning party. However, within case law it is true to say that there is often confusion about the terms to be applied when describing the vehicle for granting the interest. Lord Diplock, in *Gissing v Gissing* [1970] 2 All ER 780, stated that it was unnecessary to distinguish between which vehicle is used to permit the applicant to gain a right of ownership. What was more important was establishing whether or not that interest had arisen because of conduct or words used to induce the beneficiary to act to their own detriment in the belief that by so acting they were acquiring a beneficial interest in the land. This is a somewhat cavalier approach to the matter, but the inaccuracy in terminology has been retained, although some attempts have been made to tighten up the language.

In *Drake v Whipp* [1996] 1 FLR 826, Peter Gibson LJ comments on the types of trusts along the following lines:

- A resulting trust arises where the court presumes what the intention of the party contributing to the property was. This presumption can be rebutted.

- A constructive trust arises where the court has evidence of intention as to the ownership of the property, or this intention can be imputed. There should also be some act to the detriment of the non-legal owner.

As you can see, the concepts are quite similar, and for many non-owning spouses the terminology will not matter – all they are concerned about is getting a share in the property.

5.5.1 Resulting trusts

For Mr and Mrs Average (or Mr and Miss Cohabitee) the idea of buying a house for the other partner is probably inconceivable. Would you buy a house for your partner and relinquish all interest in it? The courts do not differ from this view and will presume a resulting trust. As Lord Browne Wilkinson states, in *Westdeutsche Landesbank Girozentrale v Islington LBC* [1996] 2 WLR 802:

> ... where A makes a voluntary payment to B or pays (wholly or in part) for the purchase of property which is vested either in B alone or in the joint names of A and B, there is a presumption that A did not intend to make a gift to B; the money or property is held on trust for A (if he is the sole provider of the money) or in the case of a joint purchase by A and B in shares proportionate to their contributions.

5.5.1.1 The presumption of advancement

This presumption can operate to rebut the resulting trust concept. All that it means is that in certain situations the court will, in the absence of any other intention, assume that the contributor or purchaser intended the conveyance to be a gift. The presumption of advancement will only arise when transfers are made between persons in particular relationships where equity recognises that the donor is under an obligation to support the donee.

Question

Who do you think would be under such a duty?

As you know, the law places spouses under a duty to maintain one another, and this is the relationship in which equity applies the presumption of advancement. However, due perhaps to the historical nature of this presumption, it works only in favour of one of the spouses.

Question

In whose favour will this presumption work?

The presumption will only apply where a husband transfers property to his lawful wife; it does not apply the other way round! Before you all rush off and reorder your ownership of your matrimonial home, you should be aware that the presumption can easily be rebutted and does not have the same strength it did in the past.

In *Pettitt v Pettitt* [1969] 2 All ER 385, Lord Diplock suggested that the presumption of advancement is rooted in history, in an age where women were not economically active and were not permitted to own property. Therefore, today:

> [I]t would ... be an abuse of the legal technique ... to apply to transactions between the post-war generation of married couples 'presumptions' which are based on intentions of earlier generations ... belonging to ... a different social era.

5.5.1.2   Illegal motivation

Question

Would an illegal motive prevent a resulting trust?

In a moral sense, perhaps it would. You may recall the court's attitude in cases such as *Whiston v Whiston* [1995] 2 FLR 268 and *J v S-T (Formerly J)* [1997] 1 FLR 402, where a spouse was not permitted to benefit from their crime. You would assume the same to be true of resulting trusts. However, this is not necessarily the case, with the court taking the view that all that has to be established to create a resulting trust was that the transfer took place at all and that the plan was for the property to be owned jointly.

In *Tinsley v Milligan* [1993] 3 WLR 126, the parties, two single women, were in a joint business venture running lodging houses. With the proceeds of the business, a property was purchased for them to live in, but with the property being in the sole name of the claimant. The understanding was that the property would be owned jointly in equity. The reason for this difference was to enable the respondent to continue to claim social security benefits, that is, acting fraudulently. After a disagreement between the parties the claimant sought possession of the property with the defendant counterclaiming on the basis that the property was held in trust in equal shares. The court found that the property was held jointly by virtue of a resulting trust; the fact that there was an illegal purpose was irrelevant. *Per* Lord Browne-Wilkinson:

Miss Milligan established a resulting trust by showing that she had contributed to the purchase price of the house and that there was common understanding between her and Miss Tinsley that they owned the house equally. She had no need to allege or prove *why* the house was conveyed into the name of Miss Tinsley alone, since that fact was irrelevant to her claim: it was enough to show that the house was in fact vested in Miss Tinsley alone. The illegality only emerged at all because Miss Tinsley sought to raise it.

5.5.2 Constructive trusts

The case of Tinsley is one that has elements of a constructive trust, in that there is evidence of an agreement between the potential joint owners. In many resulting trusts this evidence has to be implied. However, there are more factors relevant to proving a constructive trust. In the leading case of *Lloyds Bank v Rosset* [1990] 1 AC 107, Lord Bridge cited two situations where a constructive trust would arise; that is where there:

... has at any time prior to acquisition, or exceptionally at some later date, been any agreement, arrangement or understanding reached between them that the property is to be shared beneficially ... Once a finding to this effect is made it will only be necessary ... to show that he or she acted to his or her detriment or significantly altered his or her position in reliance on the agreement ...

or where there:

... is no evidence to support a finding of an agreement or arrangement to share ... In this situation direct contributions to the purchase price by the partner who is not the legal owner, whether initially or by payment of mortgage instalments, will readily justify the inference necessary to the creation of a constructive trust. But, as I read the authorities, it is at least extremely doubtful whether anything less will do.

5.5.2.1 Agreement and reliance

This is the first situation that Lord Bridge stated would give rise to a constructive trust. In relation to the agreement aspect of the test, the couple are not necessarily expected to sit down and discuss their agreement in the language or terms of a land law lawyer or equity judge. The courts recognise that this is not how Mr and Mrs Average would deal with the matter.

Question

What do you think would equal detrimental reliance?

In *Rosset*, the wife tried to claim that her participation in the renovation and decorating equalled detrimental reliance. However, you may have thought of other things – what about the payment of all household bills, while your partner pays the mortgage? What about the notion of giving up a career to raise your partner's children. Would that be sufficient since it would count as a major contribution if you were divorcing?

Mrs Rosset was unsuccessful in her claim that her actions equalled detrimental reliance, the court viewing her involvement as something a wife would naturally do. However financial contributions which enable the 'legal' owner to service the mortgage, if taken together with an agreement to share the property, are more likely to be seen as satisfying the test.

In *Grant v Edwards* [1986] 2 All ER 426, the parties had had a relationship for two years, although both were already married. Following the birth of a son, they decided to live together. A property was purchased in the name of the defendant who stated that the plaintiff's name could not be put on the deed as this would affect her dealings with her husband in divorce proceedings. The plaintiff contributed, from her earnings, to the household expenses, kept house and looked after the children. She claimed and equal share of the property.

The Court of Appeal upheld this claim stating (*per* Nourse LJ):

> ... it is clear that there was a common intention that the plaintiff was to have some sort of propriety interest in 96 Hewitt Road. The more difficult question is whether there was conduct on her part which amounted to acting on that intention or, to put it more precisely, conduct on which she could not reasonably have been expected to embark unless she was to have any interest in the house.

> ... it is in my view an inevitable inference that the very substantial contribution which the plaintiff made out of her earnings ... to the housekeeping and to the feeding and to the bringing up of the children enabled the defendant to keep down the instalments payable under both mortgages out of his own income, and moreover, that he could not have done that if he had had to bear the whole of the other expenses as well. I do not see how he would have been able to do that had it not been for the plaintiff's very substantial contribution to the other expenses.

It should be noted that the 'financial contribution' in *Grant* was not treated in the same way as a direct contribution to the purchase price.

5.5.2.2   No agreement but direct contribution

This is the second situation in which a constructive trust will arise. In *Rosset* there was no evidence of agreement. Hence, the issue was whether there had been any contribution to the purchase price from which an intention could be inferred. As the wife's activities had had nothing to do with the purchasing of the property, merely the decorating and maintenance of it, she could not show direct contributions.

In *Rosset*, only direct financial contributions seemed to be sufficient to gain an interest without an express agreement.

Question

Would any indirect financial contributions assist?

You have already come across the main type of indirect financial contributions that may result in gaining an interest: the payment of household bills in order that the other partner can meet the mortgage payments. It would appear that, provided the payment of the bills is linked to the inability of the other party to service the mortgage, this may constitute sufficient indirect detriment sufficient to gain an interest. In *Gissing v Gissing* [1970] 3 WLR 255, H and W were married in 1935. The matrimonial home was purchased by H in 1951 in his sole name. W obtained a decree absolute in 1966. Although W had made no direct contribution to the purchase of the matrimonial home, she had spent her own money on furniture, improvements to the premises and clothes for the family. W applied by originating summons for an order concerning her beneficial interest in the home. It was held by the judge that H was the sole beneficial owner and was entitled, therefore, to possession. The Court of Appeal reversed the decision and H appealed to the House of Lords. The House of Lords held H's appeal would be allowed. It was not possible to draw from the evidence any inference that H and W had a common intention that W should have any beneficial interest in the matrimonial home. Lord Reid stated:

> Why does the fact that H agreed to accept these contributions from his wife not impose a trust on him? There is a wide gulf between inferring from the entire conduct of the parties that there probably was an agreement, and imputing to the parties an intention to agree to share even where the evidence gives no ground for such an inference. If the evidence shows that there was no agreement in fact, then that will exclude any inference that there was an agreement. But it does not exclude an imputation of a deemed intention if the law permits such an imputation. If the law is to be that the court has the power to impute such an intention in proper cases, then I am content, although I would prefer to reach the same end in a rather different way. But if it were to be held to be the law that it must at least be possible to infer a contemporary agreement in the sense of holding that it is more probable than not there was in fact some such agreement, then I could not contemplate the future results of such a decision with equanimity.

Lord Diplock commented:

> The picture presented by the evidence is one of husband and wife retaining their separate proprietary interests in real or personal property purchased with their separate savings and is inconsistent with any common intention at the time of purchase of the matrimonial home that the wife, who neither then nor thereafter contributed anything to its purchase price or assumed any liability for it, should nevertheless be entitled to a beneficial interest in it.

5.6   EVALUATING SHARES IN EQUITY

In the above situations, the desired outcome for the non-owning spouse or partner will be the granting of ownership rights. As you have seen, this will result in a right to receive any proceeds from the value, or equity, in the property. However, it is one thing to state that ownership rights exist, but to what extent or value will that share be? If the non-owning party has contributed to the property in terms of money (and after *Lloyds Bank plc v Rosset* it is likely that this is the only means of evidencing a contribution), then the starting point will be the proportion of that contribution. The presumption that this is the correct starting point may be rebutted by any declaration to the contrary, that is, that the parties have agreed the property will be shared equally.

In *Midland Bank v Cooke* [1995] 2 FLR 215, H purchased a house in his sole name with a mortgage, and in addition by using a wedding gift, and by drawing on his savings. Later, the mortgage was replaced by a general mortgage in the bank's favour so as to secure H's business overdraft. W signed a form of consent which effectively gave the bank priority of rights over her own. The property was then transferred into the joint names of H and W. Proceedings, claiming payment of £52,000 with possession in default, were brought by the bank. W contended that her consent stemmed from H's undue influence. It was held by the judge that the bank had been aware of H's undue influence and that W was not bound by the signed consent. Furthermore, the judge held that W did possess an equitable interest in the house, based on her contribution to its purchase, her contribution having taken the form of her share of the wedding gift. That interest was considered to be approximately 6% of the house's value. W appealed. The court held that W's appeal would be allowed. When seeking to evaluate an equitable interest, the court should take into account the full history of the dealings between parties, relevant to their ownership and occupation of the property, and their sharing of burdens and advantages. It ought not to be bound, in arriving at a decision, by the monetary contributions of H and W where it was possible to infer some other arrangement relating to shares in the property. *Per* Waite J:

> It will take into consideration all conduct which throws light on the question of what shares were intended. Only if that search proves inconclusive will the court fall back on the maxim 'equality is equity'.

> The judge was wrong in considering W's share in the property as having been fixed according to her monetary contribution to the purchase price. Given all the evidence in the case, there appeared to be the presumed intention that H and W were to own equal shares in the house. A beneficial half interest would be granted, therefore, to W.

5.7   PROPRIETARY ESTOPPEL

In many ways, the doctrine of proprietary estoppel is similar to the concepts within informal trusts, above. The doctrine operates by preventing a person asserting their legal right (in this case, the legal right of ownership) if it would be deemed to be unjust to do so. In some situations the courts will use proprietary estoppel to transfer ownership rights but, in others, a more contractual approach is taken with tenancies granted instead.

The courts will consider criteria very similar to those in informal trusts, namely has a party to a relationship acted to their detriment, either by incurring expenditure or by some other act, in the belief that they own, or will gain an interest in, the property, with that belief being encouraged by the true owner?

The position may be complicated by payments to the mortgage loan being made if there is no express agreement or understanding as to how the property will be owned. As you have seen, indirect contributions, by way of payment of bills, may not be sufficient to increase the share of ownership. This may be particularly so with reference to cohabitees, where the court may see payments of this kind (or even contributions to the mortgage) as being nothing more than payments in lieu of rent. The issue reverts to the question of what was the intention of the parties.

In *Pascoe v Turner* [1979] 1 WLR 431, the plaintiff was a business man dealing with property. The defendant, a widow, had declined marriage when asked by the plaintiff, but had, according to the court, 'done all that a wife would do' – she helped in the business, did the housekeeping, etc. The plaintiff provided housekeeping to the defendant, but the house, and its contents, was owned by the plaintiff. The plaintiff began a relationship with another woman. The defendant claimed that she had been told the house and all its contents were hers, although the plaintiff disputed this. The court believed the defendant. Cumming-Bruce LJ stated:

> The defendant stayed on in the house. She thought it was hers and everything in it. In reliance upon the plaintiff's declarations that he had given her the house ... she spent money and herself did work on redecoration, improvements and repairs ... We would describe the work done in and about the house as substantial in the sense that the adjective is used in the context of estoppel. All the while the plaintiff not only stood by and watched but encouraged and advised, without a word to suggest that she was putting her money and her personal labour into his house. What is the effect in equity? ... So the principle to be applied is that the court should consider all the circumstances, and the counterclaimant having at law no perfected gift or licence other than a licence revocable at will. The court must decide what is the minimum equity to do justice to her having regard to the way in which she changed her position for the worse by reason of the acquiescence and encouragement of the legal owner. We take the view that the equity cannot here be satisfied without granting a remedy which assures to the defendant security of tenure, quiet enjoyment, and freedom of action in respect of the repairs and improvements without

interference from the plaintiff ... [t]his court concludes that the equity to which the facts in this case give rise can only be satisfied by compelling the plaintiff to give effect to his promise and her expectations. He has so acted that he must now perfect the gift.

Other cases that deal with these issues include *Coombes v Smith* [1986] 1 WLR 808 and *Matharu v Matharu* [1994] 2 FLR 597.

5.8   THE TLATA 1996

In the previous sections we have been looking at the methods by which to obtain a legal interest in the matrimonial (or cohabiting) home, and how to quantify the extent of that interest. This is naturally important if you wish to sell the property and realise that interest. However, not all separating couples do wish to sell up. The gaining of a beneficial interest will therefore assist if one wishes to use the FLA 1996 occupation order provisions, and also provide a means to protect against third parties. However, these benefits are not really long term, and to deal with longer term issues the TLATA 1996 will have to be utilised.

Section 12 of the TLATA provides that if one has a beneficial interest under a trust (which one will if one has succeeded in persuading the court to declare an informal trust) one has a right to occupy the property subject to s 13. This next section, s 13, establishes a trustee's powers, generally prevents exclusion of the right to occupy where it is unreasonable and establishes criteria that the trustees must consider if the right to occupy is to be restricted. This section also states that if one beneficiary's rights are restricted, the trustees can impose conditions, such as the payment of occupation rent, the payment of mortgage liabilities, etc. Under s 14 the court, subject to an application being made, can exercise the same powers in relation to the property as a trustee could have done. What may not have been obvious to you is the consequence of s 14. Considering cohabitees, if the female partner has established that, whilst not on the title deed, she has a beneficial interest, she can (as you will see in the next chapter) seek to protect her right of occupation by way of the FLA 1996, but this protection may not last indefinitely. However, she could apply under s 14 of the TLATA 1996 to obtain a right to exclusive occupation, which need not be time limited. She may be ordered to pay a rent to her ex-partner or keep up existing payments. However, do you see how similar this is to some of the orders available under the MCA 1973 to divorcing couples? Whether by intention or by oversight, it would appear that separating cohabitees, with beneficial interest in property, are in an almost identical position to divorcing couples: all that is different is the Act giving jurisdiction, the case of *Drake v Whipp* (above) being illustrative.

5.9   COHABITEES – FURTHER REFORM?

It is not just the area of land law that provides for cohabitees in a different way to married couples. As you will no doubt have gathered from your reading earlier in this chapter, cohabitees cannot utilise legislative provisions to claim financial support from one another in the event of relationship breakdown, regardless of any dependency on the other party. Rights may accrue in the context of death if one cohabitee is clearly dependent upon the other and they have cohabited for in excess of two years (the Inheritance (Provision for Family and Dependants) Act 1975, as amended). In the light of this perceived discrimination, and the increasing number of individuals who cohabit rather than marry, calls have been made to change the law to provide remedies to unmarried couples similar to those provided to married couples.

Question

What might the difficulties be in extending the law?

Despite the increasing recognition of cohabitation, it is still not clear why many individuals choose not to marry. If it is due to the assumption that cohabitees have the same status as married couples, there may be an argument for changing the law. However, could this not be dealt with by better education? If, however, individuals cohabit because they do not wish to be bound by the rules and obligations of marriage, is it fair to apply a matrimonial type regime to them?

5.9.1   Government plans

Due to the concerns about the lack of rights for cohabitees, in 2001, two, in effect competing, bills were introduced into Parliament, both of which aimed to change this area of the law.

The Relationships (Civil Registration) Bill and the Civil Partnership Bill were introduced into the House of Commons and the House of Lords in October 2001 and January 2002 respectively. Neither completed a second reading and it is unlikely that either Bill will be reintroduced into future parliamentary sessions; however the Bills do illustrate the potential scope for reform.

Both Bills applied to heterosexual and same-sex couples and while the implication was that the couples would be cohabiting, this was only a requirement in the latter Bill where six months cohabitation was needed. Couples that met the requirements would be permitted to register their partnership with a view to obtaining additional legal rights. Those rights included or related to, *inter alia*, the following:

- the ability to formally dissolve the relationship;
- the right to seek financial and property division via the court on relationship breakdown;
- clarifying the position in the event of incapacity;
- cover pensions, social security benefits and tax implications; and
- housing succession.

It is also worth noting that, unlike the law relating to married couples, both Bills enabled pre-existing agreements on property ownership to be upheld. However, in terms of the Lords' Bill, any property agreement had to be registered with the Registrar (note the Commons' Bill refers to an agreement produced to the court). If no agreement was registered, the Bill introduced an equal division of property which would arguably apply even if a co-owning couple had bought a property as tenants in common, with unequal shares, where they had failed to register this agreement. Finally, of interest was the fact that cl 13 of the Lords' Bill entitled a registered partner to make decisions for the other partner, in terms of health and care decisions. This may not sound drastic, but in fact this would have given registered partners rights that currently are not available to spouses!

5.9.2   A limited response

Despite the introduction of the above Bills, the current way forward on law reform appears to be more limited in scope. In December 2002, the Minister for Social Exclusion announced that the Government would be carrying out a consultation process into the legal recognition of certain partnerships, with the consultation period ending in September 2003 and a Bill being introduced into the House of Lords in 2004. At the time of writing this had not completed its passage through Parliament. However, only same-sex partnerships are covered in the consultation paper and Bill. The rationale, put simply, is that same sex-couples have no legally recognised status as a couple, and that the legal regime prevents them marrying. This failure to provide a legal status is deemed discriminatory, and consequently needs to be remedied. By contrast, an unmarried heterosexual couple does have a means to gain a legal status – they can get married – and therefore there is no perceived need to remedy any unfairness they suffer as a result of being unmarried.

Question

Do you agree with this rationale?

While this argument does have logic, it is questionable whether it is sufficient to dismiss the call for additional rights for heterosexual couples. It is clear that the majority of cohabiting, heterosexual couples believe they have the same rights and responsibilities as married couples – they see themselves as common law spouses – and this may account for the fact that they never marry. Is it now appropriate for the law to continue to ignore the reality of the heterosexual couple's situation and beliefs? Should the Mrs Burns' of this world, who spend most of their life playing the role of housewife and mother, and contribute their income to the family pot, in the belief that they are gaining rights in the family assets (*Burns v Burns* [1984] Ch 317), be left out in the cold? Or should the state seek to educate the population to dismiss, once and for all, the concept of common law spousehood? The fact that many of the prejudices associated with cohabitation have disappeared from society, together with the increasing popularity of cohabitation, is significant enough to warrant some form of change, and the lack of knowledge by cohabitants themselves can not be an excuse for failing to address the social changes. However, it would seem that more than this is needed to persuade the government to look at the situation of heterosexual couples.

5.10   SUMMARY

Having completed this chapter, you should be clearer about the way in which the law assists married couples with regard to financial matters, where the wide powers of the court under the divorce provisions are not applicable. The traditional approach of land law and equity is relevant to property disputes, since matrimonial law does not cover this area to any great extent. The land law rules are also applicable to cohabitees and this is the same regardless of whether they are living together or whether their relationship has broken down.

5.11   END OF CHAPTER ASSESSMENT

Simon and Janice have lived together for seven years. They bought their current house in 1993, each having sold previously owned properties. As Janice was still going through her divorce, the new house was conveyed into Simon's sole name. The relationship between Simon and Janice has now broken down, although they are still living in the same property.

The house is worth £120,000, with an endowment mortgage of £50,000. Janice contributed £40,000 towards the purchase price, with Simon contributing £30,000. Janice, despite only working part-time, has paid half of the endowment fees.

Explain how the courts will assess her claim to be entitled to a half-share in the property.

CHAPTER 6

CHILD SUPPORT

6.1 OBJECTIVES

By the end of this chapter you should be able to:

- explain the scope of the Child Support Act (CSA) 1991 (as amended by the CSA 1995);
- describe who is subject to this Act, and the situations in which the CSA 1991 takes precedence;
- evaluate the claim that the system introduced in March 2003 is fairer than the previous formulaic approach;
- compare the CSA 1991 with the scope of other statutes.

The legislation governing child support and maintenance has undergone major change over the last decade with the implementation of the CSAs 1991 and 1995, which have been amended considerably by the Child Support, Pensions and Social Security Act 2000. These Acts gave a more interventionist role to the state, and emphasised the responsibility of parents to care for their children, if only on a financial footing. The impact of the legislation has been widespread, but the CSA does not have total domination over child support: other statutes still have a supplementary role to play. You will, therefore, in this chapter concentrate on the CSAs 1991 and 1995, but will also look at the interplay between the various provisions in other legislation. This chapter will finish the discussion of financial aspects of family law.

6.2 WHAT SORT OF CHILDREN?

This may seem to be a strange heading, but do not forget that in this section we are talking about all children and not just those children whose parents are separating or going through a divorce. The obligation to support a child is not dependent upon the marital status of the parent, but purely upon the status of being a parent.

Question

Does this mean that only birth parents are liable to maintain children?

While some of the statutory provisions reflect only the birth parents' liability to support their children, the blood relationship is not necessary to create obligations. If you think about the reality of family life, many children will be cared for and supported within step-families, or possibly by other family members. From a moral perspective these carers will also have obligations towards the child or children in their care. Therefore, for each of the statutory provisions that you study, you will have to ensure that you are clear on the status of the child, or family, which is covered by the provisions. For example, as you will see, the CSA 1991 and CSA 1995 place a statutory obligation upon birth parents to support their children, whether those parents are married, separated, have never lived together or possibly even are unknown.

6.3   THE CSA 1991

By now many individuals will have experienced the impact of the CSA 1991 at first hand, or at least know someone who has had to deal with the Child Support Agency. The CSA 1991 (note that the Act will be referred to as the CSA 1991 – any references to the Child Support Agency will be to the Agency) came into force in 1993. The long term aim was to remove child support from the hands of the court and to make the assessment, collection and payment of support an administrative process. Arguably, the implementation was designed to reinforce the notion of family values and to promote the responsibility of parents towards their children. Cynically, but correctly, the CSA 1991 was also introduced to cut back the amount of welfare benefits that were being paid to single parents.

The changes that have been made by the CSA 1991 are:

- to introduce an Agency with responsibility for assessing child maintenance and enforcing payment of the same;
- to achieve consistency in maintenance payments by initially applying a strict assessment formula to all cases covered by the Agency's jurisdiction and, since March 2003, to introduce a move from a formula to the taking of a set percentage of income for child support;
- to remove the ability of other agencies – that is, the court – to make child support assessments, when the case falls within the jurisdiction of the Agency.

6.3.1   The Child Support Agency

The Agency is a national agency which 'belongs' to the Department of Social Security. It is divided into regional centres (six in all), each centre taking responsibility for the assessment of child support for individuals within its area.

The staff dealing with the collation of information and assessment of child maintenance are known as child support officers. The collation of information, assessment of levels of support and enforcement of payment is the main function of the Agency. The Agency has been the subject of much criticism for its inaccuracies in calculating assessments and its overall inefficiency in contacting non-resident parents to enforce maintenance payments. The efficiency of the Agency has improved, but is still not considered to be adequate.

6.3.2   To whom does the act apply?

The CSA 1991 places a duty on 'each parent of a qualifying child' to be 'responsible for maintaining him' (s 1(1)). To meet this duty the 'non-resident parent shall be taken to have met his responsibility to maintain any qualifying child ... by making periodical payments ... of such amount, and at such intervals, as may be determined in accordance with the provisions of [the] Act' (s 1(2)). These two extracts highlight new terminology that is applicable to the CSA 1991 and refers to those subject to the CSA 1991, namely a 'qualifying child' and 'non-resident parent'. In addition, the CSA 1991 refers to a 'person with care', just to complete the set.

Question

How would you define these terms?

These definitions are found in s 3 of the CSA 1991 and are stated thus:

    (1) A child is a 'qualifying child' if –

        (a) one of his parents is ... a non-resident parent; or

        (b) both of his parents are ... non-resident parents.

    (2) The parent of any child is a 'non-resident parent', in relation to him, if –

        (a) that parent is not living in the same household with the child; and

        (b) the child has his home with a person who is ... a person with care.

    (3) A person is a 'person with care' in relation to any child, if he is a person –

        (a) with whom the child has his home;

        (b) who usually provides day to day care for the child ...

Does this really help? The definitions provided seem a little circular. What is meant by a child? Who is a parent? The CSA 1991 further defines, in s 55, a child as being someone:

- under the age of 16; or
- under the age of 19 and receiving full-time, non-advanced education at a recognised educational establishment; and
- who has not been married.

'Parent' and 'person with care' are referred to in the interpretation section, s 54, but these further interpretations are not very helpful.

6.3.2.1   Qualifying child

The meaning of 'qualifying child' is not problematic in the sense of a 'child', but the decision as to whether the child is 'qualifying' relates to the parents.

A parent will be a legal parent, that is, a biological parent or a parent by adoption. If the child has been conceived by medical reproductive techniques, then you would need to look at the rules under the Human Fertilisation and Embryology Act 1990. A person with parental responsibility will not automatically be classified as a 'legal parent': the crucial factor is the blood link or the status of the adoptive parent (you will look at parental responsibility in a later chapter).

6.3.2.2   Non-resident parent

For a parent to be 'non-resident' they must not live in the same household as the child and the child must live with a person with care. The non-resident would in many cases be the father of the child, for example, where a married couple have separated (whether or not they divorce) and where the child remains with the mother and the father lives elsewhere. If the child in this situation were living with the paternal grandparents, then both mother and father would be deemed to be 'non-resident parents'.

6.3.2.3   Person with care

A person with care will normally be a parent, but this need not be so as you just saw in the example above. To be classed as a person with care, the child must have their home with that person, and must be provided with day-to-day care by them.

In many cases, this day-to-day care may not be consistently provided by the same person. You may have a separated couple where the mother cares for the child during weekdays and the father has contact at weekends, when the child lives with him and he provides the day-to-day care. The CSA 1991 will acknowledge such shared care situations and the assessment of maintenance payable may be altered to reflect the extent of care provided by each adult. So, in our example of the father caring for the child at weekends, he will in a year provide almost one-third of the child's care. As a non-resident parent he would be required to pay child support, but a full assessment would be inappropriate given the extent to which he provides care. The assessment would need to be amended to reflect the father's caring role.

6.3.2.4   Habitual residence

The jurisdiction of the CSA 1991 is only wide enough to cover those habitually resident in the United Kingdom (s 44(1)). All the relevant individuals, namely the non-resident parent, the person with care and the qualifying child must be resident. If one or more is not so resident, the CSA 1991 cannot be used to seek support. If this is so, the alternative legislation must be looked at to see if it can provide assistance and you will be looking at this legislation later in the chapter.

6.3.2.5   Denial of parentage

As the responsibility to make maintenance payments falls on biological parents there is clearly no requirement for the parents to be a married couple – unmarried parents cannot escape liability. (As you will learn later, an unmarried father may have no other rights or obligations towards his child other than to pay maintenance.) In some situations an unmarried father will wish to dispute paternity. The fact that paternity is denied should not be treated as a routine stage in the process, and assumptions should not be made about paternity on a basis of 'men always deny it'. If paternity is disputed, the assessment procedure should be brought to a halt to enable the paternity issue to be concluded – this means that no maintenance will be required until paternity has been established. If, however, the father only denies paternity after an assessment has been made, payments will continue as normal, but may be refunded if paternity is disproved. Hence, if paternity is to be disputed, it should be disputed at the earliest stage possible.

The procedure to be adopted in these cases is for the child support officers to interview both the non-resident parent and the person with care (who will normally be the other parent). Reduced price DNA testing will also be available. If the mother refuses to comply with DNA testing, the courts do have the power to order blood tests if they believe it will be in the child's best interests. This power was introduced into the Family Law Reform Act 1969 by the Child Support, Pensions and Social Security Act 2000. Failure to undergo testing can be used as an adverse inference in deciding the issue. If testing is undertaken, and paternity disproved, any fees incurred by the alleged father will be returned.

However, it is important to note that findings in other proceedings as to parentage can be treated as decisive on this question. For example in *R v Secretary of State for Social Security ex p West* [1998] EWHC 687 (Admin), S, the father, had applied under s 4(1)(a) of the Children Act (CA) 1989 for a parental responsibility order; this was made in his favour by consent. At a later date S returned a form to the Child Support Agency in which he denied paternity of the children involved in the earlier order. That order was discharged. The Secretary of State made a decision not to make a maintenance assessment. W, the mother of the children, made an application for a review of that decision. W's application was allowed. The decision not to make an assessment was quashed. The making of a parental responsibility order did fulfil the requirements for a finding of paternity order under s 26(2) of the CSA 1991. The question of paternity was not mentioned in the application for a parental responsibility order, but it would have been *ultra vires* the children's interests to make an order of this nature unless the judge was convinced that S was the father of W's children. There was adequate evidence for this particular finding.

6.3.3   When will the CSA 1991 be used?

This is an area that can be confusing to a student; however, by identifying the key rules, the simplicity of the system can be grasped. In theory at least, *all* payments of child support are to be dealt with under the CSA 1991 and through the Agency. To accomplish this, all existing child maintenance agreements and orders were to be taken on by the Agency by the end of the 1990s, in addition to the Agency dealing with all new cases of child maintenance. In 1995, there was a partial U-turn, and since then there has been an indefinite deferral of taking on applications where agreements already exist and where there are no welfare benefits payments. In addition to this change regarding full implementation, there are still some ways to avoid having to use the Agency.

The CSA 1991 works by establishing situations in which the person with care must apply to the Agency, and those where the person with care may apply; be careful – the difference is important. Sections 4 and 6 are the relevant provisions and state:

4   Child Support Maintenance

   (1) A person who is, in relation to any qualifying child ... either the person with care or the non-resident parent may apply to the Secretary of State for a maintenance calculation to be made under this Act with respect to that child ...

6   Applications by those claiming or receiving benefit

   (1) This section applies where income support, an income based jobseekers allowance or any other benefit of a prescribed kind is claimed by or in respect of ... the parent of a qualifying child who is also a person with care of the child.

   ...

   (3) The Secretary of State may –

      (a) treat the parent as having applied for a maintenance calculation with respect to the qualifying child ... and

      (b) take action under this Act to recover from the non-resident parent, on the parent's behalf, the child support maintenance so determined.

   ...

   (7) ... the parent shall, so far as she reasonably can, [provide the Secretary of State] with the information which is required to enable –

      (a) the non-resident parent to be identified or traced;

      (b) the amount of child support maintenance payable by him to be calculated; and

      (c) that amount to be recovered from him.

6.3.3.1 Must be used

Let us look first at the mandatory section, that is, s 6. Under this section, a parent with care must allow the Agency to make an assessment for child support under the CSA 1991 when that parent is receiving any of the following state welfare benefits:

- income support or income related jobseekers allowance; or
- other prescribed benefits (disability working allowance).

Question

What if the child is being cared for by someone other than a parent with care, but who is claiming benefits?

In this situation, the person with care is not obliged to make an application, and *may* utilise s 4 instead.

Question

What would happen if the parent with care refused to apply under the CSA 1991?

Under s 6(3) the assessment can go ahead without the parent with care actually requesting the Agency's involvement.

A parent with care may request that the Agency does not make an assessment of child maintenance under s 6(5), which states that the Secretary of State may not act if the parent with care requests him not to and that request being made in writing. The CSA 1991 does not say in what circumstances this request will be upheld. However, s 2 of the Act requires any decision within the Secretary of State's discretionary powers to take into account the welfare of the child. If a clear case can be established by the parent with care that if a child support calculation goes ahead there is likely to be significant harm caused to the child, or possibly the parent with care, it is likely that s 6(5) will be utilised.

Question

What happens if no grounds exist to prevent an assessment?

You may have thought some form of financial penalty would apply; this is exactly what happens. Under s 46 of the CSA 1991 a so-called benefit reduction will be implemented, although failure to comply will not automatically reduce the benefits payable: initially, the child support officer must serve written notification on the parent to elicit the reasons why they are not co-operating. Only if the response (if any) does not provide reasonable grounds will a 'reduced benefit direction' be made. The reduction in benefit will last for three years (it may be for a lesser period although the situations when this will happen are limited). After the expiry of those three years there is the possibility that the parent with care will be subject to another reduced benefit direction if they continue to fail to co-operate (Child Support (Maintenance Assessment Procedure) Regulations 1992 (SI 1992/1813) and Child Support (Miscellaneous Amendments) Regulations 1996 (SI 1996/1945)).

The amount of the reduction in benefit is not inconsiderable: it amounts to 40% of the income support allowances. As the total amount of income support for a single adult over 25 is approximately £55 per week (before any additional premiums), a reduction of around £22 is, it is suggested, harsh, or at least a strong motivator to co-operate.

While the welfare of the child is normally relevant to legislation dealing with children's issues, with respect to the CSA 1991 it is only applicable as a consideration when the exercise of discretion is in question. The imposition of a reduced benefit direction is arguably a discretionary matter, since s 46 states that the Secretary of State 'may ... give a reduced benefit direction'. Additionally, the question of whether the failure to co-operate is reasonable is also subject to discretion, which will necessitate the consideration of the child's welfare.

Question

Do you think it would make a difference to the exercise of discretion if there is an existing court order?

In some cases, the existence of a pre-CSA 1991 agreement or court order will prevent the Agency from acting. However, if the parent with care is claiming benefits, this is not so, and the CSA 1991 must be used, even if there is a pre-existing order. Any maintenance calculation by the Agency will overrule the previous order, and the previous order will not be capable of resurrection if the parent with care ceases their benefit claim.

6.3.3.2 May be used

If the individual with care of the qualifying child is not a parent, regardless of whether they are on welfare benefits, there is no compulsion to use the Agency. The same is true of parents with care who are not claiming welfare benefits. Section 4 of the CSA 1991 is applicable here, giving the person with care the ability to seek an assessment.

There are, however, limitations on the use that can be made of s 4. First, it cannot be used where a maintenance assessment is already in force under s 6 (s 4(9)). Secondly, s 4 cannot be used if there is a pre-April 1993 maintenance agreement or court order in force (which has been made at any time, ie, not restricted to pre-1993) and this order has been in existence for less than one year, or the parent with care is on benefit as specified for s 6 purposes (s 4(10)).

If the Agency is being used voluntarily, there may be a fee payable for the administration of the application.

Question

Can you think why someone might prefer to use the Agency?

Voluntary applications may be made due to the perception that more maintenance will be obtained from the absent parent. Equally, if there are concerns as to the reliability of payments, the fact that a formal assessment has been made may result in a more consistent payment regime. For unmarried parents, the CSA 1991 is one of only two Acts under which child support can be gained – it may be that the CSA 1991 has a higher profile and so is resorted to more often.

It is worth noting that due to the wording of s 4(10), a parent with care can in effect transfer any order granted, by virtue of legislation other than the CSA 1991 to the Agency after one year. This may well enable them to gain increased payments and will certainly assist with enforcement.

6.3.3.3 Limitations on the court

Section 8 establishes a prohibition on the court's involvement where the CSA 1991 is applicable and the Secretary of State *could* make an assessment, unless the court is being asked to make a consent order. The fact that case may be within the Agency's remit (ie, because the child is a qualifying child, etc) does not mean the Agency must assess, unless it falls under s 6.

Question

What would be the case if the applicant's request for an assessment was not taken up by the Agency?

The inability of the court to make child support orders, except by consent, may be one reason for voluntarily using the Agency. As all claims for support involving a biological child are caught by the CSA 1991 (and the other requirements met) and are capable of being assessed under this Act, there are few situations where the court can now play a role. If the Agency refuses to make the calculation of child support (even though it could), the applicant may be able to argue that the case falls outside of the Agency's remit and should be decided by the court. This would be a very tenuous argument. It is more likely the applicant would have to seek further review by the Agency.

6.3.4   Avoiding the CSA 1991

For those parents with care who are claiming benefit, it is not possible to avoid the CSA 1991 and the Agency. Those persons and parents with care who would fall within s 4 may consider using the court, provided they fit within s 8(5) which states:

... this section shall not prevent a court from exercising any power which it has to make a maintenance order in relation to a child if –

(a) a written agreement (whether or not enforceable) provides for the making or securing, by a non-resident parent of the child of periodical payments to or for the benefit of the child;

(b) the maintenance order which the court makes is, in all material respects, in the same terms as that agreement.

This sub-section permits the court to make a consent order where the person or parent with care would be a voluntary s 4 applicant. The parties must have a written agreement, which may be negotiated after April 1993. As you can see from the sub-section itself, the fact that the written agreement may not otherwise be legally enforceable is immaterial. The agreement has to be more than an expression of willingness to make payments, so if, for example, the father said he would pay £40 per week for the child, this would not amount to an agreement unless the mother has agreed to it. If this agreement were to become incorporated into a consent order, the court would have to replicate the agreement in 'all material respects' (s 8(5)(b)). The fact of incorporating the written agreement into a consent order makes it legally enforceable. If this consent order needs to be changed in the future, it is unlikely that the court would have power to vary the order as s 8(3) would prohibit it. However, there would appear to be no prohibition on the parties negotiating a new agreement to be embodied in a new consent order.

If the court order predates the implementation of the CSA 1991, the court retains its powers to vary or revoke the order because access will be denied to the CSA 1991, subject of course to the question of whether the parent with care is then on benefit. It is unlikely that the court will revoke an order simply to enable an application to be made under the CSA 1991 and especially since the CSA 1991 permits an applicant to transfer their order to the Agency after one year. Additionally, even though the courts make their orders under legislation other than the CSA 1991, they frequently adopt a CSA 1991 based calculation when assessing the application. (You will be considering the court's jurisdiction later.)

6.4   THE CALCULATION

The method for the calculation of child support under the CSA 1991 was originally a formulaic approach. However, this system required a great deal of information to be collected and helped cause the difficulties experienced by the Agency in making accurate assessments. The assessment calculation was changed in March 2003, for new cases only, by virtue of the Child Support, Pensions and Social Security Act 2000. The changes were perceived to be simpler and a fairer way of calculating child support but, due to the problems of establishing a workable computer system, implementation of this scheme was delayed past its original 2002 start date, and even though the system has been in operation for over one year, there are still problems surrounding the operation of the system.

The method of calculating the payments required by the non-resident parent are set out in Sched 1, para 2:

(1) The basic rate is the following percentage of the non-residents parent's net weekly income –

15% where he has one qualifying child;

20% where he has two qualifying children;

25% where he has three or more qualifying children;

As you can see, the system is simple – the non-resident parent is expected to pay a certain percentage of their income, dependent on the number of children they have.

Question

What if the non-resident parent has a second family?

From the White Paper that preceded the changes it seemed that the second family should not gain any greater advantage than the first, non-resident, family. However, despite this statement of intent, the method adopted in the legislation does not actually achieve this aim. Schedule 1, para 2.2 of the CSA 1991 states:

If the non-resident parent also has one or more relevant other children, the appropriate percentage referred to in sub-paragraph (1) is to be applied instead to his net weekly income less –

15% where he has one relevant other child;

20% where he has two relevant other children;

25% where he has three or more relevant other children.

Hence, as you can see, where there is a second family, that is, relevant child(ren), the set percentages are deducted from the non-resident parent's income for the benefit of the second family, and only then are the required percentages deducted for the first, non-resident children.

To show you how this works, consider the following example:

Anne and Bob have two children from their marriage. Bob left to live with Carole and they have one child. Bob earns £1,000 per week.

When calculating Bob's liability under the CSA 1999, first the relevant percentage for the second family will be deducted. As Bob and Carole have one child this is 15%. Bob would be left with £1,000 – £150 = £850. Next, the relevant percentage for the first family will be deducted. As Bob and Anne have two children this is 20%. Bob's liability to the children from his marriage is £170 per week.

In terms of how much the children receive, you will see how much more the second family in effect receives when compared to the first family.

Question

What if the non-resident parent has two non-resident families?

In this situation, Sched 1, para 6 applies:

(1) If the non-resident parent has more than one qualifying child and in relation to them there is more than one person with care, the amount of child support maintenance payable is to be determined by apportioning the rate between the persons with care.

As you can see, the CSA 1991 requires any child support to be apportioned between the parents with care. Going back to the example above, if Bob did not live with either Anne or Carole, his total child support liability would be 25% as he has three qualifying children. This 25% of income would be shared two-thirds to Anne as she has two of the three children and one-third to Carole. In terms of the figures, this would equal total support of £250 per week, with £166 to Anne and £84 to Carole.

6.4.1 Income

What is meant by income will be very important given the fact that the amount of child support payable is directly related to it.

Question

How would you define income?

Sched 1 of the CSA 1991 talks about net income, a term commonly used to cover income earned less any income tax and national insurance contributions. The Child Support (Maintenance Calculations and Special Cases) Regulations 2000 (SI 2000/155) do not really give a clear definition of net income. However, in line with the previous child support regime, net income will include the deduction of half of the non-resident parent's pension contributions.

Question

What if the non-resident parent has no income?

As the calculation depends on the income of the non-resident parent it is going to be hard to get child support if they have no income to start with!

In this case, the Secretary of State may utilise Sched 1, para 10B to treat the non-resident parent as having some form of income. This provision is very similar to other welfare benefit rules. It tries to ensure that individuals do not place a burden on the state by deliberately divesting themselves of assets, for example by having only non-income bearing capital.

An example of when this provision may be useful can be seen in the case of *Philips v Peace* [1996] 2 FLR 230. This case also illustrates how other legislation, for example, the Children Act 1989, may be utilised in situations where the Agency has no jurisdiction. We will return to those scenarios later.

Question

What about the caring parent's income?

In the majority of situations the parent with care will not have an income, other than state benefits. However, as a parent with care can use the Agency voluntarily, there will be cases where they also have an income. It is reasonable to assume that both parents' incomes will be relevant – the child is both of theirs after all. Despite this sounding logical, the CSA 1991, as amended by the Child Support, Pensions and Social Security Act 2000, does not operate in this way. As you have seen from the extracts, the CSA 1991 only refers to the non-resident parent's income. The caring parent's resources are ignored.

Question

Is this fair?

6.4.2 Variations

Question

In what situations do you think the non-resident parent should be able to apply to vary the amount of support assessed by the Agency?

The CSA 1991 does permit applications to vary the rate of maintenance payable. The situations in which this is permissible are set out in Sched 4B of the CSA 1991 and are as follows:

- where there are special expenses;
- where there has been a relevant property or capital transfer; and
- where there are additional, specified cases.

6.4.3 Special expenses

The ability to vary the calculation, where there are special expenses, is not great. The non-resident parent must be able to prove they have special expenses within the categories in the schedule which are as follows:

- costs incurred in maintaining contact with the qualifying child;
- costs attributable to a long-term illness or disability of a relevant child;
- debts of a prescribed kind incurred before the non-resident parent became non-resident;
- boarding school fees for the qualifying child;
- costs incurred in paying the mortgage on a property in which the non-resident parent no longer has an interest, but in which the child and person with care still live.

In addition, the Regulations that accompany these provisions provide limits, or rather thresholds, to the expenses before any reduction in child support will be made. Thus where the net income of the non-resident parent is more than £200 per week, the threshold is £15 of additional expenses, and if the net weekly income is less than £200, the threshold is £10.

6.4.4 Property adjustments

In addition to applications to vary the amount payable due to special expenses, the non-resident parent may seek to vary the amount payable by virtue of the fact of a capital transfer, normally of property, in the course of a divorce settlement. Prior to the implementation of the CSA 1991 this was a common way to provide for a clean break and also meet maintenance obligations. As the CSA 1991 was originally enacted, these settlements could, in effect, be overturned as the CSA 1991 overrides any previous agreements where the parent with care is on benefits. The court's approach was that any attempt to re-open the capital transfer or to prevent the Agency's involvement was impossible, since Parliament had made it clear that all child support was to be dealt with on an administrative basis.

In *Crozier v Crozier* [1994] 2 WLR 444, H and W made a clean break settlement whereby H transferred his interest (half-share) of the proceeds of sale of the family home, which was valued at around £10,000, to W in settlement of her financial claims. A nominal maintenance order was made for the child of the family, X, who lived with W. W was to accept full responsibility for maintaining X. W was receiving income support. The Department for Social Security asked for, and obtained, an order from the magistrates ordering H to make a contribution to X's maintenance. H later became liable to pay child support for X and he asked for leave to appeal out of time in order to recover his half-share of the proceeds of sale of the matrimonial home. The court held that H's application would be dismissed. A clean break agreement between H and W on the breakup of a marriage does not represent a clean financial break between a parent and their child. It may not be set aside because of the bringing into force of a new statutory enforcement body (the Agency) which regulates the amount of maintenance payable to children. No 'new event' which suffices to invalidate the very basis of a consent order is constituted by either the magistrates' order or the assessment of H's financial responsibility under CSA 1991.

The judgment in this case made it clear that spouses (and the court) are required to bring maintenance between them to an end as soon as possible (the clean break provisions). However, where a child is concerned, there is no power to achieve a clean break. The fact that parents may have made an agreement along those lines does not form a binding agreement with the state.

As a result of this perceived injustice, amendments to the assessment regime were made in 1995. The current regulations are the Child Support (Variation) Regulations 2000 (SI 2000/156) and they state that unless a property transfer has specified how much of the value is attributable to a capitalisation of child support, no relief will be given. If there is such a specification, then the child maintenance payable will be reduced by a set amount, according to how much capital was attributable to child support, with the minimum threshold being £5,000, and this may in reality be a greater figure than can be attributed to the value of the actual transfer.

6.4.5 Other assets

The CSA 1991 provides for variations to the calculation in 'additional cases', namely those set out in Sched 4B, para 4, which include where:

- the non-resident parent has assets which exceed a prescribed value;
- a person's lifestyle is inconsistent with their income;
- a person has income not taken into account in the calculation; and
- a person has unreasonably reduced the income taken into account in the calculation.

Further detail on these cases can be found in paras 18–20 of the Child Support (Variation) Regulations 2000.

6.4.6 Effect on amount payable

If a variation application has been successful, then the non-resident parent's income will either be reduced by the relevant weekly value, for example, if there are additional contact costs or a property transfer, or increased by the relevant weekly value, for example, where the non-resident parent has deliberately disposed of assets to reduce liability.

6.5 WHEN IS THE CSA 1991 NOT APPLICABLE?

As we have seen, the CSA 1991 focuses on parents and children with a biological link and bases the assessment on (almost) pure mathematical calculations.

There are situations when the CSA 1991 will not be applicable or where other legislation can be utilised in addition to the CSA 1991 and these are identified in s 8 where it states that the courts can be requested to make an order for child support even if a CSA 1991 assessment can be made:

- where the parent has already been assessed under the normal process and fully meets their child support obligations and the parent is wealthy (s 8(6));
- where the child is undergoing education or training and the maintenance order is required to meet all or some of the costs involved (s 8(7));
- where the child is disabled and the order is needed to meet the additional costs involved with the disability (s 8(8)).

Question

Can you identify any other situations where the Agency will not have jurisdiction?

There are a few more situations that you could have mentioned where the court will be the only option available to seek maintenance:

- where the habitual residence criteria are not met;
- where the child does not fall within the definition of a qualifying child – they may be a step-child, for example, or may be in excess of the age range for the CSA 1991; and
- where the parent with care is not seeking a periodical payment but a lump sum or property transfer to the child.

6.5.1 Other legislation

While the CSA 1991 does not have the jurisdiction to deal with cases in the categories listed in the above paragraph, before a court can make an order it must have the ability to exercise jurisdiction, which will be granted by statute.

Question

What other legislation can you think of that may provide jurisdiction?

Remembering what you studied earlier you should have been able to come up with two of the alternative sources, that is, the Matrimonial Causes Act (MCA) 1973 and the Domestic Proceedings and Magistrates' Courts Act (DPMCA) 1978. A third exists, being the Children Act (CA) 1989.

6.5.1.1 Status

The status of the child dictates which of the Acts apply. Both the MCA 1973 and the DPMCA 1978 state that the orders available are for the parties to a marriage and any children of the family.

Question

How would you define a child of the family?

Section 52(1) of the MCA 1973 refers to a child of the family in relation to the parties of a marriage as:

(a) a child of both of those parties; and

(b) any other child, not being a child who is placed with those parties as foster parents by a local authority or voluntary organisation, who has been treated by both of those parties as a child of their family.

Treating a child as part of the family will involve a common sense approach; for example, has the child received the level of care, physical and emotional, that would be expected from parents, etc? This would easily refer to a step-child, but may, under (b) above, cover other children who do not fit the standard norms. You should note that the MCA 1973 does not define a child of the family by reference to any legal orders that may be obtainable. The definition in the DPMCA 1978 is the same as the MCA 1973, as is the interpretation.

The final thing to note, with reference to status, is that an application can only be made under these Acts where the adults are or were married because the definition refers to parties to a marriage to which the child is a child of the family. Neither of these statutes applies to cohabiting couples and their children. Also, you should note the situations when these orders are being made, that is, either on divorce or where there has been a failure to provide reasonable maintenance, as discussed in earlier chapters.

6.5.1.2 Orders

The nature of the orders that can be obtained for children are the same as for spouses under the MCA 1973, that is, periodical payments, lump sums and property transfers (the last not being available in the Family Proceedings Court).

Question

Which of these orders is most likely to be granted?

As with spouses, the most common order made for maintenance of a child will be the unsecured periodical payments order. Lump sum and/or property transfer orders are the minority of children's orders.

Question

Why do you think this is?

In many cases, as with spouses, there will not be enough available capital to meet lump sum or property transfer orders. However, there is a more fundamental objection to the transfer of property or large financial sums, namely the fact that the award will probably extend beyond the minority of the child, which is something that is not seen as appropriate since maintenance is intended only for the child's minority.

In *Kiely v Kiely* [1988] 1 FLR 248, the parties had divorced after 12 years of marriage during which two children had been born. In dealing with the financial aspects of the divorce, W had remained in the matrimonial home with the children, with H retaining a 50% share in the home. Periodical payments were ordered in favour of W and the children. When H ceased making payments W sought a lump sum payment order with respect to the children and such an order was made, to be paid when the children reached 18 years of age. On appeal the orders were revoked, with Booth J highlighting that the court was bound to consider the factors in the MCA 1973 and that there was no evidence before the court that the children would suffer hardship or any material disadvantage if the order were not made; that there was no evidence that the children needed such a lump sum either immediately or in the future; nor were there any special circumstances requiring such an order to be made.

In *T v S (Financial Provision for Children)* [1994] 2 FLR 883, the parties were unmarried and had five children. After the breakdown of the relationship an order was made for the property in which the mother lived with the children to be held on trust until the youngest child reach 21 years of age or ceased full time education, with the benefit of the property passing to the children, following sale, in equal shares. The father claimed that this order went beyond the powers of the court since it extended the liability beyond the children's majority. Johnson J agreed that there was nothing in the circumstances of this case that justified the extended duration – the role of the court being to ensure that the children's needs were met during their minority.

6.5.1.3 Criteria

When a court is considering making an order with respect to a child, it will have to have regard to the welfare of the child as being one of the first considerations, but not the paramount one. There also will be a requirement for the court to consider the list of factors in s 25(3) of the MCA 1973 and s 3(3) of the DPMCA 1978. These lists are almost exactly the same as the factors for spouses, which have already been discussed.

One significant difference can be seen in s 25(4) of the MCA 1973 and s 3(4) of the DPMCA 1978, which will have relevance to non-biological children only. Under these provisions the court must assess the nature of responsibility taken on by the parent being asked to pay maintenance, how long that responsibility has lasted, whether it was undertaken knowing the child was not their own and whether any other person is liable to maintain the child.

Given the greater chances of serial monogamy in today's society, it is not hard to imagine a situation where a biological father is paying child support via the CSA 1991, and a step-father is being asked to pay via the MCA 1973.

6.5.2   The Children Act 1989

6.5.2.1   Status

The CA 1989 is broader than the MCA 1973 and DPMCA 1978 in that it covers a wider range of children and situations. Status is referred to more often in the context of the applicant for the order than in the context of the child themselves, as indicated in Sched 1, para 1. The child can be the product of unmarried or of married parents. The applicant can be a parent, a guardian or an individual with a residence order (residence orders will be covered in later chapters), and the respondent will be one or both of the child's parents. A child, under para 2, may themselves apply for an order when they have reached the age of 18.

Question

Does the fact that the CA 1989 permits a child to apply for maintenance once they reach majority not go against the principles of the cases highlighted previously on p 124?

An order may only be made to extend beyond a child's 18th birthday in exceptional circumstances and where the child is to be undergoing training or further education. Parents' income is assessable for the purposes of university fees already, so the CA 1989 is, in effect, merely giving the child the means to enforce payment.

6.5.2.2   Orders

The range of orders available is the same as in the MCA 1973 and DPMCA 1978 and the same difficulties exist under the CA 1989 where the settlement of property is concerned. An added problem is that if a property settlement is made in favour of a child of unmarried parents, the resident parent will gain an advantage that otherwise would not be available. This was highlighted in *T v S (Financial Provision for Children)* [1994] 2 FLR 883, when Johnson J stated: 'The sadness here is that, after a long and seemingly happy relationship, this mother of five children, never having been married to their father, has no rights against him of her own.' However, having acknowledged the problem, the order was still only granted for the children for a limited time frame. Equally, in *A v A (A Minor: Financial Provision)* [1994] 1 FLR 657, the parents were unmarried. The court ordered a settlement of a property on the child, with the property to revert to the father on the child reaching 18 or ceasing full time education. In relation to the unmarried mother Ward J stated:

> The mother's obligation is to look after A, and A's financial need is to provide a roof over the head of her caretaker. It is, indeed, father's obligation to provide the accommodation for the living in help which A needs. Consequently, it must be a term of the settlement that while A is under the control of her mother and thereafter for so long as A does not object, the mother shall have the right to occupy the property to the exclusion of the father and without paying rent therefore for the purpose of providing a home and care and support for A.

The cases of *J v C (Child: Financial Provision)* [1999] 1 FLR 952 and *Re P (Child)* [2003] EWCA Civ 837 are also illustrative on this point.

6.5.2.3 Criteria

Sched 1, para 4, of the CA 1989 sets out the factors to be considered by the court when deciding an application. Unlike the MCA 1973 and the DPMCA 1978, if the CA 1989 is being used the child's welfare will be the court's paramount consideration (s 1(1) of the CA 1989). Note: you will learn more about the CA 1989 later.

Question

Do you think that this will make a difference?

The fact that the wording of the CA 1989 is different to the MCA 1973 and DPMCA 1978 should reflect alternative approaches. However, any such distinction is hard to locate in the law reports, and so, in reality, the court seems to approach all the relevant statutes in the same manner.

6.6 SUMMARY

Child support is an issue that will, as time goes by, play a lesser role within the court system due to the implementation of the CSA 1991 and subsequent legislation. Even though cases still exist, which will remain within the court's jurisdiction, the starting points in financial terms are now expressed in the

CSA 1991 maintenance requirements. There is of course more discretion to be exercised by the court! Having completed your study of this area, you should be able to explain the CSA 1991 remit and methodology. You should also be able to discuss whether alternatives exist and those situations where the CSA 1991 does not apply at all. To ensure that you have understood all this, try the following End of Chapter Assessment questions.

6.7   END OF CHAPTER ASSESSMENT

1   In what situations can maintenance be obtained for children without recourse to the Child Support Agency?

2   Steve is 32-years-old and employed as a fireman. He is unmarried. Just over a year ago he split up from his girlfriend, Toni, and he has had no contact since. Yesterday he received a letter from the Child Support Agency together with a maintenance enquiry form asking for details of his income, etc, with regard to Toni's child, William. Toni is claiming Steve is the father of William.

Steve seeks your advice. He does not believe that he is the child's father and he wishes to know how the Agency will approach this denial. Also he wishes to know how the Agency will assess the claim if he is treated as being the father.

CHAPTER 7

DOMESTIC VIOLENCE

7.1 OBJECTIVES

By the end of this chapter you should be able to:

- appreciate the historical background to domestic violence laws;
- be aware of the multifaceted aspect of domestic violence legislation prior to the Family Law Act (FLA) 1996;
- discuss the reasons for change and how the law has changed;
- evaluate the effects of the FLA 1996; and
- understand and apply the law to hypothetical situations.

Given the links between domestic violence remedies in civil law and rights to occupy property, it is appropriate for you to look at this area of law now. You should note that these provisions, found in Pt IV of the FLA 1996, came into force in October 1997 and so have been in force for a number of years. The history of the domestic violence legislation will also be touched upon to give you an understanding of the problems surrounding this area of family law.

7.2 DEFINITIONS AND THE HISTORICAL BACKGROUND

To appreciate fully the reasons why laws to protect individuals against domestic violence have developed in the manner that they have, a historical perspective is needed.

Question

How would you define domestic violence?

Would you ever consider domestic violence to be permissible?

Within your definition you have probably referred to some form of physical violence, the assaulting of one person by another within the domestic sphere. Violence may be quite minor, such as common assault, or more severe and even includes murder. Did you think of domestic violence in the terms of psychological harm? You may feel that violence, whatever the extent, is permissible if carried out 'behind closed doors'. When speaking on the issue of reducing the age of consent for homosexual intercourse, Edwina Currie MP stated that: 'The state should be kept out of our personal lives ... everybody is entitled to his or her privacy. What my neighbours get up to in private is their business, not mine. It is not for the state to interfere.'

Despite the difference in focus, that is, homosexual intercourse, not domestic violence, is the principle not the same?

7.2.1   The wife as chattel

If you agree that domestic violence is not permissible in society, the fact that violence has been condoned within marriage is a historical fact. Wives and children were for a long time deemed to be the chattels of the husband – his property to do with as he wished. If that included beating, no one would complain. Indeed, despite commentary to discredit the belief, '... by the common law a husband was allowed to beat his wife so long as he did it with a stick no bigger that his thumb' (per Lord Denning in Davis v Johnson [1979] AC 264, at p 270). The notion of change had begun to infiltrate social thinking by 1775; again, to quote Lord Denning in Davis v Johnson, at p 271:

> He was able, Blackstone says, to give his wife 'moderate correction'. But Blackstone goes on to tell us that by this time this power of correction began to be doubted: 'Yet the lower rank of people, who were always fond of the old common law, still claim and exert their ancient privilege' (Blackstone's Commentaries on the Laws of England, vol 1, 8th edn, [1775] 1825, Butterworths).

7.2.2   Battered wives as a matter of concern

Society has now moved on from the concept of a wife as a possession: husbands and wives are now seen as equals. In addition, the use of violence within the home, or domestic life, is seen to be wrong, or uncivilised. Steps to protect victims were not taken until the mid 1970s following a Select Committee report on the issue in 1975. Legislation was enacted in 1976 with jurisdiction in the county court and the High Court, and in 1978 provisions to give jurisdiction to the magistrates' were enacted. The passing of civil legislation did not end the incidence of violence which did, and still does, continue. The influence of a patriarchal society, with its roots in the 'wife as chattel' theory, can be seen in the offence of rape. It was not until 1991 that 'marital rape' was recognised by the House of Lords as being a criminal offence. The legal validity for the proposition that rape within marriage did not exist was that when a woman consents to marriage she irrevocably consents to consortium with her husband. In the case of R v R [1991] 3 WLR 767, the House of Lords upheld a husband's conviction for raping his wife. As Lord Keith stated: 'marriage is in modern times regarded as a partnership of equals, and no longer one in which the wife must be the subservient chattel of the husband ...' Parliament took until 1994 and the Criminal Justice and Public Order Act to incorporate this ruling into statute.

As you can see, domestic violence is not a matter that has given rise to concern until quite recently. In addition, the law has responded to different issues in different ways. Legislation has been enacted as and when problems were perceived to exist. The consequence was 'a hotchpotch of enactments of limited scope passed to meet specific situations or to strengthen the powers of specified courts' (*per* Lord Scarman in *Richards v Richards* [1983] 3 WLR 173). This hotchpotch was repealed and a new and potentially clearer set of rules enacted in the FLA 1996.

7.2.3   Just battered wives?

Question

Who do you perceive to be the victim in cases of domestic violence?

The common perception will be that it is wives (or girlfriends) who will be the victims of domestic violence. This fits in with the stereotypes of the genders, that the male will be aggressive, stronger, and more prone to uncontrollable outbursts than the female. While this is often the case, the fact is that women can be violent too. In some cases the violence will manifest itself differently, and it is true to say that the way in which the law and legal processes, and indeed society, deals with violence by women against men can be different. The legislation on domestic violence is available to both genders, but would a lawyer or judge query why a man did not defend himself against such violence? Would the question of manliness be raised, not necessarily explicitly but implicitly? Would the female aggressor be treated, or castigated, in the same way as a male aggressor? In criminal law, analysis of sentencing shows that women are more likely to receive lighter sentences, or to be treated as 'mad not bad', where violence is concerned. However, for the purposes of this chapter, the victim is referred to as female.

7.3   OPTIONS TO PROTECT, OTHER THAN DOMESTIC VIOLENCE LEGISLATION

The legislation you will focus on operates within the arena of civil law.

Question

What other options for protection may be available?

Clearly, the other area of relevance is the criminal law. Domestic violence will often include the commission of an offence in criminal law that could be punishable in the criminal court. The crime may range from assault to the more serious crimes of rape or murder.

> **Question**
>
> Would you choose criminal or civil sanctions as the first option for protection?

Despite the clear criminality involved in domestic violence, in many situations the civil law will be preferred. For many years it was a general principle of the police to refrain from intervention in cases of domestic violence – perhaps this was due to the historical background you read about earlier. Although this 'principle' has now changed, prosecutions are still not always pursued. Until the Police and Criminal Evidence Act 1984 made a spouse a competent and compellable witness, evidence was difficult to adduce. It has been suggested, by Cretney and Davies, that many prosecutions still fail because the complainant fails to give evidence or withdraws the complaint, and because the prosecuting agency does not compel attendance (Cretney and Davies, 'Prosecuting "domestic" assault' [1996] Crim LR 162).

> **Question**
>
> What other reasons exist to suggest that the criminal law is not always the best option?

In addition to the evidential problems, the criminal law is a slow process. The victim of violence may wish to see the perpetrator punished, which is the aim of the criminal law, but often their aim will be to gain protection. The ability to keep a person accused of domestic violence in custody until trial is limited. If an accused is released on bail, there is always the potential for more violence to occur since the involvement of the police may exacerbate the situation and the accused may simply ignore any bail conditions imposed. Also, the charge brought may be quite minor, for example, common assault, with an equally minor sentence upon conviction that in reality will do little to help the victim. For these sorts of reasons, the civil law is generally the preferred route to take.

7.4   CIVIL REMEDIES GENERALLY

Civil law can be invoked to obtain a range of orders that attempt to provide a more suitable remedy for the victim. While statute will often be the first port of call, there is a general power of the court to grant injunctions ancillary to existing legal rights. This inherent jurisdiction may be useful to obtain protection against violence where domestic violence statutes do not provide a remedy. In *Khorasandjian v Bush* [1993] QB 727, the individuals did not come within the then existing domestic violence legislation, being merely non-cohabiting girlfriend and boyfriend, and hence the claimant had to prove the existence of some other legal right. This was the tort of nuisance. As the defendant had acted contrary to the claimant's right to be free from nuisance, the court could also grant an injunction to prevent the nuisance continuing.

The relevance of the inherent jurisdiction will diminish now that Pt IV of the FLA 1996 is in force, since the scope of possible applicants is considerably changed as you will now see.

7.5   THE FLA 1996

This Act, in Pt IV, sets out a new coherent scheme for making occupation orders and non-molestation orders, and in so doing repealed all the previous domestic violence legislation. Part IV of the FLA 1996 was added at a late stage, after the Family Homes and Domestic Violence Bill was defeated in the Lords and withdrawn (notably after a media campaign against giving cohabitants the same rights as spouses). The intention was to remove the complexity of the previous legislation and to introduce a consistent range of criteria under which applications are to be assessed.

7.5.1   Non-molestation orders

These orders are covered by s 42 of the FLA 1996 which provides as follows:

(1) In this part a 'non-molestation order' means an order containing either or both of the following provisions –

(a) provision prohibiting a person ('the respondent') from molesting another person who is associated with the respondent;

(b) provision prohibiting the respondent from molesting a relevant child.

As with the legislation that the FLA 1996 replaced, the Act does not in fact define what type of behaviour will be covered by the term 'molestation'. The approach identified in pre-FLA 1996 cases remains, in practice, good law.

Question

What would you include?

Using the approach developed by courts preceding the FLA 1996, molestation is more than just violence, and normal practice is for the order to prevent the respondent from intimidating, pestering or harassing the applicant, although the order may be expressed to prohibit specific types of contact, rather than behaviour generally. The court also has the ability to prevent the respondent entering a set or defined area and this is potentially very useful.

In *Horner v Horner* [1982] 2 WLR 914, H and W had parted although they had not divorced. The court found that prior to the separation H had been acting in a peculiar manner and had even threatened W physically. Since the separation H had harassed W by way of handing her threatening letters, intercepting her on the way to the station and hanging scurrilous posters on the school railings where W worked. In relation to the term molesting Ormrod LJ stated that: '[it does] not imply necessarily either violence or threats of violence. It applies to any conduct which can properly be regarded as such a degree of harassment as to call for the intervention of the court.'

In *C v C (Non-Molestation Order: Jurisdiction)* [1998] Fam 70, following the divorce of H and W, W published articles in the national press in which she purported to give information concerning H's relations with her and his three former wives. The articles were couched in very unflattering terms. H complained that W's intention was to humiliate and embarrass him. He applied for a non-molestation order under s 42 of the FLA 1996 so as to prevent W harassing him by publishing matter which might affect the determination of financial issues between H and W. W contended that the facts of the case did not justify the making of such an order. The court decided that H's application would be refused. Although the Act did not define 'molestation', the word seemed to imply conduct which was intended to result in a high degree of harassment of the other party and which justified the court's intervention. A mere invasion of privacy did not constitute harassment. H's concern to protect his privacy did not come within the scope of s 42; *per* Brown P:

> It is significant in my judgment that s 42 is to be found in FLA 1996 Part IV, which is concerned with the general topic of domestic violence ... The material complained of is some alleged revelations by the former wife of what she regarded as her former husband's misconduct. In my judgment it comes nowhere near 'molestation' as envisaged by s 42 FLA 1996.

7.5.1.1   The applicant

Under the terms of s 42(1)(a) and (b) of the FLA 1996, the applicant must be an 'associated person' or a 'relevant child'.

Question

Who do you think would be covered by these terms?

Unlike the range of applicants under the preceding legislation, the FLA 1996 has sought to be far less restrictive, and also to recognise that domestic violence does not just occur between spouses and cohabitants. Section 62 sets out the individuals who will be classed as 'associated' and also 'relevant children'; individuals fall within the definitions if:

- they are or have been married to each other;
- they are cohabitants or former cohabitants;
- they live or have lived in the same household, otherwise than merely by reason of one of them being the other's employee, tenant, lodger or boarder;
- they are relatives;
- they have agreed to marry one another (whether or not that agreement has been terminated but only within three years of termination);
- in relation to any child, they (the applicant and respondent) are a parent of the child or have parental responsibility for the child; or
- they are parties to the same family proceedings (other than domestic violence proceedings).

As you can see, although the section refers to the traditional spouses and heterosexual cohabitants, it also includes former spouses and cohabitants. Cohabitants are defined in s 62 as a 'man and a woman, who, although not married to each other, are living together as husband and wife'. Same-sex couples will be covered too, under the 'live or have lived in the same household, otherwise than due to being an employee, tenant, lodger or boarder' provision.

Question

Why should employees, tenants and boarders be excluded?

The view taken by the Law Commission was that it was inappropriate to include these groupings since there were thought to be more suitable remedies under property or employment legislation. While some of this reasoning may be acceptable, it is hard to understand why ex-spouses who no longer live together should be able to apply to gain protection, and yet a resident landlord who has evicted a violent tenant cannot do the same if that tenant continues to harass or molest him or her.

7.5.1.2 When can the order be made?

A non-molestation order can be made, even if it has not been formally applied for, if the court feels the order would be of benefit to a party in any ongoing family proceedings (s 42(2)(b)). Applicants may wish to apply within the context of existing family proceedings or may wish to make a freestanding application.

The court may make a non-molestation order having had regard to 'all the circumstances including the need to secure the health, safety and well-being ... of the applicant ... and any relevant child' (s 42(5)). In deciding whether or not to make an order, the court has its discretion, but must base its decision on the factors mentioned.

7.5.1.3 Duration of the order

The practice before the FLA 1996 was only to make orders for a short period of time, to allow other steps to be taken, such as issuing divorce proceedings. The FLA 1996 does not change this discretionary aspect of the order, but does clearly state in s 42(7) that the order can be made 'until further order', implying the possibility of an almost indefinite order.

In *M v W (Non-Molestation Order: Duration)* [2000] 1 FLR 107, the Family Proceedings Court had indeed made an open ended non-molestation order following application from the mother. The father claimed that the order should not be open ended, but for a limited time only. In looking at this point Cazalet J stated:

> Although I have to start from the statute, earlier decisions on the desirability or appropriateness of a non-molestation order lasting for many years may throw some light on the court's approach, although of course I bear in mind that such are concerned with different statute provisions ... the object of non-molestation orders is designed to give a breathing space for the parties and, unless there are exceptional or unusual circumstances, it should be for a specified period of time.

7.5.2 Occupation orders

These exclusion orders are dealt with in ss 33–38 of the FLA 1996 (excluding s 34). The FLA 1996 is theoretically making the legislation simpler; however, when you look at these sections you may question this fact. The basic principles for all applications are similar, what differs is the extent of the criteria to be applied and the available duration of the order.

7.5.2.1 Section 33

This section applies to those applicants who have some form of interest in the property, as set out in s 33(1). It will therefore cover, *inter alia*, spouses who have rights to occupy by virtue of their marital status, joint owners, whether married or not, or individuals who have a joint lease or tenancy agreement or where the applicant is the sole owner, leasor or tenant. Additionally, the applicant must have occupied, or have intended to occupy, the property with the respondent as their home.

The nature of the order that the applicant can seek is a regulatory one, and the order may do any of the following:

- enforce the applicant's right to remain in the property;
- permit the applicant to enter the premises, and remain there;
- regulate the parties' occupation of the property;

- prevent the respondent from exercising any rights to occupy the property, or regulate any matrimonial homes rights that the respondent may have;
- require the respondent to vacate the property; and
- prevent the respondent from entering a defined area within which the property is located.

When being asked to make an order, the court considers a statutory list of criteria in sub-s (6). These factors are:

- the housing needs and resources of the parties and any relevant children;
- the financial resources of the parties;
- the effect of the order or decision not to make an order on the health, safety or well-being of the parties or any relevant child; and
- the conduct of the parties to each other and otherwise.

In addition to the above factors, the court is required under sub-s (7), to consider what is known as the 'balance of harm' test. Thus, if the court is minded to exercise its powers to make an order, it must consider if the respondent or any relevant child is likely to suffer significant harm if the order is made, and balance the harm caused to the applicant with that caused to the respondent if the order is made. The relationship between these two sub-sections has been considered by the courts, but without a great deal of clarity.

In *Chalmers v Johns* [1999] 1 FLR 392, following a period of living together for 25 years, during which time they had occupied the family home as joint tenants for 20 years, H and W decided to separate. They had a seven year old daughter, D, and an adult son. The relationship of H and W, described as 'stormy', had involved assaults of a minor nature. W and D moved into a temporary council accommodation which was much further away from the school attended by D. D had regular staying contact with H. H and W made cross-applications for a residence order for D, and W was granted an interim occupation order under s 33 of the FLA 1996 on the ground of H's violent conduct. H appealed against the occupation order. The Court of Appeal held that H's appeal would be allowed. The court held that the judge had misdirected herself and that the application for occupation orders was to be dealt with at the substantive hearing. *Per* Thorpe LJ:

> In approaching its function under s 33, the court has first to consider whether the evidence does establish that the applicant or a relative child would be likely to suffer significant harm attributable to the conduct of the respondent if an order is not made. If the court answers that question in the affirmative, then it knows that it must make the order unless, balancing one harm against the other, the harm to the respondent or child is likely to be as great. If however, the court answers in the negative, then it enters the discretionary regime provided by s 3(6) and must exercise a broad discretion having regard to all the circumstances of the case and particularly those factors set out in the statutory checklist within sub-paras (a)–(d).

Given the facts of this case, a 'draconian' occupation order was not appropriate. A non-molestation order seemed to be the correct remedy.

In *B v B (Occupation Order)* [1999] 1 FLR 715, H and W occupied a council house where they lived with S, who was H's six-year-old son from a previous relationship, and D, the two year old daughter of H and W. Following H's violent conduct towards W, W moved, with D, into bed and breakfast accommodation. H and S remained in the home. The court issued an occupation order under s 33, ordering H and S to leave the home. The tenancy of the home was transferred to W and a non-molestation order in W's favour was granted. H appealed against the occupation order, arguing that it would cause significant harm to S under the terms of s 33(7).

The court allowed H's appeal. Weighing the likelihood of harm in relation to D and S, it was clear that the balance moved in favour of S, if an occupation order were to be made. Indeed, if S were to move, a change of school would be necessary and, further, being removed from his father was in no way a solution to the resulting problems. *Per* Butler-Sloss LJ:

> For a child of D's age, the essential security is being where her mother is. Furthermore ... W's residence in bed and breakfast accommodation is likely to be temporary ... For S, the position is much more complex. His security depends not merely on being in his father's care, but on his other day to day support systems, of which his home and school are clearly the most important ... In our judgement if, on the facts of this case, the respective likelihood of harm are weighed as far as D and S are concerned, the balance comes down in favour of S suffering the greater harm if an occupation order is made ... We have no sympathy for H ... were it not for the fact that he is caring for S, and that S has particular needs which at present outweigh those of D, an occupation order would undoubtedly have been made.

As you can see in *Chalmers*, Thorpe LJ stated that the court should first direct its attention to s 33(6) – the general list of factors, which provide the court with a wide discretion to make the order or not. If the case is more serious, and there is the risk of significant harm, Thorpe LJ suggests that the court must look to s 33(7) and balance the issue of harm. He infers that the two provisions are exclusive and that, in reality, the question of whether there is significant harm should be dealt with first. If the balancing exercise that is part of the sub-section results in no order, then the court can turn to the more general criteria in the previous sub-section. In *Banks v Banks* [1999] 1 FLR 726, the court appears to say that, under s 33(7), there was no significant harm being caused to the husband. But the court then went on to say that the harm to the wife, if the order were made, would be significantly greater. One could ask, why deal with the balance of harm test if there is no harm on the facts to begin with? In addition (and at the same time), the court stated that under the general criteria the order could not be granted. This therefore treats the two provisions as being applicable at the same time, which conflicts with the decision of the Court of Appeal in *Chalmers*. In *B v B*, the Court of Appeal again considered the two provisions and found in the husband's favour.

However, here there was no clear priority between the sub-sections or any indication as to the best method of application of the two.

The possible period for the order to last is established in s 33(10) as being that period defined by the court in the order, or the occurrence of any event indicated in the order, or until further order – meaning indefinitely unless and until the court revokes it. You should remember to link this to the powers of the courts under the Trusts of Land and Appointment of Trustees Act (TLATA) 1996 covered in the previous chapter. If the courts are likely to limit the length of the life of an occupation order under the FLA 1996, would it not be better to use the TLATA 1996?

7.5.2.2   Section 35

Section 35 covers ex-spouses where one of the couple has a right to occupy the home, while the other does not. An example where this might arise is where the husband is the sole owner and the wife has matrimonial home rights. On divorce, she would lose these rights due to the change in her status. In this situation the ex-wife would be able to make an application under s 35, only in respect of the former matrimonial home or a property which was intended to be a matrimonial home.

If an order is sought, it may be to ensure that the applicant can remain in the property if already there, or to be permitted to return to the property. It may also regulate the respondent's occupation of the property and ability to enter into the area in which the home is located.

When deciding these cases the courts will again have regard to the circumstances, including the factors in s 35(6). In addition to the factors for applicants under s 33, the court must look at the length of time since the parties separated and also the time since the dissolution of the marriage and whether any other proceedings are ongoing (that is, ancillary claims in divorce). The balance of harm test also applies to this section.

In *S v F (Occupation Order)* [2000] 1 FLR 255, H and W divorced in 1994. Their matrimonial home was in London. They had two children, S, a boy aged 17, and D, a girl aged 15, at the time of trial. H and W agreed that W would remain in the home in London with S and D in order that they might finish their education. H then moved to Kuala Lumpur, and argued that, because of his contributions, he had a beneficial interest in the London home. During a visit by S and D to H in Kuala Lumpur, W declared her intention to leave the London home and move to Somerset. S refused to move with W. D was taken by another relative to live in the countryside; S was taken in by H's sister. H was granted an order preventing the sale of the London home. H applied for an order permitting him to occupy the London home with S. The court allowed H's application. He was instructed to proceed under s 35 because of a lack of firm evidence relating to his beneficial interest. Under s 35(6) consideration had to be given to an applicant's resources and housing needs. Additionally, attention had to be given to the effect of an order on the parties' health and well-being. When the facts were balanced, the order for which H was applying would provide greater security when compared with any short-term problems likely to involve W. It had to be remembered too, that W was responsible in some measure for the existing state of affairs. H would be allowed, therefore, to return to the London home for six months; W would be given leave to apply for discharge of the order if H failed at any time to comply with an undertaking which he had given to pay the mortgage.

Question

Is it right to give an ex-wife rights in the former matrimonial home?

Naturally this would depend on how long ago the marriage was ended, and it is not envisaged that the courts will be ousting an owner 10, 15 or 20 years after the other spouse left. However, once the divorce is made absolute, if the parties are not living together, under the existing law, there is little that can be done to obtain occupation of the ex-matrimonial home. If the wife is claiming the home as part of the post-divorce financial settlement, but has nowhere else to go in the meantime, it might be perfectly justifiable to 'oust' the husband (if he can maintain himself elsewhere) until the outcome of the ancillary proceedings.

Any order made under s 35 will have a limited lifespan – initially the order can last for up to six months. It may be extended on one or more occasions for similar periods.

7.5.2.3 *Section 36*

Section 36 applies to cohabitants who are not co-owners or tenants, or former cohabitants who are not co-owner or tenants. The order that can be sought is one potentially to remove the cohabitant or former cohabitant with property rights, or to regulate their use of the property. It will be granted only after the court has considered all the circumstances of the case including the matters specified in s 36(6) (which are very similar to s 35). When the court is considering the 'nature of the relationship' under s 36(6)(e), it must 'have regard to the fact that [the couple] have not given each other the commitment involved in marriage' (s 41(2)).

Question

If the court is faced with an application to remove a partner due to their violence, should s 41(2) make any substantive difference?

As part of a package of considerations, you may agree that so far as occupation of a home is concerned, where otherwise the applicant has no rights at all in relation to the property, the fact that the couple are unmarried may be relevant. Many of you will not see the significance of commitment as having any role to play. The reasons why a couple do not marry may have nothing to do with the level of commitment they feel to one another. Arguably by including this provision, the law is prejudging cohabitation and declaring it 'second-best' and certainly not indicative of any long-term intentions. It may be suggested that this provision was included to ensure the passage of the Bill through Parliament after its earlier defeat as the Family Homes and Domestic Violence Bill.

The duration of a s 36 order is also more limited than other occupation orders. The initial order may last for six months, with the scope to extend it once only for another maximum period of six months.

Question

If a cohabitant is seeking rights of ownership via a constructive trust, could this be achieved in a 12-month period? Will the applicant necessarily have alternative accommodation after her occupation order has ended and before her property action is concluded?

Given the current state of the civil jurisdiction, and the lengthy details encountered, it may be that s 36 merely operates as a stopgap which will fall short of what is practically needed.

7.5.3 Nature of proceedings

It is possible to obtain an FLA 1996 occupation order or non-molestation order on a without notice basis. Consistent with the rest of the FLA 1996, the court's powers to grant a without notice order are set out in the Act itself, including the factors which will support the making of the order without notice. These factors are set out in s 45 and, in addition to all the circumstances of the case, include the following:

- any risk of significant harm to the applicant or relevant child, attributable to the conduct of the respondent, if the order is not made immediately;
- whether it is likely that the applicant will be deterred or prevented from pursuing an application; and
- whether there is any evidence that the respondent is aware of the proceedings and is deliberately evading service and the delay in effecting service will prejudice the applicant.

Question

Do you think these are workable?

The issues the court must have regard to before making an order on a without notice basis are founded on common sense, and probably reflect the factors that the judiciary already consider before making without notice orders generally. By the inclusion of s 45 of the FLA 1996 merely reaffirms the requirement of urgency that should be part of the making of orders in the absence of the respondent.

7.5.4   Undertakings

In many situations the court will accept an undertaking from the respondent rather than impose an order. The giving of an undertaking does not have the same 'wrongdoer' stigma as being the subject of an order, hence the popularity of undertakings. The FLA 1996 provides for undertakings in s 46 but also makes it clear when an undertaking will not be acceptable: '(3) The court shall not accept an undertaking ... in any case where apart from this section a power of arrest would be attached to the order.'

As well as this limitation, the section also states that the undertaking is enforceable as if it was an order of the court (sub-s 4). While this sub-section does not change the previous position at law relating to undertakings, the fact that this position is clearly stated may make a difference. Some respondents to domestic violence actions see an undertaking as an easy way out and, as it is not incorporated into an order, as something that can be easily broken. In practice, enforcement of undertakings is not highly successful, the best normally achievable being the making of a full order which may be seen as more 'legal'.

7.5.5   Enforcement

The breach of an order will carry certain penalties, the prospect of committal for breach being the normal one, since it is a contempt of court. As under the previous statutory provisions, the court may also attach a power of arrest to any order made, including without notice orders. The details of the court's powers are set out in s 47. The basis upon which a power of arrest may be attached requires the respondent to have used or threatened violence to the person of the applicant or a relevant child, and the court is not satisfied that in all the circumstances of the case the applicant or child will be adequately protected without such a power of arrest.

Question

Do you think this form of enforcement is sufficient?

The problem with powers of arrest is that the trigger point to arrest is an actual breach of the order. This may well mean that the applicant, the beneficiary of the order, has to, again, suffer violence to their person – not really helpful at all. However there are likely to be situations where the existence of the power of arrest does dissuade the respondent from molesting the applicant.

Powers of arrest may be granted in without notice situations. Here the only difference is that the court must believe that there is a risk of significant harm on an immediate basis. The need for significant harm is to reflect the draconian nature of attaching the power of arrest in a situation where only one party's side of the story has been heard.

In *H v H (A Child) (Occupation Order: Power of Arrest)* (2001) *The Times*, 10 January, an occupation order was made against a 17-year-old minor who had been ordered out of the family home, with a requirement not to re-enter for six months, and a power of arrest attached. The minor appealed against the attachment of a power of arrest. The Court of Appeal held that if the court had made the occupation order and it had appeared that the respondent had used violence against the applicant, then the court had to attach a power of arrest if it was needed to protect the applicant. The power of arrest was not merely there to provide a quick route into the criminal process but also enabled the respondent to be removed from the family home.

7.6   STALKING

In 1997, after much publicity, the Protection from Harassment Act (PHA) 1997 was passed which creates a new, criminally enforceable offence of stalking. In addition, the PHA 1997 introduces civil remedies, which include injunctive relief, as well as the ability for a victim to seek damages. While this Act may not be primarily focused on the domestic violence victim, the clear links with harassment and molestation may mean that it is another means to obtain protection. The victim will not have to be 'associated' in the sense of the FLA 1996; this is a clear benefit. However, although the victim may obtain civil law redress, the criminal law provisions will arguably suffer from the same problems outlined at the start of this chapter, notably the delay and the nature of the punishment that will ensue.

7.7   REFORM

The Government announced an overhaul of the current domestic violence legislation in the Queen's Speech in November 2003. The Bill to achieve this overhaul – the Domestic Violence, Crime and Victims Bill (the Bill) – was introduced into the House of Lords on 27 November 2003 and it devotes four clauses to the topic of domestic violence.

7.7.1 Proposed changes to the legislative regime

The Bill makes very few changes to the legislative regime outlined above; some of the changes to be introduced will do little to remove the confusion that exists due to the already overlapping criminal and civil jurisdictions; others will address legitimate concerns, but they certainly are not sufficiently drastic to amount to an overhaul or modernisation.

The first change will come to the non-molestation order. Clause 1 of the Bill will introduce a new section, s 42A, into the FLA 1996, and creates a criminal offence of breaching a non-molestation order: '(1) A person who without reasonable excuse does anything that he is prohibited from doing by a non-molestation order is guilty of an offence.'

The clause goes on to make clear that the person whose activities are restricted will not be subject to a criminal sanction unless they are aware of the existence of the order and its terms (see amendment to cl 1 moved by Baroness Anelay, 8 January 2004). The maximum sentence on summary conviction is six months and/or a fine and on indictment is five years and/or a fine (cl 1(5)). What the clause usefully does is ensure that any conduct which is punished under this provision by way of criminal proceedings cannot be made the subject of civil contempt proceedings (cl 1(3) and (4)).

Clause 3 seeks to extend the definition of cohabitants found in s 62 of the FLA 1996 – this being the section that establishes whether the applicant and respondent are 'cohabitants, relevant children and associated persons'. The new definition will include same-sex couples as cohabitants if their relationship is deemed 'equivalent' to that of husband and wife, implying there must be some form of intimate or sexual relationship present. For same-sex couples, who are not treated as cohabitants due to this change, they will still be associated since cl 4 extends the definition of associated persons to include those who 'have or have had an intimate personal relationship with each other which is or was of significant duration'. It should be noted that one of the amendments proposed by Baroness Anelay would change the latter part to: 'of such significance as to justify the making of an order' (amendment moved on 5 January 2004), but this has not been accepted.

In relation to occupation orders, Sched 10 of the Bill will require the court to consider making a non-molestation order if it is being asked to make an occupation order. This is to be achieved by amending s 42 of the FLA 1996.

Finally, the ability of the court to attach a power of arrest under s 47 will only relate to breaches of occupation orders not, as currently, to both non-molestation and occupation orders (see Sched 10 to the Bill).

This latter change makes sense given that breach of the new non-molestation order will automatically be a criminal offence, hence negating the need for a power of arrest. However, it is curious that only the non-molestation order, if breached, will now be classed as a criminal offence, whilst breach of an occupation order will not. The explanatory notes to the Bill justify this by saying that a 'history of violence or molestation is not a prerequisite for the grant of an order' and suggest that the requirement of the court to consider making a non-molestation order, when dealing with occupation orders, will be sufficient to protect the victim (para 26). However, as you have seen, the case law on domestic violence and the seeking of occupation orders will invariably require evidence of harm. The criteria upon which the occupation order can be granted makes this evident with the reference to the 'conduct of the parties to one another'; the effect of the decision of the court on the 'health, safety or well-being of the parties' and the requirement that the court consider if anyone is at risk of significant harm (s 33 of the FLA 1996). Added to this, the court has traditionally seen an occupation order as a draconian order since it removes the right (even if time limited) of a land owner leasee/tenant to enjoy the benefits from that status. It will hence be the rare case where the applicant cannot or will not have to show some form of harm or history of molestation to be successful in obtaining an occupation order.

It will also remain to be seen if the ability of the court to grant a non-molestation order, when there is an application for an occupation order will be used. In some cases, an occupation order is not sought at the outset of proceedings for domestic violence but after non-molestation orders have not been effective in preventing continued violence. Arguably, the fact that a breach of a non-molestation order will be punishable via criminal proceedings will reduce the need to seek the more draconian order. However, an anomaly exists in that the civil court is very reluctant to imprison for acts of domestic violence, although this may be changing. In the case of *Lomas v Parle* [2003] EWCA Civ 1804, the respondent was sentenced, under the PHA 1997, to a community rehabilitation order, whereas the contempt proceedings for breach of the non-molestation order resulted in four months imprisonment.

In addition to these changes to the FLA 1996, amendments will be made to the PHA 1997. As has been seen, the current PHA 1997 enables the court, if convicting the defendant under s 2 or s 4, to make a restraining order against the defendant – in effect achieving the same result as an injunction in the civil jurisdiction, with the advantage that breach is a criminal offence. Clause 12 of the Bill enables the court to make a restraining order if 'a person ('the defendant') is acquitted of an offence' (cl 12 – inserting a new s 5A into the PHA 1997). The main objection to this amendment to the PHA 1997 is that the defendant has not been convicted and hence has not been proven to have committed the acts of harassment. This issue is not mentioned at all in the explanatory notes, and is probably the reason why Baroness Analey moved an amendment (16 December 2003) to require that before the court does make a restraining order it 'is satisfied on the basis of facts proved on a balance of probabilities that it is necessary to make an order to protect a person from harassment by the defendant'.

It is not clear how this amendment will strengthen domestic violence remedies – surely the victim could simply use the FLA 1996 for a non-molestation order? Arguably, the incentive to permitting restraining orders in the event of an acquittal must be that not all victims will seek civil remedies (hence raising the question of whether the state should take this step for them) and not all potential victims under the PHA 1997 would fall within the criteria of applicants for a non-molestation order under the FLA 1996.

7.7.2 The overlapping jurisdiction

As can be seen, the amendments to the FLA 1996 and the PHA 1997 does not delineate between them – it will still be the case that civil proceedings may be brought under the FLA 1996 and criminal proceedings under the PHA 1997 with resulting difficulties for sentencing.

7.8 SUMMARY

Domestic violence is an issue within family law that has, over the last three decades, become more prominent. The realisation that violence does occur in the home environment led to a variety of statutes being passed to deal with specific problems as they were seen to arise. The resulting plethora of legislation led to claims of undue complexity and overlapping jurisdictions. The FLA 1996 has tried to overcome this by introducing a coherent set of rules and orders that are available to a wider range of applicants in a variety of courts.

7.9 END OF CHAPTER ASSESSMENT

Four years ago Ingrid began to cohabit with Max in his three-bedroomed house. Ingrid has no rights of ownership.

Max has always been temperamental with frequent bouts of depression. In the last 18 months these have become far more common, and Max has started to exhibit violent tendencies. Ingrid, in the last two months, has visited the local hospital's accident and emergency department twice with broken ribs, bruising and a dislocated shoulder after being attacked by Max.

Max is always apologetic when he realises what he has done and always swears never to do anything like that again.

Advise Ingrid on what rights she has to obtain protection.

CHAPTER 8

THE LAW RELATING TO CHILDREN

8.1 OBJECTIVES

By the end of this chapter you should be able to:

- discuss the notion of children's rights;
- discuss the historical background to child law and the Children Act 1989; and
- list and define the fundamental principles of the Children Act 1989.

You are now moving on to a major part of family law, and one which interlinks with the law of marriage and divorce. Childhood is seen as a time of vulnerability and one which requires protection. The law therefore seeks to protect, but preferably in a non-interventionist way. This may sound a little contradictory, but the philosophy of the law will become clear in the next few chapters. You will start by learning about the Children Act (CA) 1989, the main legislation concerning children, and the principles that the Act introduces. After you have mastered this, you will move on to orders that can be made in respect of children in both private and public law. This latter topic will be quite a long chapter and will take careful studying. You will conclude by looking at the areas of wardship and adoption. However, the whole topic of children's law is not complex once you have mastered the basic concepts. To start then, you will be considering the concept of childhood, whether children have rights and some of the fundamental principles of the CA 1989.

8.2 WHAT IS CHILDHOOD?

Question

How would you define childhood? Write down the things that childhood encapsulates.

The things you could have written down are potentially endless – much may depend on the type of childhood you yourself had.

For many, childhood reflects a period of inexperience, vulnerability, dependency, learning and inquisitiveness, lack of responsibility and innocence.

Question

Do you think childhood is changing?

The changing nature of childhood should be apparent or known to you, whether you are a parent or not. How many times do the media present the image of children who have lost their naïvety, or children who act like adults in the sense of doing adult things? Do you long for the days when childhood was a simple and innocent period in one's life? The fact that what is expected of children, and indeed what children themselves seek and desire, has changed, and that many of those changes are accepted by society as a whole, points to the idea of the concept of childhood as being 'socially constructed'. This idea gains strength when we reflect upon the attitude to, and perception of, children in the past.

As you may be aware, children were for many centuries seen as the property of the parents over whom the parents had considerable rights. Children were not perceived as having needs in the sense that we would understand today; their youthful spirits needed to be controlled and children were seen to need training, almost in the same way as we train dogs! The Industrial Revolution and the philanthropic movement of the Victorian era helped change society's views on children and childhood. The change in working patterns in the Industrial Revolution resulted in less home-working for children as part of the family. Children, due to their cheapness, were however integrated into factory employment. This did not continue since the philanthropist movement encouraged parliament to reduce working hours for children and to regulate the employment of children. In addition the increasing number of adult males needing employment encouraged a reduction in child labour. Childhood, as a period of dependency and lack of responsibility, could be argued to have been created in the 18th and 19th centuries as this is also the time when more widespread schooling was introduced, which we would see as being a more typical childhood activity.

Question

How long do you think childhood, as created in the 18th/19th centuries, lasted?

The length of childhood probably had nothing to do with the theoretical age of majority. The social class of the individual child would be crucially important. Childhood lasted much longer in the upper classes. Most children of the lower classes, even if they were lucky enough to obtain some sort of basic education, would be in employment in their very early teens (if not before).

> **Question**
>
> How does this compare with today? Which view is preferable?

Today, legally, childhood lasts until a child is 18. At least, that is the age of majority. Most children remain in education until they are 18, with a large percentage taking their studies further. The law today also places more restrictions on what children can do, when, and at what age.

> **Question**
>
> What sort of things does the law say about what a child can do?

The sort of things you could have thought of includes:

- at 10, a minor can be convicted of a criminal offence;
- at 16 a minor can marry with the consent of all those with parental responsibility, or the with courts' authority; and
- at 17 a minor can drive a car.

> **Question**
>
> Is there any clarity in the manner in which a child is treated under the law?

There appear to be as many inconsistencies with the way that the law treats children today, as in times gone past. Much will depend on a child's age and understanding, or the level of competency that the child has. The fact that the law looks at issues, such as the understanding of the child itself, indicates that there can be no clear definition of what a child is, or what can be expected of children in society, and this makes the adoption of legal principles difficult. Finally, you should note that many of the activities that are within the scope of a child's grasp are different from those in the past, which illustrates how changes in society's attitudes directly affect the legislative provisions. An example is the age of marriage which, as you may recall from earlier in this book, used to be 12 years of age.

8.3   CHILDREN'S RIGHTS

> **Question**
>
> To what extent do children have rights?

Children, being semi-autonomous individuals, are theoretical holders of rights. As you can see, at certain (normally specified) ages, children can 'do' specified things. There is also the perception of gaining rights as the child increases in age and maturity. However one of the problems with these so called rights is the difficulty that the child may have in enforcing these rights.

Question

If a 13-year-old wishes to buy a pet dog, having saved their Christmas money, and their parents say no, how can they enforce their rights?

In this situation, who could they claim against other parties than their parents? Is this the manner in which children should be encouraged to act? More to the point, if they wished to take the matter to court, could they act in person? While a child can sue through a litigation friend, generally a parent, applications by children are not permitted on a *carte blanche* basis. Some applications can be brought by a child under the CA 1989, subject to leave and to an assessment of the child's competence to make the application.

The difficulty with having rights is the specific nature of the rights in question. As stated earlier, if those rights are not truly enforceable, can they be said to be rights at all? The impact of the European Convention on Human Rights (ECHR), with regard to enforcement of the rights enshrined within the convention, is such that if a child is a victim, then they will have the right to claim breach of those rights, and therefore a remedy. Indeed, you may be aware of cases already where a child has claimed under the ECHR. If a child wishes to commence a claim, they will normally do so through their litigation friend, an adult who runs the litigation process for them on their behalf. If the child is deemed to have 'sufficient understanding', then the court may grant leave for the child to give instructions and run the case without a litigation friend.

Question

What would be meant by competence in this situation?

Competence must relate to the issue in hand; but one of the perceived dangers must be the assumption that children will lack sufficient understanding of the processes of law to seek redress through the rights in the ECHR. It may also be an issue that our system and our legislation give the rights of enforcement to others, such as the child's parents, hence removing the victim from centre stage of the proceedings.

8.4   THE STATE AND CHILDREN

In relation to protecting children's rights, there are two main 'providers' – the child's own parents and the state and it is widely accepted that the state will play a role in child care matters.

Question

Who or what is meant by the state? How much involvement should the state have?

In connection with the CA 1989, the state refers not just to the local authority social services department (this is probably the first institution you thought of), but also to the court. Under the CA 1989 principles, the intervention of the court is to be avoided unless it is necessary in the interests of the child. This 'hands off' principle is intended to realign the balance between the state and families. It could arguably be seen as regressive, returning to the state of affairs of previous centuries where children were in effect ignored. In order to assess this suggestion, and to obtain a more rounded understanding of today's child protection law, and family law for children, it is necessary to consider briefly the history of legal provisions to protect children.

8.4.1   The poor law and property

For many centuries children were seen as property belonging to their parents. For certain classes children were important for their earning capacity. Linked to the property model was the belief that only parents had a responsibility to care or provide for their children. If a parent did not provide for their offspring little would be done. The Poor Laws, which provided an early type of welfare benefit, while making provision for children who were destitute, did not differentiate between children or adult destitutes. The ability to seek 'poor relief' was seen to be the 'last resort', and where children were concerned the main obligation to provide came from the family. Where state relief was sought, and latterly this would have been via the workhouse, it was made to be so unpleasant and harsh that many were discouraged from seeking any relief at all, which meant that the poor tax was also kept to a minimum. The attitude was very much that the 'idle poor' should not be maintained by the state.

The philanthropic movement in the Victorian era, following on from a time of great exploitation of children in employment terms, saw the beginnings of larger scale state intervention. As you have seen, this was directed at regulating the employment of children, and not at the actual care of children within the family. Schooling also became more widespread although not a legal requirement. The Ragged Schools, voluntary schools for the education of destitute children, originated in about 1818, around the time that Dr Thomas Barnardo established his first home for destitute boys.

Initially, only children who lived rough were provided with care and accommodation by these institutions. This concept of provision, care and accommodation to needy children developed into the 'removal of children' who needed 'saving' from the poor care provided by their parents. At that time what was being done was illegal, and contrary to the proprietary rights which a parent had over their children. The idea of state welfare being restricted only to those who are deserving poor is very reminiscent of the attitude today. Most state benefits are reliant on availability to work, or good reason for lack of availability. The levels of benefit, despite some political comment, are set at a level designed to be at subsistence level, but also so low as to make it less worthwhile being on benefits compared to being in employment.

Legal sanctions for neglect and abuse of children at the hands of parents did not arise until much later.

8.4.2   Legislation

With regard to the prevention of cruelty to children, it would appear that the UK was behind in its thinking. Legal action had been taken in the USA, and societies founded to prevent cruelty, several years earlier. However, even the USA did not initially recognise child abuse as a problem, the first American case involving cruelty being based on US legislation designed to prevent cruelty to animals (see further Cobley, *Child Abuse and the Law*, 1995, Cavendish Publishing). The first society in the UK to work to protect children was formed in 1882. The National Society for the Prevention of Cruelty to Children was granted its Royal Charter in 1894, having been formed from a conglomeration of smaller societies. This was in fact later than the formation of the Royal Society for the Prevention of Cruelty to Animals!

The first statute to criminalise child cruelty, the Prevention of Cruelty Act, was passed in 1889. As well as making neglect or cruelty an offence, the Act authorised removal of children from their parents where this was deemed necessary. More legislation followed, with the Children Act 1908 establishing a juvenile court to deal with the cases of delinquent juveniles, and those children who were suffering neglect and cruelty. This link, between children who are delinquent and children who need care, continued throughout the 20th century. It was predicated on the view that children who acted in a criminal manner were 'deprived' in some way of the care and upbringing that they needed. Juvenile delinquents were not so much wrongdoers as individuals to whom wrong had been done, in other words they were equally 'victims'.

8.4.3   Other means of intervention

It was not just the increasing use of statute to prevent cruelty that introduced state intervention into the family. The concerns over the health of the nation also led to more state involvement. In the time of the Boer War (that is, the last 20 years of the 19th century), the physical health of the recruits was exceptionally poor and this was blamed on lack of adequate parenting. Mothers in particular were 'accused' of being ill-educated in child raising, and this lack of knowledge was placing seen as the national stock at risk.

As a result, middle class spinsters (invariably) took to 'visiting' the working class to teach them the art of child rearing and the benefits of cleanliness. From this level of intervention the origins of both social work and health visiting can be seen. These interventions have continued and have been given legal footing by legislation.

8.4.4   Up to the CA 1989

After the implementation of the Children Act 1908 no great changes occurred until the Children Act 1948, and these changes were driven by the perception that state intervention in child care was chaotic. The Curtis Committee, 1946, recommended the establishment of a centralised child care service. This was done via the Children Act 1948, and children's departments were created. There was no real distinction between delinquents and children who simply needed care, and reasons for being in care were more diverse than today. The numbers of children in care were large, with 64,000 children in care in 1952, although a large proportion of these children were there due to homelessness when their parents could not afford to pay rent. Preventive work was not as apparent as it is today in reducing the numbers of children in care.

The next major piece of legislation was the Children and Young Persons Act 1969, which came after the so-called discovery of 'baby battering', although it is unlikely that legislative changes were founded upon this (re)discovery of child abuse. Under the 1969 Act, local authority social workers were given considerable powers to act in cases of child abuse and to enable the protection of children. A child could be received into care either voluntarily or compulsorily. Under the former, no court action was needed, and following a reception of a child into voluntary care the local authority could arbitrarily gain a parental rights order giving it all parental rights over the child. Compulsory care, via the courts, was also easier to obtain than today since the criteria in the legislation were much wider.

Additionally, there also existed the place of safety order – an emergency order. This order could be granted by a magistrate, and would enable the child to be removed from its parents for up to 28 days. The criteria relevant to the making of the order was that it was suspected that the child was being ill-treated or, alternatively, the existence of any of the criteria upon which a compulsory care order could be made.

Although the 1969 Act was in force for some considerable time, it was severely criticised for being too draconian.

8.5   WHY THE CHILDREN ACT – WHY 1989?

The state of child care law had been criticised by the Short Committee which in turn led to the setting up of a government working party which produced a report, *Review of Child Care Law* in 1984. Many of the recommendations of this review were incorporated into the White Paper, *The Law on Child Care and Family Services*, published in 1987 (Cm 62, HMSO).

The primary impetus for change was the criticism that was levelled at local authority social workers throughout the 1970s and 1980s concerning the way that the 1969 Act was being used. With an increased awareness of family rights and responsibilities, the interpretation of the criteria and the lack of participation of parents when children were perceived to be at risk, were criticised. The 1969 Act focused on what *had happened* as opposed to what *might happen*. Hence, the work of social services departments was still being directed to reactive situations, the idea of preventive work was not seen as a priority. Finally, the number of high profile child abuse cases in the 1980s increased the perception that there was a lack of competent intervention by social workers or, conversely, that the state intervened too much into the lives of families.

The *Review of Child Care Law* felt that on balance there was an excess of state intervention in relation to child care. Consequently, the implementation of the CA 1989 was designed to:

* reduce the powers of the state;
* protect families from excessive state intervention;
* emphasise the support role for social services; and
* emphasise the role parents have to play when children are cared for by the state.

As such, the thinking clearly reflects Art 8 of the ECHR which requires that a citizen's private and family life be respected and that a public authority shall not interfere with this right unless necessary.

Question

The above concerns have been in relation to state involvement in family life, do you think that there were concerns about private law aspects of child law?

The level of concern about private law issues was considerably less. One of the main problems was the extent of legislation that existed in relation to children (both in public and private matters). The CA 1989 repealed many other Acts, or at minimum amended them. As well as a plethora of legislation, there was also a question mark over the extent of state involvement via the courts into private matters, principally in divorce. In the majority of divorce matters the court would be asked to make custody (as they were then called) orders even if parents were in agreement. This was not perceived to be necessary. The timing of the *Review of Child Care Law* (1984) coincided with the investigation into the state of family law by the Law Commission. The two reports were combined to produce '[T]he most comprehensive and far reaching reform of child law which has come before Parliament in living memory' (Lord Mackay, *Hansard*, HL, vol 502, col 488).

8.6 THE CHILDREN ACT 1989 – KEY PRINCIPLES

Unlike older statutes, the CA 1989 clearly identifies key principles which underpin the whole operation of the Act and these principles are found in ss 1 and 17, which state as follows:

1   Welfare of the child

(1) When a court determines any question with respect to –

(a) the upbringing of a child; or

(b) the administration of a child's property or the application of any income arising from it, the child's welfare shall be the court's paramount consideration.

(2) In any proceedings in which any question with respect to the upbringing of a child arises, the court shall have regard to the general principle that any delay in determining the question is likely to prejudice the welfare of the child.

(3) In the circumstances mentioned in subsection (4), a court shall have regard in particular to –

(a) the ascertainable wishes and feelings of the child concerned (considered in the light of his age and understanding);

(b) his physical, emotional and educational needs;

(c) the likely effect on him of any change in his circumstances;

(d) his age, sex, background and any characteristics of his which the court considers relevant;

(e) any harm which he has suffered or is at risk of suffering;

(f) how capable each of his parents, and any other person in relation to whom the court considers the question to be relevant, is of meeting his needs;

(g) the range of powers available to the court under this Act in the proceedings in question.

(4) The circumstances are that –

(a) the court is considering whether to make, vary or discharge a section 8 order, and the making, variation or discharge of the order is opposed by any party to the proceedings; or

    (b) the court is considering whether to make, vary or discharge an order under Part IV (public law orders)

  (5) Where a court is considering whether or not to make one or more orders under this Act with respect to the child, it shall not make the order or any of the orders unless it considers that doing so is better for the child than making no order at all.

    ...

17 Provision of services for children in need, their families and others

  (1) It shall be the general duty of every local authority ...

    (a) to safeguard and promote the welfare of children within their area who are in need; and

    (b) so far as is consistent with that duty, to promote the upbringing of such children by their families, by providing a range and level of services appropriate to those children's needs.

8.6.1   The child's welfare and the welfare checklist

8.6.1.1 *Welfare*

You may have believed that the interests of the child would be paramount when any question was being decided in relation to their upbringing, so why state it explicitly? Do you remember the Matrimonial Causes Act (MCA) 1973 concerning maintenance for children? Did this make the welfare of the child paramount? Not all statutes relating to children have the child's interests first and foremost: consequently it does need to be expressly stated.

Question

What is meant by 'paramount'?

Although paramount does not mean first and foremost, the Lord Chancellor explained the wording thus: 'the welfare of the child should come before and above any other consideration in deciding whether to make an order' (*Hansard*, HL, vol 502, col 1167). Lord MacDermott, in *J v C* [1970] AC 668, concluded that: 'the course to be followed will be that which is most in the interests of the child's welfare' – surely the same as saying that the child's welfare comes first? This is an even stronger argument when having regard to the factors that the court considers when establishing what is in the child's welfare. Section 1(3) sets out the welfare checklist, which contains factors comparable with Lord MacDermott's facts, relationships, risks and choices.

8.6.1.2 The welfare checklist

The purpose of this checklist is to establish what is the 'child's welfare' by focusing attention on the individual, and to ensure a greater consistency across courts and advisers when dealing with children's matters.

Question

Is the checklist exhaustive?

The factors included within the checklist cover the major issues that will be relevant to individual cases, but they are not the only factors that can be taken on board by the court. The CA 1989 says, 'a court shall have regard in particular', that is, the list is not limited.

Question

Is the court bound to consider all the factors?

Not all the factors listed in the checklist may be relevant to the particular case and so it is not necessary for the court to consider them, hence, the court has discretion as to which factors to apply and focus on.

Question

Is the list in order of importance?

Although lists normally indicate a hierarchy, this is not the case here. As you can appreciate, the wishes and feelings of the child may be unascertainable, or they may be contrary to the court's and professionals' view of the child's best interests. While the opinions of the child are to be given weight, the court is alive to the possibility of undue influence by parents. To counter this possibility, the involvement of professionals, such as children's guardians, often occurs either to assist to establish the child's wishes, or where this is not possible to provide a professional opinion as to what is in the child's best interests.

8.6.1.3 Delay

The principle of avoiding delay, as enshrined in s 1(2) of the CA 1989, is not just aimed at achieving a more efficient court system. The length of time for many child care cases to be heard was, prior to the CA 1989, almost as easy to predict as the length of a piece of string! The Law Commission proposed the inclusion of this principle since the delay and uncertainty of litigation was deemed to cause damage to the welfare of the child. Children, it is believed, need to have some form of stability in their lives and the lack of stability inherent in long-standing court action is therefore prejudicial to the child. The manner in which the court attempts to reduce this delay is by setting a timetable for child cases. This is the same regardless of whether the matter is in public or private law.

Question

How is this timetable enforced?

The timetable is not imposed without reference to the parties' legal representatives to the case as it is a negotiated arrangement. If a party is unable to meet their timetabled obligations, it is always open to them to return to the court for directions to amend the timetable. Good and appropriate reasons should be given. Failure to comply with a timetabled direction, for example, the filing of statements, may mean that the evidence within that statement will be excluded from the trial. In practice, while this is an option, it may not be deemed in the best interests of the child to exclude relevant evidence. It would appear that sanctions are rarely levied against failure to comply with timetables, and it would appear that timetabling has only been a qualified success. For example, in public law matters, the aim of 12 weeks to complete a care order application has not been met, cases routinely taking around five or six months.

8.6.1.4   No order

The principle enshrined in s 1(5) of the CA 1989 is often referred to as the 'no order' principle since it requires the court only to make an order when it is necessary to do so.

Question

Which of the criticisms of the previous legal regime is this principle designed to address?

The main purpose of the no order principle is to address the complaint that the state intervenes too much in family matters; the state referring not just to the local authority but to the court. Additionally, this principle illustrates that the CA 1989 complies with Art 8 of the ECHR. The impact of the principle has been clearly seen in relation to private law cases. According to the Judicial Statistics 1991 (the last dealing with pre-Children Act 1989 orders) 88,488 custody orders were made in that year. By 2003, 12 years after implementation of the CA 1989, the number of residence orders sought (residence orders replacing custody orders) was down to 34,474. On those applications, 31,996 orders were made, the remainder of applications having been withdrawn, refused or no order made (*Judicial Statistics*, 2003, HMSO).

While there has been a reduction in the number of orders made by nearly a third, this is not simply by the court applying s 1(5) of the CA 1989 alone. This reduction in applications indicates that the principle of no order is being reinforced via legal advice to the parties. If a potential applicant knows that they may not get their order, even if they satisfy all the criteria, they will think twice before expending money in the attempt. Also, in so far as private law is concerned, the fact that the change from custody orders to residence orders incorporated a change in the rights that were gained or lost, meant there may be little to gain from an order anyway.

8.6.1.5   The range of orders

Implicit within s 1(5) of the CA 1989 is the court's discretion to make any of the orders available under the Act when hearing an application. Indeed, in defined family proceedings the court has the power to make an order even if an application has not been made:

> 10   Power of court to make section 8 orders
>
> > (1)   In any family proceedings in which a question arises with respect to the welfare of any child, the court may make a section 8 order with respect to the child if –
> >
> > ...
> >
> > (b)   the court considers that the order should be made even though no such application has been made.

The same sort of discretion operates in public law matters, with private law orders being available on a public law application.

8.6.1.6   Social services

In s 17 of the CA 1989 you were introduced to the concept that local authorities have a duty to safeguard and promote the welfare of children in their area. The means by which this should be done, under s 17, is by the provision of services.

Question

How does the provision of services help meet the principle of reducing state intervention?

If the local authority is considering providing services, there is clearly some sort of state involvement. However, in the scale of involvement, this is not overly interventionist. It is more of a supportive role than an enforcement one. In this sense it is in keeping with the main theme of reducing state involvement. The ability to work with parents to meet their child's needs also deals with some of the criticism levelled at the preceding legislation. The reference, in s 17 of the CA 1989, to keeping children with their families continues this theme and reinforces the ideal of 'families first'.

This reluctance to intervene, and the emphasis on the responsibility of the parents and family, is reminiscent of the situation in the 19th century when child care law was in its infancy.

Question

Are we regressing with our legislation, or are we supporting an enlightened outlook on child raising and family values?

8.7   SUMMARY

You have now completed your introduction to the CA 1989 and the reasons for its implementation. As you have learnt, state involvement in the family, to support and promote good child rearing, has developed over a long period. Some of the advances in child care practices were not based on welfarist principles *per se*, but on other grounds, normally economic. The changing nature of society has caused changes in the expectations of children, with childhood being seen as a period of vulnerability and lack of responsibility and when parents have been expected to take on caring, protective duties. The failure of some parents to meet these duties, and the lack of clarity of these duties, has led to the introduction of the CA 1989. This Act operates on the basis that a child's welfare is paramount, and that the child's welfare can be assessed by reference to a checklist of factors. The intervention of the state is to be avoided if at all possible, and the simple fact of establishing the criteria needed for CA 1989 orders does not mean that the orders will automatically be granted.

At the end of this chapter, which is intended primarily to be an introductory chapter, you have two short questions to attempt. The first may be a suitable revision question once you have completed the whole of child care law in this text.

8.8   END OF CHAPTER ASSESSMENT

1   The Children Act 1989 is designed to support child rearing with families, and yet to provide the state, through the local authority, with improved powers to protect children.

Can these principles co-exist?

2   The welfare checklist in s 1(3) of the Children Act 1989 supports the concept of children's rights.

Discuss.

CHAPTER 9

THE PRIVATE LAW RELATING TO CHILDREN

9.1 OBJECTIVES

By the end of this chapter you should be able to:

- explain the concept of parental responsibility;
- advise hypothetical clients about seeking parental responsibility;
- discuss the meaning of the orders available under s 8 of the Children Act (CA) 1989; and
- answer problem questions in relation to private law matters.

If you are a lover of substantive law, you will enjoy considering much more legislation in this chapter than in the last one. We are now commencing our in-depth study of the CA 1989. Initially we will concentrate on private law matters, being the range of orders that are normally called into play due to parental separation or divorce. The principles covered earlier, within s 1 of the CA 1989, will be highly relevant to these orders. We will also need to understand the meaning and importance of 'parental responsibility' – a crucial concept under the CA 1989.

9.2 THE CONCEPT OF PARENTAL RESPONSIBILITY

9.2.1 A definition

The phrase 'parental responsibility' (PR) is one which you came across earlier in this book. In the sense that it implies a parent's moral duty over their children, its meaning should be clear. However, the nature of the moral duty and its meaning does not automatically equate to the legal definition.

Question

If you were responsible for defining the term 'PR', how would you do so?

The definition is found in s 3 of the CA 1989 which states: '(1) ... parental responsibility means all the rights, duties, powers, responsibilities and authority which by law a parent of a child has in relation to the child and his property.'

Did your definition bear any resemblance to this? If not, do not worry, since the Act's interpretation of PR is not really a definition at all if you expect a definition to provide a meaning for the phrase. Indeed, s 3(1) has been described as a 'non-definition' (*per* Lord Meston, *Hansard*, HL, vol 502, col 1172). What s 3(1) does, therefore, is to provide another set of things to be explained.

Question

What type of legal relationship does s 3(1) envisage existing between parents and children?

The phrase PR connotes a relationship of decision making by the parent for the child; it implies dependency by the child with a protective role for parents. In this regard, the CA 1989, in introducing PR, is trying to emphasise the responsibility and duty that a parent owes to the child. The term 'rights' is included in s 3(1); however, this term is in the minority, and the majority of terms give rise to an implication of a mere *power* relationship, with the child as the subservient partner. This argument can be supported by the statement by Lord Fraser in *Gillick v West Norfolk & Wisbech AHA* [1985] 3 All ER 402, when discussing how PR and the various functions within it should be utilised: 'They [parental responsibilities] exist for the benefit of the child and they are justified only in so far as they enable the parent to perform his duties towards the child ...'

Given that the phrase PR implies a mixture of rights-based powers and responsibilities or duties towards a child, the question arises: what exactly are those powers and duties?

9.2.2 What is included within PR?

Question

What are the things you think are included within PR? What do you think the consequences are for a parent if they fail in their duties?

Many of the aspects of PR are based on common law; as you have seen, statute does not provide a composite list. Things you should have thought about are as follows:

- the duty to provide the child with care;
- linked to the above duty, the duty to protect the child;
- the duty to ensure that the child is educated;
- the duty to ensure the child receives timely and appropriate medical attention (you could include this with the general care duty, above);
- the right to name the child;
- the right to choose a religion for the child;
- the right to discipline the child; and
- the right to act or bring proceedings on behalf of the child.

As you can see, these functions of being a parent have been split into duties and rights; some authors (for example, Cretney, Masson and Bailey-Harris) refer to all of them in a rights-based context. However, given that failure to comply with some of these functions can lead to criminal or civil action against the parent, it is perhaps less appropriate to talk of rights in all situations.

Some of these functions are quite easy to understand and need little by way of explanation.

Question

Is this list exhaustive?

If it is accepted that childhood is socially constructed (see Chapter 8), then it should follow that the matters within PR will be capable of change as society's views on children alter. Clearly there will be some fluidity within the concept of PR. Even if you do not agree with the notion of social construction, PR will change as the child develops. This was accepted by the Law Commission in its report (No 172):

> ... the list must change from time to time to meet differing needs and circumstances. As the *Gillick* case itself demonstrated, it must also vary with the age and maturity of the child and the circumstances of each individual case.

9.2.3   Some interpretations

9.2.3.1   The duty to care and protect

The duty to care for a child encompasses a wide range of different activities. It focuses not just on the physical care of the child, but also on the emotional and social development, which should be nurtured. The fact that emotional care is important can be seen from the welfare checklist which requires the court to have regard to the emotional needs of the child. Practically, caring for a child requires provision of suitable accommodation, the child to be adequately fed and clothed, and to be raised in as loving and stable an environment as possible. For some parents this duty will be reduced to the duty to provide financial maintenance, governed, as you are aware, by the Child Support Acts 1991 and 1995.

Question

What would be the consequences of failing in this duty?

The duty to provide care is fundamental to a child's upbringing, and the consequences for failure can be harsh. Both civil and criminal law sanctions can be imposed. Under the criminal law, if a parent neglects a child, they may be prosecuted for cruelty under the Children and Young Persons Act 1933. This Act is often used in child abuse cases, even if the harm to the child has been quite severe (including death), since it is evidentially easier to prove neglect than other more serious offences. Naturally, charges may be under other statutes, for example, the Offences Against the Person Act 1861.

Under the civil law, by failing to care for a child, the parent risks the child being removed from their care under the provisions of the CA 1989. While you will be looking at child abuse in more detail later, it is important to remember that not all cases of neglect involve true moral culpability. It is easy to blame a parent for neglecting a child, but issues of socialisation, and especially cycles of deprivation, may have a role to play. The ability to protect a child from harm is obviously part of care. If a parent does nothing to prevent a child from endangering themselves, and this is more than an isolated event, then that surely equates with neglect.

9.2.3.2   The duty to educate

Education is seen as part of the developmental process necessary for a child to pass from the status of a child to an adult. Today we accept that children should receive education until they are at least 16-years-old. The duty to ensure that a child receives an education is placed upon carers by virtue of s 7 of the Education Act 1996. The normal place for education is in a school setting.

Question

Would a parent be constrained by the Education Act 1996 to send a child to school to comply with their duty?

Despite school being the norm, it is still possible for a parent to educate a child outside the school setting. The legislation requires a child to receive an 'efficient full-time education suitable to his or her age, ability and aptitude, either by regular attendance at school or otherwise'. The ability to educate at home has always proved difficult given the reference to suitability. As Neville Harris has stated, it is now 'well-nigh impossible since the introduction of the National Curriculum' (*Law and Education: Regulation, Consumerism and the Education System*, 1993, Sweet & Maxwell, p 209). Failure to meet this duty again results in potential criminal and civil sanctions. Under the Education Act 1996, a parent can be prosecuted for their child's non-attendance at school. The penalty imposed upon parents, invariably, is quite small although there have been cases in the recent past where parents have been imprisoned for failure to ensure attendance at school by their children. Civil sanctions are to be found in s 36 of the CA 1989 and they are as follows:

(1) On the application of any local education authority, the court may make an order putting the child with respect to whom the application is made under the supervision of a designated local education authority.

...

(3) A court may only make an education supervision order if it is satisfied that the child concerned is of compulsory school age and is not being properly educated.

The education supervision order is a new order under the CA 1989 and is linked to the repeal of truancy as a ground for a local authority obtaining care of a child. This is not to say that truancy, or non-school attendance, will mean a child can never be taken into care.

In *O (A Minor) (Care Order: Education: Procedure)* [1992] 2 FLR 7, O was a persistent truant. In 1991, her parents were prosecuted and fined for not sending her to school. An interim care order was made later but did not have the desired effect. The local authority then applied for a care order under s 31 of the CA 1989. O and her parents appealed, contending that no impairment of intellectual or social development had been established by the local authority and that any harm suffered by O was not significant and that little more than might be expected in the case of a similar child. The court held that the appeal would be dismissed. *Per* Ewbank J:

> In my view it was entirely open to the justices to come to the view, as they did, that O's intellectual and social development was suffering and was likely to suffer, and that the harm which she was suffering from or was likely to suffer from, was significant ... What one has to ask oneself is whether O suffered significant harm by not going to school. The answer, in my judgment, as in that of the justices, is obvious. The second threshold condition is that the harm, or likelihood of harm, is attributable to the care given to the child not being what it would be reasonable to expect a parent to give him, or that the child is beyond parental control. In my judgment, where a child is suffering harm in not going to school and is living at home, it will follow that either the child is beyond the parents' control or that they are not giving the child the care that it would be reasonable to expect a parent to give ... In this appeal O and her parents have wholly failed in their endeavour to show that the justices came to the wrong decision.

As this case demonstrates, if the criteria for a care order can be made out, even if it is purely on the grounds of non-education, the order can be made.

Question

Does this mean that s 36 of the CA 1989 is irrelevant?

While government statistics indicate that few s 36 orders are made, it is not due to the care order route being preferred, simply that authorities prefer to prosecute under the Education Act 1996.

9.2.3.3　Medical treatment

Although this aspect of PR falls within the care function, it warrants separate consideration. Generally, due to a child's perceived lack of capacity, a parent is responsible for ensuring that the requisite consents to medical treatment are given. Without consent, unless treatment is deemed to be necessary in an emergency, that treatment will be unlawful.

If a parent fails to ensure treatment is received, they may find themselves being prosecuted under the Offences Against the Person Act 1861, or the Children and Young Persons Act 1933. If a fatality occurs, they may face murder or manslaughter charges.

The ability of parents to consent on behalf of their children raises difficult issues at law, particularly where there is an older child who may wish to have their own say on medical treatment.

Question

What do you think should be the approach in that sort of case?

In this area the law is quite complex. If you have studied medical law, you will already know the difficulties. In the *Gillick* case the *ratio* concerned the narrow issue of whether a girl under 16 years could be given contraceptive advice and treatment. The *obiter dictum* of the case referred to the wider issue of when a child would have sufficient rights to make medical decisions for themself. Lord Scarman stated:

> ... I would hold that as a matter of law the parental right to determine whether or not their minor child below the age of 16 will have medical treatment terminates if and when the child achieves a sufficient understanding and intelligence to enable him or her to understand fully what is proposed. It will be a question of fact whether a child ... has sufficient understanding of what is involved. Until the child achieves the capacity to consent, the parental right to make the decision continues save only in exceptional circumstances.

Although the other Law Lords expressed their views differently, the accepted implication of the *obiter* statements has been that where a child has the required age and understanding to make a decision on treatment (in other words has capacity), then the child's right to decide overrides that of the parent. The parent's previous rights or duties on this matter will be terminated. However, this approach has been 'watered down' in subsequent decisions on medical treatment, primarily by Lord Donaldson. Hence the current position is that children and parents will have parallel rights – the child gaining capacity does not mean that the parents' rights end. Consequently, rather than two parents being capable of making a legal decision, there are three individuals who can do so, the parents and the child. In so far as medical treatment is concerned, this is not a satisfactory principle: would doctors wish to treat a non-consenting 15-year-old?

Ultimately, the medical profession is left to decide, but the cases do ensure the doctors have freedom from suit! It is also worth noting that the court will also play a role and has the power to overrule both the parents' and the child's views. For example, in *Re R (A Minor) (Wardship: Medical Treatment)* [1992] 1 FLR 190, R, aged 15, suffered from a mental illness which resulted in severely violent and suicidal behaviour. She required medication which she often refused, on which occasions it had to be administered without her consent. Medical evidence showed that, without drugs, R rapidly became violent and had to be restrained. She was made a ward of court so that the medication could be administered with or without her consent. The judge held that he could not override the decision of a competent minor to refuse medication, but it was clear that R was *not* competent. The application to administer the medication with or without R's consent was granted as being in her best interests. The Official Solicitor appealed on R's behalf so that the relevant law might be clarified. The court held that the appeal of the Official Solicitor would be dismissed. The court was entitled, in the exercise of its wardship jurisdiction, to override the decision of a minor in relation to the giving of medication, and this was irrespective of the minor's general competence. R seemed not 'Gillick competent' and, even if R had been, the judge was right to consent to her undergoing treatment which might involve compulsory medication. The judge's order had been made correctly

In *Re M (A Child) (Medical Treatment: Consent)* [1999] 2 FLR 1097, the doctors treating M, aged 15, concluded that unless she received a heart transplant within a week, she would die. M would not consent, stating that she did not want to receive another person's heart and that she did not want to be on medication for the rest of her life. She also stated that she did not want to die. These views were expressed after the Official Solicitor had appointed a local agent to visit M and ascertain her views. An application was made for leave to carry out the appropriate emergency operation. The court held that the application would be allowed. M was mature and intelligent and weight would be given to her expressed views, but it had to be remembered that she had experienced much trauma. The risks of the operation and M's likely resentment in the future could not override the need to preserve her life. The desire to achieve what was best for M required authority to be given for the transplant operation.

9.2.3.4 Name and religion

In comparison with some of the PR issues, names and religion are normally less contentious. A parent is free to name their child in whatever manner they see fit and a child's name can be changed by deed poll (although there are some procedural rules relating to this). However, names, and family names in particular, do become more of an issue following divorce. Section 13 of the CA 1989 limits the possibility of changing names thus:

(1) Where a residence order is in force with respect to a child, no person may –

(a) cause the child to be known by a new surname ...

It is important to note that the restriction on the change of name only applies where there is a residence order in effect (under s 8). If the court has refused to make an order under the auspices of s 1(5), there would seem to be no automatic restriction to a unilateral change in name, although the court's current approach is that any change of name for a minor should be referred to them. If an order is in force then, as the section states, the change may take place where:

• written consent is given by all persons with PR; or
• the court has granted leave for the change.

The former is unproblematic, but difficulties arise where only one parent has PR; here the court has stated that where there is a dispute over a name a court order needs to be obtained.

Question

On what basis do you think the court approaches an application for a change of name?

As you may recall from your previous reading, the approach is to establish what will be in the best interests of the child. However, even though this is the case, there are certain key principles that the court has identified:

• there is an long term importance in maintaining the child's links with the paternal family;
• would changing the surname lead to any improvement from the point of view of the child's welfare; and
• the short term interests in reducing confusion, convenience and lack of embarrassment (often to the parent not the child) should not outweigh the longer term interests.

In *Dawson v Wearmouth* [1999] 1 FLR 1169, the mother had two children from an existing marriage and continued to use her husband's surname following divorce. The mother commenced cohabitation with the father of her third child, although they did not marry. The relationship ended shortly after the third child's birth. Without telling F, the child's surname was registered as that of the mother's ex-husband. F sought an order requiring the child to have his surname. The House of Lords held that an order for a change of name ought not to be made unless there was clear evidence that this would lead to an improvement from the point of view of the welfare of the child, as *per* the CA 1989. The fact that the child would have the same name as the mother and his half-siblings made the name a logical and natural choice. The Lords found no reasons to counteract this and hence could not justify the changing of the child's name.

In *Re R (A Child)* 2001 EWCA Civ 1344, again the parents of the child were unmarried. After separation the mother began to call the child by another surname rather than that of the father. In the context of proceedings to permit the removal of the child to Spain the matter of the surname was raised. Hale LJ made it clear that the choice of name is part of PR and that even if PR is not shared between both parents, they both have a right to challenge any change in name carried out by the other parent. If there is such a challenge, the role of the court is to establish if the change is justified under the terms of the CA 1989. In so doing the court is:

> ... balancing the long-term interests of a child in retaining an outward link with the parent with whom that child is not living against what are often shorter-term benefits of lack of confusion, convenience, lack of embarrassment and the like.

It was noted that the latter factors may not outweigh the benefits of the retention of the link with the birth parent. In resolving the issue in this case, the court held that the child should be known by both surnames since this would reflect the practice in Spain where the child was to live.

9.2.3.5 Discipline

Question

To what extent do you believe a parent should be able to discipline their own children?

The subject of discipline is one which raises heated debate, particularly where physical discipline is concerned. Some people fall into the 'anti-smacking' category, with others in the 'pro-smacking' category.

Currently our legislation does not prohibit physical discipline by parents, but any sort of corporal punishment in schools is forbidden. This ban was not extended to childcarers in other forms – for example, childminders, and logically they should be able to use corporal punishment if parents consent, since the doctrine of *loco parentis* and delegation of parental responsibility exists. However, this is an issue which has been considered in the court (such punishment was permitted), but is now likely to be changed so childcarers are subject to the same rules as schools.

Smacking is one thing, but what about other forms of discipline?

Question

Imagine you are a parent. Your child, who is aged eight, has 'answered you back' or perhaps sworn at you and you feel that this is bad behaviour. How would you discipline the child? Now imagine that your eight-year-old child has been caught throwing bricks through the window of the 90-year-old woman four doors down the street. How would you discipline the child?

How you respond to this will depend on your own view point on discipline. If you were asked which was the more serious act, hopefully you would have said the latter, since swearing, etc, is often a sign of testing the boundaries with parents. As the latter is the more serious act, then you may have thought about imposing a more serious form of discipline (which may or may not include physical discipline) on the child. To that end, discipline is permitted to the extent that it is commensurate to the crime and the child in question (and here naturally age would play a part).

A major difficulty for parents, however, is knowing what is acceptable by way of discipline. The ability to chastise is subject to a test of 'reasonableness' – at least in the context of criminal law proceedings, which are brought where discipline has exceeded what was reasonable and hence caused physical harm to the child. The ability of a parent to claim reasonable chastisement in criminal proceedings has been criticised by the European Court of Human Rights in the case of *A v UK (Human Rights: Punishment of Child)* [1998] 2 FLR 959. As a consequence of this case, the government issued a Consultation Paper in January 2000 – *Protecting Children, Supporting Parents, A Consultation Document on the Physical Punishment of Children* (Home Office). The main theme of this document is that parents' rights to smack or physically chastise their child would not be removed, but would be subject to stricter boundaries including:

- the nature and context of the treatment;
- its duration;
- its physical and mental effects; and
- in some instances, the sex, age and state of health of the victim.

To date, no legislation has been brought forward to incorporate these changes.

9.3   WHO HAS PARENTAL RESPONSIBILITY?

It is all very well knowing what PR is, but it is essential to appreciate who has this responsibility since without it enforceable and legally acceptable decisions cannot normally be made.

9.3.1   Automatic parental responsibility

Question

Who do you believe will have PR?

The effect of s 2 of the CA 1989 is simple: the only persons who have PR automatically are:

- the mother;
- the father if he was married to the mother at the time of the child's birth;
- the unmarried father, if he jointly registered the birth of the child with the mother (introduced into the CA 1989 by the Adoption and Children Act 2002 and covered below in section 9.3.3).

If one or both of the parents validly believe that they are married, but the marriage is in fact void, they will still have PR as of right (by virtue s 1 of the Legitimacy Act 1976).

Question

What is the situation if the birth parents marry after the birth?

In this case, s 2 of the Legitimacy Act 1976 will come into play. Under this Act, if parents of a child marry subsequently to the birth of the child, the child will be legitimated by the later marriage and PR will automatically be held by the father.

Question

Who is potentially excluded from automatic PR?

The one category of individual whom you may have thought had PR is the unmarried father. However, under s 2 of the CA 1989 the unmarried father does not have PR as of right. This will affect a great number of parents since the number of births outside marriage is increasing, with approximately one-third of births being to unmarried women.

9.3.2 The unmarried father

The idea of child raising outside of marriage is not uncommon or unacceptable today. You probably know couples with children who are 'only cohabiting'. If a child is being cared for and raised by both its parents in a stable relationship, should the law deny that father responsibility for that child? Would your response differ if the child had been conceived following a rape? This distinction between the reasons for childbirth outside of marriage is one of the factors behind the current legislation. It was believed to be preferable to enable unmarried fathers who did wish to be involved with their children to apply to be given those rights, rather than the option of giving rights and the application being to take those rights away. Section 4 of the CA 1989 sets out the way in which an unmarried father can seek PR on an almost permanent basis:

4   Acquisition of parental responsibility by father

(1) Where a child's father and mother were not married to each other at the time of his birth –

(a) the court may, on the application of the father, order that he shall have parental responsibility for the child;

(b) the father and mother may by agreement ('a parental responsibility agreement') provide for the father to have parental responsibility for the child.

9.3.2.1   Parental responsibility agreements

> **Question**
>
> For the purposes of s 4 of the CA 1989 and PR agreements, do you think it will be sufficient for the mother to agree verbally to share parental responsibility?

Normally, oral agreements are just as enforceable as written ones. This general proposition can be rebutted, and this is the case here. Before a PR agreement can be effective it must be:

- in the form prescribed by regulations made by the Lord Chancellor; and
- recorded in the prescribed manner (per s 4(2)).

Under the regulations, to be valid the agreement needs to be in the required wording, and to be witnessed. It must also be filed at the Principal Registry of the Family Division of the High Court, and following this a copy of the agreement will be sent to each party.

9.3.2.2   Parental responsibility orders

In the event that agreement cannot be reached between the parents, the unmarried father may apply to the court for a s 4 order. While the county court and High Court have jurisdiction over private law matters, the Family Proceedings Court (the magistrates' court) may be the preferred venue.

> **Question**
>
> If an application is made, what factors will the court bear in mind?

As the matter will concern the upbringing of a child, the court will have to have regard to the welfare of the child, in the sense that the child's welfare is paramount. However, the welfare checklist is not a compulsory consideration since a PR order is made under s 4 and is not caught by the provisions in s 1(4); however, it may have a subsidiary role to play. Other factors, established in case law (*Re H (Minors) (Local Authority: Parental Rights) (No 3)* [1991] Fam 151) are relevant to the decision of whether or not a father should get PR and they are:

- the degree of commitment which the father has shown towards the child;
- the degree of attachment which exists between the father and the child; and
- the reason of the father for applying for the order.

It is important to note that these factors are not absolute – a father who fulfils them all may still not get a PR order.

In *D v S (Parental Responsibility)* [1995] 3 FCR 783, X had denied Y contact with their child, C, for a year, although contact had recommenced by the date of the hearing. There was bitterness between X and Y, and a refusal to discuss any matters relating to C. Later, Y applied for a parental responsibility order in relation to C. Welfare reports suggested that such an order would be impracticable; yet the magistrates found that, in fact, Y was committed to C and that previous contact had been to the benefit of C. Y appealed against the magistrates' order of 'no order' in relation to parental responsibility. The court held that Y's appeal would be allowed. Y had demonstrated the necessary qualities (see *Re H* above): appropriate degree of commitment, a firm firm bond between applicant and child, and a genuine reason for making the application. Hostility between father and mother did not constitute an appropriate bar. Y had demonstrated that he recognised his responsibilities to the child he loved. The magistrates were clearly in error and a parental responsibility order would be made.

Question

Does it matter that the father will be in no position to do anything actively with his PR?

Where more than one person has PR, the responsibility is not shared *per se* and s 2(7) of the CA 1989 provides that: 'Where more than one person has parental responsibility for a child, each of them may act alone and without the other in meeting that responsibility ...'

Hence, although the father may get PR there is no guarantee he can use it – unless of course statute requires some form of action from all PR holders. The granting of PR does give the father a status, although often only slightly greater than that of being an unmarried father.

9.3.3 Reform

As you are aware, one of the difficulties of the legal regulation of family life is that regulation by way of law often trails behind the reality of how we live. The fact is that cohabitation and child raising outside of marriage is something that most of us take for granted – the statistics illustrate this too; but the law did not reflect the same acceptance of this reality since it did not accord full rights automatically to unmarried fathers until the amendments to the CA 1989 introduced by the Adoption and Children Act 2002.

9.3.3.1 Why change?

> **Question**
>
> Do you think the law should be changed? If so, how would you go about it?

The debate on whether or not unmarried fathers should get PR is not a recent one. In the past there has perhaps been an assumption that unmarried fathers were 'irresponsible or uninterested in their children and [did] not deserve a legal role as parents' (*Procedures for the Determination of Paternity and on the Law on Parental Responsibility for Unmarried Fathers*, 1998, HMSO). This assumption could be a remnant from the days when it was seen as a man's duty to marry a woman if she became pregnant, and that he was a cad if he did not – a somewhat outdated assumption perhaps? In addition, the fears of the complex relationships and the feelings of mothers who gave birth as a result of rape or incest produced a reaction against giving unmarried fathers responsibility.

This negative approach is now set to disappear, but not due necessarily to the enlightenment of government, but because the public are ignorant of their rights.

> **Question**
>
> Do you know any unmarried couples with children? If so, ask them who has rights over the children. Present them with a scenario where a decision needs to be made, such as a routine innoculation at the doctor's surgery, and ask them who can consent. Do you think they will give the right answer?

Because you have had the benefit of reading the preceding sections, you will know that unless s 4 of the CA 1989 has been used to gain an order or agreement, or PR has been formally delegated, the unmarried father cannot give this consent. Did the people you asked say the same? If you have managed to get a representative sample then hopefully the majority would have said the father could give consent. The lack of knowledge of the law in this area is borne out by the judicial figures on the making of s 4 orders and PR agreements.

> **Question**
>
> How many orders do you think were sought from the court for PR in 2003?

Given that the birth rate in 2003 amongst unmarried couples is over one-third of the total births per annum (of a total of 621,469 births, 257,288 were births outside of marriage), you may probably have thought quite a few applications are made. In reality, only 11,008 applications were made, with 9,524 being successful. This low figure suggests that many cohabiting couples do not realise that they do not share PR for their child.

Question

Do you think that the current system which withholds automatic PR is compliant with the European Convention on Human Rights (ECHR)?

The rights available under Arts 8 and 14 of the ECHR will be relevant to families regardless of whether the family relationship is founded upon marriage or not. *In Keegan v Ireland* [1994] 18 EHRR 342, the court stated:

> The Court recalls that the notion of the 'family' in [Art 8] is not confined solely to marriage-based relationships and may encompass other *de facto* 'family' ties where the parties are living together outside of marriage. A child born out of such a relationship is *ipso jure* part of that 'family' unit from the moment of his birth and by the very fact of it. There thus exists between the child and his parents a bond amounting to family life even if at the time of his or her birth the parents are no longer cohabiting or if their relationship has then ended.

In the *Keegan* case, the relationship between the applicant and the child's mother lasted for two years, during one of which they cohabited. Moreover, the conception of their child was the result of a deliberate decision and they had also planned to get married. Their relationship at this time had thus the hallmark of family life for the purposes of Art 8. The fact that it subsequently broke down does not alter this conclusion any more than it would for a couple who were lawfully married and who subsequently ended their relationship. It follows that from the moment of the child's birth there existed between the applicant and his daughter a bond amounting to family life.

However, the European Court of Human Rights permits a great deal of flexibility to individual states and this will mean that it is hard to argue that our law in denying certain rights to unmarried fathers does not comply. Thus, in *McMichael v UK* (1995) 20 EHRR 205, an unmarried father's lack of rights in relation to adoption proceedings was not seen to be contrary to Art 8. The aim of the relevant legislation, distinguishing between married and unmarried father's rights, was designed to identify worthy and meritorious fathers and to protect the interests of the unmarried mother and the child.

Although we do not have to change our laws to comply with the ECHR, changing the law to grant automatic PR to unmarried fathers will deal with the perceived discrimination, but also with the apathy and lack of knowledge of parents.

9.3.3.2   How to achieve the aims

To achieve the objectives of granting PR to unmarried fathers, a number of methods were highlighted in the Consultation Paper. The method ultimately adopted looks at the registration of the child's birth and who carries this out. Now that the necessary amendments to the CA 1989 (by s 111 of the Adoption and Children Act 2002) have been brought into force, an unmarried father who jointly registers the child's birth will get PR automatically. This will mean that around 80% of unmarried fathers will get PR in future. However, there will still remain some unmarried fathers who do not jointly register their child's birth who will have to use s 4 of the CA 1989 to get PR with all the attendant problems of satisfying the requirements set out in *Re H*.

9.3.4   Parental responsibility for others

The birth parents are the most likely candidates to seek PR, but PR can be obtained by others.

Question

In the following situation, on what basis can grandma exercise PR?

Anna and Bill, who both have PR, have left Christopher with grandma whilst they go on a year's vacation. Since they are backpacking, they deemed it inappropriate to take a nine-month-old child with them.

One way in which grandma could claim to exercise PR is if it has been delegated under s 2(9) of the CA 1989. However, s 3(5) may also assist:

A person who –

    (a) does not have parental responsibility for a particular child; but

    (b) has care of the child,

    may (subject to the provisions of this Act) do what is reasonable in all the circumstances of the case for the purpose of safeguarding or promoting the child's welfare.

This provision is designed primarily for temporary carers, and the carer can only do what is reasonable to safeguard the child. It would cover an emergency where PR has not been delegated. You should note that if delegation does occur, it is preferable that it is in writing, then there is less room for dispute.

If a long term arrangement for care is anticipated, it might be worth considering a residence order in favour of the carer since under the provisions of s 12(2):

Where a court makes a residence order in favour of any person who is not the parent or guardian of the child concerned that person shall have parental responsibility for the child, while the residence order remains in force.

We will look at residence orders in more depth shortly.

9.3.4.1 Step-parents

As you will know, a step-father cannot seek a PR order or agreement under s 4 of the CA 1989 because this section only relates to birth fathers. Unless the step-father seeks a joint residence order with the child's mother (or adopts), only s 3(5) provides him with any powers to act, unless the mother delegates responsibility via s 2(9). As this has been seen to create difficulties within the more complex family structures found in society, the Adoption and Children Act 2002 amends the CA 1989 to enable step-parents to gain PR without having to seek a residence order (although this provision is not yet in force). Section 112 of the Adoption and Children Act 2002 inserts a new s 4A into the CA 1989 and enables a step-parent get PR if the birth parent(s) agree for the step-parent to have PR or, alternatively, if that agreement is not forthcoming, for the court to grant the step-parent PR upon application. The approach to agreements is the same as for unmarried fathers.

The ability to take decisions on behalf of and for a child is one reason why step-parents seek to adopt their step-child, hence the ability to get PR may reduce adoption applications.

9.4 JOINT OR INDIVIDUAL LIABILITY

As we saw earlier, PR can be held by more than one person but exercising PR is something that can be done individually; there are only limited situations where the agreement of all holders of PR will be needed. This reflects the practicalities of child raising, particularly where parents with PR no longer live together.

Question

Can you think of any situations where consent from all holders of PR is needed?

If you recall, a child of 16 can only marry with the consent of all those with PR, or the agreement of the court. This is therefore such a situation.

Question

What if they cannot agree?

Inherent in a system of joint or individual responsibility is the potential for conflict. Section 8 of the CA 1989 provides a mechanism for dealing with such disputes via the specific issue order or prohibited steps order, which you will look at shortly.

9.5 LOSING YOUR PARENTAL RESPONSIBILITY

Question

How do you think a person with PR can lose it?

Anyone with children (or parents for that matter) will know that parenthood is a lifelong commitment. Legally, most responsibility for children ends when they reach 18. This can, exceptionally, be extended – for example, with regard to maintenance if a child enters higher education. PR can be lost in a limited number of ways before a child reaches 18 but, to a degree, the ability to lose parental responsibility is dependent upon how you gained PR to start with.

If you are a parent with automatic PR the only ways it can be lost, other than the child reaching majority, are:

- by the child being adopted; or
- by death, either of the child or yourself.

PR will survive divorce (the adage 'you can divorce your spouse but not your children' needs to be remembered), and it will also survive any orders made in respect of the child. If a care order, or wardship order is made, PR will not be lost, but a parent's ability to exercise that PR may be severely constrained.

If you are a parent (an unmarried father) who has gained PR by virtue of a court order (s 4) or an agreement (s 4), or any other person who has gained PR by virtue of court intervention (s 8 residence orders), the PR obtained can be lost by:

- the child being adopted;
- death; or
- the court revoking or discharging the order that originally gave you PR.

In the latter case, the PR is less permanent because what the court gives, the court can take away.

Additionally, if the unmarried father has gained PR through joint registration of the birth, the court has powers to remove that PR upon application.

9.6 PRIVATE LAW ORDERS

The holding of PR is important when it comes to seeking private law orders in relation to a child. The CA 1989 sets out who can apply automatically for orders, and who needs leave, in s 10. These rules can be summarised thus:

- parents, guardians and people with a residence order in their favour can apply for any s 8 order;
- any party to a marriage (whether or not subsisting) can apply for a residence or contact order;
- any person with whom the child has lived for the last three years can apply for a residence or contact order;
- any person who has consent from (i) the holders of a residence order, (ii) the local authority where the child is in local authority care, or (iii) all holders of PR in all other cases may apply for a residence or contact order.

In case you are wondering who is deemed a 'parent', the CA 1989 includes unmarried fathers within the definition of a parent. Thus, they have the right to apply automatically for s 8 orders.

Section 9 provides some additional restrictions in relation to s 8 orders:

- if the child is subject to a care order, the only s 8 order that may be made is a residence order;
- the local authority cannot seek a residence or contact order;
- a local authority foster carer cannot seek a s 8 order unless they have the consent of the local authority or is a relative of the child or the child has lived with them for three years (note: this will be reduced to one year, following changes in the Adoption and Children Act 2002).

9.6.1 The s 8 orders

Section 8 sets out four orders which can be sought in private law and which are:

- a residence order;
- a contact order;
- a specific issues order; and
- a prohibited steps order.

The first two orders are the most commonly sought.

9.6.2 The residence order

The residence order replaces the previous 'custody order'; however, unlike the custody order, a residence order is designed to 'settle the arrangements to be made as to the person with whom a child is to live', arguably less stringent than a custody order which gave 'custody, care and control' to one parent over the other.

9.6.2.1 The question of parental responsibility

> **Question**
>
> If married parents separate, and a residence order is made in favour of the mother, to what extent does this affect the father's PR?

As you should recall, the father's PR will not be removed. However, the fact that the parents have separated will mean that it is harder for the non-caring parent to utilise their PR. Day-to-day care, which will be within the remit of the person with the residence order, and the exercise of PR to meet that care, will fall almost solely on the caring parent. More major decisions, perhaps where the child should receive its schooling, should remain as joint decisions. This cannot easily be enforced because PR is an individual liability. However, the philosophy of the CA 1989 tries to encourage parents to work together in the best interests of the child, and that includes liaising on the future plans for that child.

9.6.2.2 Conditions

The phrase 'settling the arrangements' used within the CA 1989 provides a wide discretion for the court to include conditions, especially since the order does not now give all the rights and responsibilities to the carer (which a custody order arguably did). Additionally, the court has clear authority for this power under s 11(7) of the CA 1989 which provides as follows:

A section 8 order may –

  (b) impose conditions which must be complied with by any person –

    (i) in whose favour the order is made;

    (ii) who is a parent of the child concerned;

    (iii) who is not a parent of his but who has parental responsibility for him; or

    (iv) with whom the child is living.

> **Question**
>
> What sort of conditions do you think may be included?

The range of possibilities is almost endless but you may have thought of conditions relating to medical treatment, education and religious upbringing.

Certain conditions will be placed automatically on residence orders. You have already come across one within s 13 of the CA 1989 which prevents the changing of a child's name without the consent of all with parental responsibility, or a court order. This section also restricts the person with the residence order from removing the child from the jurisdiction for a period of more than one month without consent of all those with PR. Finally, no person with parental responsibility is able to exercise it if, by so doing, they are acting in a manner which would be incompatible with an order made under the CA 1989 (such as a residence order). This prohibition is laid down in s 2(8).

9.6.2.3 Split orders

The fact that parental responsibility is now not so closely bound up in orders relating to the person with whom a child lives, allows a greater flexibility in court orders. It is now clearly enshrined in s 11(4) of the CA 1989 that the possibility of a split residence order can be considered. Both holders of the order would have parental responsibility (which they probably would have anyway), but under a split order they will both have more ability to use it.

Question

Do you think these orders will be commonly made? If not, why not?

While these orders may be appropriate in some cases, they are not perceived as being the norm. Department of Health Children Act guidance states (at vol 1, para 2.28):

> ... it is not expected that it will become a common form of order, partly because most children will still need the stability of a single home and partly because in the cases where shared care is appropriate there is less likely to be a need for any order at all.

This highlights certain reasons for not making split orders. The notion of stability is important, since the courts must be assessing what is in the child's best interests. An order which would 'confuse' a child may not be in their interests. Also, the sharing of residence orders will normally be based upon the ability of the two carers to co-operate. If there are unresolved difficulties, or a lack of communication, it is unlikely the order would benefit the child. By contrast, if the parents or carers can co-operate, the court will look to the impact of s 1(5): the 'no order' principle. If parents can agree and work together, will there be any benefit to the child in making an order at all?

In *Re WB (Minors: Residence)* [1995] 2 FLR 1023, M and F were unmarried and had lived together for 10 years. There were two children aged 8 and 11. Care of the children was shared, following the breakdown of the relationship. F's contact with the children ceased following a severe disagreement with M. An application was made by F for a residence order and an order prohibiting the removal of the children from the jurisdiction. Later, DNA tests seemed to indicate that F was not the genetic father of the children. A residence order was made in M's favour and another order was made allowing F to have holiday staying contact and alternate weekend contact. F appealed. The court upheld F's appeal in part. There should have been a prohibited steps order preventing removal of the children from the jurisdiction. Furthermore, the magistrates were acting correctly in not making a shared residence order: once it had been decided that F ought to have limited contact only, it would have been wrong to have made a shared residence order for other purposes.

In *Re D (Children) (Shared Residence Orders)* [2001] 1 FLR 495, H and W had married in 1986 and were divorced in 1995. There were three children, aged 13, 11 and 9. The children lived with W, but had maintained substantial contact with F, including staying contact for half their holidays, and during the week. H and W had returned to the court on several occasions so as to settle matters concerning education of the children and problems relating to passports. The judge at Watford County Court had made an an order for shared residence, having concluded that the difficulties between H and W arose from W having sole residence. W appealed, arguing that there were substantial issues between the parties which had not been resolved, so that the shared residence order was premature. Shared residence orders, she contended, were appropriate only in exceptional circumstances. The Court of Appeal decided that W's appeal would be dismissed. There was no requirement, either under CA 1989 or the case law, that a shared residence order was appropriate only in exceptional circumstances. Where children spent a significant amount of time with both parents, intentionally or by accident, such an order would be appropriate if in the children's interests. In the present case the children had settled homes with H and W; the arrangement had worked well and had lasted for a considerable period of time, giving rise to a positive benefit for the children.

9.6.2.4   Criteria for orders

Question

What factors will the courts consider before making an order?

Section 8 itself does not lay down any criteria to be satisfied before the orders can be made. Hence the court is reliant on s 1 principles of welfare. The welfare checklist will apply, but is only directly called into play where the making of the order is contested.

With the impact of s 1(5), fewer residence orders are being made. While this may be beneficial in the terms of reducing state involvement, it has potential implications with reference to child abduction and utilisation of the Hague Convention on Child Abduction. Detailed knowledge of this area is beyond the scope of this work and if more information is needed, reference should be made to texts, such as Cretney, Masson and Bailey-Harris, *Principles of Family Law*.

9.6.2.5   Duration of the orders

> **Question**
>
> How long do you think a residence order will last?

There are a number of answers to this, because residence orders have a range of potential cut-off points. As the court can impose conditions on orders, it may impose a time condition, which reduces the duration of the order. If this is not done, then there are a variety of ways in which the duration of the order can be affected.

Under s 9, residence orders (and indeed all s 8 orders) will normally end on the child's 16th birthday. This is at odds with the age of majority which is set at 18. Exceptional circumstances may give rise to the extension of the order until the child is 18. However, exceptional circumstances are perceived to arise in those cases where a child is suffering from physical disabilities or learning difficulties. If a child falls into these categories then they will be unable to make decisions for themselves, hence needing care until 18.

> **Question**
>
> Can you foresee any problems with this approach?

Difficulties may arise, however, if for example a non-parent cares for a child under a residence order. Morally, once the child reaches 16, continued care should be provided but there would be no *legal* obligation to do so. A 16-year-old may find themselves without a roof over their head. Local authority accommodation may be provided, but resource shortages may limit this. Also the young adult may find themselves caught in the crossfire of local authority departments passing responsibility from one department to another. Finally, at 16 a young person cannot legally enter into a tenancy agreement; this might possibly lead to homelessness. These difficulties have been recognised in s 114 of the Adoption and Children Act 2002, which permits the court to extend the order until the child's 18th birthday where the person seeking the residence order requests such an extension.

Alternatively, the order may be discharged upon the application of the parents, the child or other party to the order. Note, however, that if the child seeks to discharge the order, they must obtain the court's leave first.

Finally, if a parent obtains a residence order, and then cohabits with the other parent for a period of six months or more, the residence order will lapse automatically (s 11(5)).

9.6.3   Contact orders

The contact order replaces the pre-CA 1989 access order with the change in terminology reflecting a change in emphasis of the law.

9.6.3.1 Rights

Section 8 defines a contact order thus:

> ... 'a contact order' means an order requiring the person with whom a child lives, or is to live, to allow the child to visit or stay with the person named in the order or for that person and the child otherwise to have contact with each other.

Question

Whose right is it to contact, and whose duty is it to see that contact takes place?

The actual definition of a contact order does not clearly refer to the right to have contact. However, a common assumption is that contact is the right of the person named in the order. Equally, it is assumed that the duty to ensure that contact occurs is placed on the person with care of the child. Only the second assumption is correct.

Question

If, therefore, it is not the right of the person named in the order to have contact, whose right is it?

If contact can be said to be a right, it is seen as being a right of the child. This principle was established well before the implementation of the CA 1989 in the case of *M v M (Child Access)* [1973] 2 All ER 81. Cases decided since the CA 1989 continue with this principle. It has been suggested that that the issue of contact as a right can be sidestepped since the definition reflects only on the duty of the carer, and that contact orders merely reflect the requirement to meet the child's needs. The child's needs will, in a majority of cases, require that some form of contact is given and the courts have worked on a presumption that contact is nearly always best. However, it is important to note that this application of the presumption of contact has not gone unchallenged in academic circles. Commentators such as Cantwell, Roberts and Young ([1999] Fam Law 226) have suggested that the adherence to the presumption by the court may in some situations cause more harm to the child – for example, where the non-caring parent uses the contact to get back at the other parent. Equally, it should be of concern that there is little research to support the contention that children do benefit from contact in all situations, and this is particularly of concern where there has been domestic violence. Indeed, the fact that the presumption of contact often seems to take priority, regardless of the circumstances, has been considered primarily of late in the context of domestic violence. The pendulum would now appear to be moving away from 'contact at all costs' to a more reasoned approach.

In *Re W (A Minor) (Contact)* [1994] 2 FLR 441, H and W married in 1988 and separated in 1989. Contact with the child created problems for H. Following W's second marriage, she attempted to end contact. She appeared to be instructing her child to accept that her second husband was the natural father. H applied for a contact order, but this was refused. W indicated that she would disobey a contact order if it were made. H appealed. The court held that H's appeal would be allowed. Contact was the child's right and, except in unusual circumstances, the judge had the duty to make an order even when faced by a mother's stubborn attitudes. By refusing to make an order, the judge had, in effect, abandoned his responsibilities under the CA 1989.

In *Re W (Minors)* (1996) CLY 568, an application had been made by W for the discharge of a contact order made in H's favour concerning their children, aged eight and nine. The application had been dismissed. Evidence had been given by a child psychologist, suggesting that any benefit accruing to the children from maintaining contact with H was not as significant as the psychological harm resulting from that contact. W contended that although the judge was empowered to reject expert evidence, in this particular case the evidence had been given by a psychologist who had extensive involvement with the family. Furthermore, the judge's decision was out of line with recommendations made by the court welfare officer. W appealed. The court held that W's appeal would be allowed in part. The judge was perfectly entitled to reach his decision on the facts, but the order was not appropriate in the circumstances. Contact would be made less frequent.

Re L, Re V, Re M and Re H [2000] 2 FLR 334, the issue of domestic violence was involved in all of the appeals and the Court of Appeal laid down some general points in relation to how the court should deal with this issue. The court stated that the conduct of the parties to one another and also towards the children, the effect on the children of the domestic violence and the effect on the residential parent, and the motivation of the parent seeking contact were all relevant factors that must be considered. If the parent seeking contact were doing so to continue the violence and/or the intimidation of the other parent, rather than seeking contact to promote the welfare and interests of the child, contact would be less likely. Also, the fact that the violent parent acknowledged the fact of their violence would be an important factor.

9.6.3.2 The implication of the ECHR

By now you should be very familiar with the right to family life enshrined in Art 8; and this Article will have the potential to bring about some subtle changes to the current judicial thinking on contact. The approach of the European Court of Human Rights (ECtHR) has been to define the right to contact (or access) in terms of the rights of the parent, not purely the rights of the child. This is quite an important difference, but the case law also illustrates that there may not be dramatic consequences for all aspects of contact since the test applied is what is in the best interests of the child – the factor currently at the heart of contact decisions made in the domestic courts.

In *Hendricks v Netherlands* (1983) 5 EHRR 231 it was stated:

> On the preliminary point the Commission recalls that, in accordance with its jurisprudence constante, the right to respect for family life within the meaning of Article 8 of the Convention includes the right of a divorced parent, who is deprived of custody following the break-up of the marriage, to have access to or contact with his child, and that the State may not interfere with the exercise of that right otherwise than in accordance with the conditions set out in paragraph 2 of that Article ... Respect for family life within the meaning of Article 8 thus implies that this contact should not be denied unless there are strong reasons, set out in paragraph 2 of that provision, which justify such an interference.

In *Peter Whitear v UK* [1997] EHRLR Issue 3, the Commission considered the factors in Art 8(2), in particular the child's mental health. The Commission considered that the best interests of the child were of crucial importance and interference with rights to access would be justified as pursuing a legitimate aim when intended to protect the child's health, in the broadest sense. Hence, here, contact was denied to the father.

9.6.3.3 What is contact?

Regardless of who (if anyone) has a right to contact, what is meant by 'contact' needs to be established.

Question

What would you include in a definition of 'contact'?

Contact falls into two categories: direct and indirect. The former should be considered the norm, and is traditionally viewed as such. Direct contact involves face-to-face meetings between the child and the person named in the order. In many situations this direct contact will involve overnight stays, or even longer term visits, especially in school holidays.

Question

What is the difference between a contact order that allows the child to stay every weekend with its father (with a residence order to the mother) and a shared residence order with the father's order specifying that he has residence for the weekends only?

In many cases where contact can be negotiated between parents amicably, the court should consider refusing to make a contact order on the basis of s 1(5) of the CA 1989. However, contact is easier to deny and is also a source of much acrimony. If a contact order is to be made, then it may appear similar to shared residence orders. In reality there may be no difference, other than in the names of the orders. If, however, the father of the child is not married to the mother, the granting of a shared residence order would automatically give him parental responsibility (s 12(1)).

In some cases direct contact, whilst seen to be in the best interests of the child, may not be appropriate if the child and adult were to be left alone. This may be because allegations of abuse have been made, or because the child does not really know the adult and may become upset, or because the caring parent is concerned and will not allow contact to happen unless supervised.

Just as direct contact may have conditions as to supervision, it may also have conditions as to time or duration or venue, all of which will be decided in the interests of the child.

Indirect contact, by contrast, does not include face-to-face meetings. The child may therefore be contacted by telephone or by letter. If this would be detrimental to the child's welfare, but it is seen as appropriate for the absent parent to have knowledge of the child, reports and photographs may be sent to them instead. Indirect contact should be considered either only where it is clear that the child would suffer as a result of contact, or as a means of establishing direct contact if none has existed before.

Question

Can the court impose conditions on the caring parent to facilitate indirect contact, that is, if the child is very young and illiterate and needs to have letters read to them?

The court can, and has imposed, conditions in such situations, although the difficulty with enforcement of the terms is recognised.

In *Re O (Contact: Imposition of Conditions)* [1995] 2 FLR 124, M and F were unmarried and had cohabited for three years. They separated before the birth of their child, who was aged three at the date of proceedings. F had been convicted in relation to the breach of a non-molestation order concerning M. M was totally opposed to any contact between F and the child. In 1994 the judge made an order for indirect contact which required M to send photographs of the child to F every three months, together with reports on progress at school, and to pass on letters and presents sent by F. M appealed on the ground that there was no jurisdiction to attach conditions of this nature to the order. The court held that M's appeal would be dismissed. It was for the court to make a decision as to whether indirect contact was in the best interests of the child; there were sufficient powers under ss 8(1) and 11(7) of the CA 1989 to make such contact orders possible. M's clear unwillingness to co-operate ought not to be allowed to defeat the court's powers. It was perfectly justifiable that the parent with care of the child ought to be obliged to report to the absent parent on the child's progress so as to invest the indirect contact with some positive meaning in these particular circumstances.

9.6.3.4 Enforcing contact

> **Question**
>
> Imagine you are a parent with care. You have two young children and the court has granted a contact order allowing contact with their father for each Saturday afternoon. You refuse to allow contact to take place since you believe that the father will abduct the children. Can you do this?
>
> What would the situation be if it were the father who was refusing to take up his contact? How could you enforce contact?

Refusal of contact is a matter that has taken up considerable judicial time in recent years. Invariably it is the refusal of contact, rather than the failure to take up contact, that is at issue.

Refusal of contact

If a caring parent does not agree to the making of the contact order, then the immediate option for that parent is to appeal. An application for discharge may be pursued, although discharge of the order may not adequately displace the presumption that contact should occur. It is far better to seek an order for no contact to clarify the situation.

If an appeal or application is unsuccessful, the immediate reaction is often to ignore the order and stop contact. If the parent with contact is still seeking to exercise the order, an application for enforcement may ensue. The range of options for the court in this case is wide. The court may:

- agree with the hostile caring parent, and refuse contact;
- amend the nature of contact, perhaps reducing the amount of direct contact time to make the order workable;
- change direct contact to indirect contact (perhaps with conditions);
- swap over the orders, so that the parent with contact becomes the parent with residence rights; or
- if all else fails, imprison the non-compliant parent.

The first option was utilised in the case of *Re H (A Minor) (Parental Responsibility)* [1993] 1 FLR 484, although this case may be confined to its facts. In many more cases the court prefers to try to obtain a workable option, even though this may mean changing direct contact to indirect contact. This may seem like 'giving in' or acting contrary to the original 'best interests of the child'. However, the assumption would appear to be that anything is better than nothing. If an alteration to the nature of contact is not effective, the court may be faced with no option but to commit the non-compliant parent to jail for the breach of the order.

Question

Is this in the best interests of the child?

For a long time, the imprisonment of the carer was seen as an inappropriate resolution; it being unlikely to be in the interests of the child. However, judicial opinion is changing, whether you agree with it or not, and failure to comply with a contact order is seen as something that will not be countenanced.

In *A v N (Committal: Refusal of Contact)* [1997] 1 FLR 533, M was appealing against and order for committal of M to prison (suspended) for failure to comply with a contact order made to F. F had played a considerable role in the child's upbringing before the parties separated. M had failed to comply with any of the numerous contact orders made by the court and had made it clear that she would never comply with them. Ward LJ's judgment was particularly robust and also clear in import. The court's view was that the mother in the case had had more than ample opportunity to enable contact to take place, and that her objections were unreasonable. As Ward LJ stated:

> The stark reality of this case is that this is a mother who has flagrantly set herself upon a course of collision with the court's order. She has been given endless opportunities to comply with sympathetic attempts made by the judge to meet her flimsy objections to contact taking place. She has spurned all of those attempts. For it to be submitted that the hardship to the child is the result of the court imposing the committal order is wholly to misunderstand the position. This child suffers because the mother chooses to make her suffer. The mother had it in within her power to save T that suffering, but she did not avail of that opportunity.

The court upheld the committal and also held that the welfare of the child is not an issue for committal proceedings – an approach that may be of surprise, but is logical.

Another innovative way to enforce contact, or perhaps to try to get the obdurate parent to reconsider their attitude to contact, was highlighted in the case of *CDM v CM, LM, DM (Children)* [2003] 2 FLR 636. Here the mother had convinced the two children that they had been sexually abused by their father and that they did not want to have contact with him. The court found there was absolutely no basis in fact for the allegations of abuse and that the mother was, in effect, brainwashing the children and that the lack of relationship with their father was causing them harm. Additionally, the court found the mother's approach was causing emotional harm to the children. In proceedings to enforce contact, the court ordered a s 37 report from the local authority. After the local authority had investigated, it was decided that the children were suffering harm due to the mothers care, and that it would be appropriate for the children to live with the father instead. Obviously this outcome fits within the list of options set out earlier, but what is interesting is the use of the local authority's investigative powers and the potential use of an interim care order.

As highlighted above, the presumption that contact is always good for the child, and mothers who object are always unreasonable, is changing and now the pendulum would appear to be moving away from 'contact at all costs' to a more reasoned approach and this is endorsed by the Lord Chancellor's Department Consultation Paper (2001) and report (2002) on *Making Contact Work*. However, it should be noted that in many cases where contact is likely to be refused, there is clear evidence of domestic violence against the caring parent and possibly against the child itself.

Failure to take up contact

Contrary to the legal armoury that has been built up in relation to failure to *allow* contact, there is nothing to rely on in relation to a failure to *take up* contact. From the wording of s 8, there is no clear implication of rights or duties, but, by placing responsibility to permit contact on the person with care, there is no means for that person to enforce contact by the person named in the order. One means by which it could be done is to threaten to stop contact completely. However, this may not have the desired effect, especially since it has been suggested that most contact will end or tail off after only about two years. That families need fathers may not be disputed, but the vocal minorities highlight the case of fathers being denied contact, not mothers who cannot ensure that it continues.

It will be interesting to see if the introduction of the ECHR will result in change. If a parent has a right to contact, does that parent not then have a duty or obligation to participate in contact arrangements? Should this be the case, then arguably the state is in breach of its ECHR obligations by not providing a remedy to the victim – normally the child – in the form of compelling attendance at contact since that child, too, has a right to family life. While this sounds an attractive argument you have probably already thought of the practical difficulties and also about the quality of that 'compelled contact' – it could be far worse than leaving be. Be that as it may, this point does illustrate the lack of finesse that exists when trying to legislate on family life and human emotions.

The fact that contact is contentious is clear and the government has published a Consultation Paper, *Parental Separation: Children's Needs and Parents' Responsibilities* (July 2004, TSO) concerning the issue of how to make contact work.

9.6.3.5 Duration of orders and criteria to be applied

Contact orders are subject to the same rules and considerations as residence orders. You should recall the fact that the court applies a positive presumption in favour of contact since it is nearly always seen as being in the best interests of the child.

9.6.4 Specific issues and prohibited steps orders

The CA 1989 defines these orders thus:

'a specific issue order' means an order giving directions for the purpose of determining a specific question which has arisen, or which may arise, in connection with any aspect of parental responsibility for a child ...

and:

'a prohibited steps order' means an order that no step which could be taken by apparent in meeting his parental responsibility for a child, and which is of a kind specified in the order, shall be taken by any person without the consent of the court.

The fact that both of these orders deal with questions of parental responsibility is clear, but the terminology of the orders is possibly confusing. Both orders seem to do the same thing: they are different sides of the same coin. The main function of the orders is to deal with any dispute between persons who hold parental responsibility. This possibility of conflict should be known to you from your work on parental responsibility earlier in this chapter. If resolution is not possible, the court can be asked to step in. The court will then make a decision based on its perception of the child's best interests.

To illustrate how the orders can be used to achieve the same ends, consider this example:

Anne and Bill cannot decide to which school Christopher should go. Anne would like to register him at the local state infant school which has reasonably good teacher/pupil ratios. Bill, however, would like him to go to a nearby private school where he could attend as a day student. Bill considers the presence of large numbers of children from the local travellers' campsite to be detrimental to a state education.

If the couple are incapable of deciding this issue, they could approach the court. Anne could seek a specific issue order (SIO) to ensure that Christopher does go to the local state school. She could alternatively seek a prohibited steps order (PSO) to prevent Bill sending him to the private school. Whichever she applies for, if she is successful, she will achieve what she set out to do.

In *Re J (Specific Issue Orders: Child's Religious Upbringing and Circumcision)* [2000] 1 FLR 571, M, the English mother of J, aged five, was granted a prohibited steps order preventing J's Muslim father, F, from making arrangements to have J circumcised without a court order. F appealed against the decision to grant the order, contending that the judge had been wrong to place greater emphasis on the fact that J had been brought up in a secular environment than on the fact that J had been born a Muslim. F argued that the judge had given too much weight to M's opposition, whilst not appreciating the impact that F's views would have on J. The court dismissed the appeal, stating that where there was a dispute concerning an important decision regarding a child, the matter should be referred to the court. Ritual circumcision was an irreversible operation which was not medically necessary, bearing physical and psychological risks, and in such cases s 2(7) of the CA 1989 stated that the consent of both parents was essential. The issue of what was in the best interests of the child would depend on the facts and, in the instant case, the judge had correctly found that circumcision, which was not medically necessary at the age of five, was not in the child's best interests.

Question

Should local authorities be able to use these orders?

As the orders refer to the use of parental responsibility, it may seem logical to prevent local authorities from utilising these provisions. However, the definitions of the orders refer to the doing of acts covered by PR, not the fact that the act in question is being done by someone with PR. This would suggest that a local authority could apply for one of these orders. This is also borne out by s 9(2) and also s 9(5) of the CA 1989 which prohibit the use of residence and contact orders by local authorities and not the other s 8 orders, subject only to the caveat that the court cannot grant an SIO or PSO to achieve a result capable of being reached via a residence or contact order. Hence, if a local authority does try to use these orders, it must restrict itself to matters of parental responsibility.

In *Nottinghamshire CC v P* [1993] 3 WLR 637, the eldest of three sisters had complained of sexual abuse by her father (F) and had made allegations that he had abused another of the sisters. Emergency protection orders were obtained by the local authority and a prohibited steps order was sought which would have ordered F to leave home and to have no contact with his daughters except under supervision of the local authority. The local authority did not, however, apply for care or supervision orders. The judge would not make a prohibited steps order because it was not in accordance with s 9. He used his residual power under s 10(1)(b) of the CA 1989 and made a residence order requiring F to leave home, with the condition that contact with the daughters would be supervised. All the parties appealed. The court dismissed the local authority's appeal, but the appeals by F and the children would be allowed. A local authority was prohibited from obtaining residence or contact orders (see s 9(2)) and, under s 9(5), could not obtain a prohibited steps order intended to have the same effect. It was the task of the local authority to apply under Pt IV of the CA 1989. The local authority's application for a prohibited steps order would not be granted. The residence order was merely artificial and, in the circumstances, without relevance.

9.6.5 Special guardianship

Special guardianship orders are being introduced into the CA 1989 by virtue of the Adoption and Children Act 2002 (s 115 inserting s 14A–G into the CA

1989). Part of the purpose behind these orders is to reduce potential adoption applications and, also, to provide an alternative to the s 8 residence order. However, quite how many of these orders are likely to be made will remain in doubt, given the lack of success of similar types of orders that existed prior to the 1989 Act.

The definition of applicant for a special guardianship order is set out in s 14A and includes:

- a (testamentary) guardian of the child;
- someone who has a residence order;
- someone with whom the child has lived for at least three years; and
- a local authority foster parent who has had the child live with them for at least one year before the application.

When an application for special guardianship is made, the local authority must be informed to enable it to assess the applicant for suitability as a special guardian and the court cannot make an order unless it has seen the local authority assessment.

If an order is made, the court can also permit the child to be known by a new surname and permit the child's removal from the UK. The effect of the order will be to give the special guardian PR for the child and to give them the power to exercise this PR to the exclusion of any other PR holders, unless the law specifically requires the consent of all PR holders (for example, in relation to marriage). The local authority will also be required to provide services to special guardians if those services are needed.

Apart from the potential benefits in relation to PR, it is hard to see what this order is seeking to achieve. The order assumes the child will live with the special guardian, given the list of applicants, but this is not made clear in the legislation. The ability to access local authority services, as provided for in s 14F, may also benefit the carer and child if the child would not otherwise be a child in need and, hence, covered by the public law remedies we will look at in the next chapter.

9.7 SUMMARY

We have now come to the end of a reasonably long chapter, and have covered a large amount of material. You will possibly find it useful to consolidate your learning by making short revision notes now. You will need to refer to the concept of parental responsibility, focusing on:

- what it is;
- who has it; and
- who can get it, and how.

Your notes should also refer to the consequences of failing to comply with one's duties and responsibilities as a parent.

The private law orders available would then form the next part of your notes. Definitions of the four s 8 orders would be needed, together with supplementary information on:

- who can apply;
- what the criteria are;
- how long the orders last; and
- any potential problems with the orders.

If you do this, you will have a suitable set of notes from which to learn. A final stage of learning for this chapter is the following End of Chapter Assessment.

9.8   END OF CHAPTER ASSESSMENT

Hussein and Jayne married 10 years ago. They have two children, Robina, aged five, and Joshua, aged three. The marriage started to deteriorate shortly after Joshua was born and now the couple have decided to separate. No divorce is planned yet, although Jayne would like to dissolve the marriage in the not too distant future. Jayne is planning to go to live with her parents, who live in Cumbria in a large farmhouse. She would therefore have plenty of space for herself and the children. Hussein is not pleased at this decision, since it would be very difficult for him to travel the 200 miles to see the children. He is also concerned about Jayne's inability to bring up the children in the Muslim faith.

Advise Hussein who wishes to prevent this move and would prefer Joshua to remain with him so he can be raised in accordance with the Muslim faith.

What advice would you give Hussein if he wished to take the children to Iran to see their paternal grandparents and other relations?

CHAPTER 10

THE PUBLIC LAW RELATING TO CHILDREN

10.1   OBJECTIVES

By the end of this chapter you should be able to:

- understand the range of child abuse;
- produce a flow diagram indicating the stages of local authority intervention;
- discuss the variety of legal orders that can be utilised by the local authority;
- evaluate the effectiveness of some of these orders; and
- apply the law to hypothetical scenarios and give relevant advice to clients.

It is now time to move to what will be a lengthy chapter dealing with the variety of legislative provisions in public law relating to child care. The principal agency you will be concerned with is the local authority social services department, which, due to the Local Government Act 1970, has the responsibility to protect children within its area. The principles you have studied under s 1 of the Children Act (CA) 1989 will all be applicable to public law (some considerations being more relevant than others). You must always remember the principles of 'non-intervention' and 'working in partnership', since these are crucial to social work practice in this field.

Remember, this is a long chapter and dividing up your study may be appropriate. Suggested sections to study together are:

Part One: 10.2 to 10.5: child abuse and investigation.

                      10.6 to 10.9: short term orders.

Part Two: 10.10 to 10.16: long term orders.

PART ONE

10.2   CHILD ABUSE

As you may remember, the 'discovery of child abuse' is linked to the passing of legislation. However, some child abuse can be seen as a recent phenomenon since some actions which are today perceived as abusive or harmful to a child have in the past been accepted as normal behaviour. In previous generations the use of corporal punishment, say by use of the belt or slipper, was perfectly acceptable. Today this attitude is questionable. The recognition of child abuse, as we understand it today, has often been linked to the 'battered baby' syndrome which was 'discovered' in the 1960s by Dr Henry Kempe. Thereafter, other forms of abuse were discovered, for example, via the investigation into ritual sexual abuse in the Orkneys and the investigation of alleged widespread sexual abuse in Cleveland. The increasing frequency of public enquiries and investigations into alleged abuse, and the increase in media coverage, has led, over a period of time, to society being more willing to accept that these sorts of things do go on. This belief may have been held before, but a major change was the public voicing of concerns.

10.2.1   What do we mean by child abuse?

Child abuse tends to be defined by category, although fitting an alleged act of child abuse into a specific definition is often an arbitrary and artificial process.

Question

What do you think are the main categories of child abuse and how would you define them?

There are four categories used for defining child abuse. They are:

- physical abuse;
- neglect;
- sexual abuse; and
- emotional abuse.

In terms of defining the acts that would constitute a particular form of abuse, it is not easy, since value judgments, cultural beliefs and individual background can all play a part in what may be seen as abusive.

Question

Looking at sexual abuse as a category, would you agree that allowing a child to watch a sexually explicit video is abusive? What about underage sexual activity – is that abusive? On what basis do you answer those questions? Are you answering on behalf of yourself and your own opinions, or on behalf of everyone? If you can, why not ask others for their views on what equals abuse.

By thinking about this, you should see that there is scope for judgments to be based on subjective positions rather than objective ones, and this is a real difficulty where child abuse is concerned.

You can also see this in the category of physical abuse where, for example, some of the indicators for abuse include:

- multiple bruising and scratches;
- injuries found to have occurred at different times; and
- linear marks and weal marks.

Clearly this is not all that is indicative of physical abuse, but you can ask yourself what would happen if a child presented with these sorts of injuries. If a child leads a reasonably active life, it is suggested that bruises and/or scratches at different times will be inevitable. (Do you recall how many times you fell off a bike whilst learning how to ride it, or fell out of a tree scrumping?) Therefore, simply having regard to the nature of the injuries cannot be sufficient, especially if only one set of injuries is presented. If the harm suffered is severe then the degree of concern may be higher; but how is the risk of harm judged, and must more than one of the indicators need to be satisfied? Additionally, and to remove the risk of incorrect diagnosis, the injuries should generally be accompanied by an inadequate or no explanation as to how they arose leading to a reasonable belief of harm being deliberately caused. Here again you return to a subjective element, and the ability to assess evidence. The link between and injury and the cause of harm may therefore be difficult to prove, particularly if a reasonable explanation can be provided. Hence, a major problem is the difficulty of proving that physical abuse is occurring.

10.2.2 The extent of abuse

> **Question**
>
> Why might it be difficult to assess the degree of child abuse that occurs in England and Wales?

There is no clear, definitive picture as to the extent of child abuse within England and Wales. Two reasons identified for the difficulty in finding 'figures' have been suggested by Cobley in *Child Abuse and the Law* (1995, Cavendish Publishing), and they are as follows:

- there is no standardised definition of the subject matter; and
- figures that are obtained are from those cases reported to the authorities or from self report surveys, which are of themselves limited.

In terms of official figures, these can be obtained from the Department of Heath statistics, and these state that at 31 March 2002 there were 25,700 children registered on local authority child protection registers. This will not reflect the true number of abused children since not all will be known to the local authority or placed on the protection register, but it does provide some form of indication of the extent of abuse.

10.3 THE LOCAL AUTHORITY'S ROLE IN CHILD PROTECTION

Despite a concentration on child abuse and child protection work, it is important to remember that not all cases where the local authority gets involved will involve abuse: the local authority's duties are much wider than that. However, the fact is that crisis work has a higher priority than it should perhaps receive. This is often due to budget and personnel constraints, which reduce the ability to act in a preventive way.

10.3.1 The basic duties: s 17 of the CA 1989

> **Question**
>
> What do you think is the basic duty of all local authorities in relation to child protection?

The duties, in general terms, are set out in s 17 of the CA 1989 and require the local authority:

(a) to safeguard and promote the welfare of children within their area who are in need; and

(b) so far as is consistent with that duty, to promote the upbringing of such children by their families by providing a range and level of services appropriate to those children's needs.

The section then refers to Sched 2 to the CA 1989, which gives more detail of the service provision. Each local authority must:

- develop a children's service plan and review that plan in relation to the services it provides;
- maintain a register of disabled children and provide services for them;
- assess children who appear to be in need of services whether under the CA 1989 or other legislation;
- take reasonable steps to prevent children being harmed or neglected;
- provide accommodation to children in order to protect them;
- take steps to reduce the need for court proceedings – especially care proceedings;

- make provision to enable children to live with their families and to provide family services such as counselling, etc; and
- provide family centres.

The provision of services and attempting to keep children with their families are consistent with the fundamental principles of the CA 1989. They are also consistent with Art 8 of the European Convention on Human Rights (ECHR) since it can be seen to support family life, although there is some state interference.

You should also try to remember that the local authority, as it is a public body, must, due to the Human Rights Act (HRA) 1998, uphold the principles within the ECHR.

Question

If services are to be provided, are they only provided to the child?

Whilst the child is the primary client of the local authority, services may be provided to any member of the child's family if 'it is provided with a view to safeguarding or promoting the child's welfare' (s 17(3)). The family of a child, for the purposes of this duty, is perhaps a little wider than the normal definition. Under s 17(10), family includes 'any person with parental responsibility [PR] for the child and any other person with whom he has been living'. This latter aspect operates to widen the potential beneficiaries of services.

Question

Does the local authority have to provide the services themselves or can they 'contract out' service provision?

While the duty to provide services rests with the local authority, the local authority can get other agencies or voluntary bodies to provide the actual service, with the local authority paying for it. Traditionally, the local authority contracts with other providers for the service, but amendments to s 17 of the CA 1989 mean that the authority can make direct payments to the family or provide vouchers to spend on getting a service for a child – for example, day care. It is important to note that in some cases the local authority can actually charge the family for the provision of services too – this is permitted under s 17(7) and (8), although in the majority of cases this would not happen.

Question

Which children will be provided with services?

As you have seen from s 17 of the CA 1989, above, the type of child to whom services can be provided is a 'child in need'. This is defined in s 17(10) thus:

> For the purposes of this Part a child is taken to be in need if –
>
> (a) he is unlikely to achieve or maintain, or have the opportunity of achieving or maintaining, a reasonable standard of health or development without the provision for him of services by a local authority ...
>
> (b) his health or development is likely to be significantly impaired, or further impaired, without the provision of such services; or
>
> (c) he is disabled.

10.3.2   Other services

> ### Question
>
> Section 17(1) of the CA 1989 makes reference to 'other duties imposed' on local authorities by virtue of the CA 1989. Can you think what these might be?

These 'other duties' are found in the following sections:

- s 18(1) and (5): day care for some children aged under five and other (older) children;

- s 20(1): provision of accommodation for some 'children in need';

- ss 22, 23 and 24(1): duties to children 'looked after' by the local authority, or 'relevant' children; and

- s 24: duty to provide advice and assistance for certain children, and s 23B and C: 'keeping in touch' with the child, including when they are no longer 'looked after'.

10.3.2.1 Day care for children aged under five and others

Section 18 provides:

> (1) Every local authority shall provide such day care fore children in need within their area who are –
>
> (a) aged five or under; and
>
> (b) not yet attending schools, as is appropriate
>
> ...
>
> (5) Every local authority shall provide for children in need within their area who are attending any school such care or supervised activities as is appropriate –
>
> (a) outside school hours; or
>
> (b) during school holidays.

As you can see, the purpose of the section is to impose a duty on local authorities to provide day care for pre-school-age children and supervised care and activities after school for school age children, if those children are 'in need' within the definition of s 17. The local authority is empowered to extend these services to other children even if they are not in need. However, these services are not commonly provided.

Question

Should they be commonly provided if this is a duty?

If this was an outright duty, local authorities would be open to legal action for failure to comply, given the general lack of such services. A careful consideration of the section shows that the duty is discretionary, that is, the local authority need only provide services 'as are appropriate'. If the local authority reasonably decides that existing facilities are appropriate, or that no facilities are appropriate, it has met its statutory requirements.

10.3.2.2 Accommodation

The general duty is specified in s 20(1):

Every local authority shall provide accommodation for any child in need within their area who appears to them to require accommodation as a result of –

(a) there being no person who has parental responsibility for him;

(b) his being lost or having been abandoned; or

(c) the person who has been caring for him being prevented (whether or not permanently, and for whatever reason) from providing him with suitable accommodation or care.

Clearly the section relates to children in need where one of the factors in s 20(1)(a), (b) and (c) applies. However, if a child is not classed as being in need under the terms of s 17, the local authority may still provide accommodation if the situation is within s 20(4) which provides:

A local authority may provide accommodation for any child within their area (even though a person with parental responsibility for him is able to provide him with accommodation) if they consider that to do so would safeguard or promote the child's welfare.

This would appear to conflict somewhat with the provision in s 20(7), which states that if any person with PR (and this will normally be someone other than the person seeking the accommodation) objects to the provision of accommodation *and* is able to provide or arrange suitable accommodation themselves, the local authority's powers are ended. Of course, there is the question of who decides on suitability! If the child concerned is the subject of a residence order under s 8 of the CA 1989, the picture is a little different. Here, if it is the person(s) with whom the child is to live who requests accommodation, then no other person with PR can stop the local authority assisting.

Question

Do you think the child should have any rights? If so, what?

Section 20 is unusual in that it gives a child a specific right with reference to accommodation. This right is, however, subject to the discretion of the local authority. Under s 20(3), the local authority 'shall provide accommodation for any child in need who has reached the age of 16 and whose welfare the authority consider is likely to be seriously prejudiced if they do not provide him with accommodation'.

It is clear that the 16-year-old faces some hurdles here, that is, they must be a child in need and they must convince the local authority that their welfare will not just be at risk, but will be seriously prejudiced if accommodation is not provided.

When the local authority is considering providing accommodation, regardless of the reason or provision for so doing, it should discuss the matter with the child and try to establish the child's wishes (s 20(6)).

Question

Is there any element of compulsion in provision of accommodation under this section?

Prior to the CA 1989, accommodation was provided either on a 'voluntary' basis or 'compulsory' basis. The distinction was that the former did not rely on any legal intervention before it could arise, whilst the latter was dependent upon an order placing the child into the local authority's care. While the terminology of voluntary and compulsory care has gone, the idea of children being cared for by the local authority in the absence of a court order continues.

Children accommodated under s 20 are provided with this accommodation on a voluntary basis. Consequently, the local authority does not gain PR, except to the extent that it is delegated by the person placing the child with it. When a parent seeks to remove the child from s 20 accommodation, there is nothing the local authority can do if it does not feel removal is appropriate, other than seek a court order.

If a child has been made subject to a legal order (that is, a care order), the local authority is obliged to provide accommodation. The local authority would, in this situation, have PR and parents, or others with PR, would not be in a position to remove the child at will. You should note that the duty to accommodate arises by virtue of the legal order made by the court, not s 20 itself.

If a child is being provided with accommodation, whether it be by virtue of a legal order or by agreement with the parents under s 20, the child will be said to be 'looked after' by the local authority. This is a generic term, and simply knowing that a child is 'looked after' will not clarify the child's status. The terminology that is appropriate to distinguish looked after children is either that the child is 'in the local authority's care', meaning subject to a legal order placing the child with the local authority, or 'accommodated', meaning that the child is being provided with accommodation under s 20, and hence on a voluntary basis.

If a child has been looked after by the local authority at any time after they have reached the age of 16, but whilst still a child, for a minimum consecutive period of three months (this period includes time prior to the 16th birthday), the local authority is under a duty to provide advice, assistance and befriending. The purpose is to promote the child's welfare when they cease to be looked after (s 24).

In addition, amendments to s 23 of the CA 1989 (made by the Children (Leaving Care) Act 2000) place local authorities under a duty to provide services to 'relevant children' that is, children who have been looked after and are 16 or 17 and not now being looked after. These duties include the provision of maintenance, accommodation and other support following assessment and development of a pathway plan. The local authority is required to take steps to ensure it keeps in touch with the relevant child by way of a personal adviser and this extends past the time frame in which the child is deemed a relevant child.

10.4   THE DUTY TO INVESTIGATE

Before a local authority can take any action toward the provision of services, it needs to establish to which families or children to direct its attention. In some situations this is easier than others, for example, the single mother requesting accommodation while she goes into hospital, or the disabled child who attends a specialist school. However, the majority of child care work is not with these types of families.

10.4.1   Section 47 of the CA 1989

> **Question**
>
> In what ways will suspected cases of abuse become known to the social services?

A case will normally become apparent via some form of referral to the local authority. Referrals may be from anyone: neighbours, friends, family, health visitor, GP, hospital casualty department, police or school.

Question

Should a doctor make referrals, or is this contrary to their duty of confidentiality?

For many professionals, the making of referrals of suspected child abuse may conflict with the ethical duty to maintain confidence. However, the public interest in disclosing abuse, and the emphasis that is placed on the welfare of the child, means that this duty may be breached. The original guidance to the CA 1989, *Working Together Under the Children Act 1989* (1991, HMSO) makes specific reference to the ethical perspective, and the duty to co-operate and to share information across different professional agencies is confirmed in s 47(9) of the CA 1989. Indeed, as the more recent inquiries into child abuse or death confirm, the lack of co-operation and sharing of information is often prejudicial to the protection of the child (see, for example, the Laming Inquiry 2003).

Once a referral is made, the local authority is under a duty to make enquiries about the child. This duty arises under s 47 of the CA 1989, which provides:

(1) Where a local authority –

    (a) are informed that a child who lives, or is found, in their area –

        (i) is the subject of an emergency protection order; or

        (ii) is in police protection; or

        (iii) has contravened a ban imposed by a curfew notice [under the Crime and Disorder Act 1998]; or

    (b) have reasonable cause to suspect that child who lives, or is found, in their area is suffering, or is likely to suffer, significant harm,

the authority shall make, or cause to be made, such enquiries as they consider necessary to enable them to decide whether they should take any action to safeguard or promote the child's welfare.

As you can see, there are several 'trigger' criteria for the commencement of a s 47 investigation, which include:

- the child is the subject of an Emergency Protection Order (EPO);
- the child is in police protection (this is covered in s 46);
- the child is in breach of a curfew notice; and
- the local authority has reasonable cause to suspect that a child is suffering or is likely to suffer significant harm.

Do not worry if you do not know about EPOs or about significant harm; we will consider all these issues later.

Question

Is the duty to investigate absolute?

While the section states that the local authority *shall* make enquiries, it then states 'such enquiries as they consider necessary to enable them to decide whether they should take any action'. The local authority may consider it unnecessary to make enquiries, and in so far as this is based on reasonable grounds, judicial review would be unsuccessful in challenging the decision.

Question

Must the child be seen?

If enquiries are considered to be necessary, it is hard to see how the local authority can assess the child's risk of suffering harm without actually seeing the child. Section 47(4) requires the local authority to:

... take such steps as are reasonably practicable –

(a) to obtain access to [the child]; or

(b) to ensure that access to him is obtained, on their behalf, by a person authorised by them for the purpose, unless they are satisfied that they already have sufficient information with respect to him.

Again, the duty is qualified, but s 47(6) does cover the consequences where access to the child is not granted. Hence the local authority, if access is denied and access is needed, is required to apply for one of a range of orders (for example an EPO) 'unless they are satisfied that his welfare can be satisfactorily safeguarded without their doing so'. Qualified duties strike again!

The purpose of the investigation, set out in sub-s (3), is to establish whether certain steps should be taken; that is:

- whether the local authority should apply for any legal order, under the CA 1989 or Crime and Disorder Act 1998, for the purpose of safeguarding or protecting the child's welfare;

- where the child is subject to an EPO and not in local authority accommodation, whether the child should be provided with such accommodation; and

- where a child is in police protection, whether an application should be made under s 46(7) which permits an application to be made for an EPO.

Hence the focus is on the possible legal orders that could be obtained.

Question

What do you think that the local authority should focus on initially in terms of investigation – should it be legal orders?

If the spirit of the CA 1989 is to be complied with, then s 47 should perhaps reflect the need of the local authority to provide services under s 17 since these may be all that is required to protect the child and safeguard its well-being.

When legal action is not to be pursued, the local authority needs to decide whether or not to review the case (s 47(7)). By including this provision, the local authority is at least directed to producing reasons why no later review is deemed necessary, and this should prevent cases being allowed to drift.

10.4.2 Section 37 investigations

Although we are looking at public law in this chapter, you should note that the private law in the CA 1989 has investigation procedures, although in the majority of cases parents will have agreed a solution. If this is not so, or the court is not happy with the parents' solution, it can utilise the services of CAFCASS (Children and Family Court Advisory and Support Service). An officer of CAFCASS (normally a social worker or court welfare officer) can be requested (under s 7) to provide a report on the family to the court. The officer will not normally have protracted contact with the family members. In some situations the court will request a s 7 welfare report direct from the local authority. However, this is generally the exception since local authority budgets do not set aside funds for this purpose.

In some private law matters, the court may believe that the child is at risk of significant harm and that the local authority needs to be involved. It might be a case where child protection is an issue, but one where the family is unknown to the local authority, or where no referrals have ever been made. In this type of situation, s 37 can be invoked. This section provides that:

(1) Where, in any family proceedings in which a question arises with respect to the welfare of any child, it appears to the court that it may be appropriate for a care or supervision order to be made with respect to him, the court may direct the appropriate authority to undertake and investigation of the child's circumstances.

Question

Why do you think that the court cannot simply make a care order?

When the law preceding the CA 1989 was reviewed it was believed that the giving of power to the court to commit a child to the care of the local authority, without necessarily having involved the local authority, or without the need to comply with specific criteria, was inappropriate. The pre-CA 1989 law also reflected an imbalance of power and responsibility between the courts and the local authority. Hence now a care order can only be made where the local authority applies for it, or the child has broken the terms of a curfew order under the Crime and Disorder Act 1998 (this is an order in relation to possible criminal activity of the child, and hence is outside the scope of the text, but you do need to be aware of its existence).

Where a s 37 investigation is carried out, the focus of the local authority should be to consider whether it needs to apply for a care order or supervision order, provide services or any other assistance or take any other action. As with s 47, the extent to which intervention is needed, and the nature of that intervention must be carefully assessed. If a child's welfare can be safeguarded satisfactorily with a minimum level of intervention, this is the path that should be taken.

Question

How long should an investigation take under this provision?

Under the terms of sub-s (4) the local authority must report back to the court within eight weeks, unless the court directs otherwise; this may mean a shorter period rather than a longer period. By contrast, there is no set time limit for s 47 investigations. While it is naturally in the child's best interests to conclude matters quickly, there is no legal obligation to finish a s 47 investigation by a specified time.

Question

If the court orders a s 37 investigation, and the local authority decides to do nothing, and the court disagrees with that decision, can the court force the local authority to act?

The courts are in a difficult position if the local authority decides to do nothing: the court itself has no powers to make a local authority apply for a care order. This was highlighted as being a major gap in the law, but as yet no moves have been made to change the situation. The gap arises simply because of the need to reduce the local authorities' powers and those of the court to remove children from the care of their parents. Such draconian state intervention should only be done in accordance with set criteria.

In *Re H (A Minor) (Section 37 Direction)* [1993] 2 FLR 541, a lesbian couple requested a residence order in relation to a child who had lived with them in their home since being born there. The court held that the situation would be regularised as far as was possible by the grant of an interim supervision and interim residence orders. The local authority was directed, under s 37(1), to make an investigation into the child's circumstances. The phrase 'child's circumstances' should be construed in a wide sense so as to include any situation which might affect the possibility of the child's being likely to suffer any significant harm in the future.

In *Nottinghamshire CC v P* [1993] 3 WLR 637, the local authority had applied for a s 8 prohibited steps order (PSO) under the CA 1989 as it wanted to prevent the father of the children residing in the same house as them and also to stop contact between the father and the children. In the original hearing the judge had stated:

> I made it perfectly plain when speaking to the manager of social services that I felt it [the supervision order] would give me teeth and powers that I did not have without their application by the local authority refused to give me the opportunity to exercise any of the powers which are ancillary to a supervision order.

The local authority was said to have persistently and obstinately refused to undertake what was the appropriate course of action, and it thereby deprived the judge of the ability to make a constructive order. Additionally, the Court of Appeal stated that:

> [it was] deeply concerned at the absence of any power to direct this authority to take steps to protect the children. Unfortunately, as appears from this case, if a local authority doggedly resists taking the steps which are appropriate to the case of children at risk of suffering significant harm it appears that the court is powerless.

The fact that a s 8 PSO had been sought to exclude the father and prevent contact was also criticised as being contrary to the CA 1989.

10.5 CHILD PROTECTION CASE CONFERENCES

The holding of case conferences is part and parcel of the child protection process.

10.5.1 What is the conference there for?

The conference is intended to:

> ... bring together the family and the professionals concerned with child protection and provides them with the opportunity to exchange information and plan together. The conference symbolises the inter-agency basis and the conference is the prime forum for sharing information and concerns, analysing risk and recommending responsibility for action (*Working Together*, 1989, HMSO, para 6.1).

In terms of who is likely to attend, this will reflect the professional nature of those involved: social work, education, health visiting and health authorities and the like. In addition the parents or persons with PR and the child will often be invited.

Question

Do you agree that the child and the parents should always be invited?

The decision to include the child in the attendees is not, nor should be, automatic although parents would normally attend. Indeed, in some cases, even if a child had reached a certain level of understanding, it would be contrary to the child's interests to attend due to the potentially harmful conflict that may arise between the child and the parents. Even if the child is invited, it is always open to exclude them from part of the conference, and this is true of the parents as well. Occasionally it may be the case that the presence of the family will inhibit the free exchange of information that is needed.

10.5.2   When will a conference be needed?

Conferences fall into two categories:

- the initial child protection case conference; and
- the child protection review.

The former needs to be convened when a referral into suspected abuse has occurred; the latter acts as a means to ensure that cases do not drift.

The initial conference is clearly part of the child protection process, but should not be used to delay protective work and it is expected that the initial conference should be held within eight days of the initial referral.

Question

Is this realistic?

Eight days is a very short time frame within which to operate, and Department of Health guidance sets 15 days as a maximum, but in many cases even this is not achieved. Despite this being contrary to the guidance, there will be no comeback. The guidance does not have the force of law. The delay is inevitable given the nature of the invitees. A conference will only work at an acceptable level if professionals can attend, and convening a conference at short notice does not promote good attendance rates.

Review conferences are subject to different time frames, since a decision has already been made, and the purpose of the review is different. Reviews will examine the existing level of risk to the child and ensure that the protection plan that has been put into effect is working.

10.5.3　What decision can be made?

There is only one decision that can be made at the conference: 'should the child's name be placed (or removed)' from the child protection register.

One of the major difficulties with case conferences is that they are perceived to be the forum within which the decision to take legal action is made. This is one decision that is *not* within the conference's remit. As you have seen, the function is to decide whether or not to register the child's name on the child protection register. If the child is already registered, the review conference will assess whether it is safe to remove the child's name from the register. As part of this decision making process, or rather as an adjunct to it, the conference can formulate a child protection plan. This plan may set out the variety of different agencies involved and the extent to which they will act. The benefit of establishing this plan is that everyone will be there, and this may include the parents.

Question

Whose decision is it to take legal proceedings?

The only decision maker will be the local authority (which is charged with this function), and in particular the social services department. The legal department of a local authority will not make the decision but merely act to advise the social workers.

10.6　SHORT TERM ORDERS

By now you will be familiar with the notion that the local authority will intervene by means of legal action only where it is necessary.

The preferred route should always be to attempt the voluntary options. In some situations a voluntary route may not succeed. Indeed, some families may actually co-operate better if subject to a court order. If legal action is needed, the local authority will approach each individual case on its facts and history. While the CA 1989 gives both short and long term orders, there will be no guarantee as to how intervention will first arise. What is clear is the requirement for local authorities to ensure that the legal action meets the standard set by the ECHR – that in determining a person's civil rights, they are entitled to a fair and public hearing within a reasonable time (Art 6). In addition, local authorities must ensure that any interference with the right to respect for an individual's private and family life is consistent with the prevailing national legislation. For study purposes, we will look at short term and emergency orders first before considering long term intervention.

10.6.1 The child assessment order: s 43

The reason for introducing the child assessment order (CAO) has been suggested by Masson and Morris as being due to 'concern that the more rigorous requirements for an EPO could mean that it was impossible to get an EPO where there was fear for the child's safety but no hard evidence' (*Children Act Manual*, 1992, Sweet & Maxwell, pp 129–30). It could be argued that by allowing the assessment of a child, the order is akin to a fishing exercise, to enable the local authority to get evidence on which to base a future application. The use of the order to gather evidence is incontrovertible. However, that it is a 'fishing exercise' is a less valid suggestion, since the CAO can only be obtained after the criteria in s 43 have been proved.

10.6.1.1 The criteria

The order is set out in s 43:

(1) On the application of a local authority or authorised person ... the court may make the order if, but only if, it is satisfied that –

   (a) the applicant has reasonable cause to suspect that the child is suffering, or is likely to suffer, significant harm;

   (b) an assessment of the state of the child's health or development, or the way in which he has been treated, is required to enable the applicant to determine whether or not the child is suffering, or is likely to suffer, significant harm; and

   (c) it is unlikely that such an assessment will be made, or be satisfactory, in the absence of an order under this section.

Question

Who do you think would be classed as authorised for the purposes of sub-s 1?

The Secretary of State is responsible for authorising agents under the CA 1989 to carry out specified functions or duties. The only agent so authorised at present is the National Society for the Prevention of Cruelty to Children (NSPCC).

The criteria for the court to consider comprise three elements:

• the applicant has reasonable cause to suspect that the child is suffering or likely to suffer significant harm;

• an assessment is needed to establish whether the child is so suffering; and

• the assessment is not likely to happen without the order.

All three elements need to be satisfied.

Question

How do you think the local authority can prove the third point in this list?

This may be proved from a variety of acts or omissions by the child's parents. For example, the local authority may be seeking to work voluntarily with the family and may have set up a series of appointments with various professionals to assess the child. The parents may refuse to assist, or fail to attend. Alternatively, the parents may simply refuse to allow access to the child. If access is refused, then the authority may go straight to an application for an EPO which is contrary to the idea of working together. Hence, a CAO may be seen as a threatening device as opposed to a 'real' order. The fact that CAOs are hardly used would support this suggestion. Is co-operation voluntary when supported with the threat of legal action?

In addition to proving the criteria set out in s 43, any applicant must also satisfy the court that the making of the order will be better than making no order at all (s 1(5)) and that the order is in the best interests of the child (s 1(1)). There is no need to go through the welfare checklist: s 1(3) is not applicable since s 43 is within Pt V of the CA 1989 and hence not referred to in s 1(4). Practically, any applicant would do well to remember the checklist and ensure that statements in support of their application make some reference to the issues within it, since the checklist is taken as indicating the factors by which the child's welfare can be assessed. (Remember that we looked at the welfare checklist earlier in the text.)

10.6.1.2 Consequences

A CAO is only available for a period of seven consecutive days. All assessments and examinations, which the local authority wishes to conduct, must be completed within this period. The applicant cannot remove the child from the parental home, unless this has been authorised by the court itself, nor will the applicant obtain PR for the child; this remains with the parents. In some cases the court, if faced with an application for a CAO, may consider the case to be too serious for a mere investigative order. In such cases, under sub-s (3), the court can treat the application as being for an EPO. This potentially reduces the effectiveness of the CAO, since the court, consisting of lay magistrates in the majority of cases, will perhaps not wish to be seen as placing a child in potential risk, regardless of the views of the applicant.

If a parent refuses to comply with a CAO, while it would be unlikely that any action to commit for breach of a court order would arise, the chances of a successful EPO or care order application would be higher.

10.6.1.3 Advantages

Question

Do you perceive there to be any advantages in seeking CAOs?

Advantages of the order are that:

- the parents keep PR exclusively;
- the child may be seen by the family doctor in a familiar environment;
- parents may co-operate with this type of order more willingly, hence the social work relationship with the family will not be damaged; and
- the child can be protected in serious but not emergency situations.

Think about these advantages for a moment. Do you agree with them?

Although there are advantages to having an order to investigate, there are difficulties. These may include the evidential difficulties in establishing lack of co-operation, through to problems with establishing working relationships with the family and the fact that this is not a protective order. The CAO is certainly not an emergency order: notice must be given of the application, and there is the time taken to prove that the parents will not co-operate. Given these criticisms, can you understand why the order is used infrequently?

10.7   EMERGENCY PROTECTION ORDERS: s 44

Whilst CAOs are under utilised, EPOs certainly are not. The EPO is a short term order, its aim being to protect in an emergency situation.

10.7.1   Criteria and applicants

Section 44(1) is often misunderstood or confused by students, primarily since they mix up the criteria and fail to appreciate how the criteria operate. The section sets out three different criteria upon which an application can be based, and dictates which type of applicant can use which of the criteria. The section states:

(1) Where any person ('the applicant') applies to the court for an order to be made under this section with respect to a child, the court may make the order if, but only if, it is satisfied that –

(a) there is reasonable cause to believe that the child is likely to suffer significant harm if –

(i) he is not removed to accommodation provided on or on behalf of the applicant; or

    (ii) he does not remain in the place in which he is then being accommodated.

(b) in the case of an application made by a local authority –

    (i) enquiries are being made with respect to the child under section 47(1)(b); and

    (ii) those enquiries are being frustrated by access being unreasonably refused to a person authorised to seek access and that the applicant has reasonable cause to believe that access to the child is required as a matter of urgency; or

(c) in the case of an application made by an authorised person –

    (i) the applicant has reasonable cause to suspect that a child is suffering, or is likely to suffer, significant harm;

    (ii) the applicant is making enquiries with respect to the child's welfare; and

    (iii) those enquiries are being frustrated by access to the child being unreasonably refused to a person authorised to seek access and the applicant has reasonable cause to believe that access to the child is required as a matter of urgency.

10.7.1.1 *The any person criterion*

Section 44(1)(a) is referred to as the 'any person criterion', since 'any person' may apply for an EPO under these grounds. There are certain elements to the criterion on which you need to be clear.

First, to be successful, there must be 'reasonable cause to believe that the child is likely to suffer significant harm'.

Question

Who has to hold that belief?

The common sense reaction would be to say the applicant. However, by reading the section carefully, you will know that it is the court that must hold that belief. The applicant's function is to convince the court that the child is at risk.

Secondly, the risk of harm must arise from the child remaining in their current accommodation, or being removed from it (s 44(1)(a)(i) and (ii) respectively).

The burden of proof to be satisfied is the civil standard.

Question

Can the local authority utilise s 44(1)(a)?

As the sub-section allows an application by 'anyone', the local authority can certainly use it to obtain an order, and frequently does. Others you may come across using it include hospitals, if they believe that the removal of a child from hospital care will be detrimental to its welfare (this falls within s 44(1)(a)(ii)), the police and family members.

If an EPO is gained by anyone other than the local authority, the court will notify the local authority of the making of the order. This will trigger the investigation of the case and the child by the local authority under the provisions of s 47.

10.7.1.2 The local authority criterion

Section 44(1)(b) is specific to the local authority. To gain an EPO under this section, the local authority must establish that:

- it is carrying out a s 47 investigation;
- the enquiries are being frustrated by access being denied; and
- it believes that access is needed as a matter of urgency.

All three elements of the criterion must be satisfied.

Question

Is this easier to satisfy than the any person criterion?

Arguably, the answer is yes. Under s 44(1)(a) it is the court that has to be satisfied that the child is at risk of harm; under s 44(1)(b) only the local authority has to believe anything. You will see that there is no mention of significant harm in s 44(1)(b); it is implicit from the fact of the s 47 investigation. Again, note the differences in wording. For s 44(1)(a), the court must have reasonable cause to believe, whereas under s 47, the local authority must only have reasonable cause to suspect. The differences are subtle, but it is suggested that suspicion implies a lower threshold than belief. The extent to which any court would question the evidence of the local authority for holding that suspicion is also a matter for conjecture.

The inability to gain access to the child is linked into the s 47 investigation. You should recall that the local authority, under s 47(4), is under a duty to see the child (unless it has sufficient information) and, if access is refused, s 47 directs the local authority to consider legal action. The question you should be thinking is, 'what is meant by access?' Naturally it will refer to physical access; but the local authority social worker may wish to see the child in the home setting, while parents will only allow 'access' at the local authority's offices. The social worker may wish to gain access to examine for injuries. The social worker may be prevented from such access if the parents refuse to allow examination or for the child to be undressed.

'Urgency' is another issue open to interpretation; it clearly means something more than the social worker wanting to see the child on a set day. Urgency will be assessed in the light of the overall situation, the history of the case, the age of the child and also whether other venues for seeing the child can be arranged and agreed between the family and the local authority.

10.7.1.3 The authorised person criterion

The final criterion in s 44 is available only to 'authorised persons', the NSPCC. The criteria to be satisfied under s 44(1)(c) are a conglomeration of s 44(1)(a) and (b). Note that there has to be some evidence supporting the suspicion of harm but here it is the applicant that must have the suspicion, not the court. Section 44(1)(c) replicates s 44(1)(b) in that there must be enquiries being carried out and refusal of access which is needed urgently.

Question

Why might the NSPCC be carrying out enquiries?

If you remember, s 47 requires the local authority, when any of the trigger criteria are met, 'to make, or cause to be made' any necessary enquiries. Hence, the local authority may 'contract out' enquiries to the NSPCC.

When the court is considering the making of an order under s 44, regardless of whom the applicant is, it must have regard to the basic s 1 of the CA 1989 principles: that the child's welfare is paramount; that the court should not delay; that it should consider whether to make an order at all. The welfare checklist is not directly called into consideration since the procedure for seeking EPOs, as with CAOs, is to be found in Pt V of the Act.

10.7.2 Consequences of making the order

10.7.2.1 Removal

Section 44(4) authorises the removal of the child by the applicant to alternative accommodation. If the child is already in suitable accommodation (that is, a hospital) the sub-section will permit the retention of the child in that place. However, this needs to be read in conjunction with s 44(10), which has the effect that if an EPO is obtained, but when the child comes to be removed there is found to be no reason for removal, the child shall remain where it is. Additionally, if the child is removed, and the source of that harm subsequently disappears, then the local authority must consider returning the child. To give you an example, consider the following situation

Anne and Bill cohabit, and have one son, Christopher. Bill is known to be violent. After a routine health visitor check-up, a referral was made to Wollham Social Services. The social worker has visited the home twice; on neither visit did she get into the house. An EPO was obtained, and Christopher removed to foster care. Two days after the order was made Anne obtained an occupation order against Bill (remember, we covered these in the domestic violence chapter). In this situation, if Anne has not been seen to be causing harm to the child, then it may be deemed appropriate to return Christopher.

Question

If Christopher is returned and Bill is accepted back into the home (contrary to the occupation order), what can the local authority do?

If the child is returned, this will not automatically result in the termination of the order. So, if the source of harm reappears, the child can be removed again for the remainder of the EPO's duration and without the need to seek further approval from the court.

Question

Would it not be better to remove a suspected abuser from the home?

If you looked at *Nottinghamshire CC v P* [1993] 3 WLR 637, you may recall that here the authority had attempted to use a prohibited steps order under s 8 of the CA 1989 to do just that (these orders were covered in previous chapter). The court held that it was not an appropriate use of the order. Now the CA 1989 has been amended to give the court power to include an exclusion order, when making an EPO (s 44A and s 44B), ordering the removal of the abuser from the home. The court will still make the EPO, but if an exclusion order is made, the child will be expected to remain in the family home. Undertakings to leave voluntarily may also be acceptable, but here too you should note that the EPO must be made by the court, presumably to enable the local authority to remove the child if the suspected abuser reneges on the undertaking or breaches the exclusion order. Additionally, a suspected abuser may be encouraged to leave, since Sched 2, para 5 of the CA 1989 permits the local authority to assist by provision of accommodation or even money to a suspected abuser, but this section is not commonly used.

10.7.2.2 Contact

If a child has been removed from their family, there is an expectation that the child will be given reasonable contact with their parents or carers during the life of the EPO (s 44(13)). It is hoped that the trauma to the child will be lessened by allowing contact. However, it may not be appropriate for contact in all cases, or certainly not for unsupervised contact. The court may therefore be asked to restrict or prevent contact for the benefit of the child. The court has the power to grant such directions under s 44(6). In this situation the local authority and the court need to remember the right of a parent to contact under the auspices of Art 8 of the ECHR.

10.7.2.3 Duration

The EPO, as its name indicates, deals with emergency situations and is, therefore, of a limited duration. This reflects the attempt to move away from the previous, and quite draconian, place of safety order. The EPO will last for *up to* eight days on the first application (s 45(1)). The applicant must be ready to persuade the court to grant the maximum duration since it is not guaranteed. During the EPO, the local authority (whether the applicant or not) should assess the child to establish whether further legal action is needed or services should be provided.

Question

Is eight days long enough to complete an assessment?

It is hard to imagine a full assessment being carried out in the currency of an EPO to enable a fully informed decision to proceed (or not) with other legal action. Indeed, as an application for a supervision order or care order needs to be made on notice, the eight days is an unrealistic proposition. If necessary, an application can be made to extend the initial order, by *up to* seven days (s 45(5)). Only one such extension is permissible.

If no other application is made (such as for a care order), then at the end of the EPO the situation will, legally, revert to normal. Practically, this may not be so since the parents may agree to work voluntarily with the local authority.

10.7.2.4 Parental responsibility

During the existence of the EPO, the applicant will obtain limited PR for the child (s 44(4)(c)). The gaining of PR will not extinguish that held by the parents. It will, however, restrict the other holders' ability to exercise it. As you should remember, the other holders will not be able to act in a manner to conflict with the order.

The extent to which decisions can be made by the applicant is strictly limited to actions needed to safeguard and protect the welfare of the child (s 44(5)).

Question

Should any liability accrue if the applicant went beyond their powers?

You might, logically, assume so; however, this was not the view of the court in the case of *F v Wirral MBC* [1991] 2 WLR 1132, although this decision was based on the actions of the local authority under the legislation prior to the CA 1989.

10.7.2.5 Appealing the order

Question

Can you appeal against the making of, or refusal to make, an EPO?

Most court orders can be appealed: the EPO cannot. This is logical given the limited time duration for the order. If an order has been made, the child, a parent of the child, anyone with PR or the person with whom the child was living before the order was made, may apply for it to be discharged (which is not the same as an appeal) (s 45(8), (9) and (10)). The discharge option is not available for all EPOs; it depends on the procedure used to get the order. If the individual(s) seeking to discharge the order had formal notice of the hearing and attended the hearing, or in relation to an extension, was present when the extra duration was ordered, then they cannot seek discharge. In any event, no application can be brought until 72 hours after the making of the order has expired. If the local authority is successful in getting the order, it will always have a minimum of three days before the order can be ended.

The situation where *no* order is made highlights the fact that gaps do exist in this legislation. The only viable option is to reapply to the court.

In *Re P (Emergency Protection Order)* [1996] 1 FLR 482, C, aged two months, was admitted to hospital after receiving injuries which appeared to be non-accidental. The judge concluded that M, one of the parents, was responsible. An emergency protection order was obtained by the local authority, but an extension was refused by the magistrates. On appeal, Johnson J commented on the refusal to extend the EPO thus:

> ... that the justices having refused to extend the emergency protection order, the Children Act 1989 lacked any effective procedure by which the local authority could challenge that decision.

A variety of options were raised, such as immediate application for a care order but, as Johnson J pointed out, these were all very cumbersome and not ideal in the circumstances.

10.7.3 Procedure

From the previous paragraphs you will know that an EPO can be obtained 'on notice'. That notice is, under Sched 2 of the Family Proceedings Rules, set at one day.

Question

Is this consistent with the notion of emergency?

You should answer this in the negative. Can it really be said that a child is being protected if parents or carers are given a day to do something worse, or disappear (if you take a very pessimistic view of human nature)? Due to the inconsistency with the concept of 'emergency', very few EPOs are sought after giving notice. Normally, they will be sought without notice; hence, most parents can seek to apply for discharge of the order.

Question

Which court will be involved?

For all public law proceedings, the starting place is the Family Proceedings Court (FPC) (magistrates). Therefore, if an order is to be sought without notice, it can be obtained out of court hours from a single magistrate. Indeed, under the Family Proceedings Rules (FPR) (SI 1991/1247) a single court clerk may be empowered to grant an out of hours EPO.

10.8   THE CHILDREN'S GUARDIAN

In certain specified proceedings, as established in s 41 of the CA 1989, the court is required to appoint a children's guardian for the child (referred to in the CA 1989 as 'an officer of the Service' – the 'Service' being the Children and Family Court Advisory and Support Services (CAFCASS)), unless the court is satisfied that it is not necessary to do so. Some of the situations where a children's guardian is appointed are where there is:

- an application for a care or supervision order or discharge of such an order or an appeal against the making of such an order;
- a s 37 investigation;
- an application to substitute a supervision order for a care order;
- a consideration of residence order being granted where the child is in care or an appeal relating to this situation; or
- an issue relating to contact to a child in care.

Appointment of a guardian may not be necessary if the proceedings are relatively simple or uncontested (primarily, agreed discharges), or if the child is considered mature enough to participate on their own behalf. The children's guardian will be a qualified social worker or probation officer but, to avoid claims of lack of impartiality, must not have worked in the particular social services department involved with the child.

The role of the guardian is to act on behalf of the child and to safeguard the child's interests. In effect, they act as an independent expert who is there to put forward their professional views as to the child's needs and welfare in a given situation. They are entitled to appoint a solicitor for the child and normally this does not cause any difficulty. However, the solicitor's client is, in fact, the child and problems can arise if, for example, there is a mature child who disagrees with the recommendations of the guardian. In this case, the solicitor would have to accept instructions from the child, not the guardian.

As guardians are independent and have a legal right (s 42) to gain access to all the social work files on a case to which they are appointed, their recommendations are given a great deal of weight in the proceedings.

10.9   SUMMARY OF PART ONE

You have now come to the end of a major part of child protection legislation. There is a lot of information here to learn and consolidate. This is not helped by the general lack of reported cases, which should not surprise you since they are mainly in the Family Proceedings Court, and EPOs are not subject to appeal. This will change when you move on to the long term orders under s 31 of the CA 1989.

PART TWO

10.10   LONG TERM ORDERS

The two orders that we are concerned with here are supervision orders and care orders, both of which are dealt with in Pt IV of the CA 1989. The section which establishes the primary criteria for seeking both these orders is s 31, although other sections deal with the consequences of the orders. In this part of the chapter you will study the criteria for, and consequences of, these orders and also a little about the process of making an order in the sense of the court's involvement.

10.11   THE CRITERIA

As indicated, s 31 provides most of the information on what is needed to get either a care or supervision order and this section states:

(1) On the application if any local authority or authorised person, the court may make an order –

   (a) placing the child with respect to whom the application is made in the care of a designated local authority; or

   (b) putting him under the supervision of a designated local authority.

(2) A court may only make a care order or supervision order if it is satisfied –

   (a) that the child concerned is suffering, or is likely to suffer, significant harm; and

(b) that the harm, or likelihood of harm, is attributable to –

(i) the care given to the child, or likely to be given to him if the order were not made, not being what it would be reasonable to expect a parent to give to him; or

(ii) the child's being beyond parental control.

(3) No care order or supervision order may be made with respect to a child who has reached the age of seventeen (or sixteen in the case of a child who is married).

Question

Before analysing the criteria in depth, which of the two orders do you think is the more draconian?

Purely from your reading of s 31(1), and without knowing any of the consequences of the orders, it can be suggested that the supervision order is the less onerous of the two. It merely places the child under the supervision of the local authority, whereas a care order will potentially remove the child from the care of their parents.

Question

Do you think it is appropriate to have the same qualifying criteria for two distinct orders?

You may find this difficult to answer at this stage, but write down your initial thoughts, and then think about this when you have studied more of the chapter.

10.11.1 Section 31(2)

You should have noticed that this subsection has two distinct elements to it. These two elements are often called the 'threshold criteria' since they form the basic evidential threshold to be reached before the court's power to make an order kicks in.

The first stage of the test is to establish that the child 'is suffering or is likely to suffer significant harm'. The second stage is to establish the reason for that harm or risk of harm. The risk of harm should be due to the 'care given to the child ... not being what it would be reasonable to expect a parent to give' or 'the child being beyond parental control', both of which relate the harm suffered by the child to the ability of the parents to care or control. Of the second element only one aspect needs to be proved, that is, that the child is not being given adequate care or is beyond control.

10.11.2 Significant harm

This is a phrase which has run throughout the criteria for orders available to the local authority and their duty to investigate.

Question

How does the reference to significant harm in s 31 differ from that in s 44?

The difference in the wording within the sections is subtle but crucial. The s 44 reference is to reasonable belief that the child is suffering significant harm. In s 47, it was only reasonable suspicion. However, in s 31 the reference is to the fact that the child *is* suffering or *is likely* to suffer. This is a more definite statement: you have gone beyond the realms of belief to actual knowledge. This higher burden is clearly necessary since you are dealing with far more interventionist orders.

10.11.2.1 The meaning of significant harm

Significant harm is defined in s 31 thus:

(9) In this section –

'harm' means ill-treatment or the impairment of health or development including, for example, impairment suffered from seeing or hearing the ill-treatment of another;

'development', means physical, intellectual, emotional, social or behavioural development;

'health' means physical or mental health; and

'ill-treatment' includes sexual abuse and forms of ill-treatment which are not physical.

(10) Where the question of whether harm suffered by a child is significant turns on the child's health or development, his health or development shall be compared with that which could reasonably be expected of a similar child.

The definition in sub-s (9) (and (10)) has been described by Masson and Morris (*Children Act Manual*, 1992, Sweet & Maxwell, p 99) as 'constructed like a Russian doll'. You may or may not agree, but it is true that the definition is not easy to deconstruct.

Harm is clearly defined in sub-s (9) as being 'ill treatment or the impairment of health or development'. These terms are then further defined. The further definitions place more emphasis, than was evident in pre-CA 1989 legislation, on the effects of emotional harm. The impairment of a child's emotional development or socialisation can therefore lead to a possible application.

Question

Do you agree with the definition of significant? Is this sufficient?

When looking at this provision, you should have noted that the means to establish whether harm is significant, given in sub-s (10), only relates to harm to a child's health or development. There is no reference to ill-treatment of the child. Also, comparing a child with another 'similar child' does not really *define* 'significant'; it merely highlights the method used to prove harm is significant.

The Royal Commission on Child Care Law stated, in relation to 'significant', that it meant 'substantial' and that:

> minor shortcomings in the health and care provided or minor deficits in physical, psychological or social developments should not give rise to any compulsory intervention unless they are having, or are likely to have, serious and lasting effects on the child (para 5.15).

Question

If the courts are required to compare one child with another, how should they pick that other child?

While many judges with experience in family matters will have a good knowledge of child development, some will have only a limited knowledge. The decision on whether a child is suffering harm will, thus, be based upon the expert evidence that is put before the court. In relation to comparison under sub-s (10), the Lord Chancellor indicated during the passage of the CA 1989 through Parliament that it referred to a child of similar physical attributes but that the background of the other child should not be brought into account. The Lord Chancellor's view is, however, contradicted by the *Children Act 1989 Guidance and Regulations* (1991, HMSO, Vol 1, Court Orders), which states that: 'the meaning of similar in this context ... may need to take account of environmental, social and cultural characteristics of the child.' This could lead to potential difficulties.

In relation to the meaning of significant harm, you have been referred earlier to the case of *Re O (A Minor) (Care Order: Education: Procedure)* [1992] 1 WLR 912, which looks at this matter. In *Humberside CC v B* [1993] 1 FLR 257, the parents of the child both had mental health difficulties. They had left their young baby, N, alone in their flat and also left her with relatives on numerous occasions. N was also found to have unexplained bruising. The court referred to significant harm by saying it should be seen in the context of all the circumstances of the case and in relation to the particular child. The court accepted the local authority's argument that the fact that the child had suffered bruising when the child was immobile and could not have caused it herself. The fact that there was no explanation and the fact that the parents required constant guidance and support which had not helped protect the child indicated that the child was at risk of suffering significant harm.

In *Re M (Care Order: Parental Responsibility)* [1996] 2 FLR 84, the fact that the parents had abandoned the child on the steps of a health clinic when the child was only a few days old was deemed to constitute significant harm.

10.11.2.2 *When will significant harm need to be proved?*

What is meant by this is at what point in time during the process of intervention must the court be able to say 'the child is suffering, or is likely to suffer significant harm'.

Question

On the diagram below, which indicates a stereotypical care order application, mark the point when you think this issue has to be satisfied.

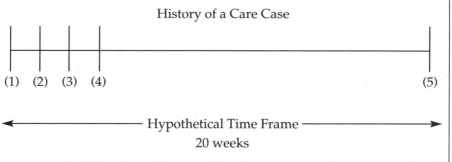

History of a Care Case

(1)   (2)   (3)   (4)   (5)

Hypothetical Time Frame
20 weeks

(1) Local authority begins an investigation under s 47 of the CA 1989.

(2) Local authority provides services under s 17 of the CA 1989.

(3) Crisis occurs, and EPO is obtained under s 44(1)(a).

(4) Application for care order made by local authority under s 31.

Between points (4) and (5), there are numerous direction hearings and appearances to obtain interim care orders under s 38 of the CA 1989.

(5) Final hearing of care order application.

The court will naturally make the decision at the time of the final hearing since this is the time when all the criteria are considered to see if the order can be made. But did you think this was the same point when the significant harm test must be satisfied? The court, if taking the date of the final hearing as the point when the significant harm test must be satisfied, may find itself faced with a situation where the child is not suffering harm since they have been removed from the harmful environment. Hence, the House of Lords has stated that the point to assess significant harm is the time at which the local authority took steps to protect the child. This makes far more sense as at that point there has been no removal from the cause of harm.

Question

Going back to the line diagram, as the local authority is working within the clear non-interventionist framework of the CA 1989, it investigated and then it provided services. Only after the services failed to achieve change was an EPO sought. Which of these events equals 'taking steps to protect'?

While it is not totally clear, and you may of course argue in a different way, it is suggested that the investigation of the family by the local authority is certainly not within the remit of 'taking steps to protect'. The provision of services is somewhat more ambiguous, and it may depend on the nature of services provided. Some services may not include sufficient intervention to be truly protective. The application for the EPO is clearly 'taking steps to protect'.

In *Re M (A Minor) (Care Order: Threshold Conditions)* [1994] 2 AC 424, the mother of a very young child, C, was murdered by the father, F. C was then fostered and a residence order was made in relation to C and three siblings in favour of the mother's cousin, X. F was convicted and recommended for deportation. X applied for a residence order. F agreed with the making of a care order which was granted. X's appeal was allowed by the Court of Appeal and the care order was discharged and replaced by a residence order in favour of X. F appealed to the House of Lords. The House of Lords decided that F's appeal would be allowed. The Court of Appeal did possess the jurisdiction to enable it to make a care order. The care order should be restored so as to allow C's general progress to be monitored by the local authority. The relevant date, under s 31(2) of the CA 1989, on which the court had to be satisfied of threshold criteria was the date on which the local authority had commenced protective arrangements concerning C.

10.11.3 Past, present or future harm?

Question

In relation to s 31(2)(a) of the CA 1989, of the three alternatives in the heading (that is, past, present or future), which do the criteria for harm fall into?

The CA 1989 is focusing on the present and the future risks to the child. It does not act retrospectively by asking what has happened to the child previously.

Question

Does this mean that 'past harm' can never be used evidentially?

The simple fact is that past harm, by itself, will never be enough to satisfy the threshold criteria: past harm must be accompanied by cogent evidence that indicates that the harm may happen in the future. When 'predicting' future harm there does not need to be certainty that it will happen, the criteria state: 'is likely to'. It is often easier to satisfy this test where cumulative harm is concerned, that is, neglect. If you are dealing with a one-off incident, it is much harder to show that it will happen again.

In *Re H and Others* [1996] 1 All ER 1, W had four children, all girls. C1 and C2 were fathered by H, whom W had married in 1979; C3 and C4 were fathered by X, with whom W had lived after separating from H in 1984. In 1993, C1, aged 15, complained to the police, alleging that she had been sexually abused by X since the age of eight. X was charged with rape and C1 was then placed with foster parents. In 1994 the local authority made an application for care orders in relation to C2, C3 and C4. X was acquitted of rape, but the local authority proceeded with their application, which was based on the alleged abuse of C1 by X. The local authority asked the judge to find that X had sexually abused C1, or, at least, that there was a substantial risk that he had done so. The application was dismissed and the Court of Appeal dismissed the local authority's appeal. The local authority appealed to the House of Lords. The House of Lords held that the appeal of the local authority would be dismissed. In order to establish that a child was likely to suffer significant harm in the future (within the meaning of s 31 of the 1989 Act) so as to enable the court to make a care or supervision order, there had to be a real possibility of risk, *based on actual facts rather than mere suspicion.*

Lord Nicholls said that he could not accept the argument that 'likely' within the meaning of s 31 meant 'probable'. 'Likely' was used in the sense of a real possibility, one which could not be sensibly ignored, having regard to the nature and gravity of the feared harm in the particular case. The standard of proof required here was the ordinary civil standard of on the balance of probabilities. To decide that C2, C3 and C4 were at risk because there was a possibility that C1 was abused would be to base a decision not on fact, but on the suspicion that C1 *might* have been abused. That would be to lower the threshold prescribed by Parliament. Parents were not to be at risk of having a child taken from them and removed into the care of the local authority on the basis of suspicions only.

Lord Browne-Wilkinson (dissenting) said that if legal proof of actual abuse was a prerequisite to a finding that a child was at risk of abuse, the court would be powerless to intervene to protect children in relation to whom there were the gravest suspicions of actual abuse but where the necessary evidence legally to prove such abuse was lacking.

Lord Lloyd (dissenting) said that the question was whether, on all the evidence, the court considered that there was a real possibility of the child's suffering significant harm in the future. If so, the threshold criteria were satisfied. The court did not have to be satisfied, on the balance of probabilities, that the child had in fact suffered significant harm in the past, whether by sexual abuse or otherwise, even where the allegation of abuse was the foundation of the local authority's case for a care order.

In the case of *Re D (A Minor) (Care or Supervision Order)* [1993] 2 FLR 423, there was evidence of previous harm to another child but not a sibling. Despite no evidence of harm to the child in question, the court made the care order due to the high risk the father posed. Of particular importance were the nature of the injuries, the criminal conviction, the lack of acknowledgment by the father that he had caused harm, and also the lack of acknowledgment by the mother and wider family that the father posed a problem.

10.11.4 The standard of care by parents

The second element of the threshold criteria concentrates on the cause of harm to the child. This may either be poor care or lack of control.

Question

With regard to the care available to the child, what is the nature of the test?

Poor parenting has for some time been ground for intervention, and the standards to be imposed have, in the past, reflected a very middle class attitude. Even today, it can be questioned whose values of what makes good parenting are being applied.

The standards required are not those of the perfect parent; this is reflected in the fact that minor problems are to be ignored when assessing harm. However, the test to be applied is clearly of an objective nature, that is, not what is *this* parent capable of providing, but what is *a* parent capable of providing by way of care?

Question

Why is 'beyond parental control' included in the criteria?

This existed as a means to obtain a care order under the preceding Children and Young Persons Act 1969, but today it will only be applicable where the child is suffering significant harm. It could be suggested that a child who is beyond control is not being provided with adequate care, and that therefore this duplicates s 31(2)(a). This may be the case, but it is also true to say that parents may be doing all they can for a child, and all that a reasonable parent would do, and still be left with a child beyond their control.

In *M v Birmingham CC* [1994] 2 FLR 141, the child had a history of making allegations against others, including family members, of being harmed, abused or bullied, most allegations being withdrawn. She self-harmed and was admitted to hospital and was later voluntarily accommodated by the local authority. From there she repeatedly absconded. The court was clear that the child was suffering significant harm and also that this was due to her being beyond parental control. There was no evidence to indicate that the harm was due to the level and standard of care that the parents had tried to provide for the child.

10.11.5 Age

Although it is only a short sub-section, you should not overlook the importance of s 31(3), which prohibits the making of a care or supervision order once a child has reached the age of 17 years, or 16 if the child is married. This point needs to be remembered since it is somewhat out of sync with other legislation, and also begs the question of how can the local authority protect children in this age range.

10.11.6 Why the 'threshold' criteria?

Question

Can you think why the criteria are described in this way?

This should not be difficult as you have encountered the reasons before. The answer is simply that the proof that a child may be suffering significant harm, and that this is due to the parents, is only the first hurdle that needs to be overcome. Thereafter, the court is required to consider the welfare of the child, the welfare checklist (since the order is within Pt IV), and the no order principle. Linked to the welfare checklist is the need to consider all other options or other orders that would be available under the CA 1989. Proving the threshold criteria may not result in the order sought.

10.11.7 Other situations where care orders can be made

Following the implementation of the Crime and Disorder Act 1998, a new set of criteria for the making of a care order has been introduced. Prior to the CA 1989, a care order was a legitimate response in criminal proceedings in the juvenile court. As a method of sentencing, it was not popular and so following the *Review of Child Care Law* (1985, HMSO), the powers of the criminal court to make this civil order were removed. However, the 1998 Act has, in a way, reintroduced the civil response to a criminal act.

The 1998 Act creates some new orders with regard to children. You have already come across the curfew notice in relation to s 47 of the CA 1989 investigations. In addition, the 1998 Act introduces the child safety order (CSO). The circumstances when a CSO can be made by the magistrates' court are set out in s 11(3) of the 1998 Act as:

- the child has acted in a criminal manner but because the child is below 10 cannot be charged with a criminal offence;
- the order is necessary to prevent the child committing a criminal act;
- the child has breached a curfew notice, so has been in a public area covered by the curfew notice between the relevant hours and without a responsible adult; and
- the child is behaving in an anti-social manner.

If the local authority seeks a CSO the court will have regard to the factors in s 12 of the Crime and Disorder Act 1998, but it is of note that these do not address issues such as the child's welfare or child's needs *per se*. All that is mentioned is the need to consider the child's family circumstances.

In the event of a breach of the CSO by the child, the CSO may be enforced by the local authority via a responsible officer. The court's powers are set out in s 12(6) and (7) thus:

(6) Where a child safety order is in force and it is proved to the satisfaction of the court which made it or another magistrate's court ... that the child has failed to comply with any of the requirement included in the order, the court

(a) may discharge the order and make in respect of him a care order ...

(7) Subsection (6)(a) above applies whether or not the court is satisfied that the conditions mentioned in section 31(2) of the 1989 Act are fulfilled.

The important thing to note is that if the court makes a care order under the Crime and Disorder Act 1998, it is not required to consider whether the threshold criteria are met, thereby bypassing completely the provisions of the CA 1989. This is a major change, and one that may have significant repercussions for children and local authorities.

10.12   THE PROCESS

As you have seen from the earlier line diagram, a care order application will take a considerable time to complete its passage through the court. This time has, however, been somewhat reduced since the implementation of the CA 1989.

Proceedings for care or supervision orders do not, generally, begin without there having been any involvement with the family by social services. In many local authorities, if an EPO is obtained by way of crisis management, a care order application will invariably follow. However, the gaining of an EPO or CAO is not a prerequisite to the application; neither is the provision of s 17 services.

10.12.1 The applicant

> **Question**
>
> Who is the applicant?

Only two possible applicants exist: the local authority or the NSPCC, as an authorised person (s 31(1)).

As you know, the court cannot make an order of its own motion (again, s 31(1)) and the court cannot make the local authority apply for an order (*Nottinghamshire CC v P* [1993] 3 WLR 637).

By introducing these restrictions, the amount of state involvement should be reduced.

10.12.2 Where to apply and when

Again, you will know that the local authority must make the application to the Family Proceedings Court. Whereas applications for EPOs and CAOs will normally remain in the Family Proceedings Court, in the majority of cases applications for care orders and supervision orders can be, and often are, transferred to other courts. If a case is perceived to be complex, that is, if it will last over three days' duration, if it will involve expert evidence and cross-examination, or if there are other family proceedings with which the application can be consolidated, it may move to the county court or the High Court. Only certain county courts are authorised to deal with care applications, and these courts are named as designated care centres. Any judge dealing with these issues will concentrate on family cases.

Applications must be made on notice which, according to the Children Act rules, will be three days – but these are clear days' notice.

10.12.3 Who will be involved?

The parties to the proceedings will be the child, all persons with PR and, of course, the local authority. If there is a parent without PR (an unmarried father), that parent will be told that the proceedings are taking place. That party may then seek leave to be joined to the proceedings. Once the application has been made, if it was not preceded by an EPO, the court will appoint a guardian for the child.

10.12.4 Directions

The first hearing that will take place in court after the application has been filed, will merely establish the timetable for the running of the matter. The court, having consulted with the parties, will set the dates for the filing of statements, expert reports, the guardian report and the final hearing. Several weeks may be taken up with the process of gathering and exchanging evidence. For the guardian the evidence is crucial since they know nothing or very little about the case at the time of their appointment.

The gap between their initial application and the final hearing is also important to the local authority, which will probably still be in the process of investigating and formulating a future plan for the child.

10.12.5 Care plans

In addition to the production of various statements for the court, the local authority will be required under s 31A to produce a document known as a care plan in relation to the child:

(1) Where an application is made on which a care order might be made with respect to a child, the appropriate local authority must, within such time as the court may direct, prepare a plan ('a care plan') for the future care of the child.

The care plan must contain certain information, as prescribed under statutory instrument. As yet, the requirement to file a care plan is not yet in force, having been inserted into the CA 1989 by the Adoption and Children Act 2002. However, prior to this provision, care plans were required by virtue of case law and so an indication of what will be required can be established. The sort of information required will include:

- the proposed placement: type and details;
- the arrangements for contact and rehabilitation with the family;
- the duration of placement;
- the contingency plans in case of breakdown; and
- the details of the parents' role in day-to-day arrangements.

In *Re J (Minors) (Care: Care Plans)* [1994] 1 FLR 253, the local authority was asking for final care orders in relation to M's four children. The judge was satisfied that the threshold criteria had been met and felt that, in the interests of the welfare of the children, they should be removed from M's care and final orders made. However, a care plan made by the local authority had been modified a few days before the hearing. It proposed placements with foster parents, although no complete matching of the children and foster parents had been undertaken. The guardian opposed final care orders, suggesting the alternative of interim care orders.

The court held that final care orders would be made. The local authority plan must be in line with guidance structures issued by the Department of Health. The threshold criteria had clearly been satisfied and, on the facts, final care orders as issued seemed to be the appropriate course of action to be taken in relation to the four children. In relation to the care plan Wall J stated that:

A properly constructed care plan is not only essential to enable the court to make its decision based on all the known facts; it will or should have been compiled either in consulation with the parents and other interested parties, including where appropriate the child or children involved, or at the very least after taking their views and wishes into account.

The care plan should also, wherever possible, be supported by evidence.

The problem with care plans is the difficulty of enforcing them; if the local authority changes its mind, there is little the court can do. This is because once the care order is made, all control passes to the local authority. The most practical solution, if the care plan is altered, is for an application to discharge the care order to be made by the child's parents or possibly the child themselves. This would seem to be the best means to get a court review. The alternative of judicial review would be more complicated and perhaps less likely to be successful. However, failure by the local authority to comply with the care plan may also result in proceedings under the ECHR since there are Art 8 rights at issue.

Question

What happens if the court does not agree with the local authority's proposals?

Several alternatives could be suggested:

- the court refuses to make the order;
- the court adjourns the final hearing to allow reconsideration;
- the court makes the care order but with conditions attached; or
- the court makes a private law order under s 8 of the CA 1989 (covered in the previous chapter).

Whether any of these are suitable remedies depends upon the nature of the situation, the child's best interests, and the legality of the remedy. Now the court has also to consider the issue of compatibility with the ECHR when deciding on the outcome of the care proceedings.

In *R v W and B (Children) W (Children)* [2001] HRLR 50, the appellants in two cases appealed against the making of full care orders arguing that the CA 1989 was potentially incompatible with Sched 1, Pt 1 of the Human Rights Act 1998, and if not incompatible, that pre-existing case law governing the interpretation and operation of the 1989 Act must be modified. In the first appeal, the care plan had subsequently broken down whilst, in the second appeal, the plan had been made without full and sufficient information and had also failed. It was argued there were potential breaches of the right to respect for family life under Art 8 and of the right of access to the courts under Art 6, as once the care order had been made, all responsibility for the child passed to the local authority and the role of the guardian was removed, which left the children potentially without representation. The absence of an overriding mechanism in the event of a care plan failing was raised as a hurdle in the way of a court which otherwise would have sought to remedy the situation. The Court of Appeal held that the CA 1989 was not fundamentally incompatible with the HRA 1998. The provisions of the CA 1989 were not problematic, but the philosophy surrounding the legislation of the division of responsibility between the court and the local authority raised potential breaches of the HRA 1998. These potential breaches could be avoided by two major adjustments in the application of the care order provisions. First, it was important that judges had a wider discretion to order interim care and were free to defer the full order. Secondly, the development of the care plan should be collaborative, elevating important milestones to a 'starred status'. If these highlighted factors, ie, those with starred status, were not achieved within a reasonable time, the matter should return to the court.

Despite this view, creating or elevating key factors to a 'starred status' is not happening in practice.

10.12.6 What happens to the child whilst proceedings are ongoing?

While all this investigation and report writing is proceeding, the child will have to be cared for.

Question

If the application is for a care order, will it be appropriate for the child to remain with its parents?

In some cases, the child may be left with their parents, but these are likely to be the minority of cases. If a child has been removed under an EPO it is very unlikely that a return will be planned until the s 31 proceedings are concluded. Hence, the court can make interim care orders under the provisions of s 38 of the CA 1989. The section provides two situations where an interim order may be made:

- where care or supervision order proceedings are adjourned; and
- where the court has requested a s 37 investigation.

It is very important to be aware of the limited situations in which the court's powers to make interim care orders (ICOs) arise. A local authority cannot apply for an ICO as a stand alone order, and so an ICO is not a protective option in that sense.

In both situations, under s 38(2), the court must have reasonable grounds for believing that the threshold criteria are satisfied.

> **Question**
>
> Does this mean that the making of an ICO will guarantee that a full care order is made?

When an ICO is made, it is made without the benefit of all the relevant evidence. Hence, the burden to be satisfied regarding the threshold criteria is lower. The court is not looking for absolute proof that the threshold will be satisfied, but the reasonable belief that it will – not the same at all. The making of a s 38 order will not, therefore, mean that the full order will necessarily be made.

It is worth remembering that when the court makes an interim care order, it has discretion to include an exclusion requirement (s 38A). This works in a similar way to exclusion requirements for EPO's under s 44A (if you cannot recall these, re-read the relevant pages).

The court can, therefore, leave a child in its home with a carer who the court believes is able to meet the child's needs, and yet exclude others who the court believes are responsible for the harm being suffered by the child.

The court may also accept an undertaking to leave the property from the person viewed as being the source of harm (s 38B).

To comply with the 'no delay' principles of the CA 1989, ICOs are time limited. To prevent a child drifting in care due to the court system, under s 38 an ICO can initially be made for a maximum of eight weeks. It may be necessary to renew this order, and any renewals can be for up to four weeks' duration. On each renewal the court must reasonably believe the threshold criteria to be met.

10.12.7 Assessments

Under s 38(6), the court can give directions as to assessments that are to be undertaken during the course of the ICO. The CA 1989 refers specifically to medical and psychiatric assessments.

> **Question**
>
> Could the court order a residential assessment, that is, one whereby the mother (and sometimes father) are observed and supervised in a residential setting (often called mother and baby units)?

An assessment of this sort is clearly focused on the capabilities of the parents, and yet the section indicates that the assessment must be of the child. This issue is one which has led to judicial comment in the case of *Re C*

(Interim Care Order: Residential Assessment) [1997] 1 FLR 1, decided by the House of Lords, where the view was that such assessments were within the remit of s 38, since without such an assessment the court would be prevented from having all the relevant evidence to hand. However, the opinion of the House of Lords could lead to some difficult decisions for local authorities, especially when financial constraints are taken into account. Is it right to spend several thousands of pounds on assessing one child's parents, especially if the result can be predicted as being negative, and deprive several other children from receiving services or preventive work? The decision in *Re C* did not rule out the costs argument being successful; it has just made it harder to run.

10.13   THE FINAL HEARING: WHAT ARE THE OPTIONS?

If the court is satisfied, at the final hearing, that the local authority has proved the threshold criteria at the time when steps to protect the child were taken, it may then make the order sought.

Question

What are the other issues or factors that the court must consider before making the order?

You should have thought of:

- the welfare of the child;
- the welfare checklist;
- the other options available under the CA 1989; and
- no order at all.

10.13.1 No order

Question

If a court has found that the threshold criteria have been satisfied, can it ever be said to be in the child's interests for the child to return to the parents without the making of an order?

The concepts may seem contradictory. However, the court may believe that the parents will co-operate in a satisfactory manner to ensure the child's welfare is protected (in many cases of this sort the court will make a supervision order). In addition, there is a growing body of research which would suggest that the removal of a child from their home environment by virtue of a care order is more damaging to the long term welfare than leaving the child where they are. Also, the very nature of the care system may result in longer term harm. Many children who have been through the care system have lower than average qualifications, little or no real employment prospects and a higher chance of being involved in crime.

10.13.2 Other options

Despite the proceedings being commenced in the public law domain, the court can make a s 8 residence order if it deems it appropriate. In developing its care plan, the local authority should have regard to the extended family of the child, and consider whether suitable carers can be found from this category of individuals. The fact that the local authority may support the placement of the child within the wider family does not necessarily mean that it will not wish to have a care order. In some cases though, the local authority will be perfectly amenable to the making of a s 8 of the CA 1989 residence order (covered in the previous chapter). To illustrate this, consider the following example:

> Anne had a relationship with Bill and conceived a child. They split up before the birth of Christopher. Bill has so far played no role in the child's life. Anne presents at the casualty department of her local hospital with Christopher and non-accidental injuries are diagnosed. Anne is believed to have beaten and burnt Christopher repeatedly. The local authority commences care proceedings. They give notice of the application to Bill, but as an unmarried father without parental responsibility he is not a party to the proceedings. Bill has now settled down, has a stable relationship and a reasonable job. He and his new girlfriend wish to care for Christopher. The local authority assesses the couple and agrees that their care would be appropriate, as does the children's guardian. At the final hearing the local authority recommends the making of a s 8 order.

If the court agreed with the local authority and the children's guardian on the outcome, a s 8 order could be made, without Bill having even been party to the proceedings. However, in the majority of cases where a s 8 order is sought, the party seeking it will apply for leave (if necessary) to be joined to the proceedings. One difficulty with the making of s 8 orders is that the local authority has no means to control or dictate how the child is cared for. Hence, the court may consider the need to impose conditions on the residence order, or combine it with a supervision order. However, in the main, the use of private law remedies in public law cases seems to work. If Bill and the local authority were at odds on the outcome, it would definitely be necessary for him to seek leave to join the proceedings in order to ensure that his case was fully explored.

10.13.3 Care versus supervision

Under s 31(5) the court has the power:

  (a) on an application for a care order, [to] make a supervision order;

  (b) on an application for a supervision order, [to] make a care order.

The ability of the court to do this stems from the fact that the criteria to be fulfilled to obtain the orders are exactly the same. However, the court, as arbiter, may disagree with the 'expert' opinion of social workers and the children's guardian when it comes to the nature of the state intervention and the welfare of the child. The debate over care orders or supervision orders is frequently found within the law reports. In the following cases, some of the factors that led the court to their decision are highlighted:

- *Re D* **[1993] 2 FLR 423**
  - the father's history of violence and failure to acknowledge the same;
  - the father's failure to undergo therapeutic treatment;
  - the mother's inability to accept the level of risk posed and also her inability to protect the child;
  - the family's poor relationship with social services;
  - the ability of the local authority to leave the child living with parents under a care order; and
  - poor enforceability and safeguards under a supervision order.

- *Re O (Care or Supervision Order)* **[1996] 2 FLR 755**
  - the limited duration of the supervision order would mean more overseeing by the court;
  - the improvements that had occurred in relation to weight gain;
  - the co-operation with other agency workers (family centre); and
  - the need to build a good relationship with the social workers.

- *Re B (Care or Supervision Order)* **[1996] 2 FLR 693**
  - the fact that the father had kept away from the children and the home;
  - the fact that if the father were to return, EPOs would be applied for;
  - the effect on the mother if care orders were made; and
  - the ability of the local authority to meet the children's needs under the supervision order if the order was subject to conditions.

Naturally, these cases will only give you an illustration of the sorts of things that will be relevant to the balancing exercise that the court will undertake. In all the cases there was a strong emphasis on the children's welfare.

10.14   THE CONSEQUENCES OF THE ORDERS

One of the fundamental distinctions between these two orders lies in the consequences, some of which you will have gleaned from your reading to date.

10.14.1 Care orders

The consequences of making a care order are set out in ss 33 and 34 but do not raise many theoretical difficulties and, in reality, they do not seem to raise many practical difficulties.

10.14.1.1 Section 33: suitable accommodation; parental responsibility

Once a care order is made, the child is to be placed in the care of the local authority. Due to this, the local authority has a duty to provide suitable accommodation for the child.

Question

What types of accommodation are potentially suitable?

There are several possibilities with regard to accommodation for a child in care. The child may be placed in foster care, which acts as a substitute family. If the local authority's care plan set out a rehabilitation scheme for the child and their family, then short term fosterers would be used. If rehabilitation is unlikely, long term fosterers would need to be found. All foster carers must be approved by the local authority before they can act as such (there are situations where a child can be placed without the requisite approvals, but this is where it is an emergency). Linked to long term fostering, the child may be seen as suitable for adoption. Here the child may be placed with foster parents until an adoptive placement is identified. Children's homes are uncommon nowadays and, if used, tend to focus on older children, and often those who will shortly be reaching adulthood. Children's homes are also subject to approval and must comply with certain regulations. The local authority may decide to place a child with their wider family; even though there may be a blood tie, this would in effect be nothing more than a foster placement. Finally, the child may be returned to their parents. This is permissible but, before the placement can take place, the local authority must comply with the requirements of the Placement of Children with Parents etc Regulations 1991 (SI 1991/893).

Following the making of a care order the local authority will gain PR under s 33(3) and may determine the extent to which parents can utilise their PR. The making of the care order will not extinguish the parents' PR, but the local authority can restrict the use made of it by parents. To all intents and purposes, the local authority will be the parent. The ability to restrict the parents is dependent upon the placement. If the child is returned to its parents, the local authority will not be in a position to make all decisions for the child, but would expect to participate in major decisions. Likewise, good social work practice (and compliance with the ECHR) would indicate that where a child is in care, the local authority endeavours to encourage parental participation in major decision making.

> **Question**
>
> When would this be unsuitable?

The continued involvement of parents would need to be assessed in the light of the child's welfare. In addition, if the plan for the child is adoption, it could be argued to be unfair to parents to continue to allow participation in decision making if ultimately all links will be ended (you will learn more about adoption in Chapter 11).

Not all decisions that form part of PR can be taken by the local authority. Section 33(6) and (7) restricts the local authority in that they are unable to change the child's religion; consent to the child's adoption; appoint a testamentary guardian (a person appointed to care for a child in the event of the parents' death, the appointment being made normally in a will); change the child's surname; or remove the child from the UK for over a month. The last two are permitted if the agreement of all with PR is obtained or the court agrees to it.

10.14.1.2 Section 34: reasonable contact

Under s 34 there is a presumption that reasonable contact will take place and hence there is no automatic need for an order. It is only where the parents or the individual seeking contact and the local authority disagree as to what is reasonable, or the local authority does not believe contact to be in the best interests of the child that an order should be sought.

The issue of contact should be included within the care plan that is produced by the local authority for the final hearing and the court is specifically required to consider contact under s 34(11) before making the order. Failure to address this point may lead to the application being dismissed (at worst), and almost certainly being adjourned. This issue is also clearly linked to the jurisprudence from the European Court of Human Rights.

> **Question**
>
> Can the local authority prohibit contact?

If the child is to be adopted, or the parents' behaviour to the child is such as to cause distress and harm, the local authority may wish to stop contact totally. This will need to be brought before the court, as the presumption of contact can only be rebutted by the making of an order. That order, for 'no contact', will be under s 34. However, in some cases the need to terminate contact may only arise as a matter of urgency; for example, if the child makes an allegation of abuse, claiming that the abuse happened during the contact. In this situation the local authority can terminate contact, without the need to go to court, for a maximum of seven days (*per* s 34(6)).

In *Berkshire CC v B* [1997] 1 FLR 171, the care order had been made with contact to M. The local authority appealed against the making of the contact order. The court held that there were a range of cases that came before them regarding contact; those where the child needs a new family and contact with the birth family will bring no benefit to the child and impede the placement of the child; those where the child is likely to return home so contact is essential to ensure this happens and those where although a return home is not likely, the relationship with the birth family is of importance to the child and hence some form of contact should be maintained. The requirement in these latter cases is for the advantages of contact to be balanced against the disadvantages that will arise, bearing in mind that contact may result in difficulties finding a suitable placement. The local authority cannot approach contact on a take it or leave it basis.

10.14.1.3 *Duration of the order*

You will recall, from your earlier reading, that no court can make a care order in respect of a child who is aged 17. However, despite this restriction, a care order will, unless brought to an end earlier, last until the child reaches majority at the age of 18.

It can be ended earlier by the court making a s 8 residence order (which you may recall from s 9 of the CA 1989 is the only s 8 order that can be made with respect to a child in care). The care order may also end by being discharged (and on discharge the situation returns to how it was before the care order). Section 39 of the CA 1989 deals with discharge and who can apply. Most discharge applications are commenced by local authorities. However, you should note the implication of sub-ss (4) and (5) of s 39, which permit the court to substitute a supervision order for a care order without the need to establish the existence of the threshold criteria. The same is not true of converting a supervision order into a care order.

10.14.2 Supervision orders

10.14.2.1 *Consequences under s 35*

The main consequence of the supervision order is that the local authority will have to appoint a supervisor whose role is to advise, assist and befriend the child. Sched 3 to the CA 1989 states the child may also be subject to conditions in relation to residence, attendance at specified places or participation in specified activities. Medical and psychiatric assessments may also be carried out on the supervised child, although in respect of these conditions the mature child can in effect veto them (para 4(4)). Treatment may also be specified, but only for the purposes of treating the child's mental health. It is interesting to note that this power overlaps with the powers available under the Mental Health Act 1983 to permit detention for treatment, and yet under the 1983 Act treatment can be given in the face of opposition whereas under the CA 1989 a mature child can veto treatment.

Question

Does the local authority get PR under a supervision order or the power to remove the child?

The answer is no, unless of course the order permits the supervisor to require the child to live in a specified place (which may not be with the parents). In this situation PR for the child on a day-to-day basis will have to be delegated by the parents to the temporary carer, or s 3(5) will need to be utilised.

10.14.2.2 Enforcement

Question

What powers do you think the supervisor has in the event of non-compliance?

Section 35 states that one of the functions of the supervisor is to consider whether or not to apply for the variation of the supervision order or for its discharge in the event that the order is not wholly complied with (s 35(1)(c)(i)). However, the variation of the order is restricted to obtaining the right to impose conditions if conditions were not initially imposed. The success of the order with new conditions is questionable if the first attempt at supervision has failed.

Question

Can the supervisor apply for the order to be varied to a care order?

Although the supervision order can only be obtained after proving the same threshold criteria as for a care order, the 'trading up' of orders is not permissible. As we saw in the section on the duration of care orders, the opposite is available, ie, trading a care order for a supervision order, but this is justifiable only on the basis that the orders are being 'traded down' from care to supervision. If a care order is believed to be necessary, a supervision order having failed, a new application must be made and the threshold criteria satisfied. The failure of the supervision order will, of course, be evidence of the need to make an order, but the making of the care order is not a certainty. The lack of enforcement powers for a supervision order may tip the balance in favour of a care order in some cases.

It has been suggested that a supervision order will only work if co-operation already exists. If that is the case, then to what principle should the court have regard?

You should immediately have thought of s 1(5), the no order principle.

Duration

As the supervision order is less draconian than the care order, it lasts for a shorter period of time.

Question

How long do you think the supervision order lasts?

The initial time limit on a supervision order is one year (Sched 3, Pt II, para 6(1)). It may, however, be extended upon the application of the supervisor for a period not in excess of two years (para 6(3)), although any extension cannot take the supervision order beyond the child's 18th birthday or give a total period in excess of three years.

This necessity to renew the order, whilst it may be argued to be a time wasting exercise, at least requires the local authority to review the matter and to deliberate on the case. Again, this supports the idea of limiting the amount of time during which child care matters may be allowed to 'drift', and also supports the reduction of state intervention.

In addition to this time limit, the order may be brought to an end by an application to discharge by the same range of applicants as for care orders.

10.15   APPEALS

Unlike the EPO, the making of, or failure to make, a care order or supervision order may be appealed. The court will have the power to make certain orders pending the appeal being heard, that is:

- to permit the care order to take effect whilst the appeal is ongoing; or

- to continue the existence of an ICO (if one was in operation at the time of the final hearing) pending the outcome of an appeal against the refusal to make a full care order or supervision order (s 40 of the CA 1989).

10.16   SUMMARY OF PART TWO

You have now finished the bulk of your studying on the public law intervention into families in respect of children and their care. We will look at post-care matters and options for the local authority outside of the CA 1989 in Chapters 11 and 12 when you consider adoption law and wardship. These areas also cover private law too. However, you should now be able to advise clients, whether they be individuals or local authority social workers, in respect of the legal means to protect children. You should always commence your thought processes by considering voluntary action or the legal steps which have the least draconian intervention by the state. You should also be able to identify situations where a voluntary or 'softly-softly' approach is inappropriate.

10.17   END OF CHAPTER ASSESSMENT

Helen is grandmother to Imogen (nine). Imogen lives with her mother, Janet, and has no knowledge of her birth father who was in fact married to someone else at the time of Imogen's birth. Five months ago Janet's boyfriend Kevin moved into the house. Helen has become increasingly concerned about Imogen since then as Imogen has told her that she is not allowed to talk at meal times and if she does not clear her plate she is slapped by Kevin and that this hurts. Imogen has also told Helen that Kevin locks her in the garden shed if she has been naughty and has left her there for several hours. More recently, Imogen has complained that she has been locked in the back garden when Janet and Kevin have friends round to the house when they smoke 'something with a funny smell'. Helen has tried to raise her concerns with Janet but was told to mind her own business and that Kevin is merely trying to teach Imogen good manners. Helen did not accept this and has contacted the social services.

Discuss the legal powers and duties that the social worker will have available to them.

CHAPTER 11

ADOPTION

11.1   OBJECTIVES

By the end of this chapter you should be able to:

- provide an explanation of adoption, what it is and what the effects are;
- describe the procedures for arranging adoptions;
- explain the legal requirements in adoption;
- highlight the distinctions between legal and non-legal requirements in relation to local authority placements;
- relate the adoption legislation to the provisions of the Children Act (CA) 1989; and
- advise hypothetical clients.

The topic of adoption is one which will overlap both public and private law, although it will more frequently be more of an issue in public law since local authorities may regard adoption as the best means of promoting the long term care of children. In private law, the majority of cases arise where step-parents wish to adopt their step-children. The law regarding both situations is fundamentally the same; there are a few small distinctions with procedures, which will be made apparent during this chapter. Your studying will take the form of considering the main issues involved in adoption law and this will be on the basis that the Adoption and Children Act 2002 (ACA 2002) is fully in force, although full implementation is not expected until late 2004. Hence, all references will be to the ACA 2002 unless indicated otherwise.

11.2   WHAT IS ADOPTION?

11.2.1   A recent phenomenon

As a legal procedure, adoption was only introduced into our system in 1926 in the Adoption of Children Act 1926, although many children, prior to this were, in fact, in what would be perceived as adoptive relationships. The nature of adoption introduced in 1926 was not the same as today, the legal consequences being somewhat different. As child protection and the role of the local authority developed, adoption was increasingly seen as a means of providing a caring environment for children who could not otherwise live with their parents. The Adoption of Children Act 1926 was repealed and since then we have had several Acts dealing with adoption. The latest, the

ACA 2002, replaced the Adoption Act 1976, following several years of debate on how a modern adoption law should be framed.

11.2.2   A declining phenomenon

Adoption was very popular and the 'heyday' for the process was in the late 1960s. In 1968 the number of adoption orders made reached nearly 25,000. By 2003 the total number of adoption applications had reduced to 4,870 with only 4,713 orders made, less than one-fifth of the 1968 figures. It is evident that for some reason adoption is losing popularity.

Question

Can you think of any reasons why this might be?

Some reasons for the decline in adoptions are: the change in society's attitude to single parenthood, and 'illegitimacy'; the possible opportunities for women to work and raise children; and, possibly, the availability of welfare benefits. It is now no longer unusual for single women to keep their children. This is true for women, and girls, of all ages. Neither is it expected that single mothers will put their babies up for adoption, or be pressurised into doing so. Those single women who did not wish to have their children adopted, but wished to hide the fact of their illegitimacy, were able to do so by adopting their own child, as a single person. The law recognised the child as legitimate. This can still happen today.

Additionally, today there exist other orders which may achieve similar aims to adoption. The residence order, under s 8 of the CA 1989, is a potential alternative to adoption for step-parents or other familial carers. Despite these alternatives, step-parents still seem keen to seek the 'security' that an adoption order can bring, with 1,287 applications and 1,172 orders in 2003. The amendments to the CA 1989 to permit a step-parent to gain PR without the need for getting a s 8 of the CA 1989 order may result in a reduction to these figures although this remains to be seen.

11.2.3   Who is adopted?

With the trend away from adoption, there has also been a change in the type of children who are adopted.

Question

If you had to give a stereotype of an adopted child, what would it be?

For the majority of people, the image of an adopted child is a baby, or very young child, who will be adopted by a childless couple. However, that is not the reality; so called 'baby adoptions' are in the minority of all adoptions. In 2002 only 5% of adoptions were in respect of this group, with a total of 76% of adoptions being in relation to children under 10 years at the time of the order.

Adoption is now a potential long term option for children in care, who are unlikely to be rehabilitated with their birth families, and the government would like to see the numbers adopted from care increased dramatically. In many cases, though, these children will have behavioural problems, or may be suffering from varying degrees of impairment, which may make adoption harder to achieve. This changing face of adoption has led to the implementation of the ACA 2002 and to a change in emphasis on the assessment of who wants to adopt and the qualities expected from adoptive parents.

11.3   WHAT ARE THE EFFECTS OF ADOPTION?

Question

What do you think are the consequences of adoption?

Section 67 sets out the primary concept of adoption, that is, an adopted person is to be treated in law as the child of the adopter(s) and is the legitimate child of the adopter(s). The order is one which gives parental responsibility (PR) to the adoptive parent(s) and extinguishes any PR held by the birth parents (or anyone else) (s 46(1)). Hence it is, in effect, recreating the legal relationship between child and adoptive parents that would otherwise have existed between child and birth parents.

Question

Will this relationship end when the child reaches their majority?

Whilst in strict legal terms PR does end on majority the practicalities of life mean that the relationship, which an adopted child has with its adoptive parents, will continue after the age of 18. Indeed, because the adoption order recreates a legal relationship, the rules on succession and intestacy will apply to the new adoptive family, and will last until death. Hence, an adoptive child becomes a child for the purposes of their adoptive parents' wills or death intestate (ss 69 and 70). The ability to inherit on intestacy from the birth family is, accordingly, extinguished. Other such areas of law where the fact of adoption may have an impact are set out in ss 69–76 of the ACA 2002.

There are situations where links will be retained with the birth family, that is, where there exists a peerage, dignity or title which is hereditary (not likely to affect many cases of adoption), and the ability to marry. An adopted child will remain within the prohibited degrees with all the specified birth family members in Sched 1 to the Marriage Act 1949 (s 74(1)) and, in addition, will be prevented from marrying their adoptive parents. However, there is no prohibition on an adopted child marrying his or her adoptive sibling.

11.4   WHO CAN BE ADOPTED?

Whilst we have already seen that the nature of adoption has changed over the last decade or two, it is important to be aware of the legal restrictions on who can be adopted.

The limitations in law relate to the child's age and status. A child must be below 19-years-old (although this provision (s 47) does mean an adult of 18 may be adopted!) and cannot be adopted if they have been married. The reference to marriage presumably means a valid marriage or a voidable one. In addition, the ACA 2002 establishes a minimum age for adoption, and this is related to the requirement that the adopted child live with the applicants before the application can be granted. These restrictions are set out in s 42 and require:

- 10 weeks residence before application if the child is placed via a local authority placement for adoption, or by order of the High Court, or the applicant is the child's parent;
- six months if the applicant is the partner of the child's parent; or
- one year if the applicant is a local authority foster parent and the placement was for the purposes of foster care, not adoption.

Finally, it is worth remembering that until the child is six weeks old the mother cannot give valid consent to the adoption – we will be looking at consent in more detail later.

11.5   WHO CAN ADOPT?

The legal requirements concerning who can adopt are potentially weaker than the requirements placed on prospective adopters by the local authorities who arrange adoptions. Any local authority, which operates as an adoption agency, may establish its own policy guidelines. The legal requirements are set out primarily in ss 49–51 and state:

- an application can be made by a couple or one person;
- at least one of the couple, or the single applicant, must be domiciled in part of the British Isles;
- both of the couple, or the single applicant, must be habitually resident in part of the British Isles for a minimum of one year;

- both the couple, or the single applicant, must be 21 years of age unless the application is by a couple and one is the parent of the child and they have reached the age of 18 years, provided the other is 21;
- a married person can apply as a single applicant if their spouse cannot be found, they are separated and this is likely to be permanent, the spouse is unable to apply due to ill-health; and
- the applicants must be deemed suitable with reference to any relevant regulations.

Unlike the previous Adoption Act 1976, where a step-parent is seeking to adopt a step-child, the application need not be by the parent and the step-parent; s 52(2) permits the application to be by the step-parent alone. Also, the ACA 2002 tries to restrict birth parents adopting their own children (and, hence, ensure they are legitimate) by requiring that a birth parent may only adopt their own child if:

- the other parent is dead or cannot be found;
- due to the impact of the Human Fertilisation and Embryology Act 1990 there is no other parent (for example, where the birth parent has received fertility treatment as a single person using donor gametes and, hence, under the 1990 Act any resulting child will have only one legal parent, that is, the mother); or
- there is a reason why adoption by a parent is deemed necessary.

In *Re B (Minor) (Adoption by Natural Parent)* [2002] 1 WLR 258, the House of Lords considered the sort of situations when one of the natural parents should be excluded from the life of the child. Although in connection with the Adoption Act 1976, the court stated that: 'there had to be some reason justifying the exclusion of the other natural parent and that reason had to outweigh the adverse consequences of such an order upon the child's life.'

Question

What about a homosexual or lesbian couple: can they adopt jointly?

Before the ACA 2002, if a same-sex couple wished to adopt a child, the only means to do so would be for one applicant to apply as a single person and if the adoption were to be granted, for the couple to seek a joint s 8 residence order under the CA 1989. Generally, there was some concern about a child being raised in this type of environment, although far less than in the past.

In *AMT (Known as AC) (Petitioners for Authority to Adopt SR)* [1994] Fam Law 225 (a case under Scottish law although the provisions were the same as in England and Wales), the child was disabled and had been taken into care at birth. Difficulties had been encountered in finding a suitable placement, and eventually the child was placed with the petitioner and his long term male partner. The application for an adoption order was refused on the basis that the mother was reasonable in refusing consent and that adoption by a homosexual applicant, who planned to raise the child with a same-sex partner, was contrary to principle. On appeal, in relation to the latter point, the court stated that there was no fundamental objection to an adoption order in these circumstances. The legislation did not prohibit an application by a homosexual and the requirement to take on board the characteristics of the parties cannot prevail over the need to meet the needs of the child. Hence, the adoption order would be granted.

The prospect of adoptions by same-sex or cohabiting couples proved to be one of the main areas of contention in the passing of the ACA 2002. However, despite attempts by the House of Lords to prevent non-married couples adopting, s 50 does not require the couple to be married, hence enabling same-sex and heterosexual cohabiting couples to apply jointly. They will however have to satisfy s 45, which states:

> (2) In particular, the regulations [on suitability] may make provision for the purpose of securing that, in determining the suitability of a couple to adopt a child, proper regard is had to the need for stability and permanence in their relationship.

Although this can be directed at married applicants, it is inevitable that there will be an emphasis on non-married couples establishing the permanence, etc, of their relationship.

Question

What are the potential difficulties in permitting non-married couples to adopt?

One of the main concerns expressed at the time the Bill was passing through Parliament was what would happen if the relationship ended, with some commentators suggesting that the child would have to go back into local authority care. However, both the adoptive parents would be treated as legal parents, both would have PR, and both would be able to access s 8 of the CA 1989 orders to regulate where and with whom the child should live. In other words, the situation would be exactly the same as if the adoptive couple had been married.

Question

These are the legal restrictions in relation to applicants. Can you think of any others that may be imposed by an adoption agency?

As mentioned above, any body acting as an adoption agency may impose its own requirements on potential applicants. While local authorities fulfil the major role in acting as agencies (indeed, under s 3 of the ACA 2002 every local authority has to establish services for adoption or secure them via an approved adoption agency), other bodies may be approved to act as such. In many cases these adoption societies are part of a religious body.

Frequently imposed criteria include the following:

- a maximum age: often 35 or sometimes 40 if there are already adopted children in the family;
- the requirement that couples are childless or infertile or not undergoing fertility treatment;
- the requirement that potential adopters are non-smokers;
- a certain level of physical fitness, and that adopters are not obese;
- a preferred religion; and
- an unwillingness to use corporal punishment.

You may have thought of other possible conditions.

When an applicant wishes to adopt, there will be a variety of reports prepared on them, including such matters as health and lifestyle. You may therefore query why there need to be additional requirements such as those listed above. The primary reason is linked to the long term welfare of the child. If a parent is unfit, unhealthy and overweight, it does not bode well for the future health of the child (or so the reasoning goes). It is also more likely that such a parent would be at greater risk of early death or disability or permanent ill-health.

Question

If an applicant is classed as being too old, on local authority guidelines, can they challenge the decision?

As the policy guidelines are not statutory, the only means of challenging the decision is by way of judicial review, arguing that the decision is unreasonable, or one that no reasonable authority would have reached on the facts. In addition, as the policy should be discretionary, it can be argued that applying it without recognition of the individual case and facts is a fettering of discretion. This argument was tried in the case of *R v Lancashire CC ex p M* [1992] 1 FLR 109, but without success.

As we saw earlier, there is currently government concern at the delay and inefficiencies within the adoption service. Children who would benefit from adoption are not identified as being suitable, or, if they are, cannot be matched with 'ideal adopters'. The use of policy to restrict the range of adopters is a matter that has been addressed by the Department of Health in its various policy documents and guidance, with the National Adoption Standards – policy with the force of law – being one of the most important produced. One of the more contentious aims of the new standards is for all children looked after by local authorities to have permanence planning once they have been looked after for six months. What this will mean is that all local authorities will have to plan possible adoption for children they are looking after, even if there is the prospect of rehabilitation with the birth family.

11.6 WHO CAN ARRANGE ADOPTIONS?

There are strict rules governing the placement of children for adoption, although, of course, ways around the provisions can be found. However, establishing the rules is not easy under the new ACA 2002.

The following are expected to be the main methods of placing a child:

- via an adoption agency, with or without a placement order;
- via an order of the High Court;
- with a partner of the child's parent; and
- via placement for the purposes of fostering where the applicants are foster carers and have had the child living with them for the required length of time.

Where a local authority is arranging an adoptive placement, it will have to have regard to the suitability of the prospective adopters in light of the legal requirements under the ACA 2002 and also its own policy guidelines. The assessment of the adopters is not solely done by social workers acting on behalf of the local authority, since all prospective adopters must also be approved by an adoption panel (or similar if the placement is by a non-local authority agency). The panel will comprise social workers, a member of the local authority social services committee, medical adviser, and two independent persons. The panel will not only consider the adopters, but also the suitability of this placement with these adopters and this individual child.

11.6.1 Placement by the adoption agency

Unless the child is being adopted by their step-parent, the majority of adoptions will arise due to the placement of the child for adoption through the local authority acting as adoption agency. Section 18 of the ACA 2002 permits the agency to place children only if the agency is satisfied that the child ought to be placed for adoption (sub-s (2)). Before the placement can occur the agency must ensure compliance with s 19, which states:

(1) Where an adoption agency is satisfied that each parent or guardian of a child has consented to the child –

(a) being placed for adoption with prospective adopters identified in the consent, or

(b) being placed for adoption with any prospective adopters who may be chosen by the agency,

and has not withdrawn consent, the agency is authorised to place the child for adoption accordingly.

However, if the child is subject to care proceedings or, subsequent to the giving of consent, a care order or placement order has been made, the local authority cannot act on any parental consent to place for adoption other than by seeking a placement order for the child (placement orders are covered below).

For the purposes of placement (and the making of the adoption order) consent is defined in s 52(5) as being: '... consent given unconditionally and with full understanding of what is involved; but a person may consent to adoption without knowing the identity of the person in whose favour the order will be made.'

Unconditional consent is a concept that was in place in the Adoption Act 1976 and requires that the parent must understand the full extent and impact of the adoption order, and not try to place restrictions on it, such as agreeing only on condition that contact will be continued post-order.

If the parent(s) do not give consent to the placing of the child for adoption, or the child is subject to care proceedings, the only way the agency can proceed is by applying for a placement order. These orders are covered in s 21, which defines the order as being one that authorises the agency to place with prospective adopters of the agency's choosing. The order can only be made if:

> (2) (a) the child is subject to a care order;
>
> (b) the court is satisfied that the conditions in s 31(2) of the 1989 Act ... are met; or
>
> (c) the child has no parent or guardian.
>
> (3) The court may only make a placement order if, in the case of each parent or guardian of the child, the court is satisfied –
>
> (a) that the parent or guardian has consented to the child being placed for adoption with any prospective adopters who may be chosen by the local authority and has not withdrawn the consent; or
>
> (b) that the parent's or guardian's consent should be dispensed with.

Hence, if the child is subject to a care order made after the consent to placement was given, or the agency believes that the criteria for making a care order would be met, they must seek a placement order to which the parent(s) can consent. If the care order has been made before consent to placement is given by the parents, the agency can place without a placement order under the terms of s 22(3), but this is anticipated to be an unusual practice – inevitably the agency will seek the order. If the parent(s) will not give consent to placement, the agency can seek to have that consent dispensed with. The grounds for dispensing with consent, a notion that was in the previous legislation, have been narrowed considerably. Under the terms of s 52, the court:

> (1) ... cannot dispense with the consent of any parent or guardian of a child to the child being placed for adoption or to the making of an adoption order in respect of the child unless the court is satisfied that –

(a) the parent or guardian cannot be found or is incapable of giving consent; or

(b) the welfare of the child requires the consent to be dispensed with.

We will look at the welfare test shortly; the first ground for dispensing with consent is, however, unproblematic.

11.6.2 Placement via other means

As you are aware, only half of the adoption orders made each year are as a result of placement via the adoption agency. The remainder arise from other forms of placement, the most common being where a child lives with one of their birth parents and a step-parent.

In these circumstances the local authority will still be involved in the adoption proceedings since the ACA 2002 requires the prospective adopters to give notice of intention to adopt under s 44. According to this section: '(5) On receipt of a notice of intention to adopt, the local authority must arrange for the investigation of the matter and submit to the court a report of the investigation.' This investigation will focus on the suitability of the adopters, and also the welfare of the child.

There are time limits specified in the ACA 2002 as to how far before the application to adopt is made that this notice of intention must be given.

11.7   THE MAKING OF THE ADOPTION ORDER

In relation to the making of the order, the court is primarily required to consider two issues, ie:

* whether the conditions for making the order under s 47 been met; and
* whether the child's welfare requires them to be adopted.

Naturally, there are other things the court will have to confirm, for example, are the adopters actually qualified to adopt under the terms of the legislation, and these are factors that should also be confirmed by the agency before placing the child, or during their investigation under s 44 of the ACA 2002.

11.7.1   Conditions for making adoption orders

Under s 47, before a court can make an adoption order it must be satisfied that one of three conditions is met. These are stated thus:

(2) The first condition is that, in the case of each parent or guardian of the child, the court is satisfied –

(a) that the parent or guardian consents to the making of the adoption order,

    (b) that the parent or guardian has consented under section 20 (and has not withdrawn the consent) and does not oppose the making of the adoption order, or

    (c) that the parent's or guardian's consent should be dispensed with.

      ...

(4) The second condition is that –

    (a) the child has been placed for adoption by an adoption agency with the prospective adopters in whose favour the order is proposed to be made,

    (b) either –

        (i) the child was placed for adoption with the consent of each parent or guardian and the consent of the mother was given when the child was at least six weeks old, or

        (ii) the child was placed for adoption under a placed order, and

    (c) no parent or guardian oppose the making of the adoption order.

      ...

(6) The third condition is that the child is free for adoption by virtue of an order made [under the law of Scotland or the law of Northern Ireland].

In relation to the opposing of orders, this can only be done with leave of the court.

As can be seen, the conditions relate to the giving of consent or the existence of a placement order where consent to adoption will have already been considered. The reference to s 20, in the first condition, refers to a provision whereby a parent can consent to the making of the adoption order at a very early stage, even as early as giving consent to placement, and then in effect drop out of the picture.

11.7.2   The welfare of the child

As you may recall, one of the criticisms of the Adoption Act 1976 was that the welfare of the child was not given the same prominence as it is in the CA 1989. This has been addressed by providing a similar sort of checklist for the court in the ACA 2002 for the court as can be found in s 1(3) of the CA 1989. Hence, in s 1 of the ACA 2002, where the court is coming to a decision relating to the adoption of the child it must have the child's welfare, throughout its life, as the paramount consideration. To establish what will be in the child's welfare the court must have regard in particular to the following:

- the child's ascertainable wishes and feelings regarding the decision (in the light of the child's age and understanding);
- the child's particular needs;
- the likely effect on the child of being adopted and ceasing to be a member of its birth family;

- the child's age, sex, background and any characteristics that the court considers relevant;
- any harm the child has suffered or is likely to suffer;
- the relationship the child has with relatives or other relevant individuals including whether continuation of that relationship will be valuable, the ability of relatives to meet the child's needs and the wishes and feelings of such relatives; and
- the child's religious, cultural, racial and linguistic background.

Naturally, these are only indicative and not an exhaustive list of the factors the court will have to take on board. The list is different to the CA 1989 welfare checklist, but this is to be expected given the more draconian consequences of adoption. The fact that the child's views, and those of relatives, will be taken into account is also important since many children to whom this Act applies will have a fully formed relationship with their parents, etc, due to their age – remember that baby adoptions are rare!

As this is a new checklist, the approach by the courts remains to be seen. The court will still have to be very clear as to how it has balanced the various factors in reaching its decision.

11.8   OTHER ORDERS

Section 1(6) of the ACA 2002, as with the similar CA 1989 requirement, requires the court to consider the whole range of orders available to it under both the 2002 and 1989 Acts, and to only make an order if it would be better for the child than doing nothing at all.

This continues the approach from the previous Adoption Act 1976 where courts were able to use s 8 orders of the CA 1989 instead of adoption, or to supplement adoption, although this was not common.

The main alternative to adoption *per se* will be the making of a s 8 residence order or possibly a special guardianship order (which we looked at in earlier chapters). These alternatives may not be as effective, however, since PR is shared, the order does not fully transplant the child into the new family and may be perceived to provide inadequate security. Indeed, the failure of step-parents to use residence orders was one of the criticisms of the working of the Adoption Act 1976.

The type of order the court may have to consider more frequently will be that of contact, primarily due to the changing face of adoption being for older children rather than babies. These children will know and have relationships, with parents and other relatives, and those relationships may still have value to them, even if these relatives may not be able to provide full-time care for the child. As we have seen earlier, consent to adoption cannot be made conditional on the granting of a contact order, but it can be raised and considered under the welfare criteria. These 'open adoptions' can be successful, but in some cases the extent of contact with the birth family can prevent full integration into the new adoptive family leading, ultimately, to placement breakdown. Most open adoptions, therefore, provide for limited contact and only occasionally will the contact be face to face – provision of annual letters, school reports and the like being most commonly ordered.

Contact is not just considered at the adoption stage, but also at placement, with ss 26 and 27 covering contact in placement situations.

Once an adoption order has been made, without other CA 1989 orders, the birth parents of the child will lose their status to make applications under the Act unless they are able to gain leave to do so. Hence, if contact or other such orders are required, they need to be applied for in the adoption proceedings to which the parents are parties.

11.9 REVOCATION

> **Question**
>
> Can an adoption order be revoked?

The principles behind adoption are clearly that it is an irrevocable process. The ACA 2002 states that an adopted child may be made subject to a second adoption order, but there are no provisions to permit the first order being overturned. This is not to say that the exceptional case will never arise where overturning the order on appeal is warranted. One such exceptional case arose in *Re K (Adoption)* [1997] 2 FLR 221, in connection with a Bosnian refugee, where the adoption order was overturned on the basis that it had been obtained without the true facts being known. However, even where the situation may have profound effects on the child, in many cases revocation will not occur.

In *Re B (Adoption Order: Jurisdiction to Set Aside)* [1995] 2 FLR 1, B's parents were Arab. He had been placed with, and adopted later by, a Jewish couple. Several years later he learned that his parents were Arabs and made application for an order which would nullify the adoption order. B's application was refused on the ground of a lack of jurisdiction. B then appealed. The Court of Appeal held that B's appeal would be dismissed. The court did not have the jurisdiction which would have enabled it to nullify the adoption order, which had been made in a correct manner, simply because of a mistake relating to B's ethnic origins. If such an application were to be allowed it would assist in the impairing of the adoption system, which accepted adoption orders as existing for life. An order might be set aside only where it clearly involved a denial of natural justice.

11.10 SUMMARY

You are now almost at the end of your study of family law. Adoption fits in to both public and private law spheres and is perceived to be a valuable means to achieve permanence in a child's life, especially in local authority care cases. You have seen how the law lays down a variety of regulations that must be complied with before an order can be made. Agencies, which carry out a large number of placements for adoption, often impose their own, often more rigorous, conditions. Placement for adoption is subject to strict criteria which the agency must comply with. If the agency is not placing a child for adoption it is still required to assess the suitability of adoptive parents – for example, where a step-parent is seeking to adopt. The consequences of adoption are permanent transplantation from one family to another and an order, once made, can rarely be revoked.

To consolidate your knowledge of adoption, complete the End of Chapter Assessment.

11.11 END OF CHAPTER ASSESSMENT

Why are adoption applications from step-parents and relatives seen with some disquiet? What problems can arise from this sort of application and what alternatives exist?

CHAPTER 12

THE INHERENT JURISDICTION – WARDSHIP

12.1 OBJECTIVES

By the end of this chapter you should be able to:

- explain the meaning of the inherent jurisdiction;
- place the order of wardship within the inherent jurisdiction;
- highlight the situations where wardship may be used, in comparison with other orders; and
- explain who may be subject to the jurisdiction and the consequences.

In this final chapter we will be considering the inherent jurisdiction of the court to make orders in respect of children. As an area of law, the importance of the inherent jurisdiction has waned in recent years, in the main due to the impact of the Children Act (CA) 1989. There still exist situations where this jurisdiction is useful, and so you need to study them. This chapter will be comparatively short and you will not be expected to complete an End of Chapter Assessment.

12.2 WHAT IS THE INHERENT JURISDICTION?

> **Question**
>
> Do you understand what is meant by the inherent jurisdiction of the court?

The jurisdiction is historically based and stems from the sovereign's powers to act as 'father to the nation' (acting as *parens patriae*) and to protect minors and those incapable of making decisions for themselves from harm or injury. The Crown, and now the state, acted in the sovereign's place in making those decisions. Hence, under the inherent jurisdiction the court could do whatever it felt was necessary to protect the interests of the child (or adult if looking at, for example, domestic violence). As such, the concept of the inherent jurisdiction is very similar to the rules of equity, that is, doing right in a situation even if statutory powers do not exist.

In so far as children are concerned, the use of wardship is the normal means by which the inherent jurisdiction is invoked. Wardship is part of the inherent jurisdiction, but is also an entity in itself since it has its own rules and consequences.

Question

What orders would you expect to fall within the inherent jurisdiction of the court in addition to wardship?

One such order should be easily identifiable, that is, the injunction which seeks to prohibit certain types of actions. However, you may not have identified the opposite type of order: a declaration which is permissive in nature.

12.3   INJUNCTIVE OR DECLARATIVE ORDERS

Question

Can you think of any situations where these types of orders may be used?

You could have mentioned any of the situations where an application for a specific issue order (SIO) or prohibited steps order (PSO) could be made, as these orders under the CA 1989 do much the same thing as those under the inherent jurisdiction. However, the case law would seem to indicate that in many of the cases where the inherent jurisdiction, instead of CA 1989 remedies, is used there is a question relating to medical treatment of the child. While the inherent jurisdiction declaratory relief could be used, it is also common for wardship to be used in this type of case.

For example, in *Re J (A Minor) (Child in Care: Medical Treatment)* [1992] 4 All ER 614, J was aged 16 months. He was microcephalic, blind and severely epileptic. Medical opinion was unanimous in advising that he could well deteriorate and that his expectation of life, although uncertain, must be short. The local authority was granted leave, under s 100 of the CA 1989, to invoke the inherent wardship jurisdiction of the High Court so as to determine whether artificial ventilation and/or life-saving measures should be given to J if he suffered a life-threatening event. The judge had ruled that, pending a further hearing, the status quo should be observed. The local authority appealed. The Court of Appeal held that the local authority's appeal would be allowed. *Per* Lord Donaldson:

> The fundamental issue in this appeal is whether the court in the exercise of its inherent power to protect the interests of minors should ever require a medical practitioner or health authority to adopt a course of treatment which in the *bona fide* clinical judgment of the practitioner concerned is indicated as not being in the best interests of the patient. I have to say that I cannot conceive of any circumstances in which this would be other than an abuse of power as directly or indirectly requiring the practitioner to act contrary to the fundamental duty which he owes to his patient. This, subject to obtaining any necessary consent, is to treat the patient in accordance with his own best clinical judgment,

notwithstanding that other practitioners who are not called upon to treat the patient may have formed a quite different judgment or that the court, acting on expert evidence, may not agree with him ... I have no doubt that all the doctors concerned [in this case] would agree that situations can change, and that if and when a decision whether or not to use mechanical ventilation has to be taken, it must be taken in the light of the situation as it then exists. This is what clinical judgment is all about ... So long as those with parental responsibilities consent to J being treated by the health authority's medical staff, he must be treated in accordance with their clinical judgment.

As the court proceedings in inherent jurisdiction are still classed as family proceedings, the court will have the power under the CA 1989 to make a s 8 order, subject only to the restrictions imposed by the CA 1989 itself. This is where difficulties arise for the local authority especially, since the CA 1989 has placed severe restrictions on the use that can be made of the inherent jurisdiction by the local authority (which we will look at shortly).

12.4   WARDSHIP

In practice, this is the most frequently used area of the inherent jurisdiction in respect of children and, until the implementation of the CA 1989, over half of the applications to make a child a ward were made by a local authority. From this you can surmise that wardship (and the other orders within the inherent jurisdiction) will be available in private law.

12.4.1   Who is covered?

> **Question**
>
> Who you think can be made a ward and who can apply to make a child a ward?

You should have recognised that you must be talking about a child, who will be an individual below 18 and who has never been married. A child must also have an independent existence from their mother before they can be made subject to an order. In *Re F (In Utero)* [1988] Fam 122, an application was made by a local authority to make an unborn child a ward. The application failed due to the child not being in existence, in the sense of not yet being separate from its mother and independent. The child does not need to be habitually resident in the jurisdiction, nor does the child have to be in the jurisdiction when made a ward of court. It is unlikely that a child will be made a ward whilst abroad unless, of course, the child has been abducted.

The applicant, who is seeking to make the child a ward, does not need to have any relationship or connection to them. However, if an application is lodged where there is no link, or a very tenuous one, the court may not be minded to make the order unless it is clear that making the child a ward is in the child's interests. For example, in the case of *Re D (A Minor) (Wardship: Sterilisation)* [1976] Fam 185, the applicant was an educational psychologist, and in *Re B (A Minor) (Wardship: Medical Treatment)* [1981] 1 WLR 1421, the applicant was a doctor.

As you can see, the nature of the applicant's profession may suggest why they were seeking to make the child a ward.

12.4.2 Where to apply

The jurisdiction to grant wardship orders lies primarily with the High Court Family Division, although many aspects of wardship may be dealt with in the county court (s 38 of the Matrimonial and Family Proceedings Act 1984). The procedure will involve one or more directions hearings prior to the final hearing, and it is these directions appointments that will take place in the lower court, generally before a district judge. The final hearing is normally dealt with by a High Court judge, although it is possible that a county court judge (acting as a High Court judge) may deal with the matter.

12.4.3 When does wardship become effective?

> ### Question
>
> Imagine that you are the aunt or uncle of a young child. The parent, your sister, is a drug addict. Because of her addiction, you believe that she should not care for the child. You do not really want to involve the social services, so you apply to make the child a ward. When would you expect that wardship to become effective?

Most legal orders only become effective once they have been made at the final hearing. If action needs to be taken prior to the final hearing, interim orders may be made. Wardship does not quite work like that. The child will become a ward of court, and subject to all the consequences of wardship, as soon as the application has been lodged at court, regardless of whether it is served on the other parties and regardless of a hearing. This state of affairs does not last indefinitely – this temporary protection will only remain for 21 days after the application has been filed at court – hence, within this time frame, the applicant must ensure that a hearing takes place, at least to decide if the wardship should continue.

> ### Question
> What happens if an issue needs deciding immediately?

Not all cases of wardship involve emergency situations but if something needs to be done as a matter of necessity or urgency, then a without notice hearing can take place (that is, a hearing where only the applicant is present, the respondent parents would be absent). Such a without notice hearing would not act to satisfy the requirement of the Family Proceedings Rules that a hearing take place within 21 days to prevent the wardship lapsing.

The fact that wardship is 'immediate' in its effect is one of its great advantages. In private situations this immediacy can be used if, for example, the child has been abducted and it is believed the child will be removed from the jurisdiction.

Question

Would any CA 1989 order be as effective?

While a s 44 of the CA 1989 emergency protection order (EPO) could be sought, it will invariably involve a few hours' delay. This in itself may not be such a detriment to warrant the more expensive High Court application, but the fact that the wardship will last at least 21 days (unless there is a hearing in that time) is certainly more advantageous.

When non-emergency cases are dealt with, the use of CA 1989 orders may increase, although it may be arguable that the use of wardship jurisdiction is preferable. In the case of *Re K (Adoption and Wardship)* [1997] 2 FLR 221 (a case you have come across in the previous chapter), following the revocation of the adoption order the need to protect the child and ensure the reintroduction to her Bosnian family was a high priority. By retaining wardship, the court could be in control of the process.

The procedures for concluding wardship applications are not subject to the timetabling requirements of the CA 1989 and, in practice, it would seem that many wardship cases will take much longer to reach a final hearing than s 8 residence orders and, particularly, s 31 care orders. This would certainly be the situation in *Re K*, dealing as it did in private law and the possible long-term reintroduction to the Bosnian family.

12.4.4　Consequence of wardship

The nature of wardship may be another reason for its being preferred in some situations to the CA 1989 remedies. When a child is made a ward of court, the court will in effect 'step into the shoes' of the parent and no act can be taken with respect to the child without the court's permission or authority. Any exercise of parental responsibility by anyone else, unless in accordance with the directions of the court, will be unlawful. The only sanction, presumably, would lie in contempt proceedings.

Question

If the court takes over the parental role, does this mean the court will provide day-to-day care, etc?

Practically, the court cannot fulfil a parental role in full, but must delegate some of the parental duties and responsibilities to others. This would include the day-to-day care of the child. The issue of providing care for the child may be one which would necessitate a without notice application when the wardship application is filed, if the protection of the child was at issue. In many cases, the person to whom care will be delegated will be the applicant.

12.5 THE LOCAL AUTHORITY AND THE INHERENT JURISDICTION

12.5.1 Restrictions

As mentioned earlier, the use of wardship has been restricted in the case of local authorities by virtue of s 100 of the CA 1989 in sub-ss (2) and (3). The latter sub-section simply prevents any application under the inherent jurisdiction by a local authority unless the local authority has obtained the leave of the court. Leave may be granted in the situations covered by sub-s (4), which is discussed below.

The court is also prevented from using the inherent jurisdiction to involve the local authority in child care. Thus, under sub-s (2) of the CA 1989:

- the court cannot use the inherent jurisdiction to put a child into the care of a local authority;
- the court cannot use the inherent jurisdiction to put a child under the supervision of the local authority;
- the court cannot use the inherent jurisdiction to put the child into accommodation provided by or on behalf of the local authority;
- the court cannot use the inherent jurisdiction to make a child subject to a care order a ward of court; and
- the court cannot use the inherent jurisdiction to confer parental responsibility or any aspect of parental responsibility on the local authority.

Even though this is directed at the court, it provides a severe limitation on local authorities too.

12.5.2   Why s 100?

The restrictions that have been created by s 100, being so comprehensive, must have some justification.

> **Question**
>
> Can you think of any?

You were told earlier that almost half of the applications in wardship pre-CA 1989 were made by local authorities. This extensive use of the procedure was one reason for seeking to reduce the powers of the court and the local authority in respect of inherent jurisdiction. Local authorities had come to utilise wardship to combat the perceived problems with the Children and Young Persons Act 1969 which provided their powers of intervention for child protection. The grounds available under the 1969 Act were thought to be inflexible and backward looking. Wardship with its ability to consider future perceived harm (without the existence of past harm), its speed and the variety of options once made was a more attractive proposition. With the implementation of the CA 1989, and the new powers to take a child into protective care, the faults of the old law were removed. The intention was that the CA 1989 powers should be perfectly sufficient for the local authority to act to protect a child, without the need to resort to the inherent jurisdiction.

12.5.3   When can the inherent jurisdiction be used?

As we have seen, there exists a means by which the local authority can use the inherent jurisdiction, having obtained leave to do so and this is covered in s 100(4) and (5) of the CA 1989.

The local authority must satisfy two criteria before leave will be granted for the application. The granting of leave, you must remember, does not mean that the order will be granted; it is just the first hurdle to overcome. The first condition is that the making of an order under the inherent jurisdiction will achieve something that the local authority could not do using the orders available to it under the CA 1989. In other words, the inherent jurisdiction is being used to plug gaps that exist in the legal regime. Secondly, the making of the order will prevent the child suffering significant harm which would otherwise be suffered.

> **Question**
>
> Can you think of any examples when the inherent jurisdiction will, or could, be used?

From your earlier reading on public law you will have come across a couple of situations where the inherent jurisdiction would be the only means of protecting a child.

Do you recall who can be made subject to a care order or supervision order? Under the CA 1989, a court cannot make either of these orders if the child has reached their 17th birthday. If a child of 17 is believed to be at risk of suffering significant harm, how can the local authority protect them? The only conceivable way would be to use the inherent jurisdiction, since the local authority cannot be expected to use s 44 EPOs repeatedly.

Other cases where the inherent jurisdiction will commonly be used are medical treatment matters, that is, where children require medical attention and are either refusing to consent or their parents are refusing consent. However, here the local authority may wish to apply only for a declaration, rather than wardship, and arguably should really be applying under the CA 1989 since a SIO or a PSO is available as a remedy to the local authority.

12.6   SUMMARY

As you have seen, the inherent jurisdiction can be used in both public and private law cases, although following the CA 1989 the use made of it by local authorities has declined. The inherent jurisdiction is used in respect of children usually by declaring the child a ward of court. In so doing, the child's parents or others with parental responsibility are usurped from their role and the court becomes the decision maker for the child. Wardship is used primarily where a range of decisions needs to be made, as it is a more rounded order, since wardship covers *all* decisions relating to the child. In contrast, the inherent jurisdiction will be used where a specific question needs to be decided or referred to the court. As a residuary power, and as a means to plug any apparent gaps in the statutory code, the inherent jurisdiction is crucial.

CHAPTER 13

END OF CHAPTER ASSESSMENT
– OUTLINE ANSWERS

END OF CHAPTER ASSESSMENT – MARRIAGE
– THE STARTING POINT

'[M]any of the procedures [relating to marriage] are unnecessarily complex and restrictive': *Registration: A Modern Service*, Government Green Paper, Cm 531.

Discuss the validity of this statement.

Outline answer

To answer this question you are not only required to discuss the procedures or formalities relating to marriage, but also to evaluate whether they are or are not restrictive and complex. Hence, to start, you should identify the core formalities to marriage.

Starting with the pre-marriage formality of notice, the question requires you to identify the different types of notice that can be given in relation to the various religious or civil ceremonies. These would be:

(a) Marriage under a superintendent registrar's certificate (seven days' residence and 15 days' notice).

(b) Marriage under a registrar's general licence (relevant to deathbed marriages or those where the individual cannot get to the registered place for the ceremony).

(c) Marriage after banns have been called (banns called for three successive Sundays in the parish of residence and celebration of the marriage if different).

(d) Special licence or 'Archbishop's licence', which permits deathbed marriages or marriages in churches where there is no connection for the parties.

With respect to all notice provisions, the issue of payment of fees and length of residence or time between giving notice in an area and the actual ceremony are key features. Complexity arises in the sense that there are different notice periods in existence in terms of types of ceremony. If a couple can fit into all three categories then they may find it hard to make a choice – but this is hardly 'complex'. The notice periods appear to cater for different needs (and products) and if this is accepted, then the process is not harsh.

The question of restrictiveness is somewhat different. The time periods are also restrictive in the sense that they require some sort of planning of the marriage, but this should be evaluated in the light of why notice periods are needed. If the notice periods are designed to enable impediments or objections to be given, then they should be retained. However, given the general ineffectiveness of the process, you may agree that they are not really needed. To suggest this is not to agree that they are restrictive or complex.

Looking now at the formalities of the marriage ceremony itself, the requirements you should have focused on were:

- the qualification of celebrant;
- the place of marriage;
- the wording and the witnesses; and
- hours for the ceremony and open doors.

In all but Quaker and Jewish ceremonies, the law lays down requirements to meet the above requirements. If the celebrant, whether it is a civil marriage or religious, is not qualified and this is known to the parties, the marriage will be invalid. This would not appear to be too complex. As to restrictive, surely the parties will decide what type of ceremony to have in light of the celebrant they want.

The place of marriage is restricted by virtue of the type of notice given. In 1994 the law widened the scope of venues for marriages. You may argue that the nature of the regulations are too limiting – a marriage cannot be conducted on a beach or at the top of Snowdon (although a marriage can be blessed), which may be the preferred place. You may believe that these sorts of venues are inappropriate but you should also have linked this to the proposed changes to be brought about by the Civil Registration White Paper (*Civil Registration: Vital Change: Birth, Marriages and Death in the 21st Century*).

Turning to the wording, the legal requirements are not draconian. It is, however, strange that a so-called 'simple contract' needs to have a minimum of two witnesses. The reference to 'no lawful impediment' may result in a perjury charge if there was, in fact, a known impediment.

Thus, these requirements can be classed as complex or restrictive since, especially where wording is concerned, there is nothing to stop the rest of the ceremony being in the couple's chosen wording.

The hours for marriage and the 'public' element of open doors could, arguably, be seen as irrelevant. If a couple wish to marry, have the necessary licence, does it matter what time the ceremony takes place? Equally, is it relevant that the public can gain access when there are the required witnesses? Whilst you may believe these formalities are unnecessary, especially given the lack of sanctions if they are broken, this does not mean the requirements are complex, although they may be restrictive.

Finally, look at past marriage requirements – that of registration. The purpose of registration is to provide public evidence of a change in status. Marriage confers additional rights and obligations, which are not otherwise available, so registration is necessary. The process of evidencing a marriage, with handwritten certificates and filing of copies is, arguably, complex but, more relevantly, far too outdated.

In your conclusion you should draw all these threads together. In isolation, the requirements are not overly complex or restrictive of an individual's freedom. Taken together, a picture of more complexity may build up, but even so, it can be suggested that the Law Commission's statement does not reflect the truth of the situation when taken at face value. By broadening out the evaluation of the reason and need for the requirements, it is easier to agree that the formalities need to be changed.

END OF CHAPTER ASSESSMENT – NULLITY AND LEGAL SEPARATION

1   Alfred has been undergoing medical treatment for clinical depression. The drug regime has made him intermittently 'hazy' and he has difficulty in understanding or making sense of things. Last week Alfred went through a register office wedding with Bernadette. After the ceremony they booked in to an hotel nearby and the marriage was consummated. They have not lived together beyond that first night. Alfred has now sought your advice on bringing the marriage to an end.

2   To what extent can an individual marry whomsoever they wish, wherever they wish?

3   Andre is married to Steffi and the marriage took place eight months ago. Shortly after the marriage Andre confessed he was bisexual. Due to this, Steffi insisted Andre have an HIV test. This has been returned with a positive result. No sexual intercourse has taken place. Advice Andre, who wishes to set up home with Phillip and to relinquish all his marriage ties.

4   Four years ago Paramjit and Ravi married in their local temple, the marriage having been arranged by their respective families. The couple had not met prior to the ceremony. Ravi was not keen on the prospect of marrying but, due to her age at the time (28), her parents were constantly telling her of the shame that she was bringing on the family. The marriage has never been a happy one; Ravi has never felt able to have physical contact with Paramjit, and sexual intercourse has never taken place. Again, due to the family concerns, Ravi agreed to be artificially inseminated and has borne one child, Amandeep, now eight months old. Advise Ravi on her chances of bringing the marriage to an end.

Outline answers

1   The issues within this answer will revolve around whether the marriage is void or voidable. You must always be aware of who you are advising since not all the grounds for voidable marriages are available to both parties. Here you are advising Alfred.

Looking initially at void marriages, reflect upon s 11 of the Matrimonial Causes Act (MCA) 1973. You would not be expected to list all the grounds upon which a marriage can be avoided under this provision, but to consider if any of them are relevant. The advantage for Alfred of falling within s 11 would be that the marriage has never existed and hence he would not need to do anything to 'end' the marriage. A decree of nullity would be proof that the marriage was in fact invalid from the start. Does Alfred fall within the section?

Unfortunately, there are no grounds for declaring the marriage void that can be identified from the facts given. Whilst the facts are not very detailed, there is no indication of the couple being within the prohibited degrees, they appear to be of the requisite ages, have complied with the formalities (they may, of course, have lied to obtain the necessary licence to marry), and there is no reference to a previous marriage that is still existing.

Consequently, you would need to turn your attention to the provisions in s 12 of the 1973 Act. This concerns voidable marriages. These are marriages that are valid, unless and until they are avoided by one of the parties to the marriage. The grounds that are given in s 12 refer generally to some pre-existing defect which affects the basis of marriage. Again, pick out the most appropriate grounds suitable to Alfred's case, and indicate why others may not be relevant.

Section 12(a) and (b) are not applicable in this scenario, since the facts given show that the marriage has been consummated. You may find more mileage in the next ground in s 12(c). It is unlikely that the marriage can be avoided by Alfred on the basis of mistake or duress, but there may be a way to avoid the marriage on the basis of Alfred's 'unsoundness of mind'. You are told that Alfred has been undergoing treatment for clinical depression and, in particular, that the drug regime has affected his ability to make sense of things. It could be argued that this haziness resulted in Alfred not understanding what he was doing when he went through the ceremony. In other words, he was not mentally capable of consenting to the marriage. Remember that under this ground in s 12 you are looking at the ability to consent. Also remember that marriage is a simple contract (*Re Park*), and so Alfred's incapacity must be quite severe. Alfred would be able to utilise this ground since it states that 'either party' may rely on unsoundness of mind.

The next ground, under s 12(d,) may also be applicable to Alfred. Again, this provision reflects the mental capacity and mental health of one of the parties. The distinctions between this ground and the one in s 12(c) is that under s 12(d) there must be a recognisable mental illness as defined by the Mental Health Act 1983. Clinical depression, whilst only a minor mental illness, would fall within the 1983 Act's provisions. The issue will be whether or not this mental illness makes Alfred 'unfit for marriage'. This does not relate to an impediment at the time of the marriage but one which is discovered later. It can be relied on by Alfred, even though it is his own mental state, since the provision states that 'either party' could suffer from a mental incapacity.

The other provisions of s 12 (venereal disease (VD) and pregnancy) would not seem to be applicable to Alfred's situation.

Finally, you would need to mention whether or not Alfred's application to annul the marriage would be prevented under s 13 of the MCA 1973. From the facts given, it would not seem that Alfred has acted in such a way as to lead Bernadette to believe that he would not seek to annul the marriage. Also, the marriage has not existed for more than three years and hence s 13(2) is not applicable.

To gain extra marks, a brief consideration of the consequences of a voidable marriage would be necessary. For example, you could discuss the fact that ancillary relief can be obtained and that any children born of the marriage will be legitimate.

2   This, again, reflects void and voidable marriages. The question looks at two issues – the marriage to whomsoever an individual chooses, and where the marriage can be conducted.

Dealing with the first issue, you should have looked at s 11 of the MCA 1973 and, in particular, discussed the following categories:

(a) s 11(a)(i) – that the parties are within the prohibited degrees of relationship. Explain what is meant by this, and who is caught by the provision. Refer to the loosening up of the restrictions in the degrees of affinity by the Marriage (Prohibited Degrees of Relationship) Act 1986. Clearly, these provisions do restrict the freedom of an individual to marry whomsoever they choose. The provisions do not, however, prohibit the cohabitation between individuals within these categories;

(b) s 11(a)(ii) – the age of the parties and being below the age of 16. This again is restrictive in the sense that if one of the parties is below the age of 16 no marriage can take place. This can be justified on social grounds, and also if a marriage does take place, the question of unlawful sexual intercourse may arise. You could suggest that this provision is less restrictive than the former, since it is open to the couple to wait until they both become of age;

(c) s 11(b) – one of the parties is already married. This provision, whilst again restricting the freedom to marry, is linked to criminal law, and the notion that marriage is the union of one man and one woman, forsaking all others. On public policy, the restriction is not unwarranted, and can be resolved by the married party obtaining a divorce;

(d) s 11(c) – that the parties are not male and female. This links in to the concept mentioned above, that marriage is the union of one man and one woman. The restriction on same-sex marriages does deny homosexuals and lesbians the ability to obtain the same rights and status as married heterosexual couples. It is a restriction, but one which would be justified on public policy grounds.

Moving now to the restriction as to where a marriage can be conducted, this relates to the formalities of marriage. Note that marriages can only be carried out in specified and registered premises. Failure to comply with this requirement, when done wilfully and knowingly, may invalidate the marriage. The nature of the restriction, you may suggest, is not that draconian. Since the Marriage Act 1994 authorised the granting of licences to premises other than churches and registry offices, the ability to marry where an individual wants is quite wide.

3   Steffi and Andre's situation falls within the provisions of s 12 of the Matrimonial Causes Act 1973. Section 11 is not relevant since none of the grounds are applicable. As with question 1, concentrate on the grounds which may be utilised rather than simply discussing all of them.

The marriage has not been consummated, and so your attention should be drawn to s 12(a) and (b). Andre is the person seeking advice, and under s 12(a) either party can be incapable. Andre could, therefore, rely on his own incapacity. The issue would be whether he is in fact incapable of consummating the marriage. The facts are not clear on this, so you would have to explain the meaning and interpretation of this ground.

With regard to wilful refusal to consummate, Andre would have to show that it is Steffi who is refusing to consummate the marriage. From the facts this would appear to be a more likely scenario since she was the one who requested the HIV test. You may also explore the issue of whether the refusal to consummate is refusal *per se*, or whether Steffi refuses intercourse unless Andre uses a condom. The latter would not amount to wilful refusal and hence Andre would not be able to utilise this ground.

Finally, the issue of HIV needs to be discussed. As you should have mentioned, if a party to the marriage is suffering from VD in a communicable form, then the marriage can be annulled. There are two problems with reference to this scenario. First, Andre has HIV, and so would be unable to rely on s 12(e) since he is the petitioner, and the provision refers to the respondent having VD. Secondly, there is a question mark over the meaning of VD and whether this in fact includes HIV. Whilst the AIDS virus is normally passed on through sexual contact, this is not the only means whereby the disease will be transmitted. Also, is HIV a disease in its true sense? Medical opinion is not clear, but it can be suggested that HIV is merely the precursor to the disease of AIDS.

4   This question should have been relatively easy to answer, given the work you have done in the previous three questions.

The main issue is whether the marriage is voidable for lack of consent on the part of Ravi under s 12(c) of the MCA 1973, or whether it is voidable for the lack of consummation under s 12(a) or (b). Unlike the earlier questions, you should have focused on s 13 more closely here.

Dealing first with duress under s 12(c), mention the reason why duress can invalidate a marriage. The duress should go to the heart of consent to the marriage. The cases of *Szechter* and *Hirani* are relevant authority to quote. Ravi's difficulty would be the influence of s 13(2), since the marriage has been in existence for more than three years. In addition, under s 13(1) it may be argued that the fact that Ravi agreed to artificial insemination indicates that she has conducted herself in such a way as to lead the respondent to believe that the marriage would not be annulled.

The fact that Ravi has been artificially inseminated would not prejudice an application under s 12(a) or (b) since artificial insemination is not within the definition of 'consummation'. She would not be able to rely on wilful refusal since she is the one who is refusing intercourse. To succeed on incapacity, she would have to prove that she is psychologically repugnant to the idea of intercourse. This would be difficult since it is harder to show mental difficulties compared to physical difficulties.

END OF CHAPTER ASSESSMENT – THE LAW ON DIVORCE

1   Joyce and Ralph married 10 years ago and approached their relationship on an 'open marriage' basis. Consequently, both partners have had casual relationships outside the marriage. Last year Ralph began to have a change of heart and decided that he would not participate in any such casual relationships. Joyce did not concur with this decision and has continued to act in the same way, much to Ralph's disgust. Recently he learnt that for the last seven months Joyce has been having an affair with Anne-Marie.

Advise Ralph on his rights in relation to divorce. Is there any way that Joyce could prevent a divorce?

2   Peggy and Tony married 15 months ago and stayed together for two months before Tony left the matrimonial home. He has recently contacted Peggy and asked to give the marriage a second chance. Advise Peggy how this would affect her potential rights to seek a divorce.

3   Anne and Ben married four years ago, having cohabited for the 14 years preceding the marriage. Carl, their son, was adopted by Anne seven years ago, and Ben has a joint residence order with Anne. Three years before they married, Anne adopted Carl.

Their relationship was deteriorating when the adoption took place – not having a child was one reason why the difficulties were occurring. The situation did improve for a while, but not for long. The marriage was a method to achieve a reconciliation. This has not happened. Anne and Ben have slept in separate rooms for the last five years. Ben has now met Diana and would like to commence a relationship with her.

Advise Ben on ending his marriage.

Outline answers

1   As with the answers to the questions in the previous chapter you should always remember who you are advising. Ralph is your client in this scenario. He is seeking a divorce and for the purposes of this question you need to consider the divorce legislation under the Matrimonial Causes Act (MCA) 1973.

To commence, you would have to advise him that there is only one ground for divorce under s 1(1) – that the marriage has broken down irretrievably. From the facts in the question, it would appear that as far as Ralph is concerned the marriage has broken down.

However, you would need to advise him that to prove irretrievable breakdown, one or more of five facts will need to be proven too. It would be unnecessary to recite all the facts under s 1(2); you should focus on the relevant ones. In this case, s 1(2)(a) or (b) would seem to be the most appropriate to discuss.

Section 1(2)(a) deals with the respondent's adultery and the fact that the petitioner finds it intolerable to live with the respondent. Ralph and Joyce have previously enjoyed an open marriage. Whilst this constitutes adultery, it would be questionable whether Ralph found it intolerable to live with Joyce. As you should have commented, the fact of intolerability is not related to the adultery.

Also mention that it would not be possible for Ralph to cite Joyce's current relationship with Anne-Marie as being adulterous. For adultery to take place the intercourse must be between a male and female, one of whom is not a party to the marriage. Clearly, therefore, a lesbian relationship will not count as adultery. The date when Joyce last had intercourse with a male partner would need to be identified, and also whether or not Ralph knew about it. This refers to the content of s 2(1). Under this section a party to a marriage cannot rely on the other's adultery if, knowing that the adultery has occurred, they have lived together for a period of six months after the last act of adultery.

Given that the success of a petition under s 1(2)(a) seems in doubt, the fact in s 1(2)(b) may be more applicable. Under this fact the breakdown can be shown by proving that the respondent has behaved in such a way that the petitioner cannot reasonably be expected to live with them. The fact that Ralph has now changed his opinion as to open marriages may be sufficient, together with the continued actions of Joyce with her lesbian partner. The question you may like to pose is whether it is unreasonable to expect Ralph to live with Joyce, using the authority of *Ash*, since he too has had relationships outside the marriage. Would it make a difference that Joyce's new partner is female if Ralph has always had heterosexual relationships in the past? The fact of continued 'living together' could detract from the reasonableness of the expectation of cohabitation, but as Ralph is seeking to take action shortly after discovering the facts of the relationship this is unlikely.

If Joyce wished to prevent the divorce, she would have to rely on s 5 or s 10 of the MCA 1973 Act. The former section acts as a power to refuse a decree of divorce, and s 10 acts as a delaying tactic. Joyce, unfortunately, will be unable to avail herself of these provisions, since they relate purely to the separation facts in s 1(2)(d) and (e).

2   In this situation you are focusing on the separation facts and also the reconciliation provisions of s 2(5). If Peggy is contemplating a divorce, there are two facts which she could be advised to apply under in future. The first would be desertion, under s 1(2)(c), for a period of two years. To be successful there must be no just cause for Tony's leaving the matrimonial home, and Peggy must have been willing for the marriage to continue. If at this stage she refuses to accept Tony's return, he could argue that it is Peggy who is now deserting rather than himself! A better option would be two years' separation with consent. The difficulty would be, not in proving that the couple have lived apart, but in getting consent if Tony continues to request a reconciliation. If consent is not forthcoming, then the only option would be to wait for a total of five years.

Insofar as the wish to reconcile is concerned, the MCA 1973 does attempt to promote the saving of marriages by permitting trial reconciliations, without necessarily affecting the fact that is to be relied upon. Under s 2(5), where desertion or separation is to be relied upon:

> ... no account shall be taken of any one period (not exceeding six months) or of any two or more periods (not exceeding six months in total) during which the parties resumed living with each other, but no period ... shall count as part of the period for which the parties to the marriage lived apart.

Therefore, if the reconciliation is not successful, Peggy will still be able to rely on s 1(2)(d) but will not be able to count the period of reconciliation as part of the two year separation.

3   In dealing with ending the marriage, you should note they married four years ago and hence meet the s 3 one year bar. In terms of satisfying the MCA 1973 there needs to be discussion on whether the marriage has irretrievably broken down and which, if any, of the five facts in s 1(2) apply. Behaviour or two years separation should be the main facts discussed, and you should relate the latter to the cases of *Mouncer* and *Fuller*. You may also comment on the fact that if both parties are willing to accept the marriage is over, then using behaviour or adultery may be possible, given the lack of verification under the special procedure, and if one of the couple are willing to perjure themselves. You should also note the possibility of mediation if one or both of the couple are seeking state funding to finance either the divorce or the proceedings to deal with property or finance. You may also have considered the issue of nullity since the marriage may not have been consummated.

END OF CHAPTER ASSESSMENT – PROPERTY AND FINANCE ON DIVORCE

Anna and Bob have been married for 18 years and together have built up a successful business. They have two children: Carmen, 20, and David, 16.

Both children live in the matrimonial home. Carmen is currently finishing her university degree and David is soon to start college.

Anna has worked in the family business since the time of the marriage, although she has never received a proper salary. The matrimonial home is owned jointly in equal shares, although Bob has been the major contributor financially to the acquisition and upkeep of the house.

The marriage began to deteriorate several years ago and Bob has been living in a separate annex to the matrimonial home for the last six years.

Advise Anna on:

(a) her ability to seek a divorce;

(b) the principles the court would apply in assessing her claims for ancillary relief; and

(c) the types of order the court could make.

Outline answer

This question is not that difficult, but requires the ability to relate law to facts and to be able to choose the relevant law, rather than simply writing all you know about the topic.

Hence in part (a), you need to explain to Anna the process of divorce under the Matrimonial Causes Act (MCA) 1973 and to illustrate which of the five facts would be suitable to her situation. You should also have advised on the minimum duration of marriage (one year), the ground for divorce and also highlight the fact that if she used the fact of separation for five years, Bob had the right to seek to delay, or seek to prevent the divorce due to hardship; these latter points being somewhat irrelevant on the facts, due to the financial status of the couple.

In part (b) you need to apply the relevant factors from s 25 of the MCA and also to consider the issues of mediation. While it would be unlikely that Anna would need to seek state funding for the ancillary claims, this cannot be ruled out. In any event, if private funding were used, the solicitor may suggest mediation. In going through s 25, the key is to highlight those factors that are relevant – the issue of disability, for example, is not relevant at all, so why include it? Also important is to at least consider what Bob's needs and requirements will be. When considering ancillary relief, there are always two parties! Conduct is relevant since Anna has contributed positively to the business and her contributions to the family should not be ignored. While the case of *White* may also assist, remember that Mrs White owned substantial assets of her own before the marriage; this is not the case with Anna, although *Lambert* may have overtaken some of the *White* points. The issue of starting points also should be mentioned, as well as the clean break principles, since this is a case where there may be sufficient assets to permit a clean break, even with a minor child (the more so as he is 16).

Finally, when dealing with part (c), there needs to be an application of the law to the facts. Rather than simply listing the orders, it is better to suggest which will be most suitable. So periodical payments may be necessary but might be time limited. If there is sufficient capital, a lump sum order could easily be used to create income for Anna so she has no ongoing links with Bob, which will support the concept of clean break. Insofar as the house is concerned, while there are several possible orders, a *Mesher* order or an immediate sale may be the most suitable. A *Mesher* order will not disadvantage Anna greatly as the youngest child may end education in a couple of years, and this type of order presupposes that the children will remain with Anna, not a guaranteed outcome. The immediate sale may be warranted if there is sufficient equity to enable Anna to purchase alternative accommodation (and the same for Bob). One range of orders that must also be considered are those for pension funds – given that the petition will be filed after 1 December 2000, then Anna could seek a pension sharing order, or have a pension attachment, or simply an increased lump sum.

END OF CHAPTER ASSESSMENT –
PROPERTY AND FINANCE WITHOUT DIVORCE

Simon and Janice have lived together for seven years. They bought their current house in 1993, each having sold previously owned properties. As Janice was still going through her divorce, the new house was conveyed into Simon's sole name. The relationship between Simon and Janice has now broken down, although they are still living in the same property.

The house is worth £120,000, with an endowment mortgage of £50,000. Janice contributed £40,000 towards the purchase price, with Simon contributing £30,000. Janice, despite only working part-time, has paid half of the endowment fees.

Explain how the courts will assess her claim to be entitled to a half-share in the property.

Outline answer

This is not a difficult question to answer and, hence, you may find the outline here somewhat short! The issue for discussion is the application of constructive or resulting trust doctrines to Janice's case. As Janice does not have her name on the title deeds to the property, and there is no evidence on the facts given that a declaration of trust has been executed, it is to be assumed that Simon is the legal and beneficial owner. To claim entitlement, Janice will have to prove that in reality the beneficial entitlement is shared between them. Your answer will consequently consider the way in which the courts approach the doctrine of constructive trusts.

The first thing that the court will need to establish is whether there was a common intention that the property should be shared (*Gissing v Gissing*). In relation to this test, the court may look for direct evidence of intention or implied evidence. The former is naturally easier to establish. The types of direct evidence that the courts will look for are as follows:

- express declarations;
- contribution to the purchase monies; and
- payment for substantial works or renovation.

Janice may fall within one of these categories.

There does not seem to be any express declaration on the facts presented to you. Janice has, however, provided a large contribution to the purchase monies, being £40,000 of the purchase price, and subsequent payments to the mortgage. Even if purchase money has been paid by the party claiming a beneficial share, it is still open to the other party to argue that the money was a loan or even a gift. Fortunately for Janice the presumption of advancement operates in marital relationships only and, anachronistically, only in favour of the wife.

The payment of purchase monies may be sufficient to satisfy the courts that the couple did have a common intention to share the property beneficially, and therefore it may be unnecessary to consider the implied evidence to satisfy the courts. However, it would be useful to mention the nature of that evidence, that is, conduct, especially undertaking substantial works to the property (bearing in mind *Lloyds Bank v Rosset*) or financial contribution to the relationship (again bearing in mind that a cohabitant's payment of bills, in the absence of an express declaration, may be treated as the equivalent of rent).

There is no evidence that Janice has done any work of improvement, or paid for the same. However, following *Rosset*, the carrying out of works on premises is of a lesser evidential weight. Paying for the work increases the weight of the evidence.

The second element to the test is to establish if the party claiming the beneficial entitlement has acted to their detriment. This test is often subsumed into the first. Here it is arguable that Janice has acted to her detriment since she paid a large sum of money to help purchase the property and has continued to pay the endowment.

Finally, having established that a common intention exists, the court will have to assess the extent of that beneficial ownership. As you will recall, there has been a split in the way that the courts approach this, one line of argument being that a purely financial view is taken – what percentage the claimant put in equals what they will get out. The second line of argument considers what the parties intended the percentage share to be. The latter system includes a degree of crystal ball gazing and may be deemed inappropriate. However, following *Midland Bank v Cooke*, this seems to be the line that the courts are taking. On the basis of Janice's contributions, she will qualify for a 30% share in the equity of the property. More difficult to assess would be the share she should receive by virtue of her payments towards the mortgage (on the assumption that the court views this as right-bearing rather than as occupation rent). The question states that she is paying half the endowment fees, which leaves Simon paying the other half, together with the interest on the capital sum. Without precise figures, you cannot estimate the exact share this would entitle her to. This purely financial calculation would result in less than the half-share she is claiming. If the court approaches the claim on a *Cooke* basis, she may well get her half-share, but it is unlikely that she would get any more.

END OF CHAPTER ASSESSMENT – CHILD SUPPORT

1   In what situations can maintenance be obtained for children without recourse to the Child Support Agency?

2   Steve is 32 years old and employed as a fireman. He is unmarried. Just over a year ago he split up with his girlfriend, Toni, and he has had no contact since. Yesterday he received a letter from the Child Support Agency together with a maintenance enquiry form asking for details of his income, etc, with regard to Toni's child, William. Toni is claiming Steve is the father of William.

Steve seeks your advice. He does not believe that he is the child's father and he wishes to know how the Agency will approach this denial. Also he wishes to know how the Agency will assess the claim if he is treated as being the father.

Outline answers

1   In this answer you have to consider all the situations where the Child Support Agency (the Agency) does not have jurisdiction to make an assessment for support or, in the event they have jurisdiction, fail to make an assessment. Consequently, you need to mention a variety of different statutes under which maintenance can be ordered, as well as the fact that voluntary arrangements may be made.

To start with, it may be useful to state briefly when the Agency does have to be approached – those cases where a parent with care is receiving one of the specified state benefits and there is an absent parent. The existence of a pre-1993 court order or maintenance agreement will not prevent the Agency's involvement if the parent with care is on benefits, and any Agency assessment will override and extinguish the previous arrangements. In this case the compulsory involvement is due to the operation of s 6 of the Child Support Act 1991.

If a parent with care is not on benefits (or the child is being cared for by someone who is not a parent), then under s 4 of the 1991 Act, an application for assessment by the Agency can be made as the Agency has jurisdiction, but this is not compulsory.

If a pre-1993 written maintenance agreement exists, or there is an existing court order for child support, then a parent with care who is not on benefit cannot seek an assessment by the Agency unless that court order has been in existence for a minimum of one year. If there is a pre-existing agreement or order, the correct approach is to re-negotiate the agreement, or return to court to seek a variation of the order.

If there is no pre-existing agreement or order, then the parent with care may seek maintenance through the Matrimonial Causes Act (MCA) 1973, the Domestic Proceedings and Magistrates' Court Act (DPMCA) 1978 or the Children Act (CA) 1989. Factors that would be crucial to mention in your answer are:

- The inability of the court to make provision, other than in consent orders, in respect of child support. In other words if the parties disagree then the matter will have to go to the Agency.

- The possibility of making a non-court sanctioned written maintenance agreement, again by consent, which would deal with the child support payments but may be harder to enforce if not subsequently embodied in an order.

- The status of the applicant since the MCA 1973 and the DPMCA 1978 are only available to married parents – non-married parents must utilise the CA 1989.

- The factors and criteria to be applied by the court under these Acts when assessing the appropriateness of the consent order with respect to child support.

- The ability of the court to make property adjustment orders under these Acts, which cannot be made by the Agency, although the reluctance of the court to do so should be mentioned.

If the Child Support Act 1991 does apply the court may be used to seek a 'top-up' to the maintenance assessment made under the CSA formula. As the percentage slice does not adequately deal with wealthy parents (the percentage deduction only applies to a set amount of income) it is permissible to go to court for an additional award of child support to be paid. This is not subject to the same requirement of consent as under s 4 of the 1991 Act. This 'top-up' may involve additional periodical payments or may also involve the making of a property adjustment order.

You should also refer to the other situations where the court has jurisdiction over additional child support, that is, the situations set out in s 8 of the CSA 1991 and refer to educational fees and the disability of the child.

Finally, there are certain situations where the Agency has no jurisdiction at all, and where the courts must be used. These situations will arise where the definitions of qualifying child and absent parent or parent with care do not apply. Hopefully, you have mentioned the possible liability of a step-parent who has treated a step-child as a child of the family, to pay maintenance under the 1971 and 1978 Acts. In addition, if the child is over 16 then they do not class as a qualifying child and support will have to be sought through the courts or a voluntary agreement.

2   This question concerns other aspects of the Child Support Act 1991 and its operation by the Agency. In this question you are focusing more on the practicalities of the making of the assessment and the formula approach.

To start with, advise Steve with regard to the question of paternity. If Steve has been declared the child's father in any other proceedings, the Agency is able to presume that he is the father and continue the assessment on that basis. If Steve is adamant that he is not the father and no other presumption of paternity exists, then the Agency is required to stop the assessment until the matter of paternity is concluded.

Paternity will be decided by reference to DNA testing. This can be provided at reduced cost from the Agency, but if Steve is found to be the father then any costs will need to be paid by him. Only if the results of the testing prove him not to be the father will the cost be borne by the Agency. If Toni refuses to co-operate and will not allow blood tests, then adverse inferences can be made to the effect that Steve is not in fact the father.

Assuming testing goes ahead and shows that Steve is the father, you need to explain the assessment process and the fact that only Steve's income is assessed and he will have to pay on a percentage basis. You would also need to mention the consequences of Steve failing to co-operate or return forms quickly, that is, he would be assessed on an interim basis which invariably is much higher than a full assessment.

The possibility of departure from the percentage slice also has to be covered. It is unlikely that many of the departure grounds will be applicable; Steve will not have a pre-1993 property adjustment to consider, nor are his travel to work costs likely to be higher than the requisite mileage. He may have excessive expenditure on property, which will entitle Toni to claim under the departure regulations.

END OF CHAPTER ASSESSMENT – DOMESTIC VIOLENCE

Four years ago Ingrid began to cohabit with Max in his three-bedroomed house. Ingrid has no rights of ownership.

Max has always been temperamental with frequent bouts of depression. In the last 18 months these have become far more common, and Max has started to exhibit violent tendencies. Ingrid, in the last two months, has visited the local hospital's accident and emergency department twice with broken ribs, bruising and a dislocated shoulder after being attacked by Max.

Max is always apologetic when he realises what he has done and always swears never to do anything like that again.

Advise Ingrid on what rights she has to obtain protection.

Outline answer

Starting with the physical violence, Ingrid can still seek a non-molestation order under s 42 of the Family Law Act (FLA) 1996 as she will be an associated person (the definition of associated person is found in s 62). The acts that will provide evidence for an order are not specified, hence the meaning of molestation will be the same as under the case law for the Domestic Violence (Matrimonial Proceedings) Act (DV(MP)A) 1976. The violence inflicted upon Ingrid by Max will clearly be caught by the FLA 1996. The court has to consider certain criteria before it can make the order. These are set out in s 42(5) as being 'all the circumstances including the need to secure the health, safety and well-being [of the applicant]'. In reality, the application of the criteria will not make that much difference, although that the health, safety and well-being factors promote a more victim-centred approach to the order. The FLA 1996 does not set a minimum or maximum duration for the order, and hence it is still open to the court to make short duration orders in the expectation that the parties will sort the matter out by themselves (presumably by reconciling or by divorce, etc). The court still retains the ability to attach a power of arrest to the non-molestation order, although it is important to note that there seems to be a greater emphasis in the FLA 1996 on the court so doing. Powers of arrest are covered in s 47 and are expressed thus:

(2) If –

(a) the court makes a [non-molestation] order; and

(b) it appears to the court that the respondent has used or threatened violence to the applicant

it shall attach a power of arrest ... unless satisfied that in all the circumstances of the case the applicant ... will be adequately protected without such a power of arrest.

Hence, the indication within the Act is that a power of arrest should be made unless it is unnecessary. It would seem that it is for the respondent to show this, rather than under the previous scheme where the applicant had to show the need for a power of arrest to be attached. Equally, the respondent does not have to have used violence, the mere threat will be sufficient to trigger s 47. There still remains the possibility for the court to accept an undertaking from Max, rather than to impose a non-molestation order. Undertakings are dealt with in s 46 and are little changed. However, it should be noted that if the court attaches a power of arrest to an order, then it cannot accept an undertaking from the respondent.

On the procedural side, the court can still be approached to make the order on a *without notice* basis. The ability of the court to make orders *without notice* is dealt with in s 45, which lays down factors for the court to consider before making the order requested. These factors include, *inter alia*, the risk of harm to the applicant if the order is not made immediately or the respondent is deliberately avoiding service of proceedings. It should also be noted that the courts empowered to make orders for non-molestation (and orders dealing with occupation of the home) have been widened – it may be possible to obtain the orders from magistrates sitting as the Family Proceedings Court.

With regard to occupation of the 'matrimonial home', the FLA 1996 lays down a series of different regimes and factors for the court to apply when deciding to 'oust' one party from the home. The FLA 1996, therefore, tries to avoid the complexity of the previous mixture of statute and case law. The key to advising Ingrid is to establish the status of the two parties and fit this to the legislation. As Ingrid and Max are not spouses or former spouses, ss 33 and 35 will not be relevant. Max has a right to occupy the home due to his ownership – Ingrid has no such rights. Therefore, you will be advising Ingrid under s 36 of the FLA 1996, which applies to cohabitants or former cohabitants with no existing rights to occupy. Under s 36 Ingrid can seek to remove Max from the home and for her to remain there, or to re-enter the property if she has been excluded by Max. Before the court will make an occupation order under s 36 there are several factors to be considered. These are set out in s 36(6) and (8). In addition to the factors within the section itself, the court is also required to have regard to the fact that the couple have not shown the commitment involved in marriage (s 41). In addition to the FLA 1996 establishing clear criteria or factors for making the order, it also establishes clear periods of duration for the order. As Ingrid is a cohabitant, she will be entitled, on the first application under s 36, to an order of a maximum period of six months' duration. She will be permitted to apply for an extension to the order and the court can make one such extension. This, too, will last for a maximum of six months. Thereafter, she will have no rights to the property under the FLA 1996. The court can attach a power of arrest to the occupation order (using the same criteria as for the non-molestation order) and can also consider making the order *without notice* (again using the same criteria as for the non-molestation order).

END OF CHAPTER ASSESSMENT – THE LAW RELATING TO CHILDREN

1   The Children Act 1989 is designed to support child rearing with families, and yet to provide the state, through the local authority, with improved powers to protect children.

    Can these principles co-exist?

2   The welfare checklist in s 1(3) of the Children Act 1989 supports the concept of children's rights.

    Discuss.

Outline answers

1   This is not an easy question to answer, and hence it might be a good idea to return to it as a revision question having completed the rest of the child law chapters.

At this stage all that you can discuss is the concept of non-intervention and the principle of working in partnership with parents.

The notion that the best place for a child to be reared is with their family reflects the existing social structure, that of privacy and reduced state intervention. You may question the basis for this perception. Does the modern way of living, with less support from the extended family, and with many parents both working either full- or part-time, mean that we have moved away from the family structure when it was deemed best for children to be raised within the family at all costs? Or is the support for the family a result of the move away from the traditional family unit? Is it a means to reproduce the concept of father as breadwinner and mother as homemaker? You may also reflect upon the extent to which the state intervenes in any event. Currently the state intervenes by way of health visitors, ante-natal care, public health measures and guidance. This intervention is subtle and far less intrusive than that perceived from the social services, but it still exists to reproduce a consistent and focused direction to parenting and child development.

The Children Act (CA) 1989, through s 17 and the accompanying schedule, promotes the concept of partnership, and directs that a local authority should endeavour to reduce the need to take proceedings. This implies a proactive role for the authority, but you may raise the question of resources, and the fact that the authority operates more on a reactive basis. In working with a family on a voluntary basis, inevitably there will be a tension between the legal background to the local authority's work and the parents' role. You could highlight the fact that the local authority can always resort to the CA 1989 to take proceedings if parents do not comply. Does this, therefore, mean that parents will comply because of the threat of legal action? If this is so, then is this really a voluntary arrangement?

The tension that can be identified here is such that the principle of partnership and keeping children within the family cannot always be met within the framework of the existing legislation. Indeed, you may conclude that the mere existence of powers to protect children by removal from the home shows the principles behind the legislation are in tension from the start.

2   This question concentrates on a very small part of the CA 1989, but one which is central to the whole operation of the legislation. As well as assessing the impact of s 1(3), you may also find it useful to discuss the concept of children's rights and what is meant by this term.

There is a difference between promoting a child's rights in a moral sense to rights that are enforceable in law. On what basis does the CA 1989 promote children's rights? It can be suggested that the rights included are more legal than moral and, in addition, that there are not many rights at all. However, many of these legal rights stem from the ability to seek orders under the Act, which are not apparent from the face of s 1.

The contents of the welfare checklist are more directed towards the moral rights of the child – the right to be heard. Section 1(3) starts by referring to the 'ascertainable wishes and feelings of the child (in the light of his age and understanding)', which clearly does not introduce any real enforceable right. The list of factors in s 1(3) is not in order of priority, nor is the list exhaustive. It is also a matter for the court's discretion how much weight is to be placed upon each individual factor. Where a child's wishes and feelings are concerned, the child may be considered unable to express their wishes and feelings if of tender years. Even if an opinion can be given, the court, or any professional involved with the case, may question that opinion on the basis of age and understanding. Children are seen as potentially malleable, and hence their opinions susceptible to disbelief. You may have referred to issues such as a parent influencing the child's voice in divorce and contact disputes.

Given this general atmosphere of mistrust, the idea of s 1(3) supporting a child's rights is somewhat misplaced. The welfare checklist may provide the child with a voice, but it is one which can be overridden by adults and professionals who know better than the child. In many cases, the adults will know best, but each case must be decided individually. You should be able to question whether or not lip-service is being paid to the concept of rights not only in s 1, but throughout the CA 1989.

END OF CHAPTER ASSESSMENT – THE PRIVATE LAW RELATING TO CHILDREN

Hussein and Jayne married 10 years ago. They have two children, Robina, aged five, and Joshua, aged three. The marriage started to deteriorate shortly after Joshua was born and now the couple have decided to separate. No divorce is planned yet, although Jayne would like to dissolve the marriage in the not too distant future. Jayne is planning to go to live with her parents, who live in Cumbria in a large farmhouse. She would therefore have plenty of space for herself and the children. Hussein is not pleased at this decision, since it would be very difficult for him to travel the 200 miles to see the children. He is also concerned about Jayne's inability to bring up the children in the Muslim faith.

Advise Hussein who wishes to prevent this move and would prefer Joshua to remain with him so he can be raised in accordance with the Muslim faith.

What advice would you give Hussein if he wished to take the children to Iran to see their paternal grandparents and other relations?

Outline answer

The issue for consideration in this question is the ability to obtain orders with respect to the children, which will enable Hussein to care for Joshua and take the children abroad with him.

First, it is always advantageous to clarify the position regarding parental responsibility in any family problem question. As Jayne and Hussein are married, and the children were born after the marriage took place, under the provisions of s 2 of the Children Act (CA) 1989, both parents will automatically gain parental responsibility. This can be exercised independently and without the consent of the other. Part of parental responsibility is the duty to provide care for the child, which will naturally include physical care and the provision of a home. In the current situation, there is nothing to prevent Hussein taking the children to live with him – equally, there is nothing to prevent Jayne moving to Cumbria with both children.

It is also important to mention that orders under the CA 1989 can be obtained regardless of the existence of divorce proceedings. Any applications can be made to the Family Proceedings Court or the county court. It is for the party applying, on the advice of their legal representative, to decide where to commence proceedings.

The application that will be required, in the absence of any agreement, is for a s 8 residence order. In the circumstances highlighted in the question, agreement between the two parents is unlikely to occur. Explain or discuss in your answer the consequences and meaning of a residence order. Consider the criteria and factors taken into account by the court when deciding whether to make an order or not. These are found in s 1 of the CA 1989.

The primary factor is that the welfare of the child is the court's paramount concern. Linked to that is the welfare checklist in s 1(3) – a list of non-exhaustive considerations used to establish what is in the best interests of the child. Discuss the checklist in the light of the children in question. Here, you may have to look at the needs of the two children separately since Hussein appears to be more concerned to care for Joshua than for Robina. Look at a few of the issues that will be relevant. You have the ages of the children to consider: both are young and generally there is a tendency for young children to be placed in the care of the mother. There is also a strong tendency for siblings to be placed together, and here there is the possibility of them being cared for by different parents. This may be contrary to their welfare. The question of religious upbringing is important in this scenario, but the court will be concerned to evaluate whether the need for Joshua to be brought up in the Muslim faith necessitates his possible separation from his mother. It might be perfectly feasible for Jayne to ensure he is brought up as a Muslim. The court would also be careful to consider the actual arrangements for care of the children – to what extent is Hussein able to provide full-time care for one or both children? The court may believe that it will be too stressful for the children to be cared for by Hussein and possibly another carer rather than just Jayne and the maternal grandparents.

As well as the welfare checklist, the court must have regard to the possibility of delay, which can be harmful to the children, and this is relevant here since Robina is of school age, and it will be important to settle her at a new school quickly. The court must also have regard to the no order principle – however, it is unlikely that the court will find it appropriate to make no order if the parents are unable to agree or decide issues with respect to the children amicably.

The question of contact is also important here and it would appear to be somewhat insurmountable. However, in many situations one parent will be the inevitable 'loser' with regard to child care and contact. The court, even if it has only been asked to deal with a question of residence, may make a contact order. The CA 1989 enables the court to make orders without the need for an actual application. If Hussein is unsuccessful in obtaining a residence order, he may be more successful in gaining a contact order.

Turning to the question of taking the children to see the paternal grandparents and relatives in Iran, the ease with which this can be done depends on the outcome of any residence order application. If there were no order made, there would be nothing to prevent Hussein taking the children abroad. The only way Jayne could stop this would be by seeking a prohibited steps order under s 8 of the CA 1989.

If, however, a residence order is made, then under s 13 certain limitations are placed on those with parental responsibility, regarding the children's names and removal from the jurisdiction. Under s 13(1)(b) and (2) where a residence order is in force, a child can only be removed from the jurisdiction for periods of up to one month. If a period of removal is to be longer than this, or permanent, the consent of all with parental responsibility, or the consent of the court, is required. Only the person with the residence order is permitted to remove the children from the jurisdiction.

In advising Hussein, you would have to explain all this and the fact that if Jayne is granted the residence order, he will be unable to take the children to visit their relatives in Iran unless he has Jayne's permission, or seeks an order permitting the visit from the court. You may also mention that if any such application is made, Jayne may object on the basis of potential abduction by Hussein. If this is deemed to be likely, the court may fail to give consent to the visit taking place.

END OF CHAPTER ASSESSMENT – THE PUBLIC LAW RELATING TO CHILDREN

Helen is grandmother to Imogen (nine). Imogen lives with her mother, Janet, and has no knowledge of her birth father who was in fact married to someone else at the time of Imogen's birth. Five months ago Janet's boyfriend Kevin moved into the house. Helen has become increasingly concerned about Imogen since then as Imogen has told her that she is not allowed to talk at meal times and if she does not clear her plate she is slapped by Kevin and that this hurts. Imogen has also told Helen that Kevin locks her in the garden shed if she has been naughty and has left her there for several hours. More recently, Imogen has complained that she has been locked in the back garden when Janet and Kevin have friends round to the house when they smoke 'something with a funny smell'. Helen has tried to raise her concerns with Janet but was told to mind her own business and that Kevin is merely trying to teach Imogen good manners. Helen did not accept this and has contacted the social services.

Discuss the legal powers and duties that the social worker will have available to them.

Outline answer

This question covers a wide remit in terms of local authority duties and powers. Although it may not seem the most logical place to start, a brief discussion as to the position on parental responsibility (PR) is appropriate, since this will mean that when it comes down to the issue of who is party to the proceedings the local authority may take, you have already looked at PR. So, Janet as the birth mother will have PR automatically; Kevin will not have PR – although Janet may have delegated some powers of decision making to him; Helen will not have PR.

When the local authority is first contacted by Helen, they will need to consider if an investigation under s 47 of the Children Act (CA) 1989 is necessary, or if the situation is bad enough to warrant an immediate application to court for an emergency protection order (EPO). It would check the child protection register to establish if Imogen has been subject to investigation before and check records to see if they have dealt with Kevin as a possible abuser in the past.

If, as is most likely the case, the local authority decides to investigate, it will need to be mindful of its duties and powers under s 47 and the purpose of s 47 investigations. Hence, it will be making enquiries to see if Imogen is 'in need' and if any services need to be provided to Imogen (and the family) as a result of this; it will also be looking to see if legal steps need to be taken to protect Imogen if the provision of services would be insufficient to safeguard her welfare. You should refer to the need to work voluntarily with the family and the requirement, wherever possible, to keep the child with their family (although, of course, this does include the wider family and so would cover Helen). You should refer to the manner in which the investigation should take place and the consequences for Janet if she fails to co-operate. One of the main aims for the local authority is to see Imogen on her own and to verify the reports from Helen. They would also liaise with other agencies – for example, the school – to see if Imogen's behaviour had deteriorated or they had noticed or been told anything by Imogen.

The local authority will also have to hold a child protection case conference within seven days of the referral if guidance is followed strictly.

However, compliance with this time frame is unlikely since they will have to see the family, etc, in order to have information to present to the conference! Remember, the conference is only able to decide if Imogen's name should be placed on the child protection register.

If the local authority is unsuccessful in seeing Imogen, then under the terms of s 47 it should consider whether it needs to apply for an EPO under s 44 – and if it does, it will most likely be using the local authority criteria under s 44(1)(b). If having seen Imogen the local authority believes that she is at risk of suffering significant harm it can apply to the Family Proceedings Court (FPC) for an EPO under the s 44(1)(a) criteria. You would need to go through these criteria and explain the differences that exist between them, and clarify who would be a party to the proceedings (referring back to who has PR). You will also have to have regard to the issue of whether the s 1 welfare checklist is applicable to the case before the FPC. You should also cover the effects of the order if granted, these being the same regardless of which trigger criteria is used for the proceedings. If Kevin alone is seen as being the cause of risk or harm to Imogen then the court does have the power to order him out of the premises, but there would need to be consideration of Janet's ability to keep him out of the home.

In the event that an EPO is granted, you would need to mention the longer term possibilities, since the EPO can only last a maximum of 15 days (this is, where an extension has been granted). If the local authority has been successful in obtaining an EPO it is highly likely that they will, as a matter of routine, apply for a care order, given the need for notice. As the facts in the problem question are not that detailed you should not go into a detailed explanation of the requirements to be satisfied to get a care order – reference to the section that applies and the basic criteria and the consequences would be more than sufficient here.

END OF CHAPTER ASSESSMENT – ADOPTION

Why are adoption applications from step-parents and relatives seen with some disquiet? What problems can arise from this sort of application and what alternatives exist?

Outline answer

In this question you are looking at the category of individuals who adopt in approximately half the adoptions made in England and Wales.

You should identify that placements with relatives is a permissible way to establish a placement under the Adoption and Children Act (ACA) 2002, as is placement via an order of the High Court, where the placement is made by an adoption agency, or where the carer is a local authority foster parent. Given that a placement with relatives is allowed, you should then identify why these types of placement are questionable. The difficulties that arise depend on whether it is a step-parent applying to adopt because they are married to the natural parent, or a relative of the child say, for example, a grandparent or an aunt or uncle.

Taking the situation of an application of a step-parent and natural parent first, the perceived difficulties arise by virtue of the consequences of the adoption order. The effect of the order will be to terminate all the legal links between the other birth parent and to recreate them with the adoptive step-parent. In a step-parent adoption this will mean that one birth parent (normally the father) will lose all rights and responsibilities with respect to the child. The question has to be whether it is right for this to happen and whether the making of the order is in the interests of the child under s 1 of the ACA 2002. It could be suggested that as the ACA 2002 permits the step-parent alone to make the application (before it had to be a joint application by the step-parent and the birth parent), the legislation will, in fact, encourage more applications and, hence, the interests of the child will be more contentious.

One of the major criticisms of step-parent adoptions is that it does sever the legal links between the child and one birth parent, and this is seen as detrimental to both child and parent. This is more so if the child has had some form of relationship with that parent. The need to know about one's origins is currently perceived as very important (and hence the ability to trace birth parents is being made available to adopted children), and is something that may be lost on adoption.

The reasons behind the step-parent seeking to adopt can also be criticised. In some cases the adoption is predicated by a wish to change the surname of the child (officially) since this is not easy to achieve under the Children Act (CA) 1989. The adoption may be sought (and agreed to by the birth parent) in order to avoid the intervention of the Child Support Agency or simply to exclude the birth parent from the new family. However, this should not suggest that all step-parent applications are based on inappropriate reasons; many are sought to cement the new family unit, and to highlight the step-parent's commitment to the family.

Whilst the first three reasons mentioned are in themselves seen to be problematic, the more 'beneficial reasons' are still not viewed as being totally acceptable. Many second marriages break down with the result that the children will lose yet another parent. This loss arises regardless of the adoption order, but is often deemed more serious since there may have been no contact with the birth parent since adoption. You may not agree that this is a valid concern sufficient to justify restrictions on step-parent adoptions. Also, it is stated that the security of the family unit can be created and maintained by use of other orders.

Those other orders will be the s 8 residence order in favour of the step-parent, and possibly a s 8 contact order to the non-caring birth parent. You should discuss the effect of these orders and also highlight the differences between them and the adoption order to illustrate why they may not be utilised fully. Such differences include the fact that parental responsibility is not exclusive to the adoptive parents, that the order will only last until the child is 16 whilst adoption is for life, the fact that both step-parent and birth parent need to apply, etc. The fact that under the ACA 2002 the step-parent can seek parental responsibility (PR) may be seen as sufficient to reduce the need for adoption applications but, again, PR may not provide enough 'security' in the parental relationship, especially if the child is young.

Turning to relative adoptions, the major criticism that is leveled at this type of application is the potential distortion of the family structure post-adoption. When there was a greater stigma on illegitimacy, situations would arise where grandparents would adopt an illegitimate grandchild. This would then result in the child's mother becoming the child's sister – a situation that is not viewed favourably. In addition, if the relatives adopting the child are somewhat older, there is the risk that the child will be left without a full-time carer in the future (this being one of the reasons why adoption agencies place a maximum age limit on prospective adopters). Other criticisms that can be made concern contact with the birth parents(s). If the birth parent was a poor carer, or even an abuser, the adoption by a relative may raise further concerns over contact. Will a relative be sufficiently strict to ensure that no harm will arise from continued contact? An advantage of relative adoptions over stranger adoptions is that the child will remain within the wider birth family and, hence, have (potentially) greater knowledge of their origins.

The alternatives to adoption, where a relative is involved, again are to be found in s 8 of the CA 1989. You would not be expected to go through another explanation of the orders if you have already done so with regard to step-parents. You should however point out that the problems with s 8 may be the same.

INDEX

access order 183
  See also contact orders
adoption
  adopters 248–52
  adoption agencies 251, 252–54
  age of adopters 251
  alternative orders 256–57
  baby adoptions 246–47
  birth family links 247–48, 256–57
  by birth parent 249
  care orders and 240
  cohabiting couples 250
  conditions
    for order 254–55
  consent 248, 252–54, 255
  decline in 246
  dispensing with
    consent 253–54
  history 245–46
  judicial review
    of decision 251
  legislation 245–46
  making adoption
    order 254–56
  minimum age 248
  parental responsibility 247
  placement with extended
    family alternative 256
  placing for 252–54
  religious upbringing 256
  residence order
    alternative 246, 256
  revocation of order 257
  same-sex couples 249–50
  step-parent 249, 254
  succession and
    intestacy rules 247
  welfare/wishes
    of child 255–56
  young children 247
adultery
  cohabitation after 48
  divorce fact 37, 38, 40–41
  intolerability 41
  time limits for
    petition 47–48
advancement,
  presumption of 95–96

affinity, degrees of 17
after-acquired assets
  divorce 70–71
ancillary relief
  public funding 53–54
  void marriage 31–32
  See also financial provisions
Ancillary Relief Protocol 82
annulment of marriage 15–16
  applicants 30
  bars to 30
  consequences 31–32
  existing pregnancy 29
  gender recognition 29, 30
  lack of consent 26–28
  mental incapacity 28
  non-consummation 23–26
  polygamous marriages 22–23
  time limits 30
  venereal disease 29
  void marriage
    See void marriage
  voidable marriage
    See voidable marriage
anti-social behaviour 230
appeals
  care orders 243
  emergency protection
    orders 219
  financial provisions
    on divorce 80–82
  supervision orders 243
assessment for
  child support 116–21
  income 118–19
  property adjustments 120–21
  second families 117–18
  special expenses 120
  unreasonable reduction
    in income 121
  variation of amount 119–21
assets
  after-acquired 70–71
  disclosure 69
  of new partner 71–72

'baby battering' 153, 196
banns 2, 5
Barnardo, Dr Thomas 151
'battered baby'
  syndrome.................. 153, 196
battered wives 130
behaviour
  divorce fact............. 37, 38, 41–44
  financial
    provision and............ 67, 76–77
  irretrievable
    breakdown.................... 42
  negative 42, 76
  positive..................... 42, 76
  unreasonableness
    of cohabitation................ 42
'beyond parental
  control' 222, 228–29
'big money cases'............... 72–73
bigamy 19, 32
breach of curfew
  notice 204, 230

care orders
  adoption of child................ 240
  age of child................. 229, 266
  anti-social behaviour 230
  appeals 243
  applicants....................... 231
  assessments 235–36
  beyond parental
    control................ 222, 228–29
  breach of curfew
    notice....................... 230
  care plans................... 232–34
  consequences................. 239–41
  courts........................... 231
  criteria for making 221–30
  directions 232
  duration of order................ 241
  final hearing................. 236–38
  interim 234–35
  juvenile court
    sentence 229–30
  no order made............... 236–37
  non-education 165
  parental responsibility........... 239

parents, continuing
  involvement............... 240–41
parties to proceedings 231
placement with
  extended family............... 237
procedure................... 230–36
reasonable contact 240–41
significant harm 222, 223–25
standard of care
  by parents................. 228–29
suitable accommodation 239–40
supervision order or.......... 237–38
threshold criteria............. 222–29
variation 242
with notice applications.......... 231
carers
  committal of.................... 189
  parental responsibility........... 176
  See also extended family
case conferences
(child protection)
  attendees...................... 209
  child protection
    register 210
  decisions...................... 210
  initial 209
  purpose.................... 208–09
  review 209
chattel
  child as 148, 151
  wife as........................ 130
child abuse 195–96
  corporal punishment 169, 196
  emotional 196
  extent of 197–98
  investigation duty of
    local authority 203–08
  neglect........................ 196
  physical.................... 196–97
  sexual 196
  See also child protection
child assessment order
  advantages..................... 213
  authorising agents 211
  consequences................... 212
  criteria for.................. 211–12
  reasons for 211
  refusal to comply 212

child protection

accommodation
  provision. 201–03
advice and assistance. 200
breach of curfew
  notice and. 204, 230
care plans 232–34
case conferences 208–10
child assessment order. 211–13
'child in need' 200
child protection
  register 210
child safety orders. 230
children's guardian 220–21, 231
contracting out
  services 199
courts and. 220–21
  investigations. 206–07
  See also inherent jurisdiction
day care provision 200–201
duties of local
  authorities 198–200
emergency protection
  orders. 204,
                        213–20, 263
investigations
  by CAFCASS 206
  by court. 206–07
  See also investigation by
    local authority
legal proceedings,
  decision to take 210
legislation. 151–53
local authorities 151, 159–60,
                        198–203
long term orders
  See care orders; supervision orders
'looked after' children 200, 203
place of safety orders 153
placement with extended
  family 237, 256
provision of services. 199
referrals. 203–04
'relevant children'. 203
residence order
  with conditions 237
reviews 209
s 37 investigations. 206–08

short term orders
  See child assessment orders;
    emergency
    protection orders
trigger criteria 204
welfare reports 206
See also child abuse
child protection register. 210
child safety orders 230
Child Support Agency 108–09
assessment
  See assessment for child support
benefit reduction penalty 113–14
collation of information. 108–09
denial of parentage. 111
DNA testing. 111
habitual residence. 110–11, 122
income. 118–19
jurisdiction. 110–11, 122
limitations on court
  involvement. 115
mandatory
  applications 112, 113–14, 116
non-resident parent 109, 110
person with care 109, 110
pre-CSA 1991
  agreement or order. . . . 112, 114, 116
property adjustments. 120–21
qualifying child 109, 110
reduced benefit
  direction 114
request for assessment
  not to be made. 113
s 8 orders 122
second families 117–18
shared care. 110
special expenses 120
step-families. 122
unreasonable reduction
  in income 121
variation of
  assessment 119–21
voluntary
  applications 112, 114–15, 116
welfare benefits
  requirement. 112,
                        113–14, 116

See also financial provisions,
  children

childhood

duration 148–49

meaning 147–49

children

abused

See child abuse

adoption

See adoption

age of majority. 149

anti-social behaviour 230

'baby battering' 153, 196

as chattels 148, 151

child assessment order. 211–13

child of the family 123

Children Act 1989 155–94

competency 149, 150

contact

See contact orders

corporal punishment 169, 196

courts and. 151

delay, avoidance of. 157–58, 235

discipline 169–70, 196

divorce and 154–55

education 164

emergency

protection orders 192, 204,
213–20, 263

employment of 148, 151

financial provision for

See Child Support Agency;
financial provisions,
children

Gillick competency 166, 167

health visiting 152–53

historical treatment of 151–53

legislation to protect. 152–53

litigation friend 150

marriage 10–11

medical treatment. 166–67, 266

name 167–69, 181

non-intervention

principle 158–59

orders 159, 172–73

parental responsibility

See parental responsibility

paternity issues 111

poor law and 151

prohibited steps

See prohibited steps orders

protection

See child protection

religious upbringing 191–92, 256

residence orders

See residence orders

rights of. 149–50

section 8 orders

See individual orders,
eg, residence orders

shared care. 110, 181–82

social services and 159–60

social workers 152–53

special guardianship

orders 192–93

specific issues

orders 190–92, 260

truants. 164–65

wards

See wardship

welfare checklist 157

welfare of child 155–60

children's guardian **231**

appointment by court. 220

independence 221

role. 220–21

Church of England

marriage

banns. 2, 5

common licence. 5–6

pre-marriage

requirements 2, 3, 4–6

special licence 5, 6

'clean break' **60**

deferred 61, 79

financial provision and 78–79

cohabitees

adoption by 250

civil partnerships 103–04

civil registration of

relationships 103–04

common law marriage. 104–05

financial provision 88, 91

non-molestation orders 135

occupation rights 103–05

social security benefits 91

common law

marriage 1–2, **104–05**

consanguinity,
  degrees of........................ 17
consent
  adoption................ 252–54, 255
  divorce 37, 39
  marriage..................... 10–11
    duress 26–27
    mistake 27–28
    unsoundness
      of mind 26
  medical treatment........ 166–67, 266
constructive trusts
  agreement
    and reliance 97–98
  common intention................ 98
  detrimental reliance 97–98
  direct contribution 98
  indirect contribution.............. 99
  matrimonial home 97–99
consummation of marriage
  definition 24–25
  incapacity...................... 25
  just excuse 25–26
  voidable marriage............. 23–26
  wilful refusal 25–26
contact orders
  brainwashing of child 189
  committal of carer.............. 189
  conditions.................. 187–88
  criteria for issue................ 190
  definition 184
  direct...................... 186–87
  duration 190
  enforcement................. 188–90
  European Convention on
    Human Rights............. 185–86
  failure to take up.............. 190
  indirect 186, 187
  refusal of contact............. 188–90
  rights......................... 184
corporal punishment.......... 169, 196
curfew notice, breach of....... 204, 230
Curtis Committee (1946)........... 153
custody order 179
  See also residence orders

defending a divorce
  disputing evidence.............. 47
  grave financial hardship 48, 79
  other hardship.................. 48
  reasons 47
desertion 37, 38, 44
disciplining a child
  child abuse and................. 196
  corporal punishment........ 169, 196
  reasonable
    chastisement 169, 170
divorce
  adultery.............. 37, 38, 40–41,
                                47–48
  after-acquired
    assets..................... 70–71
  behaviour.............. 37, 38, 41–44
  'by a process
    over time' 50
  collusion.................... 39–40
  consent 37, 39
  counselling.................... 51
  defending................. 47, 48, 79
  delaying 79–80
  desertion................. 37, 38, 44
  facts................... 37–38, 45–47
  FLA 1996
    framework 51–52
  FLA 1996
    reforms 50–51
  ground 37–38, 45–47, 51
  historical
    perspective................ 35–36
  information
    meeting.................... 51–52
  investigation
    obligations 39
  irretrievable
    breakdown 37, 42,
                              46–47, 51
  legislation...................... 35
  matrimonial
    offences.................... 36, 37
  MCA 1973 .... 37–38, 49–51
  mediation
    See mediation; mediators
  numbers 35, 36

parental
  responsibility and 178
pensions 48, 67, 77–78
pre-nuptial
  agreements 82–84
process 38–40
purpose of
  legislation 36–37
reconciliation 48
reflection and
  consideration 50, 52
reforms 49–52
separation
  with consent 37, 38, 44–45
  without consent 38, 45
'serial monogamy' 36, 125
special procedure 38–40
statement of
  marital breakdown 52
stopping clock 48
time bars 47–48

domestic violence
battered wives 130
children
  See child abuse; child protection
civil remedies 132–33
criminal law 131–32
Domestic Violence, Crime
  and Victims Bill 143–46
enforcement of orders 142–43
female aggressor 131
FLA 1996 133–43,
                           145–46
historical
  development 129–30
marital rape 130
non-molestation
  orders 133–36,
                         141–42, 144
occupation
  orders 133, 136–43, 144
physical violence 129
powers of arrest 142–43,
                              144–45
protection from
  harassment 143, 146
psychological harm 129
reforms 143–46

restraining orders 145–46
stalking 143
undertakings instead
  of order 142
wife as chattel 130
**Domestic Violence, Crime
and Victims Bill 143–46**

education
care order for
  non-education 165
corporal punishment 169, 196
parental duty 164–65
truants 164–65
**emergency protection
orders 204, 263**
any person criteria 214–15
appeals 219
applicants 213–14
authorised person
  criterion 216, 231
burden of proof 214
consequences 216–19
contact with family 217
duration 218
local authority
  criteria 215–16
'on notice' 219
parental responsibility
  and 218
procedure 219–20
prohibited steps
  orders and 192, 217
reasonable cause
  to believe 214
removal of child 216–17
without notice 220
estoppel, proprietary 101–02
**European Convention
on Human Rights**
contact orders 185–86
parental responsibility 175
extended family
adoption and 256
placement with 237, 256
residence orders 246

financial provisions,
  children
  blood relatives 107
  child of the family. 123
  Children Act 1989. . . . . 123, 125–26
  disabled child 122
  DPMCA 1978. 123
  legislation. 107
  lump sums 123, 124
  MCA 1973. 123
  non-biological
    children. 125
  obligation to support 107–08
  periodical payments. 123, 124
  property transfers. 123, 124
  status of child. 123, 124
  step-families. 108, 122
  training or further
    education 125
  welfare of child 125
  See also Child Support Agency

financial provisions, divorce
  after-acquired assets. 70–71
  age of parties 67, 74
  Ancillary Relief
    Protocol. 82
  appeals 80–82
  assets
    after-acquired 70–71
    disclosure 69
    of new partner. 71–72
  'big money cases' 72–73
  'clean break'. 60, 61, 78–79
  cohabitation of
    payee (recipient) 61
  conduct of parties 67, 76–77
  contributions to
    marriage 74–75
  death of party 61
  decision of court 65–79
  delaying divorce 79–80
  disability of parties. 67, 74
  disclosure of assets 69
  duration of
    marriage 67, 74
  enforceability. 84
  equality and
    fairness 67

financial needs,
  obligations and
  responsibilities 66, 68, 72–73
financial resources 66–67, 69–72
FLA 1996 reforms 82–84
inheritance
  (potential). 70–71
loss of benefits 67
loss of future benefits. 77–78
lump sum orders. 60, 62
maintenance concept 59–60
maintenance
  pending suit. 62–63
matters taken
  into account 65–79
Mesher orders. 64, 65
mutual obligation
  to support. 59–60
new partners 71–72
one-third rule. 68
orders available. 60–65
pensions 48, 67, 77–78
periodical
  payments 60, 61
permanent
  maintenance. 60
potential
  inheritance 70–71
pre-nuptial
  agreements. 82–84
presumption of
  equal division 68
preventing divorce 79
property orders. 63–65
reasonable
  requirements 68
reforms 82–84
remarriage
  of party. 61, 62, 71–72
return to
  workforce. 70
second families 72
settlement of
  property 63–65
standard of living 67, 74
statutory criteria 66–67
time of issue
  of order. 79

transfer of property 63–65
variation of orders 80
financial provisions,
without divorce
claimants 88–90
cohabitees.................... 88, 91
common law duty
to maintain.................. 87
consent orders.................. 90
DPMCA 1978................. 89–90
duration of order.............. 88, 89
family home
See matrimonial home;
occupation orders
fixed term payments.............. 88
lump sum payments 88, 89
MCA 1973.................... 88–89
periodical payments.......... 88, 89
remarriage of party............... 89
social security benefits 91

gender reassignment/
recognition
annulment of marriage 29, 30
birth certificate change........... 20
void marriage 19–22
voidable marriage............. 23, 29
'gender recognition
certificate' 21, 23, 29
Gillick **competency** 166, 167
guardian *ad litem*
See children's guardian

hardship
divorce defence............ 48–49, 79
grave financial.................. 48
not financial................. 48–49
religious grounds 48–49
social grounds 49
harm
See significant harm

information meeting
divorce 51–52
inherent jurisdiction
declarative orders............. 260–61
injunctive orders............. 260–61

local authorities and.......... 264–66
meaning 259–60
restrictions 264–65
See also wardship
interim care orders.............. 234–35
investigation by
local authority
access to child 205, 215
duration of
investigation 207
duty........................ 203–08
purpose....................... 205
review of cases................. 206
time limits.................... 207
trigger criteria 204
welfare reports 206
irretrievable breakdown........ 37, 42,
46–47, 51

judicial review
adoption decision 251
jurisdiction
Child Support Agency.... 110–11, 122
inherent
See inherent jurisdiction

Laming Inquiry (2003) 204
legal help...................... 53–54
legal separation 32
litigation friend 150
local authorities
accommodation
provision.................. 201–03
advice and assistance............ 200
breach of curfew
notice and................ 204, 230
care plans 232–34
case conferences 208–10
child assessment
order 211–13
'child in need' 200
child protection 151, 159–60,
198–220
child protection
register 210
contracting
out services.................. 199

day care provision 200–01
duties..................... 198–200
emergency
   protection orders 192, 204,
                 213–20, 263
inherent jurisdiction.......... 264–66
investigation
   See investigation by local authority
legal proceedings,
   decision to take 210
long term orders
   See care orders; supervision orders
'looked after' children 200, 203
placement with
   extended family 237, 256
prohibited steps
   orders 192
provision of services............ 199
referrals.................... 203–04
'relevant children'.............. 203
residence order
   with conditions 237
reviews 209
short term orders
   See child assessment orders;
      emergency protection orders
specific issues orders 192
trigger criteria 204
lump sum payments
children................... 123, 124
divorce 60, 62
instalment payment 62
remarriage of payee
   (recipient).................... 62
without divorce................. 88

maintenance
divorce and
   See financial provisions, divorce
without divorce
   See financial provisions,
     without divorce
maintenance pending suit....... **62–63**
marital rape..................... **130**
marriage
affinity........................ 17
age of parties 10–11, 18
banns........................ 2, 5

bigamy 19, 32
ceremonies
   See marriage ceremony
common law 1–2, 104–05
consanguinity 17
consent
   See consent, marriage
consummation
   See consummation of marriage
divorce
   non-compliance.......... 11–13, 18
gender reassignment 19–22
invalid...................... 11–12
legal separation 32
legislation regulating 2
male and
   female parties 19–22
mental capacity 28
minors...................... 10–11
non-compliance with
   formalities 11–13, 18
notice
   See notice of marriage
nullity
   See annulment of marriage
polygamous.................. 22–23
pre-marriage
   requirements 3–7
pre-nuptial agreements 82–84
prohibited degrees 16–18
registration..................... 10
under certificate
   without licence 4
venereal disease 29
void
   See void marriage
voidable
   See voidable marriage
marriage ceremony
approved premises.............. 8–9
authorised person.................. 7
Church of England 2, 3, 4–6,
                  9–10
churches other
   than C of E 3–4, 10
civil marriages.............. 3–4, 7–9
common licence................. 5–6
Jewish 10

'open doors' 7, 9
Quakers........................ 10
reforms 9
register office 7
religious,
    other than C of E 10
'required declaration'......... 7, 9–10
secular procedure 2
special licence 5, 6
times 7, 9, 13
venues..................... 7, 8–9

matrimonial home
bank foreclosure
    on mortgage.................. 91
common intention................ 98
constructive trusts............. 97–99
contribution, direct
    and indirect 98
detrimental reliance 97–98
evaluating shares
    in equity 100
informal trusts
    of land..................... 94–99
mortgage payments 98, 99, 101
ownership rights........... 91, 92, 94
presumption of
    advancement 95–96
proprietary estoppel.......... 101–02
resulting trusts................ 95–97
third party rights.............. 91, 93
TLATA 1996................... 102
See also occupation rights

mediation
divorce 51, 52–57
function...................... 55–56
public funding after 53–54, 55
unsuitable situations 54–55

mediators..................... **51, 53**
lawyers as.................... 55–56

medical treatment
children................. 166–67, 266
refusal of consent 266

Mesher **orders** **64, 65**

minors
See children

mortgages **91, 98, 99, 101**

name of child **167–69, 181**

**National Society for
the Prevention of
Cruelty to Children** **152,
211, 216, 231**

non-molestation
orders **133–36**
applicants................... 134–35
cohabitees.................... 135
Domestic Violence,
    Crime and Victims
    Bill reforms............... 144, 145
duration of order................ 136
enforcement.................. 142–43
former partners 135
instigation of court 135–36
nature of
    proceedings 141–42
powers of arrest 142–43,
    144–45
undertaking instead 142
when order made 135–36

notice of marriage **3–4**
banns........................ 2, 5
declaration
    to accompany.................. 4
emergency notice 6
joint notice 7
periods 7
purpose........................ 6
reform....................... 6–7
religious marriages............... 10

nullity
See annulment of marriage

occupation orders................. **133**
cohabitants or former
    cohabitants............... 140–41
Domestic Violence,
    Crime and Victims
    Bill reforms............... 144, 145
duration of order................ 141
enforcement.................. 142–43
ex-spouse with no
    right to occupy 139–40
nature of
    proceedings 141–42

powers of arrest 142–43,
    144–45
spouses with right
   to occupy 136–39
undertaking instead 142
occupation rights **91–93**
cohabitees 103–05
effective against later
   creditors only 93
exclusive occupation 102
non-owning spouse 92
notice on register 93
occupation order 92–93
registration 93
TLATA 1996 102

parentage
DNA testing 111
parental responsibility
acquisition 178
acquisition by father 172
adoption 247
agreements 172
automatic 170–71
care orders 239
care and
   protection duty 163–64
carers 176
definition 161–62
discipline 169–70
divorce and 178
duties 162–70
education duty 164
emergency protection
   orders and 218
European Convention
   on Human Rights and 175
grandparents 176
individual liability 177–78
joint liability 177–78
legitimated children 171
loss of 178
medical treatments 166–67, 266
name of child 167–69
reforms 173–76
religious
   upbringing 191–92
rights 162–70

s 8 orders
   See individual orders
step-parents 177
supervision orders 242
unmarried father 171–76, 178
paternity
Child Support
   Agency 111
DNA testing 111
parental responsibility
   order and 111
pensions
attachment 77–78
divorce 48, 67, 77–78
earmarking 77
hardship from
   loss of 48
loss of benefit 67
splitting 78
periodical payments
children 123, 124
divorce 60, 61
secured 60, 61, 88
unsecured 89
without divorce 88, 89
place of
safety orders **153**
polygamous
marriages **22–23**
powers of arrest
domestic violence 142–43,
   144–45
pre-marriage
requirements
banns 2, 5
certificate without
   licence 4
Church of England 4–6
churches other
   than C of E 3–4
civil marriages 3–4
declaration to
   accompany notice 4
non-compliance 11–13, 18
notice of marriage 3–4
notification
   procedure 10
purpose of notice 6

pre-nuptial
agreements **82–84**
pregnancy
annulment ground 29
presumption of
advancement................ **95–96**
prohibited degrees,
marriage.................... **16–18**
affinity........................ 17
consanguinity 17
prohibited
steps orders............ **190–92, 260**
emergency protection
order and 192, 217
local authorities.............. 192
property
child as 148, 151
divorce and 63–65
Mesher orders............... 64, 65
transfer and settlement
children 123, 124,
125–26
divorce 63–65
wife as....................... 130
proprietary estoppel
doctrine **101–02**
public funding
ancillary relief 53–54
assessment for 54
mediation
requirement........... 53–54, 55

rape, marital **130**
reconciliation
stopping clock 48
registration
marriage...................... 10
occupation rights............... 93
religious upbringing
adoption..................... 256
children.............. 191–92, 256
remarriage of party
financial provisions
without divorce.............. 89
lump sum orders............... 62
periodical
payments 61

residence orders **176–77,**
179–83
adoption alternative............ 256
change in name
of child 168, 181
conditions.............. 180–81, 237
criteria for orders 182
duration 183
extended family............... 246
shared care................ 181–82
shared residence 182
split orders................ 181–82
step-parents.................. 246
restraining orders.............. **145–46**
resulting trusts
illegal motivation 96–97
matrimonial home 95–97
presumption of
advancement.............. 95–96

same-sex couples
adoption by 249–50
civil partnerships 103–04
non-molestation
orders 135
second families
assets of new partner 71–72
Child Support Agency........ 117–18
financial provisions on
divorce and 72
secured periodical
payments
divorce 60, 61
without divorce................. 88
separation
divorce 37, 38, 44–45
five years without
consent 38, 45
legal separation................. 32
two years with
consent 37, 38, 44–45
'serial monogamy' **36, 125**
'sex change'
marriage and 19–22
significant harm
long term order
criterion 222, 223–25

meaning 223–25
past, present or
    future harm 226–28
time when needs to
    be proved 225–26
social security benefits
cohabitees 91
liable relative 91
mandatory CSA
    applications 112, 113–14
reduced benefit
    direction 114
special guardianship
orders **192–93**
adoption alternative 256
applicants 193
specific issues orders **190–92, 260**
local authorities 192
stalking. **143**
statement of marital
breakdown. **52**
step-families
child support 108, 122
parental
    responsibility 177
step-parent
adoption by 246, 249, 254
residence orders 246
supervision orders
age of child 229, 266
appeals 243
applicants 231
assessments 235–36
attendance at
    specific places 241
'beyond parental
    control' 222, 228–29
care order or. 237–38
care plans 232–34
conditior 241
consea⁻ 241–43
courts 231
criter⁻ 221–30
direct. 232
duration 243
enforcement 242
final hearing. 236–38

medical assessment 241
mental health
    treatment 241
parental responsibility 242
parties to proceedings 231
procedure 230–36
psychiatric assessment. 241
residence
    requirements 241
significant harm 222, 223–25
standard of care by
    parents 228–29
supervisor
    appointment. 241
threshold criteria. 222–29
variation 242
with notice
    applications 231
transsexuals, marriage **20–21**
truants. **164–65**
undertakings
domestic
    violence and 142
unmarried father **171–76, 178**
venereal disease **29**
violence within family
See domestic violence
void marriage. **11–12, 15,**
                            16–23
age of parties 18
ancillary relief 31–32
application for
    annulment 30
bigamy 19, 32
consequences of
    annulment 31–32
disregard of
    formalities 11–13, 18
gender reassignment 19–22
not male and
    female parties 19–22
parties' rights. 31–32
polygamous
    marriages 22

prohibited degrees 16–18
transsexuals 20–21
voidable marriage **15, 23–29**
applicant for
   annulment 30
consequences
   of annulment 32
existing pregnancy 29
gender
   reassignment 23
gender recognition 29
incapacity 25, 28
lack of consent 26–28
parties' rights 32
refusal
   to consummate 25–26
venereal disease 29

wardship
applicant 261–62
consequences 263–64
delegation of
   parental duties 264
emergency situations 262–63
High Court
   Family Division 262
immediately effective 262–63
welfare of child **155–60**
adoption 255–56
financial provision 125
welfare reports **206**
wives
battered 130
as chattels 130
marital rape 130
'moderate correction' 130